D.D. HOME: HIS LIFE, HIS MISSION

D.D. HOME: HIS LIFE, HIS MISSION

BY

MADAM HOME

Edited, with an Introduction,
by Sir Arthur Conan Doyle

D. D. Home: His Life, His Mission

White Crow Books is an imprint of
White Crow Productions Ltd
PO Box 1013
Guildford
GU1 9EJ

www.whitecrowbooks.com

Text design and eBook production by Essential Works
www.essentialworks.co.uk

ISBN 978-1-907355-16-5
eBook ISBN 978-1-907355-76-9

Religion & Spirituality

Distributed in the UK by
Lightning Source Ltd.
Chapter House
Pitfield
Kiln Farm
Milton Keynes MK11 3LW

Distributed in the USA by
Lightning Source Inc.
246 Heil Quaker Boulevard
LaVergne
Tennessee 37086

Contents

Introduction

I HAVE FELT IT TO BE AN honour to be allowed to edit this new edition of the Life of D. D. Home. The book is so vital that it went much against the grain to excise any part of it, but our first task is to make it easy for the public to get the information which they need, and in its original form the book was a little difficult on account of occasional redundancy and repetition. This I have endeavoured to correct, but I foresee the time when the full text will be restored and I censured for having tampered with what is a very valuable record. Meanwhile this shorter version gives the reader all that is essential.

Home has himself left three books to the world, the first and second series of *Incidents in my Life* and *Lights and Shadows of Spiritualism.* The latter contains the most earnest protest against the abuse either of mediumship or of Spiritualism which the most conservative critic could utter. Personally I am of opinion that Home took a somewhat narrow view of mediumship, failing to realize its protean aspects, so that when he found any which differed from his own he was inclined to put it down to bad observation or to fraud. At the same time he sets us an example of that alert and critical intelligence which every spiritualist should cultivate. In *Incidents in my Life* will be found a most interesting autobiography including his controversy with Sir David Brewster from which the man of Science emerged so badly. Very especially the second series is commended to the student of Home, because in it will be found all the actual papers dealing with the Home-Lyon lawsuit, showing conclusively how honourable was the action of Home, in spite of the severe remarks by Lord Gifford, which were the result of his own ignorance and prejudice. To quote them against Home's character is like quoting the remarks of a Roman judge upon an early Christian. A spectator has told me that Gifford asked Home's counsel: "Do I understand that your client claims to have been levitated?" Upon the counsel assenting, Lord Gifford made a wild gesture of his arms, very much as the High Priest rent his garment of old. The reader who consults the evidence for levitation given in this volume will certainly have no doubt as to Home's power or as to Gifford's bumptious ignorance.

Home is a man to whom the human race, and especially the British public, owes a deep apology. He was most shamefully used by them. He came as one of the first and most powerful missionaries who have set forth upon the greatest of human tasks, to prove immortality, to do away with the awful mystery of death, to found religion upon positive knowledge, and to break down the dense materialism which was as great within the Christian Churches as outside them. All this he felt that he could do by those same personal demonstrations of spiritual power which were used for the same ends in the early age of the Church, before form and ritual smothered the living reality. He devoted his life to this end in spite of failing health and comparative poverty. Never did he receive any reward for his splendid, self-sacrificing work save indeed those personal souvenirs from Royalties which were given not in payment but in friendship. He left a trail of religious conviction and of human consolation behind him wherever he went. He was admirable in every relation of life, a good husband, a devoted father, a beloved friend, a charitable helper, a worker upon the battle fields, a lover of art and of all that is beautiful. And yet when he died worn out at the age of 51 there was hardly a paper in Great Britain which did not speak of him as if he had been a Cagliostro, who had spent a life of intrigue and deception. Those who read this life will surely echo my words that we owe him a deep apology, and recognize that in this Spiritual tide which flows so strongly today we find much which undoubtedly found its spring in his unselfish labours. His influence was admirably summed up by Mrs. Webster, a well known resident of Florence, when she wrote: "He is the most marvellous missionary of modern times, and the good that he has done cannot be reckoned. Where Mr. Home passes he bestows around him the greatest of all blessings, the certainty of a future life."

One or two of Home's aphorisms may be quoted to show the mind of this man who is even now hounded down by ignorant traducers, especially Materialists who cannot forgive the shattering blow which he inflicted upon their whole philosophy a death-blow, as it will prove. "Follow Christ's teaching and carry out His mission." "Religion is to worship something outside and beyond yourself." 'Try all communications by the help of your conscience and your reason." The sanity as well as the essential piety of the man shines through such sayings. Surely it is the outworn case of a beautiful soul which lies under the slab in Paris on which is carved the words: "To another, discerning of spirits." Cor. xii. 10.

A. C. D.
MARCH, 1921

NOTE. In reading this edition of D. D. Home, His Life and Mission *it is necessary to remember that the book was originally written nearly forty years ago. It is thus necessary to make allowance for dates and occurrences referred to as of comparatively recent occurrence, the original language being retained.*

Prologue

IN THE REALM OF SPIRIT as well as in the exact sciences, our age demands facts that can be verified. I reproduce, in all its authenticity, as much as possible of the testimony that has been borne to the phenomena investigated in the presence of D. D. Home. A crowd of theories, more or less ingenious but none satisfactory have been created to explain away the facts, without explaining them in the least. The perverted understanding which takes that which is not for the reality, and the reality for a chimera, can alone lead men into this singular denial of the possibility of a truth that, by their own avowal, it would give them the greatest happiness to recognize. Undoubtedly the most hideous cancer of our age is its materialism that, eating constantly deeper, leads men more and more into the denial of their immortality. Spiritualism was not regarded by Home as a fantastic or poetic reverie. He suffered cruelly for his mission, without having any other object in view than to give an irresistible impulse to the consoling belief in a future life. A multitude of irrefutable facts were demonstrated in his presence which science tested and admitted. By sacrificing himself to every description of research, he enabled scientific investigators to establish the existence of forces that until his day had remained unknown; and he founded belief in a spirit-world on those remarkable evidences of identity that will remain the bases of the true modern Spiritualism. No sophistry can avail to show that the well-established and well-attested facts contained in this work have had no existence. It will be seen how great a number of well-known personages have investigated the subject, and have been convinced. The fact that many of these names are now for the first time published, will prove to what degree Home carried his consideration for others, suppressing their names in order to spare them from ignorant abuse, and tranquilly encountering the host of calumnies that were directed against him in consequence. Where is there another man, who, with the means in his possession of proving how false were the assertions made concerning him, would have thought of others, rather than of himself?

There are very few celebrated men whose real character has been so strangely misunderstood, and concerning whom false reports have more persistently been spread abroad. The extensive correspondence he has left even the small portion of it I have found space to print proves how blameless his life must have been, how irreproachable his honour, and how elevated his sentiments. No one was ever more happy in doing good, or was more beloved. In every country persons who were not Spiritualists pronounced his name with respect; and the social position he occupied in the world is the best proof of the estimation in which he was held.

Spiritualism, as demonstrated by Home, gives a serenity of mind that death cannot destroy. The edifying proofs of identity contained in the communications received through him tend to change our life and modify our actions, by giving fresh strength to love and charity. The Spiritualism which is incapable of being investigated under scientific, or, at least, trustworthy conditions, and confers no moral benefit, is not Spiritualism. If tokens of spirit identity and phenomena established under such conditions as are described in this volume can rarely be met with, and the truth is, in consequence, derided as fiction, this only illustrates a fact established by the history of humanity in every age that the possessors of such a diversity of gifts as were bestowed on Home are makers of epochs. Home never had the ambition to create a sect, although nothing would have been easier to him. For him who understood the teaching of the Saviour, there could be no question of honour and prominence; and the acts of his life show that he was a Christian in the full acceptation of the word. His aim was the propagation of Spiritualism, especially among those who have lost the innate perception of spiritual things, that inner light whose revelations all Nature confirms. He sought to save us from the emptiness of a selfish life, and to give us in this world less of suffering and more of joy.

D. D. Home did not teach; he proved.

CHAPTER 1

Scotland and America

DANIEL DUNGLAS HOME was born near Edinburgh, March 20, 1833. His parents both came of ancient Scottish families. Through his mother, whose maiden name was McNeill, he was descended from a Highland family in which the traditional Scottish gift of the "second-sight" had been preserved. Mrs. Home possessed it herself; and while her son was still an infant she had a vision concerning him that found fulfilment more than twenty years later at Fontainebleau. An aunt, who had no children of her own, adopted Home; and his infancy was passed in her care at Portobello. When he was nine years old, she and her husband emigrated to America, and took with them the boy whose life was destined to be so wonderful. He was a sensitive, delicate child, of a highly nervous temperament, and of such weak health from his infancy that he had not been expected to live. His frail health, however, no more affected his natural sweetness of temper and gaiety of spirits than did the bitter trials of after years. "I remember him," writes to me a schoolfellow of his, Mr. J. W. Carpenter, Mayor of Norwich, Connecticut, "as one of the most joyous, affectionate, and whole-souled boys among my whole circle of acquaintances, always ready to do a kind act. He was fond of his studies; but when out of the schoolroom spent all his time in the wood and beside the streams, with one or two chosen companions. His nature was very sensitive, and he was easily grieved at any act of unkindness done to others or to himself. I never saw anything of Spiritualism," adds Mr. Carpenter, "and am therefore a disbeliever myself; but I know that my old friend was thoroughly honest and sincere in his belief. I know of no one of my many schoolmates whose career I have more carefully followed, and whom I have been more proud to call my friend, than D. D. Home." Greeneville, Connecticut, where Home received his first impressions of America, has been swallowed up in the growth of the adjoining city of Norwich. Forty years ago, when he lived there with his uncle and aunt, Greeneville existed as a separate village; and close at hand were the woods to which he escaped at every opportunity, spending there hours in that study of nature which always charmed him. Nothing escaped his observation and his prodigious memory. He always looked back on those days as the happiest of his boyhood. His studious and dreamy habits separated him from most other children of his age; but he had a chosen companion in these rambles, a school fellow a little older than himself, of the name of Edwin. A strong friendship grew up between the two; and they were always together, until Home went with his relatives to live at Troy, in the State of New York, some three hundred miles from Norwich. A few weeks before this separation, Home was, as usual, with his friend Edwin in the woods. The two boys were both great readers; and when either of them had found anything in a book that interested him, it was sure to be communicated to the other On this occasion it was in April, 1845 or 1846 Edwin was full of a ghost-story that he had just read. The event it related to is associated with the history of a noble English family; and I am told that it furnished Sir Walter Scott with the groundwork of one of his ballads. A lady and her lover had mutually agreed that, if there were a life beyond this, the one who died first should appear to the survivor. In pursuance of his vow, the lover, within a few days of his death presented himself to his mistress. She treated the vision as a delusion of her senses; on which the spirit stretched forth his hand and laid it on hers, leaving there a mark that was ineffaceable. Many years after lie had listened to this legend in the woods of Norwich, Home met in England a member of the family to which it related; and was assured that the history was well authenticated, and that a portrait of its heroine still existed, known in the family as "the lady with the black ribbon," from a covering she had always worn on her wrist, to conceal the mark. When Edwin's story was told, the two boys set themselves to discuss it, and also the possibility of such apparitions of departed spirits appearing to those whom they had loved on earth. With the romance of their age, they ended by agreeing to bind themselves by the same promise that the two lovers in the legend had taken; and exchanged vows on the spot, in the most solemn manner they could devise. A few weeks later, Home went to live at Troy. He was then about thirteen years of age. In the month of June following, he had been spending the evening at a friend's house, and on returning to that of his aunt; found that she had already retired to rest. Fearing to be scolded for being late, her nephew hastened to follow her example. It was a lovely summer's night, and the moon, shining through the curtainless window of his room, rendered a candle unnecessary; but at the moment when the boy, having finished his prayers, was slipping into bed, her light was suddenly darkened. Startled by the phenomenon, Home looked up, and beheld a vision that he has described in the opening chapter of his *Incidents in My Life*, published in the year 1863 by Messrs. Longman:

"I was about to draw the sheet over me," he writes, "when a sudden darkness seemed to pervade the room. This surprised me, inasmuch as I had not seen a cloud in the sky; and on looking up I saw the moon still shining, but it was on the other side of the darkness, which still grew more dense until through the darkness there seemed to be a gleam of light, which I cannot describe; but it was similar to those which I and many others have since seen when the room has been illuminated by spiritual presence. This light increased; and my attention was drawn to the foot of my bed, where stood my friend Edwin. He appeared as in a cloud of brightness, illuminating his face with distinctness more than mortal. He looked on me with a smile of ineffable sweetness, then, slowly raising the right arm, he pointed upward; and making with it three circles in the air, the hand began slowly to disappear. Then the arm, and finally the whole body, melted away. The natural light of the room was then again apparent. I was speechless, and could not move, though I retained all my reasoning faculties. As soon as the power of movement was restored I rang the hell, and the family, thinking I was ill, came to my room, when my first words were 'I have seen Edwin -he died three days ago.' A day or two afterwards a letter was received, announcing the death of Edwin after a very short illness. The second such vision that befell Home was in the year 1850. By this time his aunt had returned to Norwich; and at Waterford, some twelve miles off, were settled his father and mother, who had followed their relatives to America. One day Mrs. Home, when alone with her son, told him that she would leave him in four months' time. "Your little sister Mary," she went on, "came to me in a vision, holding four lilies in her hand; and allowing them to slip through her lingers one after the other, till the last one had fallen, she said 'And then you will come to me.'" I asked her whether the four lilies signified years, months, weeks, or days, and she told me "months." The death of little Mary had taken place under the saddest of circumstances. The mother went out for a few hours, leaving the child at home. On returning, she had to cross a small stream near the house; and while on the bridge, saw what seemed to be some loose clothes floating in the stream. She ran down the bank, and drew from the water the body of her child. In the fourth month after her vision, Mrs. Home was called away to visit some persons at a distance; and when her family were expecting her return, they received instead a telegram announcing her serious illness. Her husband started at once on its receipt; her son could not accompany his father, for he was himself confined to bed in the house of his adopted parents by an affection of the lungs. The same evening, his aunt heard the boy calling loudly for her; and on hurry into his sickroom, found him in the greatest distress and agitation. "Auntie," he said, "mother died to-day at twelve o'clock, because I have seen her, and she told me so." His aunt, as most persons would have done in her place, thought her nephew delirious. "Nonsense, child," she said, "you are in, and this is the effect of a fevered brain." It proved to be sad reality. Mrs. Home had died that day at twelve o'clock, without one of her family near her even as she had predicted to her son four months before. After the loss of his mother, Home's thoughts occupied themselves more and more with the life beyond this; and he was constant in attending the religious exercises of the body to which he belonged. Much to the displeasure of his aunt, who was a member of the Kirk of Scotland, he had joined the Wesleyan communion; but her opposition to this step was so persistent and violent, that her nephew finally compromised matters by leaving the Wesleyans for the Congregationalists, whom she regarded with less dislike. One night, on going to bed, he heard three loud blows struck at the head of the bedstead. Thinking some one was hidden there and trying to frighten him, he rose and searched, but found nobody. While he could still hardly realize that he was actually the only person in the room, the three blows sounded again in the same place, and then, after a moment's pause, they came a third time. The listener spent a sleepless night in watching for their recurrence and in repeating to himself that the phenomenon was a something not of earth; but the strange sounds were heard no more by him. In the morning he came down to breakfast pale and fatigued; and his tired looks were noticed by his aunt, who set them down to the account of a prayer meeting he had attended the evening before, and began to lecture on the evil results of religious excitement. She was interrupted by a volley of raps on the table at which the two were seated. "What is this?" was her astonished demand. Her nephew, almost as startled as herself, could not answer; but if he had no interpretation of the marvel to furnish, his aunt soon found one. "So," she exclaimed, drawing away from him in horror, "you have the devil in you too, have you? And you have brought him to my house! '"About two years earlier, the knockings at Rochester had attracted public attention. Home's aunt had heard of them from some of her neighbours, and believed them to be works of the evil One. She put the same construction on the strange sounds now heard in her own presence, and considered her nephew to be possessed. It was some hours before she could get over the shock of having, as she fancied, entertained one or more fallen angels unawares; but in the afternoon she began taking steps to drive the visitors from her house. There were three pastors in the village of Greeneville, a Congregationalist, a Baptist, and a Wesleyan. Forgetting for the moment her prejudices against one and the other persuasion, she sent for all three, and requested their advice and ministrations. Two of the three were perfectly of her opinion as to the source of the phenomena; and one of these two, the Baptist, proceeded to question Home. "It is Satan who possesses you," he began. "What have you done to bring him to you?" His catachumen could only protest that it was out of his power to give any explanation of the mysterious sounds; and seeing his agitation, the Congregationalist minister interposed. "Don't be frightened," he said kindly; "if this is the work of Satan, it is your misfortune and not your fault." "In any case," said the

Baptist, "let us seek to drive him forth by our prayers"; and he proceeded to offer up a supplication in which he desired Home to join.

"Whilst we were thus engaged in prayer," writes Home, "there came gentle taps on his chair and in different parts of the room; while at every expression of a wish for God's loving mercy to be shown to us and our fellow creatures, there were loud rappings as if joining in our heartfelt prayers. I was so struck and so impressed by this, that there and then, upon my knees, I resolved to place myself entirely at God's disposal, and to follow the leadings of that which I then felt must be only good and true, else why should it have signified its joy at those special portions of the prayer? This was, in fact, the turning point of my life; and I have never had cause to regret for one instant my determination, though I have been called on for many years to suffer deeply in carrying it out. Astonished and perplexed by the result of their prayers, the three ministers departed. The Congregationalist offered no opinion as to the origin of the phenomena; saying only that he did not see why this young member of his flock should be persecuted for what he was unable either to prevent or cause. The Baptist a Mr. Mussey shook his head, but was so bewildered by the thought that his prayers had seemed to call forth the sounds, instead of silencing them, that he had little to say; and only the Methodist remained firm in his first belief, declaring that these wonders were the work of Satan, and telling Mrs. McNeill Cook that her nephew was a lost sheep. "He was so unkind," says Home simply, "that I derived no comfort from him." From that day the rappings were heard frequently; but familiarity with the sounds had no effect in diminishing the terror with which the aunt of Home regarded them. After a time the furniture began to be moved about without visible agency. On one occasion, when a table was moving across the room with no one near it, the aunt ran to the family Bible, and placed it on the table with the triumphant exclamation, "There! That will drive the devils away!" "To her astonishment," writes Home, "the table only moved in a more lively manner." As yet, no one seems to have thought of trying to ascertain whether the sounds heard were controlled by intelligence. The first experiment in this direction was made at the house of another relation of Home's, a widow who lived near the aunt who had adopted him. One evening, while with this second relative, raps were heard, and the alphabet was called over. The letters indicated by the raps were written down; and in this way intelligent communications were received, and replies obtained to questions put.

The people of Greeneville had heard by this time of what was occurring. "They took to besieging the house," says Home, "in a way that did not tend to soothe the religious susceptibilities of my aunt." Among them came a Mrs. Force, in whose presence the name of her mother was spelt out by the raps. A message followed, reproaching her with having forgotten a sister who had gone west with her husband some thirty years before, and had not since been heard of. The name of the town where this long-lost relative lived was added; and on the astonished Mrs. Force writing there, she received a letter from her sister in reply.

It has been objected *ad nauseum* that it is ridiculous to suppose that a disembodied spirit would seek to communicate with us by sounds made on a table or a wall. Why ridiculous? Contrary to the pre-conceived opinions of many, it may be; but then, those opinions are themselves based on no grounds but prejudice and sentiment, while the assertion that spirits do thus seek to communicate is based on evidence. The question was ably discussed in the year 1863, in a preface contributed to Mr. Home's *Incidents in My Life*, by a distinguished man of letters, who, as a result of his investigations with Home, had become a Spiritualist the late Dr. Robert Chambers. It was in no credulous spirit that this well-known writer had commenced has inquiry. For a great part of his life Dr. Chambers was a materialist of materialists, and was known among his friends to have been the joint author with Leitch Ritchie of one of the most sceptical works of the day, *The Vestiges of Creation*.

"There remains a great stumbling-block to many," wrote Chambers in his anonymous preface to Home's book, "in the manner in which the communications are most frequently made. It seems below the dignity of a disembodied spirit to announce itself and speak by little pulsatory noises on a table, or wainscot. It might, however, be asked if it be not a mere prejudice which leads us to expect that the spirit, on being disembodied, suddenly, and of necessity, experiences a great exaltation. We must, moreover, remember that we know nothing of the conditions under which spirits can communicate. This may be the most readily available mode in most instances. Beyond doubt, in certain circumstances of difficulty, the most exalted of living persons might be glad to resort to such a mode of telegraphy."

Home's aunt did not treat the phenomena in the spirit of those critics to whom the remarks of Dr. Chambers were addressed. She saw them to be real, she feared them to be unholy; and, far from finding in the sounds heard in the house and the sights seen there a matter of ridicule, they distressed her mind beyond endurance. The siege laid to her house by her neighbours was the last straw; and declaring that, since the spirits of which she had such a horror would not go, her nephew must, she turned him out of doors.

Home found a temporary refuge in the house of a friend in the neighbouring town of Willimantic. In most natures, the cruelty of such treatment as his aunt had dealt out to him under the impulse of perverted religious feelings would have excited abiding resentment; but Home's temper was too sweet and generous not to forgive and forget. He remembered only her kindness of former years; and the old age of his aunt was passed in a cottage that he bought for her. She died in 1876, of the shock caused to her by reading in the American papers a false report of his death.

While Home was at Willimantic, he was constantly beset by curious intruders; and offers of money were made to him, which he refused. He felt that his mysterious gift was not a thing to be trafficked in, and had already laid down the rule to which he adhered all his life, that he would never take payment for a séance.

Much against his will, an account of some extraordinary phenomena witnessed at Willimantic was contributed to the local newspaper. Shrinking from the publicity thus forced on him, he cut short his visit and went to Lebanon. "There," he writes in his *Incidents in My Life,* "I was received in the family of an old resident."

Very few names are given in the *Incidents,* for Home's chivalrous delicacy towards others made him prefer to suffer from the misconception of the world himself, rather than expose a friend to ridicule or abuse. This consideration for the feelings of others sometimes led him to refrain from availing himself of the permission when granted, especially in the case of ladies. His generosity was, as a rule, its own reward. When a cry for more names of witnesses was raised by the press on the publication of the *Incidents*, very few of those witnesses had the courage of their opinions.

The results of numerous applications made to the friends of Mr. Home in both the Old and New Worlds, together with the correspondence preserved by him, enable me to supply most of the names omitted in the *Incidents*, and in various cases to add the personal testimony of investigators concerning their experiences. In this way I shall be able to render these pages a record of attested facts. My only difficulty will be to contain the record of a life so full of wonderful and varied incident within the limits of a single volume.

It was in the spring of 1851 that Home left Willimantic for Lebanon, where he became the guest of a family named Ely, who had a farm in the neighbourhood. His health was in a most delicate state, and trying scenes through which he had just passed had intensified the symptoms of lung disease; but quiet and the healthy influences of a country life wrought a change for the better. More unselfish and considerate than some of his friends of later years, the Ely family discouraged their young visitor from holding séances too frequently. It was a fact of which Home soon became conscious, that some power or force passed from him during the occurrence of the phenomena; or, as Mr. William Crookes put it in 1871; "The evolution of psychic force is accompanied by a corresponding drain on vital force." Repeated séances meant the serious injury of Home's health; but for that health the majority of his friends had very little consideration; and his unselfish good nature again and again led him to comply with their entreaties for séances, when his vital force was already at the lowest ebb from previous sittings. "Were I in Springfield, I should be a very discordant element," writes one of the Ely family to him in March, 1852, "if you continued very long to sit in six circles a day, you invariably pay the penalty fainting when you do so, and why can you not say 'No'?"

Near Lebanon, in 1851, the first of many remarkable cures was wrought through the agency of Home; the life saved being that of a Mrs. Bill. The facts of this case are recorded in the *Incidents*, without names being given.

In June 1851, Home accepted the invitation to pay him a visit, of Mr. W. Green, living at Boonton, New Jersey. While there, he had frequent visions and trances, at which times he beheld the lost friends of many persons who were perfect strangers to him, and described them with such accuracy that they were immediately recognized.

From. Boonton, Home, about the middle of July 1851, went on a visit to Mr. J. W. Carrington, a resident (then and now) of Brooklyn, New York. During this visit he met Professor George Bush, a distinguished theologian and Oriental scholar. Mr. Bush, who had been educated with a view to taking orders in the Episcopal Church, but had abandoned the design in consequence of the change wrought in his views by an acquaintance with the works of Swedenborg, took deep interest in observing the phenomena connected with Home. The communications he received were of such a nature as to render him assured that they proceeded from friends who had passed from earth. I will give an instance of their character. Home had one evening fallen into a trance. In this condition he saw one who had been the schoolfellow of Professor Bush forty years before. The name was given through Home, and the Professor was reminded of a strange dream that he had had on the very night his friend passed from earth.

"The spirit," writes Home, "now told through me the whole of the Professor's dream, which was that, whilst they were playing together, he suddenly saw his schoolfellow taken from him, and heard his voice saying, 'I leave you, George, but not forever.' A dream of forty years previously was thus brought to his remembrance. The Professor was so strongly impressed with this that he called on me next day, and wished to have me reside with him for the purpose of studying for the Swedenborgian ministry. I went to his house with the intention of so doing; but within forty-eight hours I saw in my waking state the spirit of my mother, who said to me, 'My son, you must not accept this kind offer, as your mission is a more extended one than pulpit preaching.' On seeing the good Professor, I told him of this spirit message. He expressed regret, but no surprise; so I returned to my friend Mr. C. '(Carrington)', and remained with him till the end of August.

"I frequently afterwards saw Professor Bush, with whom the most kindly inter-course was interchanged."

From Brooklyn, Home returned to Lebanon. The youngest of his friends there, the Ely family, was a boy of about his own age, named Ezra. In September 1851, Ezra fell ill. The family were under no alarm, the illness appeared so slight; but Home had a vision that forewarned him his friend would be gone within three weeks. On the nineteenth day of his illness Ezra passed from earth tranquilly and happily.

"His extraordinary composure," records Home, "remained with him throughout. I had told the family of my vision, which prepared them for the coming change. About two days before his leaving us, the doctor asked me to break it to him, when I informed him that Ezra had long been aware of it. He doubted this, from seeing him so composed; and I desired him to stand at the door and hear what I would say to Ezra. I then went to his bed, and told him that the doctor had left some news for him. He laughingly said, 'I suppose it is to tell me that I am going. Little does he imagine that I have already decided who my bearers are to be.' The doctor now came into the room, and taking his hand, said, 'my dear boy, if I had not heard this, I could not have believed it. You have everything to make life happy, and yet you are so willing to leave it.' A few hours after this a deacon of the church visited him. He argued with the dying boy, trying to take away his happy belief, but fortunately without the slightest success."

Home remained at Lebanon till the end of January 1852, and then went to Springfield, Massachusetts, where he became the guest of one of the best known residents, Mr. Rufus Elmer. The Elmers, unlike the Elys, took no account of the drain on the vital force of Home that went on during séances. They threw open their house to all inquirers, and urged him to sit morning, noon, and night. A passage in *Incidents in My Life* indicates the exhausting and hurtful nature of Home's surroundings at Springfield:

"I stayed with them '(Mr. and Mrs. Elmer)' for some time," he writes, "and great interest was excited by the accounts given by the very numerous witnesses who came to see the manifestations. Whilst here the power was very strong, and frequently I had séances six or seven times a day. The house was besieged by visitors, and often outside in the street there was a concourse of anxious inquirers. People came from a distance, even from the extreme west and south of America, having seen the accounts given of me in the newspapers of the previous year." Among them came the celebrated American poet, Bryant, accompanied by Professor Wells of the University of Harvard, and two other persons. They were, one and all, thorough sceptics as to the reality of the phenomena; and their investigations, which extended over several sittings with Home, were as searching as a determined incredulity could render them. Constrained at length to yield to the testimony of their senses, Messrs. Bryant, Wells, and their coadjutors had not only the candour to own that they had witnessed phenomena which could not have been produced by trickery, but the fairness to state so publicly. Their conduct might have been imitated with advantage by Lord Brougham, Mr. Ruskin, and many other subsequent investigators, on whose lips timidity set a seal. The narrative published by Bryant and his friends restricted itself to the phenomena witnessed at a single séance with Home, the most remarkable. I append it, with the exception of a passage I reserve for another chapter, in which I shall have occasion to cite instances of the particular phenomenon this passage attests:

"The undersigned, from a sense of justice to the parties referred to, very cordially bear testimony to the occurrence of the following facts, which we severally witnessed at the house of Rufus Elmer, in Springfield:

"The table was moved in every possible direction, and with great force, when we could not perceive any cause of motion.

"It (the table) was forced against each one of us so powerfully as to move us from our positions together with the chairs we occupied in all several feet.

"Mr. Wells and Mr. Edwards took hold of the table in such a manner as to exert their strength to the best advantage, but found the invisible power, exercised in an opposite direction, to be quite equal to their utmost efforts.

"Mr. Wells seated himself on the table, which was rocked for some time with great violence, and at length it poised itself on two legs, and remained in this position for some thirty seconds, when no other person was in contact with it.

"Three persons, Messrs. Wells, Bliss, and Edwards, assumed positions on the table at the same time, and while thus seated, the table was moved in various directions.

"Occasionally we were made conscious of the occurrence of a powerful shock, which produced a vibratory motion of the floor of the apartment in which we were seated it seemed like the motion occasioned by distant thunder, or the firing of ordnance far away causing the table, chairs, and other inanimate objects, and all of us to tremble in such a manner that the effects were both seen and felt." In the whole exhibition, which was far more diversified than the foregoing specification would indicate, we were constrained to admit that there was an almost constant manifestation of some intelligence which seemed, at least, to be independent of the circle.

"In conclusion, we may observe that Mr. D. D. Home frequently urged us to hold his hands and feet. During these occurrences the room was well lighted, the lamp was frequently placed on and under the table, and every possible opportunity was afforded us" for the closest inspection, and we admit this one emphatic declaration we know that we were not imposed upon nor deceived.

"W. M. Bryant, B. K. Bliss, W. M. Edwards, David A. Wells."

Similar, but still more striking phenomena were witnessed on the 28th of February, 1852, at the house of the Elmers, and attested in a declaration signed by John D. Lord, Rufus Elmer, Henry Foulds, and eight other persons. One evening a visitor from New York, Mr. S. B. Brittan, was at the Elmer's residence. There was no thought of a séance; the party were sitting talking to each other, when their conversation was interrupted by a startling incident. The person most intimately concerned, Mr. Brittan, subsequently published the following account of his memorable experiences at Springfield:

"While spending a few days at the house of Mr. Rufus Elmer, Springfield, I became acquainted with Mr. Home. One evening Mr. Home, Mr. and Mrs. Elmer, and I were engaged in general conversation, when suddenly, and most unexpectedly to us all, Mr. Home was deeply entranced. A momentary silence ensued, when he said, 'Hannah Brittan is here,' I was surprised at the announcement; for I had not even thought of the person indicated for many days, or perhaps months, and we parted for all time when I was but a little child. I remained silent, but mentally inquired how I might be assured of her actual presence. "Immediately Mr. Home began to exhibit signs of the deepest anguish. Rising from his seat, he walked to and fro in the apartment, wringing his hands and exhibiting a wild and frantic manner and expression. He groaned audibly, and often smote his forehead and uttered incoherent words of prayer. Ever and anon he gave utterance to expressions like the following: 'Oh, how dark! What dismal clouds! What a frightful chasm! Deep down far, far down, I see the fiery flood. Save them from the pit! ... I set no way out. There's no light! The clouds roll in upon me, the darkness deepens! My head is whirling!' . . . "During this exciting scene, which lasted perhaps half an hour, I remained a silent spectator, Mr. Home was unconscious, and the whole was inexplicable to Mr. and Mrs. Elmer. The circumstances occurred some twelve years before the birth of Mr. Home. No person in all that region knew aught of the history of Hannah Brittan, or that such a person ever existed. But to me the scene was one of peculiar and painful significance. She was highly gifted by nature, and endowed with the tenderest sensibilities. She became insane from believing in the doctrine of endless punishment; and when I last saw her the terrible reality, so graphically depicted in the scene I have attempted to describe, was present in all its mournful details before me.

"Thirty years have scarcely dimmed the recollection of the scene which was thus re-enacted to assure me of the actual presence of the spirit. That spirit has since informed me that her present life is calm, peaceful, and beautiful, and that the burning gulf, with all its horrible imagery, existed only in the traditions of men, and in the fitful wanderings of her distracted brain."

Home was now nineteen years of age. Since quitting his aunt's house, he had been the guest of one or other friend; but from the suggestion of seeking to turn his gift to pecuniary account he invariably recoiled, and was as poor as on the day when he began his wanderings. Some extraordinary cures wrought through him at Springfield turned his mind towards the medical profession. If he were to train himself for that profession by the usual course of study, the beings who guided him would surely, he reasoned, be able to turn his training to account.

He spoke of his plan to Mr. and Mrs. Elmer, who, without entirely disapproving of it, responded by an unexpected proposal. They had learned to feel a great affection for their young guest, and they were rich and childless. They offered to adopt Home and make him their heir, on condition of his changing his name to that of Elmer.

It was a tempting prospect to be held forth to one who had neither home nor means, but after anxious thought he decided to decline it. Before doing so, he wrote to ask the advice of his friends, the Ely family, who replied in a letter now before me: "You can never feel anything but unbounded gratitude for Mr. Elmer's kindness still it would be a pity to do anything hastily which might eventually become irksome to either party. Your name is a very good one as it is, and why not be distinguished by it? The words echoed Home's own thoughts. He was unwilling to change his name, and his sensitive and independent nature had already pictured the offer of adoption as .an impulse of which the Elmers might afterwards repent. The result was that he gratefully refused the proffered adoption, and soon after-wards left Springfield for New York. There was no break of friendship between him and the Elmers; he spent a few days with them the following autumn, and, at their pressing invitation, paid them a long visit in the spring of 1854.

In New York, Home met, among other distinguished Americans, Professor Hare, the eminent chemist and electrician, inventor of the oxy-hydrogen blowpipe; Professor Mapes, noted for his researches in connection with the application of chemistry to agriculture; and Judge Edmonds, of the United States Supreme Court. All three investigated the phenomena that occurred in

Home's presence, and all three became fully satisfied, not only of their genuineness, but of their spiritual origin. Yet they had approached the subject as utter sceptics. Judge Edmonds, who devoted three years to a painstaking series of researches into Spiritualism, wrote in the *New York Herald*, August 6, 1853: "I went into the investigation originally thinking it a deception, and intending to make public my exposure of it. Having from my researches come to a different conclusion, I feel that the obligation to make known the result is just as strong."

Professor Hare had accepted the experiments of Faraday as conclusive; but meeting with facts for which the explanations of the English philosopher would not account, he set himself to devise more ingenious apparatus than Faraday's, that should, as he expected, conclusively establish that no force was exerted during a séance but that of the sitters present. The results of his manifold experiments he published in a volume that passed through five editions. Vary the experiments and apparatus as he might, he found it demonstrated that there was a power at work not that of the human beings present, and that this power was governed by intelligence.

Another inquirer who sought Mr. Home's acquaintance at New York in 1852 was Dr. John Gray, a leading American physician. "For Dr. Gray," wrote Home in his autobiography, "I have ever had the deepest affection and esteem. He and his kind wife have given me counsel and befriended me at all times and under all circumstances. From his character and attainments he was eminently suitable as an investigator of phenomena requiring a calm, dispassionate judgment."

Dr. Gray encouraged his young friend to carry out his plan of entering on a course of medical study, but a chain of unforeseen circumstances for some time prevented Home from following the advice. The first was a pressing invitation from a Dr. Hull, who had been present at a séance in New York, to visit him at his residence on the Hudson. Home accepted, and did not see New York again till the autumn of 1853.

Dr. Hull lived at Newburgh on the Hudson. He had offered Mr. Home a considerable remuneration in proposing the visit, which was, of course declined; Home informing him that he had never been paid and never would be, but that he should be happy to pay a visit t Newburgh if all suggestions of payment were dropped. Some very interesting séances were held there; and the result was that Dr. Hull and others of Home's new friends united in a kindly-meant project. They proposed that, as his education had naturally been somewhat neglected, he should place himself in their hands to go through a course of ordinary study, before entering on the medical training that he had in view. Home accepted the offer; but having made promises to visit numerous persons during that autumn and winter, he was obliged to defer availing himself of it till the following year.

In August 1852, after spending a week at Springfield, where he was prostrated by severe illness, he went on a visit to Mr. Ward Cheney of South Manchester, near Hartford, Connecticut, one of the most eminent of American manufacturers. The Cheney family were soon numbered among his fastest friends in America; and when Home left the States, one or other of its members was always among his correspondents. In 1869, Ward Cheney, then a friend of seventeen years' standing, visited him in England; and manifestations occurred that were recorded by Lord Dunraven. Those attending Home's introduction to the Cheneys were somewhat remarkable.

As he entered the hall of their residence at South Manchester, a sound resembling the rustling of a heavy silk dress attracted his attention. He looked round, and was surprised to see no one.

A few minutes later, when talking to Mr. Cheney in one of the sitting rooms, Home again heard the rustling of the dress, and again sought in vain for anything that might account for such a sound. His host noticed his startled look, and naturally asked him the reason of it. Home, unwilling to make much of the matter, only replied that he had been very ill, and his nervous system was probably out of order. He had hardly spoken the words, when looking through the open door into the hall, he saw standing there a little, active looking elderly lady, clad in a heavy dress of grey silk. The apparent mystery was explained; and as the thought passed through his mind, the dress again rustled.

This time Mr. Cheney also heard the sound. "What is that?" he asked, looking towards the hall. "Oh," said Home, who, from the life-like distinctness of the figure, had not the slightest thought that it could be other than of flesh and blood, "only the dress of that elderly lady in the grey silk rustling."

Mr. Cheney made no response; and his guest's thoughts were diverted from the subject by the entrance of the other members of the family. The lady of the grey silk was not among them; nor, to his surprise, did she appear at dinner. He expected that his host would make some remark about her, but nothing was said; and this singular reserve naturally set the visitor wondering who she might be.

As he was leaving the dining room, the dress again rustled, close to him; and he heard a voice say very distinctly, "I am annoyed that a coffin should have been placed above mine."

Astonished beyond expression, Home repeated this strange message to Mr. and Mrs. Cheney, and related what he had previously seen and heard. His listeners stared at him, and at each other in mute astonishment, till finally Mr. Cheney broke silence.

"The style of dress," he said, "we perfectly recognize even to the peculiar colour and heavy texture; but as for this story of a coffin having been placed on hers, it is as incorrect as it's ridiculous."

Home did not know what to answer. Till he heard the words, he had not for a moment suspected the visionary character of the figure; and even now he was not aware what relationship existed between the mysterious visitant and his hosts. He waited to see what would happen next; and what happened was that, an hour later, the voice again sounded in his ear, uttering the self same words. This time, however, it added: "What is more, Seth had no right to cut that tree down."

Home repeated the message from first to last. Mr. Cheney seemed greatly perplexed. "Certainly," he said, "this is very strange. My brother Seth did cut down a tree that rather obstructed the view from the old homestead; and we all said at the time that the one who claims to speak to you would not have consented to his felling it had she been on earth. As for the rest of the message, it is sheer nonsense."

Just before the party separated for the night, the message was again given, and again met by a point-blank contradiction. "I went to my room," writes Home, "feeling greatly depressed. It was the first time an untrue message had been received through me; and even were it correct, it astonished me that a liberated spirit should occupy itself with such a matter. I could not sleep for thinking of the occurrence." In the morning he made known to his host how much the matter had troubled him. "I am just as sorry about it," answered Mr. Cheney; and resumed "I am now going to demonstrate to you that, if it were the spirit it purports to be, it is sadly mistaken. We will go together to the family vault, and you shall see for yourself that, even had we desired to do so, it would be impossible to place another coffin above hers."

The two went at once to the burying-ground. The person who had the care of the vault was sent for, and its owner desired him to open it. As he placed the key in the lock, the man seemed to recollect something; and turning, said in a half-apologetic tone, "By the way, Mr. Cheney, as there was just a little room above the coffin of Mrs–.

"(The old lady in the grey silk)," I have placed the coffin of Mrs. L.'s baby there. I suppose it's all right, but perhaps I ought to have asked you first about it. I only did it yesterday."

Mr. Cheney turned on his companion a look that Home could never forget. "It's all true, then it's all true!" were the only words he could utter.

Home related this strange incident in his *Lights and Shadows of Spiritualism*, published in 1877. He gave the scene of its occurrence, Hartford, Conn., but omitted naming the Cheney family.

"The same evening," he writes, "the spirit once more made known her presence. 'Think not,' ran the message now delivered, 'that I would care were a pyramid of coffins to be piled on mine. I was anxious to convince you of my identity, once and forever'."

Ward Cheney, Home's host of 1852, died at South Manchester in 1876. Shortly after his departure from earth, Home received a communication that I shall give in a future chapter.

While staying with the Cheneys in 1852, the first instance of Home being lifted in the air occurred.

"During these elevations or levitations," he wrote, "I feel no hands supporting me, and since the first time, I have never felt fear; though, should I have fallen from the ceiling of some rooms in which I have been raised, I could not have escaped serious injury. I am generally lifted up perpendicularly; my arms frequently become rigid, and are drawn above my head, as if I were grasping the unseen power which slowly raises me from the floor."

On taking leave of his new friends at South Manchester, Home passed the remainder of the year 1852 in paying various visits he had promised. It was at this time that he first saw Boston, where converts to Spiritualism were becoming numerous. The manifestations witnessed there were similar to those already recorded, with the addition that on more than one occasion strains of music were heard during a séance when no instrument was near, a phenomenon often subsequently attested.

Early in the year 1853, Home returned to Newburgh to commence the course of study proposed to him by Dr. Hull and his other friends there. In this retired and beautiful spot, which lies among the highlands of the Hudson and not far from West Point, the spring and summer were tranquilly but laboriously spent. He had entered the Theological Institute as a boarder, though he did not attend the classes; and, under the direction of Dr. Hull, was commencing the acquirement of the French and German languages.

"While here," wrote Home in 1863, "I had an extraordinary vision, which is still "so vivid that I remember it in all its details." The Institute was built on an eminence commanding a view of peculiar beauty; below lay the city; on the right the river was lost in its windings among the rocky hills surrounding West Point; on the left it lay in expanse, and could be traced for a distance of many miles; behind spread out the country, with its pretty little farmhouses dotted here and there. I have sat for hours of an evening watching their lights, and endeavouring to picture the lives and emotions that crossed those thresholds. "One evening I had been pondering deeply on that change which the world calls death, and on the eternity that lies beyond, until, wearied, I found relief in prayer, and then in sleep. It appeared to me that, as I closed my eyes to earthly things, an inner perception was quickened within me, till at last reason was as active as when I was awake. I, with vivid distinctness, remember asking myself the question whether I was asleep or not? When, to my amazement, I heard a voice which seemed so natural that my heart bounded with joy as I recognized it for the voice of one who, while on earth, was far too pure for such a world as ours, and who, in passing to that brighter home, had promised to watch over and protect me. And, although I well knew she would do so, it was the first time I had heard her voice with that nearness and natural tone. She said, 'Fear not, Daniel; I am near you: the vision you are about to have is that of death, yet you will not die.' The voice became lost; and I felt as one who at noonday is struck blind. As he would cling even to the last memories of the sunlight, so I would fain have clung to material existence not that I felt any dread of passing away, nor that I doubted for an instant the words of my guardian angel; but I feared I had been over-presumptuous in desiring knowledge, the very memory of which might disturb my future life. This was but momentary, for almost instantaneously came rushing with a fearful rapidity memories of the past; my thoughts bore the semblance of realities, and every action appeared as an eternity of existence. During the whole time I was aware of a numbing and chilling sensation which stole over my body; but the more inactive my nervous system became, the more active was my mind, till at length I felt as if I had fallen from the brink of some fearful precipice; and as I fell, all became obscure, and my whole body one dizzy mass, only kept alive by a feeling of terror, until sensation and thought simultaneously ceased, and I knew no more.

"How long I had lain thus I know not; but soon I felt that I was about to awaken in a most dense obscurity. Terror had given place to a pleasurable feeling, accompanied by a certitude of some one dearly loved being near me, yet invisible. Instinctively I realized that beyond the surrounding obscurity lay an ocean of silver-toned light.

"I felt that thought and action were no longer connected with the earthly tenement, but that they were in a spirit-body in every respect similar to the body which I knew to have been mine, and which I now saw lying motionless before me on the bed. The only link which held the two forms together seemed to be a silvery light, which proceeded from the brain. As if it were a response to my earlier waking thoughts, the same voice, only that it was now more musical than before, said: 'Death is but a second birth, corresponding in every respect to the natural birth; and should the uniting link now be severed, you could never again enter the body. As I told you, however, this will not be. You did wrong to doubt, even for an instant, for this was the cause of your having suffered; and this very want of faith is the source of every evil on your earth. ... Be very calm, for in a few moments you will see us all; but do not touch us. Be guided by the one who is appointed to go with you, for I must remain near your body.'

"It now appeared to me that I was waking from a dream of darkness to a sense of light, but such a glorious light! Never did earthly sun shed such rays, strong in beauty, soft in love. This heavenly light came from those I saw standing about me. Yet the light was not of their creating, but was shed on them from a higher and purer source, which only seemed the more adorably beautiful in the invisibility of its holy love and mercy thus to shower every blessing on the creatures of its creation. And now I was bathed in light, and about me were those for whom I had sorrowed. One that I had never known on earth then drew near, and said, 'You will come with me, Daniel?' I could only reply that it was impossible to move, inasmuch as I could not feel that my nature had a power over my new spirit-body.

"I was wafted upward, until I saw the earth, as a vision, far, far below us. Soon I found that we had drawn nearer, and were just hovering over a cottage that I had never seen; and I also saw the inmates, but had never met them in life. The walls of the cottage were not the least obstruction to my sight; they were only as if constructed of a dense body of air, yet perfectly transparent; and the same might be said of every article of furniture. I perceived that the inmates were asleep; and I saw the various Spirits who were watching over the sleepers. I was most deeply interested in all this, when my guide said, 'We must now return.' When I found myself near the body, I turned to the one who had remained near my bed, and said, 'Why must I return so soon, for it can be but a few moments I have been with you; and I would fain see more and remain near you longer?' She replied, 'It is now many hours since you came to us; but here we take no cognisance of time, and as you are here in spirit, you, too, have lost this knowledge;

we would have you with us, but this must not be at present.' ... "I heard no more, but seemed to sink as in a swoon, until consciousness was merged into a feeling that earth with its trials lay before me, and that I, as well as every human being, must bear my cross. And when I opened my eyes to material things, I found that the little star I had lain watching had given way to the sun, which had been above the horizon about four hours; making in all some eleven hours that this vision had lasted. My limbs were so dead that at least half an hour elapsed before I could reach the bell-rope to bring anyone to my assistance, and it was only by continued friction that, at the end of an hour, I had sufficient force to enable me to stand upright. "I merely give these facts as they occurred; let others comment on them as they may. I have only to add that nothing could ever convince me that this was an illusion or a delusion; and the remembrance of those hours is as fresh in my mind now as at the moment they took place."

In the autumn of 1853, Home quitted Newburgh for New York, with the intention of beginning a course of medical study. One after the other, various hindrances linked themselves together into a chain of circumstances opposing the fulfilment of his wish; until, convinced that another career was destined for him, he began to feel the necessity of abandoning his cherished plan.

His friends at Newburgh had wished him to promise that, during his residence in New York, he would give no séances without their express consent. Impressed by the cures already wrought through him, they were eager to see him become, as Dr. Hull expresses it in one of his letters, "a physician who would do honour to his race;" and in the hope of developing speedily and remarkably his gift of healing, they insisted on his pursuing a course of severe and solitary study. But of all natures, the joyous, affectionate, social temperament of Home was most unfit for solitude, and suffered most from the effects of a life unhealthy to all, and to him repulsive. In January 1854, he fell ill. "I had been so left to myself in solitude and study the whole winter," he records in the *Incidents*, "that mind and body were alike disturbed. I wrote to my friends saying that I could not think of continuing the life I then led; and after many letters had passed between us, I was again left to myself to decide as to my future course. I had friends in Boston, who, as soon as they knew what my intentions were, generously offered to do all that my other friends had been doing, and to allow me perfect liberty to see whom I might please."

On recovering his liberty of action, he stayed for some time with the Elmers at Springfield, where manifestations occurred of which an account was published by one of the witnesses, Dr. Gardner, of Boston. "With the room well lighted," he wrote, "we were many times touched more or less forcibly, producing a peculiar and indescribable sensation. Some of us distinctly felt the form of the spirit hand, a soft, delicate, elastic, yet powerful touch, which cannot be described, but must be felt to be appreciated. "The reader," added Dr. Gardner, "will bear in mind that the hands of every person present were in plain view on the top of the table."

Home passed much of the spring and summer of 1854 in Boston, where frequent and remarkable séances took place, the rare phenomenon of the apparition of a phantom form being observed on more than one occasion. For part of the summer he lived at Roxbury; and as his health seemed gradually improving, he reverted, in spite of former obstacles and disappointments, to his wish of studying for a medical diploma. Among his correspondents at this time and subsequently, was one of the most distinguished of American preachers and theologians, Dr. T. M. Clark, now Bishop of Rhode Island, who, in the years 1853 and 1854, was residing at Hartford, Connecticut. South Manchester, the home of the Cheney family, is not far distant; and Dr. Clark was a friend of the Cheneys, in whose views a revolution had been wrought by their experiences with Home. The wonderful particulars communicated to him determined Dr. Clark to inquire into the subject; and he availed himself of the various visits of Mr. Home to Hartford and its neighbourhood to carry on in his own house a patient and searching investigation of the phenomena. As to the results of that inquiry, I may leave the following letter from Bishop Clark to Home to speak for itself:

"Hartford, June 2, 1854."

"My dear Daniel, It is a glorious June morning, and I think that I will have a little chat with you. I can imagine you looking out from your elevation in Roxbury upon the distant sea, and then up into the more distant heavens, to see who are looking down upon you from above. I can also imagine you squaring away at your table, digging into French and German.

"One law, if I were you, should be as the laws of the Medes and Persians. I would not 'sit' but twice a week for anybody. You have been over excited of late, and now 'the grasshopper is a burden.'

"Don't allow yourself to be too sensitive as to the opinions and notions of other people. I think that this is perhaps the source of your greatest trouble. You have the consciousness of integrity: let that suffice for the present the future will settle the rest. You have the pleasant assurance of having been the instrument of conveying incalculable joy and comfort to the hearts of many people. In the case of some you have changed the whole aspect of their existence; you have made dwelling-places light that were dark before; you have, then, a right to be happy yourself.

"And again, you never ought to feel that you are living in a state of dependence upon others. For you give infinitely more than you receive. Never have one distrustful thought as to the future. You will see bright sunshine yet.

"Every evening, as we sit down in our snug parlour, we say as a regular chorus, 'Oh, if Dan were only here!' We intend to drive to Manchester in a day or two. My book is posted up to that last night in your chamber. Those tangible demonstrations cannot be recorded on paper.

"Write me as soon as you can.

Very affectionately yours,

Thomas M. Clark.

The excellent advice of Dr. Clark, that he should lay down a law to hold at most two séances a week, Home could not act upon. He was surrounded by eager inquirers, who were determined that he should not act upon it. As for that sensitiveness in which his correspondent justly discerned a source of trouble to him, it was one of the conditions of his phenomenal life a hard condition, but one of which no effort would have enabled him to divest himself. He was created to feel both joy and sorrow more keenly than other men, and his life was so ordained that the sorrow should largely predominate over the joy.

A few weeks later, Dr. Clark writes to Home again:

"Hartford, June 25, 1854."

"My dear Daniel, I expect to be in Newbury port on the Fourth of July, and shall return here on the 5th, by way of Boston. Please to let me know whether I shall find you home on Wednesday, the 5th. How I wish that you could only drop in upon us this quiet Sunday evening! It seems hardly possible that we can ever have any more of those wonderful scenes which we passed through with you. When I recall the incidents as they occurred, they appear too great to be believed. Do you get anything new that is, anything different in kind from what we have experienced? It is rather hard for us to be deprived of all that is going on in Boston and Brooklyn. I have been so occupied with other matters, that I have now a strong appetite for something a little spiritual."

What were the wonderful scenes, it will be asked, to which the Bishop refers? Dr. Clark does not afford me any information; not that he denies the evidence of his senses any more than he did in 1854, but that those who were too timid to give their names to the world, when the impression made by the phenomena was fresh, are still more unwilling now. I will relate briefly the remaining events of Home's life in America, and then conclude this chapter with an extract from the scanty information in my possession concerning the séances at Hartford. Home kept no record of those séances or of any others; he left the phenomena to speak to the beholders, and the beholders to speak in their turn to the world, if they had the courage. Not very many displayed that courage; and with regard to the Hartford manifestations, there are few now left on earth to speak of what they saw and tested in Home's presence more than thirty years ago.

Home spent the winter at New York, going much among the poorer classes, and holding séances with them. He had again entered on his medical studies, and again they were interrupted by the failure of his health. The winter that year was unusually bitter; and by January 1855, the symptoms had grown so alarming that all thought of continuing his studies had to be abandoned. A year previously, his left lung had been pronounced diseased. Dr. Gray of New York, and other eminent medical friends whom he now consulted, united in declaring that the malady had made such progress as to render his condition one of grave danger, and in recommending, as the best hope of prolonging his life, a voyage to Europe.

That recommendation was the sole and sufficient reason why Home quitted America. It cost him a hard struggle to follow the advice so pressingly tendered. "I was to be separated from those who would have tended me with every affection," he writes, "and to be thrown as it were a stranger in a strange land. My family had by this time all been residents of America for some time, and I knew no one friend in all England."

His many friends in the States wrote, as soon as the verdict and advice of the physicians became known to them, to express their deep grief at the news and press him to pay them parting visits before he sailed. I quote a few words from a letter in my possession written to Home early in 1855 by Mrs. Clark:

"I am grieved at the result of Dr. Gray's examination, for I had always tried to persuade myself that no serious difficulty existed. But oh, it cannot be that you are to pass away from us soon. I will not think of it. I am sure that, with care and a quiet course of life, you may be spared to us many years yet, and enjoy a good degree of health, as many do under such circumstances."

February and March 1855, were passed by Home in paying farewell visits to his friends; they and he both thinking it was the last time they should meet on earth. In March he was at Hartford, Conn., and held one or two last séances there. Three years later a lengthy narrative of one of these séances was published in the Hartford Courant (March 6th, 1858), but as the writer only signs himself "D." I have been unable identify him. The editor of the Courant prefixed to "D.'s" narrative the following introductory remarks. Perhaps they may enable some American readers to identify the "D." to whom they refer:

"The gentleman who signs the subjoined communication was appointed by the Secretary of War a member of the Board of Examiners of the national military school at West Point last summer (1857). At West Point he was selected by the Board of Examiners from their number to deliver the parting address to the cadets. We mention these facts as significant of the mental calibre and culture of the writer."

"The friend to whom I was indebted for an introduction to Home," writes "D," "being well acquainted with my scepticism upon these matters, arranged that the 'circle' should sit in my own house, that all suspicion of machinery or any other underhanded contrivance might be removed at the outset. It was also left for me to determine who should compose the circle. I selected a party of ladies and gentlemen of whom it was presumed that two, from previous investigations with Mr. Home, admitted the reality of these phenomena, and were inclined to believe in the spiritualistic solution. The remaining eight scouted both the theory and the facts.

"I could not help consoling Home when I saw him, a youth at the age of twenty, pale, emaciated, and suffering from consumption, confronted by such an array of mature, hard headed scoffers at his pretensions."

The séance, relates "D.," was held in a room lighted by a gas chandelier with four burners; and the party sat at a large oral table, seven feet eight inches in length. The table vibrated, loud raps were heard, and various phenomena succeeded, which "D." minutely describes. Among them, an accordion played in "D.'s" hand, he holding the instrument by the end farthest from the keys. "Home was seven feet eight inches from me," "D." writes, "and could not have reached me even if his entire body had been extended in my direction."

"These spiritual phenomena," continues "D.," "had so repeatedly refused to appear in my presence and respond to my wooing, that in regard to then I was inclined to reject all testimony. One sitting with Mr. Home disabused me of this incredulity, and convinced me, not of the alleged spiritual agency, bat that the marvels which attend him are genuine, and cannot be explained by jugglery, collusion, deception, or hallucination, but must be solved, if solved at all, by some law of nature or of mind as yet undiscovered. I affirm this of no other medium but Home, for my attempts to extract miracles from other professors of this art have proved most signal failures."

Home spurns every inducement to invest his wonderful power in business, and engage in rapping as a trade. He is rather too wary of his rare gift, and displays it only on urgent solicitation, as a favour to those he likes, or as a grace to the psychological inquirer.

"It is less preposterous to my mind," declares "D.," in terminating his account of the séance, "to adopt even the spiritual hypothesis than to believe that Home could accomplish all this by his feet, while twenty suspicious eyes were fastened upon him."

Throughout this narrative, Home's name is spelt "Hume," a mistake made by many persons besides the writer in the *Hartford Courant.* Home always wrote his name "Home," but he retained the ancient Scottish pronunciation of that name, "Hume;" hence the difference between his own mode of spelling it and that sometimes mistakenly adopted by others. He was much amused when, on one occasion, a very oracular acquaintance wrote to some American newspaper to settle, once and For ever, the question whether the name were Home or Hume, by announcing that with his own ears he had heard the bearer of that name pronounce it Hume, and that those persons who spelt it Home, only showed that they had never met its owner.

In Mr. Home's *Incidents in My Life,* published in 1863, is contained (pp. 56–61) the narrative of a séance that took place at Hartford, Connecticut, on March 14, 1855, within a few days of the other séance described by the *West Point Examiner* "D." The name of the witness who furnished this narrative was not published in the *Incidents.* He was Mr. Frank L. Burr, editor of the *Hartford Times,* and has kindly sent me a letter attesting the facts narrated in the *Incidents,* and adding some further particulars to the description there given by him.

This Hartford séance of March 14th, 1855, was one of the last perhaps the very last held by Mr. Home in the States before he sailed. I extract a portion of Mr. Burr's narrative as published in the *Incidents.* The sitters on this occasion consisted of Mr. and Mrs. Burr, and Mr. Home:

"A paper was taken from the floor, slowly lifted up, and placed upon the table, as I can affirm, without the aid of a human hand. Sitting at the end of the table where this was done, I was enabled to see the whole of this proceeding. The paper was placed upon the edge of the table, and so near my hand as to touch it. I saw plainly and clearly the hand that held the paper. It was evidently a lady's hand, very thin, very pale, and remarkably attenuated. The conformation of this hand was peculiar. The fingers were of an almost preternatural length, and seemed to be set wide apart. The extreme pallor of the entire hand was also remarkable. But perhaps the most noticeable thing about it was the shape of the fingers, which, in addition to their length and thinness, were unusually pointed at the ends; they tapered rapidly and evenly towards the tips. The hand also narrowed from the lower knuckles to the wrist, where it ended. All this could be seen by the light that was in the room, and for a few moments the hand was holding the paper upon the edge of the table. "The hand," continues Mr. Burr, "presently took a pencil and began to write. This was in plain sight, being only shaded by one of the circle who was sitting between the paper on the table, and the fire. The hands of everyone present were upon the table, in full view, so that it could not have been one of the party who was thus writing. Being the nearest one to the hand, I bent down close to it as it wrote to see the whole of it. It extended further than the wrist. With a feeling of curiosity natural under the circumstances, I brought my face close to it in the endeavour to see exactly what it was, and, in so doing, probably destroyed the electrical or magnetic influence by which it was working; for the pencil dropped, and the hand vanished. The writing was afterwards examined, and proved to be the name, in her own proper handwriting, of a relative and intimate friend of one of the circle, who passed away some years since." ("My wife's cousin a lady who died some five years before," says Mr. Burr in a letter to me of April 1887.) "Other marks were also made, and the word 'Dear' had been written just as the pencil dropped. This writing has been preserved, and remains as an evidence of the reality of the fact. That it was produced by no hand of any one bodily in that room I know and affirm." A daguerreotype portrait of Mrs. Burr's cousin, taken shortly before her death (from consumption) was presented to Mr. Home subsequently to the séance. It has been preserved, and is now in my possession. The hands and fingers in the daguerreotype have the very same wasted look and singular conformation so minutely described by Mr. Burr. "The hand," says Mr. Burr in concluding his narrative published in the *Incidents*, "afterwards came and shook hands with each one present. I felt it minutely. It was tolerably well and symmetrically made, though not perfect; and it was soft and slightly warm. IT ENDED AT THE WRIST."

In his letter to me of April 6, 1887, Mr. Burr gives some additional particulars concerning the séance, and relates in detail the examination he made of the spirit-hand when it grasped his.

"Mr. Home came to our house rather late in the evening," he writes, "having been at the house of Mr. Day, then the editor of the *Hartford Courant*, all the evening. I invited him into the parlour for a séance. Nobody was present but Mrs. Burr and myself and Mr. Home."

Mr. Burr then details the phenomena of the séance as in his description written thirty years before; and on arriving at the point where the narrative given in the *Incidents* concludes, he subjoins the following particulars:

"The hand white as marble, and not visibly attached to any arm reached out to my hand, and shook hands with me; a hearty human shake. Then the hand sought to withdraw from mine. I would not let it. Then it pulled to get away, with a good deal of strength. But I held it firmly, resolved to see what it was. (All this time Mr. Home did not move, more than a dead man. He was too far back in his chair to reach me, without bending over forward.) When the hand found it could not get away, it yielded itself up to me for my examination; turned itself over and back, shut up its fingers and opened them; letting me examine the fingernails, the joints, the creases. It was a perfect human hand, but white as snow, and ENDED AT THE WRIST. I was not satisfied with the sense of sight to prove this I wanted the concurrent testimony of other senses; and I swung my hand and arm up and down, where the arm belonging to this hand should have been had it been of flesh and bone, but no arm was there. Even then I was not satisfied. Turning this strange hand palm towards me, I pushed my right forefinger entirely through the palm, till it came out an inch or more visibly, from the back of the hand. In other words, I pushed my finger clear through that mysterious hand. When I withdrew it, the place closed up, much as a piece of putty would close under such circumstances leaving a visible mark or scar, where the wound was, but not a hole.

"While I was still looking at it the hand vanished quick as a lightning-flash. It was gone!"

The remarkable séance above was also described by Mr. Burr, in 1875, in the *New York Sun*; his narrative being headed "A Strange and Startling Story."

CHAPTER 2

England and Italy

Arrival in England. Séance at Cox's Hotel. Controversy with Sir David Brewster. Damaging testimony against Sir David. Lord Brougham. Lord Dunraven's testimony. Browning and Sludge. Lord Lytton's experience. Thompson's opinion. Experience of the Trollopes, mother and son. Journey to Florence. Attempted assassination.

IN APRIL 1855, Home landed in England. "I never can forget my feelings," he writes in his first volume of *Incidents*, "as I looked around me, and saw only joy beaming on the faces of my fellow-passengers; some there were who were about to reach their home, and the thought of kind friends waiting to welcome them brought the smile of joy to their countenances. I stood there alone, with not one friend to welcome me, broken down in health, and my hopes and the fairest dreams of youth all, as I thought, forever fled. The only prospect I had was that of a few months' suffering, and then to pass from earth. I had this strange power also which made a few look with pity on me as a poor deluded being, devil-sent to lure souls to destruction, while others were not chary in treating me as a base impostor. I stood there on the ship's deck amongst the crowd of passengers, and a sense of utter loneliness crept over me, until my very heart seemed too heavy for pie to bear up against it. I sought my cabin, and prayed to God to vouchsafe one ray of hope to cheer me. In a few moments I felt a sense of joy come over me, and when I rose I was as happy as the happiest of the throng."

Home's presence in London soon became known, and without having courted it, he found the notice of English society attracted to him. More requests for séances were pressed upon him than he could gratify; and among other noted personages of the day, Lord Brougham expressed a desire to investigate the phenomena. An afternoon séance was appointed, and Brougham requested and received permission to bring with him a scientific friend, Sir David Brewster. In full daylight, these two shrewd inquirers sat with Home, the proprietor of the hotel in Jermyn Street where he was staying being also present. This was Mr. W. Cox, a most worthy and excellent man, who had speedily become, and remained till the day of his death, the fast friend of Mr. Home. The effect produced on the minds of the two investigators by what they witnessed was subsequently attested by Mr. Cox in a letter to the *Morning Advertiser*, dated October 15, 1855.

"I assert," he wrote, "that both Sir David and Lord Brougham were astonished at what they heard, saw, and felt. I assert that Sir David, in the fullness of his astonishment, made use of the expression, 'This upsets the philosophy of fifty years.' ... I assert that Lord Brougham was so much interested that he begged me to arrange for him another sitting, and said he would put off every engagement for the purpose of further investigation."

After the séance, Mr. Home wrote to a friend in America a description of his English experiences, in the course of which he very naturally and truly stated of Lord Brougham and Sir D. Brewster, that both had brought the whole force of their keen discernment to bear upon the phenomena with a view to accounting for them by natural means, and had been unable to so. The letter was published and commented upon in America, and the statements of the American press presently found their way into English journals. Long before they did so, Home had left Jermyn Street on a visit to Mr. Rymer of Baling; a London solicitor in large practice; and at Baling, Sir D. Brewster was present at a second séance. A few days later Mr. Rymer received a letter, of which the following are the first few lines:

"Sir, In consequence of a very remarkable account given by Sir David Brewster of the extraordinary powers of Mr. Home, together with two or three friends I am anxious to have an interview with him. If he can make it convenient to come to my house, No. 80, Eaton Square, on Thursday or Saturday next, at two o'clock, I should be glad to make an appointment for either of those days, your obedient servant,

Edward Buller."

A still more' decisive testimony to the effect produced on Sir

David's mind is on record.

"I was so struck," wrote the late Earl of Dunraven, "with what Sir David Brewster with whom I was well acquainted had himself told me, that it materially influenced me in determining to examine thoroughly into the reality of the phenomena. I met him one day on the steps of the Athenaeum; we got upon the subject of table turning and he spoke most earnestly, stating that the impression left on his mind from what he had seen was that the manifestations were to him quite inexplicable by fraud, or by any physical laws with which we were acquainted, and that they ought to be fully and carefully examined into."

As yet, the assertion that Sir David had been converted to a belief in Spiritualism had not been copied from the American press by the English; and the philosopher, with the first feelings of wonder and bewilderment strong in his mind, had the frankness, as the words of Lord Dunraven and Mr. Buller show, to confess to his friends that the phenomena he had witnessed in the presence of Mr. Home were inexplicable by the theory of fraud. At last, in September, 1855, the *Morning Advertiser* reproduced the American statements; and Sir David at once wrote to that paper to disclaim all belief in Spiritualism, and to set down to imposture the very phenomena that he had assured Lord Dunraven could not have been produced by trickery and were inexplicable by any physical laws with which he was acquainted.

A lengthy correspondence followed. Sir David, in a second letter, declared that, had he been allowed to look under the table, he might perhaps have been able to expound the riddle of the phenomena. "I assert," replied Mr. Cox of Jermyn Street, "that no hindrance existed to Sir David looking under the drapery of the table; on the contrary, he was so frequently invited to do so by Mr. Home, that I felt annoyed at Mr. Home's supposing that either he or I could be suspected of any imposition." So much for the séance in Jermyn Street. Sir David was requested to verify the absence of concealed mechanism, but declined a curious mode of conducting a scientific investigation. Yet he afterwards assumed its presence. Was it honest of him to do so in view of his refusal to examine, and still more in view of the fact that at Baling he actually did examine? Invited by Mr. Rymer to give his testimony to facts, the well-known author, Mr. T. A. Trollope, responded as follows, in a letter written for publication:

"I declare that at your house at Ealing, on an evening subsequent to Sir David Brewster's meeting with Mr. Home at Cox's Hotel, in the presence of Sir David, of myself, and of other persons, a large and very heavy dining table was moved about in a most extraordinary manner; that Sir David was urged, both by Mr. Home and by yourself, to look under the cloth and under the table; that he did look under it; and that while he was so looking, the table was much moved; and that while he was looking, and while the table was moving, he avowed that he saw the movement.

"I should not, my dear sir," ends Mr. Trollope, "do all that duty, I think, requires of me in this case, were I to conclude without stating very solemnly that, after very many opportunities of witnessing and investigating the phenomena caused by, or happening to Mr. Home, I am wholly convinced that, be what may their origin, and cause, and nature, they are not produced by any fraud, machinery, juggling, illusion, or trickery on his part."

Sir David was as fully convinced of that, in his secret soul, as Mr. Trollope, but he had a scientific reputation to lose, and he feared ridicule; so, after declaring in private that the manifestations could not have been produced by jugglery, he declared in public that they could, and wrote, "Were Mr. Home to assume the character of the Wizard of the West, I would enjoy his exhibition as much as that of other conjurors." On which Mr. B. Coleman of Bayswater wrote to the *Morning Advertiser*:

"I was as much astonished at what I saw, felt, and heard in the presence of Mr. Home as any man; and when I found that Sir David Brewster had been a witness of similar phenomena at the house of my friend, I called upon Sir David, accompanied by my neighbour; and in the course of conversation Sir David said, that what he and Lord Brougham saw 'was marvellous quite unaccountable.'

"I then asked him, 'Do you, Sir David, think these things were produced by trick?'

'No, certainly not,' was his reply.

'Is it delusion, think you?'

'No, that is out of the question.'

'Then what is it?'

To which he replied, 'I don't know; but spirit is the last thing I will give in to.'

"The publication of this letter naturally made Sir David very angry, and he wrote to contradict it in part, not denying the substantial accuracy of the above statements, but challenging the writer's reproduction of the description that Sir David had given him of the phenomena in Jermyn Street. Brewster then continued:

"In reply to Mr. Cox, I may take this opportunity to answer his request by telling him what I have seen, and what I think of it. At Mr. Cox's house, Mr. Home, Lord Brougham, and myself, sat down to a small table, Mr. Home having previously requested us to examine if there was any machinery about his person, an examination, however, which we declined to make. When all our hands were upon the table, noises were heard rappings in abundance; and, finally, when we rose up, the table actually rose, as appeared to me, from the ground. This result I do not pretend to explain; but rather than believe that spirits made the noise, I will conjecture that the raps were produced by Mr. Home's toes, . . . and rather than believe that spirits raised the table, I will conjecture that it was done by the agency of Mr. Home's feet."

This from the man who had declared so emphatically to Lord Dunraven and Mr. Coleman that he could not suppose the phenomena were produced by trickery!

Sir David then described, the remaining phenomena that he had witnessed in Jermyn Street, and continued: "How these effects were produced neither Lord Brougham nor I could say, but I conjecture that they may be produced by machinery attached to the lower extremities of Mr. Home."

Which machinery a keen and sceptical observer like Brewster could not detect in broad daylight! Nor could he say, in full daylight, whether a table rose in the air or not, but only that it "appeared "to him to rise.

All through this newspaper warfare Lord Brougham preserved an inflexible silence; and Sir David Brewster did not venture to appeal to him. Is not the inference certain that Sir David dared not and that his lordship would not speak, though requested by Mr. Home to do so, and though he had half-promised to publish an account of the séance, because his testimony must have been unfavourable to his friend? That Lord Brougham's views were not in accordance with those of Brewster may be inferred from the fact that in 1860 or 1861 Brougham was again present at séances with Home, and from his remarkable declaration made in a preface written by him for Mr. Groom Napier's work, *The Book of Nature*: "In the most cloudless skies of scepticism, I see a rain cloud if it be no bigger than a man's hand: it is Modern Spiritualism."

Said the *Spectator*, when the whole correspondence was republished by Mr. Home in his first volume of *Incidents*: "It seems established by the clearest evidence that he" (Sir David) "felt and expressed, at and immediately after his séances with Mr. Home, a wonder and almost awe, which he afterwards wished to explain away. The suppression of Lord Brougham's half-promised testimony, though challenged by Mr. Home, is on the whole unfavourable to Sir David, as it might be presumed that Lord Brougham would support his friends testimony as far as possible. Nor does the passage-at-arms between Sir David and Mr. T. A. Trollope concerning the subsequent séance at Baling, seem to us quite creditable to Sir David. The hero of science does not acquit himself as we could wish or expect."

How could he? Sir David was not conducting the controversy in the interests of truth, but in the interests of David Brewster. When compelled to decide whether he would tell the truth and be laughed at, or prevaricate and have the world on his side, the philosopher did not hesitate for a moment. But it so happened that he had already placed his honest opinion of the Jermyn Street séance on record; and the letter that contains it was published by his daughter, Mrs. Gordon, in her Home Life of Sir David Brewster. As there could not be a better witness against Sir David than himself, I append the words in which he contradicts the statements he had made in the *Morning Advertiser.*

"Last of all, I went with Lord Brougham to a séance of the new spirit-rapper, Mr. Home, a lad of twenty. Mr. Home lives in Cox's Hotel, Jermyn Street, and Mr. Cox, who knows Lord Brougham, wished him to have a séance, and his lordship invited me to accompany him in order to assist in finding out the trick. We four sat down at a moderately sized table, the structure of which we were invited to examine. In a short time the table shuddered, and a tremulous motion ran up all our arms; at our bidding these motions ceased and returned. The most unaccountable rappings were produced in various parts of the table; and the table actually rose from the ground when no hand was upon it. A larger table was produced, and exhibited similar movements. ... A small hand-bell was laid down with its mouth on the carpet; and after lying for some time; it actually rang, when nothing could have touched it. The bell was then placed on the other side, still upon the carpet, and it came over to me and placed itself in my hand. It did the same to Lord Brougham.

"These were the principal experiments. We could give no explanation of them, and could not conjecture how they could be produced by any kind of mechanism."

Written with no idea that it would ever see the light, this letter undoubtedly contains Sir David Brewster's true impression of the phenomena he had witnessed. He could not explain them: he could only see that they were not, as he subsequently and dishonestly suggested, due to trickery on the part of Mr. Home.

It should be added, with regard to Sir David's "conjecture" that the table might have been lifted by the feet of Mr. Home, that at the Ealing séance the table used was a dining-table twelve feet long; that Sir David Brewster, Mr. T. A. Trollope, I, and Mr. Rymer did, as a matter of fact, experiment on it after the séance to see whether it were possible to move the table or to raise it with their feet, and that it could not be stirred by the united efforts of the feet of all three.

No doubt thousands of tables have been tilted by human feet and hands, and Faraday's famous theory of the action, unconscious or conscious, of the sitters, was applicable to many séances, but never to those of Mr. Home. Only those who have witnessed the phenomena can realize how startling and peculiar they were in his presence. Many persons have attested the facts detailed in the following description, and many more could bear witness to its exactitude had they the courage to come forward.

The phenomena that marked the commencement of a successful séance were, as a rule, as follows:

While the hands of Mr. Home and the other persons present rested on the table, a curious phenomenon would fix the attention of the circle. The table did not move, it was neither tilted nor raised; but the hands resting on it felt it quiver and tremble as if instinct with life. When the power was strong, these vibrations affected not only the table but everything in the room, and often the floor and walls also shook. Some have compared the vibrations to the beating of a pulse; others to the ripples that pass over a sheet of water when its surface is lightly stirred by the wind. The phenomenon was well described by Dr. J. Garth Wilkinson, or rather by his daughter, in his *Evenings with Mr. Home and the Spirits*, published at the time of the Brewster controversy.

"In a minute or two the same inward thrill went through the table as I have described in the first séance, and the chairs also, as before, thrilled under us so vividly that my youngest daughter jumped up from hers, exclaiming, 'Oh, papa, there's a heart in my chair!' which we all felt to be a correct expression of the sensation conveyed."

Presently the tremors would cease, and raps were forthwith heard, as if the vibrations that passed through the table had marked the period occupied in charging it with some subtle force, electrical or otherwise, that was now given off in these tiny detonations. The raps were as varied in their character as human nature is varied, timid, bold, clear, muffled, changing with every intelligence that produced them; just as in this world no two persons will knock at a door in a manner exactly similar. "I have heard," wrote Mr. W. Crookes, F.R.S. "delicate ticks, as with the point of a pin; a cascade of sharp sounds as from an induction coil in full work; detonation in the air; sharp, metallic taps; a cracking like that heard when a frictional machine is at work; sounds like scratching; the twittering as of a bird, &c."

When the power was present in great force, not only did the largest and heaviest tables repeatedly rise from the ground when the hands of the sitters were on them; but a mass of evidence is on record that at séances with Mr. Home tables, chairs, and many other objects have been seen in strong light to move about the room or to rise in the air, when neither Home nor any other of the human beings present was touching them. The world is slow to attach credence to such a fact, but a fact it is, if human eyesight and human testimony count for anything. Sir David Brewster, one of the most hostile and sceptical of inquirers, attests the phenomenon in the letter published by his daughter; and Mr. Crookes wrote: "I have had several repetitions of the experiment considered as conclusive by the committee of the Dialectical Society, that is to say, the movement of a heavy table, in full light, the backs of the chairs being turned towards the table, at about a foot away from it, and each person kneeling on his chair, his hands placed on the back, above the table, but without touching it."

Means were often adopted by inquirers to test the correctness of Professor Faraday's theory in the case of Mr. Home. For instance, in 1868, Mr. J. H. Simpson of Campden Grove, Kensington, a gentleman of considerable scientific attainments and a disbeliever in Spiritualism, placed rollers on the table, and on these a large flat music-book. The fingers of Mr. Home and the other sitters rested lightly on the music-book, and while the result of this experiment was watched above, Mr. Simpson lay down on the floor to see that no foot touched the table below. The table moved more violently than before, and Mr. Simpson quite satisfied himself that the movement, to whatever cause due, was independent of any person present. This experiment, it will be seen, was made three years before Mr. Crookes employed a different apparatus with similar results.

At séances with Mr. Home, when the table tilted, the tilting was almost always accompanied by a very startling phenomenon. No matter how acute the angle, the various articles on the table, such as pens, pencils, paper, lamps, candlesticks, etc., would remain in their place as if glued to it. This has been seen to occur again and again in the strongest light; and at the demand of persons present the force retaining the article in its place has been instantaneously relaxed, and the substance so released has slipped from the inclined surface of the table. Sometimes it would be requested that a particular article might thus slide down, while others on the table kept their places; and the invisible forces at work always complied with the request.

The Earl of Dunraven wrote, in describing a séance in 1867, at which he, Mrs. Thayer, and Mr. Earl, the latter a total disbeliever in the phenomena, were present with Mr. Home: "The room was lighted by a fire, a large lamp standing on the piano, and two wax candles on the table. The table was repeatedly tilted up at an angle, I should say, greater than 45. The surface was smooth, polished mahogany, yet the candles, paper, and pencil did not move. Home asked that the candles might slip (as they naturally would), and they did slide down the table until near the edge, when at his request they remained stationary."

In 1860, Robert Bell wrote in his famous article "Stranger than Fiction," contributed to the *Cornhill Magazine* while Thackeray was editor:

"Of a somewhat similar character is another movement, in some respects more curious, and certainly opening a stranger field for speculation. The table rears itself up on one side, until the surface forms an inclined plane, at an angle of about forty five degrees. At this altitude it stops. According to ordinary experience everything on the table must slide off, or topple over; but nothing stirs. The vase of flowers, the books, the little ornaments are as motionless as if they were fixed in their places. We agree to take away our hands, to throw up the ends of the cover, so as to leave the entire round pillar and claws exposed, and to remove our chairs to a little distance, that we may have a more complete command of a phenomenon which, in its marvellous development at least, is, I believe, new to us all. Our withdrawal makes no difference whatever; and now we see distinctly on all sides the precise pose of the table, which looks like the Tower of Pisa, as if it must inevitably tumble over. With a view to urge the investigation as far as it can be carried, a wish is whispered for a still more conclusive display of the power by which this most extraordinary result has been accomplished. The desire is at once complied with. The table leans more and more towards the perpendicular; two of the three claws are high above the ground; and finally the whole structure stands on the extreme tip of a single claw, fearfully overbalanced, but maintaining itself as if it were all one solid mass, instead of being freighted with a number of loose articles, and as if the position had been planned in strict accordance with the laws of equilibrium and attraction instead of involving an inexplicable violation of both."

The evidence of various other witnesses of this phenomenon will be found in subsequent chapters.

Before the Brewster controversy begun, Mr. Home had left England, and was passing the autumn of 1855 at Florence, while his assailants and defenders were filling the columns of the *Morning Advertiser*. After leaving Cox's Hotel, he had spent the summer with the Rymer family at Baling, and the warm affection with which these new English friends soon learnt to regard their young guest is repeatedly, expressed in their letters subsequently written to him. Many years later one of those pitiful creatures who invent and publish falsehood, but forget to sign their names to them, set afloat a story that soon went the round of the American press. It was said that Mr. Horn had ordered in the name of Mr. Rymer a fur-coat, value £50, and had left his generous host to pay for it.

"A lie that is all a lie may be met and fought with outright, but a lie that is half a truth is a harder matter to fight."

And so Mr. Home found. The half-truth in this particular slander was that a gift of £50 had entered into his relations with the Rymer family. But it was not the value of the apocryphal fur-coat, and so far from having received a gift of £50; Mr. Home had made it, under the following circumstances:

A few years after the séances at Baling, business embarrassments and the conduct of others involved Mr. Rymer in absolute ruin. His being a declared Spiritualist was against him in England; and despairing of finding an opening at home; he went to Australia to try his fortune there. His wife and children were longing to join him, but had not the means. In her distress Mrs. Rymer wrote to Mr. Home, recalling old days at Baling, and entreating him in memory of them to aid her. This was in the autumn of 1859, and on November 1st of that year Mrs. Rymer was able to write to Mr. Home a letter now before me. I quote only as much of it as is necessary for my purpose:

"My dear Dan, I cannot in words express my thanks for your affectionate liberality, which enables me to follow my beloved husband to the new country. Most heartily, most sincerely do I thank you for what you have given; also, Dan, for your prayers and good wishes. Believe, with affectionate greetings and many prayers, how truly I am always, dear Dan, in this or a far-off country, your sincere and grateful friend,

Emma Rymer."

The sum that Mr. Home sent was £50. This gift of £50 to Mrs. Rymer is the only traceable foundation for the falsehood that he had wronged her husband. It was but one of a thousand slanders circulated concerning him.

During his stay at Ealing, frequent séances were held, and remarkable manifestations occurred. It was at this time that he made the acquaintance of Dr. Garth Wilkinson, who published in a very interesting pamphlet, *Evenings with Mr. Home and the Spirits*, an account of the phenomena he had witnessed and the striking communications he had received. Dr. Wilkinson gave no names in his pamphlet, and at the distance of thirty years it is impossible to recover them, or I would have supplied them in the following extract:

Dr. Wilkinson relates that he was present at the séance with Mr. Home, where there was spelled out by touches on his knee, a message from "an intimate friend of mine, once a Member of Parliament, and as much before the public as any man in his generation, who died on the 30th of June last"(1855). "I said, 'Have you any message to your wife, whom I shall probably see in a few days?' Again affirmative touches, five in number, therefore calling for the alphabet. Mr. Home now called over the alphabet, and this was spelled out: 'The Immortal Loves'. "I remember at the time thinking that this was rather a thin message; but the next time I saw Mrs. I told her the circumstances, and gave hex the words. Her son was sitting with her, and said, 'That is very characteristic of my father, for it was a favourite subject of speculation with, him whether or not the affections survive the body; of the immorality of the soul itself he never doubted; but the words, the immortal loves, show that he has settled the problem of his life.' Such was the import which the family of the deceased quite unexpectedly to me conferred upon the phrase."

Lord Lytton, then Sir E. B. Lytton, was perfectly convinced of the genuineness of the phenomena he witnessed in Mr. Home's presence, and even of their spiritual origin, but too timid to avow his convictions publicly. Mr. Home was his guest for a short time at Knebworth in 1855, and several séances took place there, no record of which is available. Home never wrote down an account of a séance, but left it to others to speak; and when, from fear of the world or fear of ridicule, they preferred to remain silent, he acquiesced in their silence with the easy good nature that characterized him. His mission, as he understood it, was to convince people of the facts: if they were bold and honest enough afterwards to declare what they had witnessed, that was as it should be; if they kept silence, it was their affair, not his. Almost any other man in his place would have laboured to accumulate all the names and data possible; not perhaps for publication in his lifetime, but at any rate that the full story of his life might he told when he had quitted earth. Home collected nothing, published in his two volumes of *Incidents* such séances as friends chose to give him, or had already made public; and let the memory of the rest perish, many of them more remarkable than those given to the world. These facts explain why nothing can be said here of the séances at Knebworth. Mr. Home kept no record of them; and Lord Lytton, though he probably preserved one, never published it.

In the years 1860 and 1861, Lord Lytton was again present at many séances with Mr. Home, both at Knebworth and in London. Of the latter I can give some details, obtained from other persons who were present; and shall do so in the proper place.

At Baling, Sir E. B. Lytton took part in at least one séance at the house of the Rymers. During the lifetime of this celebrated man, Mr. Home published in his first volume of *Incidents* the following description of what occurred; and as Lytton remained silent though; the press at once detected his identity, and called on him either to deny or affirm it may be presumed that the account was absolutely correct. In a matter of this kind to be silent was to affirm, and that Lord Lytton could not but know.

"Whilst I was at Ealing," says Mr. Home, "a distinguished novelist, accompanied by his son, attended a séance, at which some very remarkable manifestations occurred that were chiefly directed to him. The rappings on the table suddenly became unusually firm and loud. He asked, 'What spirit is present?' The alphabet was called over, and the response was, 'I am the spirit who influenced you to write Z -(Zanoni). 'Indeed,' said he, 'I wish you would give me some tangible proof of your presence.' 'What proof? Will you take my hand?' 'Yes,' and putting his hand beneath the surface of the table, it was immediately seized by a powerful grasp, which made him start to his feet in evident trepidation, exhibiting a momentary suspicion that a trick had been played upon him. Seeing, however, that all the persons around him were sitting with their hands quietly reposing on the table, he recovered his composure, and offering an apology for the uncontrollable excitement caused by such an unexpected demonstration, he resumed his seat."

Immediately after the above phenomenon, another equally remarkable occurred. "We wish you to believe in the" was spelt out, and there the message stopped.

"In what am I to believe? "asked Lytton. "In the medium?"

"No."

"In the manifestations?"

"No."

"As this second negative was returned, Sir Edward felt himself gently touched on the knee, and on putting down his hand a cross was placed on it, by way of finishing the sentence. The cross, which was of cardboard, had been lying with other articles on a table at the end of the large room in which the party were seated. Lytton, apparently much impressed, turned to Mrs. Rymer, and asked her permission to retain the cross as a souvenir.

"She assented, saying that its only value to her was that it had been made by her boy, then recently deceased; but she could have no objection to him keeping it, if he would remember the injunction.

"He bowed his assent, and placing the souvenir in his breast-pocket, carried the cross away with him (*Incidents in my Life, Vol. I*).

The following undated note preserved by no process of selection, but at random, as the mass of Mr. Home's correspondence was preserved or destroyed belongs evidently to this period:

"1 Park Lane, Wednesday."

Dear Sir, I am very anxious to see you for half an hour. It would be very kind of you so to favour me.

"You said you would try and see if you got en rapport with me. Has any such been established? I would come to you at Baling if more convenient, whenever you like to appoint. Yours truly,

E. B. Lytton."

Perhaps none of the thousand falsehoods circulated concerning Mr. Home has been more persistently repeated than the assertion that he was found cheating by Mr. Robert Browning. Mr. Browning himself, in his unpoetic effusion, "Mr. Sludge, the Medium," appeared to lend a certain colour to the fable, or it would probably soon have died the death natural to slanders that have not a grain of fact in their composition. The press, on the appearance of "Mr. Sludge," insisted that he was meant for Home. Had this been an error, Mr. Browning, as an honourable man, would of course have written to some leading English journal to correct it.

"It is 'a blot on the scutcheon'," wrote the American authoress, Mrs. Whitman, on the publication of Mr. Browning's prose-verse, and a harsher term might with justice have been used of the incoherent attack that was declared by the English journals of the time to be directed against Mr. Home as the foremost living exponent of Spiritualism. Flattered into an opinion of his own infallibility by his admirers, Mr. Browning has probably long been in the habit of considering that the truth of any proposition which he may advance is self-evident, or he would have felt that even the angriest poet who chooses to write as follows, should have been prepared to back up his poetical flights, when challenged to do so, with the plain prose of facts:

"Now don't, sir! Don't expose me! Just this once! This was the first and only time, I'll swear, Look at me, see, I kneel, the only time, I swear, I ever cheated."

"Well, sir, since you press (How you do tease the whole thing out of me!) now for it, then."

"I cheated when I could, Rapped with my toe-joints, set sham hands at work, Wrote down names weak in sympathetic ink, Rubbed odic lights with ends of phosphor-match, And all the rest."

Mr. Browning's poetic eye, in its "fine frenzy rolling," saw, in the retirement of his study, more than the thousands of keen inquirers who so narrowly, and in many cases so sceptically, investigated the phenomena during a period of thirty years in the presence of Mr. Home. In all that time, no person present at a séance with Mr. Home, sceptic or Spiritualist, ever found him rapping with his toe joints, or setting sham hands at work, or writing names in sympathetic ink, or rubbing odic lights with phosphor match, "and all the rest of it."

Let any reader, however stubborn his incredulity as to the reality of the phenomena, trv to consider calmly what is involved in the proposition that, year after year, Mr. Home continued to manufacture sham hands and set them to work, but that none of the thousands of persons who both saw and touched these hands ever detected them to be an imposture! I shall speak more fully of these spirit-hands in other chapters: here it is enough to say that they have again and again appeared under circumstances that made detection an absolute certainty, had they been, as some ingenious theorists have surmised, wax casts, or stuffed gloves manipulated with wires, or, in fact, anything but what they were, a marvellous phenomenon, inexplicable by any known physical laws.

The late Robert Bell was quite as shrewd, intelligent, and honest a man as Mr. Browning. He described in the *Cornhill* his experiences with Mr. Home; and his friend, Thackeray, a keen and intensely sceptical observer, who had also witnessed various phenomena in Home's presence, endorsed his declarations by publishing with them the note: "As editor of this magazine, we can vouch for the good faith and honourable character of our correspondent, a friend of twenty-five years' standing."

Says Mr. Bell: "Soon after, what seemed to be a large hand came under the table-cover, and with the fingers clustered at a point, raised it between me and the table. Somewhat too eager to satisfy my curiosity, I seized it, felt it very sensibly, but it went out like air in my grasp. I know of no analogy in connection with the sense of touch by which I could make the nature of that feeling intelligible. It was as palpable as any soft substance, velvet or pulp; and at the touch it seemed as solid, but pressure reduced it to air."

Would that Mr. Browning had seized the hands he saw at Baling, whose action, in placing a wreath on the brow of his wife and omitting to crown his own, may possibly have given him deep offence! Had the poet been a man of large and liberal nature, he would have forgiven the want of discernment the spirits showed reflecting that, while all the world does homage to the genius of his wife, the larger half of it fails to comprehend his own.

Mrs. Browning, it is well known, accepted Spiritualism as a fact. In her *Notes on England and Italy*, Mrs. Hawthorne, the wife of Nathaniel Hawthorne, writes: "Mrs. Browning introduced the subject of spiritism, and there was an animated talk. Mr. Browning cannot believe, and Mrs. Browning cannot help believing."

When the Browning Society has succeeded in explaining the other poems of Mr. Browning to the world if it ever accomplishes that herculean task perhaps it will be bold enough to take the poem (or prose) of "Mr. Sludge, the Medium," in hand, and explain why Mr. Browning had the bad taste to write it. There is nothing in the account of the single séance at which Mrs. and Mr. Browning were present at Ealing, given by Mr. Home in his second volume of *Incidents*, vouched for by Mr. W. M. Wilkinson, and never challenged by the poet, to explain either Mr. Browning's conduct or his motives.

"Mr. and Mrs. Rymer and their family," writes Mr. Home, "were present at the séance, which began by several of the ordinary manifestations. Mr. Browning was requested to investigate everything as it occurred, and he availed himself freely of the invitation. Several times during the evening, he voluntarily and earnestly declared that anything like imposture was out of the question. Previously to the arrival of Mr. and Mrs. Browning, some of the children had been gathering flowers in the garden, and Miss Rymer and I had made a wreath of clematis. During the séance this wreath was raised from the table by supernatural power in the presence of us all, and whilst we were watching it, Mr. Browning, who was seated at the opposite side of the table, left his place, and came and stood behind his wife, towards whom the wreath was being slowly carried, and upon whose head it was placed in full sight of us all, and whilst he was standing close behind her. He expressed no disbelief; as, indeed, it was impossible for any one to have any of what was passing under his eyes; whilst Mrs. Browning was much moved, and she, not only then but ever since, expressed her entire belief and pleasure in what then occurred. All that was done in the presence of eight persons besides Mr. and Mrs. Browning, all of whom are still living, and are ready to testify to the truth of every word here written, if it should be gain said by Mr. Browning."

Was Mr. Browning annoyed that to him there came no crown? All the Rymer family thought so, at least. Yet the invisible wreath-bringers were probably only anticipating the verdict of posterity, both in their neglect of him and in crowning his gifted wife.

At any rate, Mr. Browning subsequently elaborated a theory to account for the manifestations; and, forgetting that he had voluntarily and earnestly declared that anything like imposture was out of the question, his theory, if Mrs. Hawthorne and the *Notes on England and Italy* may be trusted, was that the hands were in some way "affixed in Mr. Home's chair, with his legs stretched far under the table." It was natural to some minds, as Sir David Brewster had already shown, to grasp eagerly, when the first sensation of Bonder had passed away, at any explanation of the phenomena, however ridiculous and futile, that did not involve a belief in the spiritual.

It would be a complete waste of time and labour to contradict one by one the many calumnies that have been circulated concerning Mr. Home; and I dwell on the above incidents only because so many fabulous versions of the single séance with Mr. and Mrs. Browning have been circulated, both in England and America. It may be interesting to quote here the following extract from a letter written to Mr. Home by an old friend, a well-known English medical man, so long after the Ealing séance in 1870:

"Since I saw you I have been in the Isle of Wight. I went to lunch with Alfred Tennyson, and had two or three hours' talk with him. He says that if he and you and I could have a sitting or two in daylight, or in a strong artificial light, and he convinced himself of the facts, he should have no hesitation in proclaiming his belief in any way. Meantime he says that he is much more inclined to believe than to disbelieve. He had all those tales about you from Browning, including one that you went on your knees, wept, and confessed your imposture in a certain thing. I told him Browning was mad about the matter, and he admitted that B's manner led him to credit his prejudices more than his statement."

I do not know what prevented Mr. Home from gratifying Lord Tennyson's wish to investigate, but probably the fact that in 1870 his time was much occupied and he was absent more than half the year from England. I pass now from the subject of the calumnies that have been invented and circulated concerning Mr. Home, with the determination not to recur to it, but to relate simply the facts of his life, and leave them to speak for themselves.

In the pamphlet of Dr. Garth Wilkinson, already referred to, the doctor, like Robert Bell, relates how he, on one occasion, grasped a spirit-hand. The result was the same as in the case of Mr. Bell.

"Every hand but my own being on the table, I distinctly felt the fingers, up to the palm, of a hand holding the bell. It was a soft, warm, fleshy, substantial hand; such as I should be glad to feel at the extremity of the friendship of my best friends. But I had no sooner gasped it momentarily than it melted away, leaving my hand void, with the bell only in it. ... As a point of observation, I will remark that I should feel no more difficulty in swearing that the member I felt was a human hand' of extraordinary life, and not Mr. Home's foot, than that the nose of the Apollo Belvedere is not a horse's ear."

In the early autumn of 1855, Mr. Home went to Florence on a visit to the well-known writer, Mrs. Trollope, accompanied by the son of his Baling host, Mr. Rymer. The invitation had been given by Mrs. Trollope during her stay at Baling; she and her son, Mr. T. A. Trollope, having come from Italy to London that summer expressly to investigate the phenomena occurring in the presence of Mr. Home. She left England convinced of their genuineness; and Mr. T. A. Trollope, as I have already shown, shared her certainty. As to the theory that the manifestations might be produced by trickery, that accomplished gentleman wrote, at a period subsequent to the manifestations at Baling and Florence: "I may also mention that Bosco, one of the greatest professors of legerdemain ever known, in a conversation with me upon the subject, utterly scouted the idea of the possibility of such phenomena as I saw produced by Mr. Home being performed by any of the resources of his art." And in a letter to the Athenaeum, written from Florence eight years later (March 21, 1863), Mr. T. A. Trollope said: "I have been present at very many 'sittings' of Mr. Home in England, many in my own house in Florence, some in the house of a friend in Florence. My testimony is this: I have seen and felt physical facts wholly and utterly inexplicable, as I believe, by any known and generally received physical laws. I unhesitatingly reject the theory which considers such facts to be produced by means familiar to the best professors of legerdemain."

In Florence the interest aroused by the arrival of such a visitor was even greater than in London. Society talked of nothing but his wonderful powers; and though some shunned him in the fear that they were of demoniac origin, the great majority eagerly sought the acquaintance of Mr. Home, and made every effort to be admitted to his séances.

Mr. Hiram Powers, the celebrated sculptor, writes as follows concerning the séances held in Florence:

"I recollect we had many séance at my house and others, when Home was there. I certainly saw, under circumstances where fraud, or collusion, or prearrangement of machinery was impossible in my own house, and among friends incapable of lending themselves to imposture very curious things. That hand floating in the air, of which all the world has heard, I have seen. There was nothing but moonlight in the room, it is true; and there is every presumption against such phenomena, under such circumstances. But what you see, you see; and must believe, however difficult to account for it.

"I recollect that Mr. Home sat on my right hand; and besides him there were six others, round one half of a circular table, the empty half towards the window and the moonlight.

"All our fourteen hands were on the table, when a hand, delicate and shadowy, yet defined, appeared, dancing slowly just to the other side of the table, and gradually creeping up higher, until, above the elbow, it terminated in a mist. The hand slowly came nearer to Mrs., at the right side of the table, and seemed to pat her face. 'Could it take a fan?' cried her husband. Three raps responded 'Yes,' and the lady put her fan near it, which it seemed trying to take. 'Give it the handle,' said her husband. The wife obeyed; and it commenced fanning her with much grace. 'Could it fan the rest of the company? Someone exclaimed; when three raps signified assent, and the hand, passing round, fanned each of the company, and then slowly was lost to view.

"I felt, on another occasion, a little hand it was pronounced that of a lost child patting my cheek and arm. I took hold of it; it was warm, and evidently a child's hand. I did not loosen my hold, but it seemed to melt out of my clutch." Powers' testimony corroborates that of Robert Bell and Dr. Wilkinson. In 1871 the experience of Mr. William Crookes, F.R.S was exactly similar. I shall refer in another chapter to the researches of Mr. Crookes; here I content myself with citing a few words from his narrative. The phenomena that he describes are attested by him to have occurred in a strong light.

"I have retained one of these hands in my own," writes Mr. Crookes, "firmly resolved not to let it escape. There was no struggle or effort to get loose, but it gradually seemed to resolve itself into vapour, and faded in that manner from my grasp." Dr. Wilkinson (of whom the *Spectator* said, March 14, 1863, "In the honour of his personal character we have good reason to believe") grasped one of these hands in 1855, Hiram Powers in the same year, Robert Bell in 1860, and Mr. Crookes in 1871. In each of the four cases the result was the same: there was no effort at withdrawal, but the warm, life-like hand that had been seized melted in the grasp. Set against these facts the contradictory declarations of Mr. Browning, during and after the single séance he attended, and to which side does the balance of testimony incline? If still further evidence be asked for, let the reader turn to the narratives in subsequent chapters of this work, and read the accounts furnished to me of these unearthly hands by observers quite as sceptical as Browning, but more reasonable and less prejudiced. If he wishes to balance poet against poet, let him turn to the letter in which the distinguished Russian poet, Count Alexis Tolstoy, relates how he travelled to London in the year 1860 expressly to meet Mr. Home; how, at a séance at Mrs. Milner Gibson's, he seized a hand that appeared and touched him, and what was the result of this decisive method of verifying the phenomenon.

Whatever the Italian peasant may have become since the political redemption of Italy, he was in 1855 an extremely bigoted and superstitious creature. At Florence in that year his fears and passions were worked on to the prejudice of Mr. Home. He was told perhaps by the priesthood that Home was a vile necromancer, who administered the sacraments of the Church to toads, in order, by spells and incantations, to raise the dead. In January, 1856, Signor Landucci, Minister of the Interior to the Grand Duke of Tuscany, warned Home of these reports and the excitement they had created among the peasantry; but he had already received a terrible proof of the fact that his life was in danger in Florence.

The winter of 1855 was very severe there. Late one bitter night that of the 5th of December Mr. Home was returning to his rooms alone through the deserted streets, when, just as he reached the house where he was staying, a man stepped from the adjoining doorway. In the *Incidents*, Home describes what ensued:

"I was on the step leading to my own door, and was looking up at the window to see if the servant was still up, when I received a violent blow on my left side, the force of which, and the emotion caused by it, threw me forward breathless in the corner of the doorway. The blow was again repeated on my stomach, and then another blow on the same place; and the attempted assassin cried out, 'Dio mio, Dio mio!' and turning with his arm outstretched, he ran. I distinctly saw the gleam of his poignard; and as he turned, the light of the lamp also fell full on his face, but I did not recognize his features. I was perfectly powerless, and could not cry out or make any alarm; and I stood thus for at least two minutes; after which I groped my way along the wall to the door of a neighbour, where I was admitted. I thought I must have received some serious injury; but on examining myself I found that the first blow had struck the door key, which I happened to have in my breast pocket, immediately over the region of my heart. I wore a fur coat, and this had chanced to be twice doubled in front. The second blow had gone through the four folds of it, through a corner of my dress coat, my waistcoat, and the band of my trousers, without inflicting any wound. The third blow had penetrated the four folds of my coat, and also my trousers and linen, and made a slight incision, which bled, but not freely."

It appears by the following letter that an accident to an acquaintance was the cause of Mr. Home being alone on the night in question:

"Casa Salviata, Via Chiara," Friday, December 7, 1855.

"My dear Home, I should have certainly have gone to see you, were I not laid up with a sprained ankle, which prevented my meeting you at the Colombia on Wednesday evening, and coming home with you that evening. Perhaps there being two, might have prevented the accident that happened to you. I am delighted to hear you came almost miraculously out of it; and though I do not think that I am of a revengeful nature, still I sincerely wish the cowardly scoundrel to get what he deserves; and, could I in any way be of use to you, pray dispose of me. Believe me to be, dear Home, yours very truly. "C. T. Fuller."

The attempted murderer was never arrested. Probably superstitious bigotry was the passion that inflamed him; though some persons thought robbery to have been the motive of the crime; and it was even suggested that Mr. Home might have been mistaken for another man.

CHAPTER 3

Italy and France

Temporary cessation of Home's powers. Conversion to Roman Catholicism. Napoleon III. Return of his powers. Séance with the Empress Eugene. Fontainebleau. Refusal of, 2,000 for a sitting. Cure of a deaf boy.

EARLY IN 1856, HOME, who was then suffering severely in health from the trying winter and the shock to his sensitive temperament of the dastardly crime from which he had so narrowly escaped, made the acquaintance at Florence of a Polish nobleman, Count Branicka, and of his mother, the niece of the famous Potemkin. The Count, with his family, was about to visit Naples and Rome, and invited his new friend to accompany him. Hardly had the invitation been given and accepted, when Home's power left him. His conduct under these unexpected circumstances was characteristic of the self-respect and delicacy of his nature, and met with a worthy response from Count Branicka.

"The spirits," writes Mr. Home in the *Incidents*, "told me that my power would leave me for a year. This was on the evening of the loth of February 1856. Feeling that the Count and his family must have felt an interest in me arising only from the singular phenomena which they had witnessed in my presence, and that this cause being removed, their interest in me would have diminished, I wrote the following morning to inform them of what I was told, and to say that I could no longer entertain the idea of joining them. They at once told me that it was for myself, even more than for the strange gift I possessed, that they had become interested in me. I went to them; and in a day or two we left Florence for Naples."

Either there or previously at Florence, Mr. Home made the acquaintance of Prince Luigi, the brother of the King of Naples, who presented to him one of the numerous souvenirs that he was destined to receive from royal personages, in token of their esteem and friendship. It was a ring set with a ruby shaped in the form of a horseshoe; and his Highness at the same time had a second ring exactly similar wrought for himself, and always wore it. The ruby is a brittle gem; and it was so difficult to shape two horseshoes from it, that, before the Prince's orders could be carried out, seven stones were broken.

These presents from crowned heads and members of royal families had no other value in Home's eyes than the memories attached to them. They were marks of gratitude and esteem; and as such he cherished them, preferring, in the moments of his greatest poverty, to support any hardships rather than part with a single stone. It is a mistake to suppose that these jewels were an indirect recompense for séances. He never accepted recompense for a séance, direct or indirect. The three most valuable rings that Home possessed were presented to him by the Emperor Alexander II, and in each case the circumstances under which the gift was made rendered it doubly precious. One ring was the wedding-gift sent by the Czar in 1858, at the time of Home's first marriage. The following year, on the birth of a son, his Majesty presented an emerald set with diamonds; and thirteen years later, in 1871, the Emperor, on the occasion of our marriage, sent to Mr. Home a ring set with a sapphire of great size, surrounded with diamonds. The sapphire Home retained in the ring; the diamonds he caused to be set in an exquisite ornament of his own design, and presented this to me as a marriage gift.

Nothing could have been more gracious and delicate than the Czar's behaviour to Home on every occasion when the latter was his Majesty's guest. I relate in another chapter an incident connected with Mr. Home's presentation to the Emperor of Russia in 1858, which not only does honour to both the Czar and himself, but would alone explain why Home always remembered Alexander II with peculiar esteem and gratitude, and received with the profoundest grief and horror the news of the hideous crime that in 1881 deprived Russia of her beloved sovereign.

Naples, so beautiful to look on and so unpleasant to live in, was Home's residence for six weeks in the early spring of 1856. In addition to Prince Luigi, he became intimate with the Hon.

Robert Dale Owen, American Minister at the Neapolitan Court; to whom he had a letter of introduction from Owen's father, whose life was consumed in the heroic attempt to prove that in England Socialism is possible. The elder Robert Owen, then almost a dying man, had been staying at Cox's Hotel when Home was there; and in his letter to his son he speaks very warmly of the kind attentions his young acquaintance had shown him.

I have not Mr. Dale Owen's work, *Footfalls*, before me, and cannot say with certainty whether the manifestations he describes himself as having witnessed in Mr. Home's presence occurred in 1856, or two years later, when Home returned to Italy. More than probably the latter, as his power had quitted him at the time of the earlier visit; though it may be remarked that there were a few detached phenomena during the twelvemonth of its absence, notably the "Gregoire" manifestation that summer at Paris, which Home recorded in the *Incidents*, but mistakenly gave the date as 1857.

From Naples, the Branicka family and their guest went to Rome, where the Catholic influences that surrounded him exerted themselves constantly and effectively to turn his thoughts towards seeking refuge in the Church. They were aided by the cruel experiences he had recently suffered. The falsehood of friends to whom he was much attached had wounded him keenly, the occurrences that closed his stay at Florence had profoundly saddened him; and while these clouds darkened the natural sunshine of his spirit a veil had been suddenly dropped between him and the world beyond, and all counsel and comfort from it was withdrawn. In this gloomy moment, Catholic advisers suggested to him that the peace of mind he longed for might perhaps be found in the Church of Rome, and he sought and read with intense eagerness works relating to her doctrines. "Finding them expressive of so many facts coincident with my own experiences," he writes, "I thought that all contending and contradictory beliefs would be for ever set at rest, could I but be received as a member of that body. My experiences of life and its falsity had already left so indelible a mark on my soul, from my recent experiences of it at Florence, that I wished to shun everything which pertained to this world, and I determined to enter a monastery. After two or three weeks of serious deliberation on the part of the authorities, it was decided that I should be received as a member of the Church, and I was confirmed."

Pius IX gave an audience to the young convert, and received him with the most benign favour. An English prelate, Monsignore Talbot, accompanied Home to the Vatican. "The Pope questioned me much regarding my past life," writes the neophyte. "He pointed to a crucifix which stood near to us, and said: 'My child it is upon what is on that table that we place our faith.'"

There was nothing said of demoniacal possession. Possibly, in welcoming her new son, the Church had hopes that she might one day canonize in him a worker of miracles.

It was Monsignore Talbot to whose counsels Home had chiefly recourse in this important moment of his life; and I find among his papers a letter from that prelate, dated on the eve of his confirmation, and giving directions to him concerning it.

Not only did Pius IX favour Mr. Home with an audience, and converse with him in the most benignant manner, but he subsequently sent him his special blessing, guaranteeing to Home and to his relatives an entry into Paradise. Home preserved this interesting document, and it is now in my possession.

Whom the king smiles on, courtiers smile on; and the gracious bearing of the Pope was imitated by all the hierarchy of Rome, from cardinals downwards. The path that led the young convert up to the monastery gates was strewed with roses, and, amidst the applause and encouragement of all round him, he might have finally seen those gates close on him, but that the nearer he drew to the monastic life the less that life allured him, and the stronger became his misgivings. He had hoped to find peace in it; but his hopes soon changed to fears that peace very rarely inhabits the cell of the monk. Did not Christ set the example of living in the midst of the world and is not the task of following that example less agreeable and more difficult? Convinced that to shut himself in a monastic cell would be a fatal error, he drew back and refused to enter. This determination was no sooner arrived at than he quitted Italy; and in company with the Branicka family, betook himself to Paris, in June 1856.

Although Home had renounced his purpose of entering a

monastery, the Pope's interest in him did not cease. Perhaps his Holiness hoped that he might yet be persuaded to take the vows; what is certain is that, before Home left Rome for Paris, Pius IX had personally counseled him to select for his confessor there one of the most excellent and eloquent of French priests, the celebrated Père de Ravignan. In him Home found a kind friend, whose lofty piety delighted him and in whose society he took great pleasure. There was but one point on which he and the good Father differed. It had been foretold to Home when his power left him, that it would return exactly a twelvemonth later, on the 10th of February, 1857, and he was convinced that the promise would be kept; but when he said so to Père de Ravignan, the priest always confidently replied: "Have no fear of that, my child so long as you go on as you are now doing, observing carefully all the precepts of our holy Church, they will not be allowed to return."

During the winter Home again fell ill; and Dr. Louis, one of the most celebrated physicians in France for consumptive cases, decided on auscultation that the left lung was diseased, and advised a more genial climate. His patient was without the means of acting on his advice, and remained in Paris, where for some time he was confined to his bed.

"On the night of the 10th of February, 1857," he writes, "as the clock struck twelve, I was in bed, to which I had been confined; when there came loud rappings in my room, a hand was placed gently upon my brow, and a voice said, 'Be of good cheer, Daniel; you will soon be well.' But a few minutes had elapsed before I sank into a quiet sleep, and I awakened in the morning feeling more refreshed than I had done for a long time. I wrote to the Père de Ravignan, telling him what had occurred; and the same afternoon he came to see me. During the conservation, loud rappings were heard on the ceiling and on the floor; and, as he was about to give me his benediction before leaving, loud raps came on the bedstead. He left me without expressing any opinion whatever on the subject of the phenomena."

The predicted return of Home's power on the 10th of February 1857 was known at the French Court; and the following day the Marquis de Belmont, chamberlain of the Emperor, presented himself to inquire if he had regained it. An Imperial invitation to the Tuileries followed; and he was presented to the Emperor and Empress. This was on the 13th of February; and certain personages of the Court were selected by their Majesties to be present at a séance held the same evening.

No account was published of this or any séance at the Tuileries; but a few of the particulars became known in the Parisian world; and as they passed from lip to lip a thousand fabulous details were added, until, in the imagination of French society, Home assumed the proportions of a necromancer with a host of familiar spirits at his command, over whom he exercised the authority of a Manfred or a Faust. It was in vain for him to make known again and again, in the most emphatic terms, the fact that he was nothing but the instrument of the phenomena, and had never pretended to evoke spirits or exercise any influence over them; the world of Paris would have its way; and in the journals and caricatures of 1857, Home, who was perfectly unable to say at the commencement of a séance whether there would be manifestations or not, figures always as the imperious summoner of a legion of familiars, who are his very humble servants. Now he is evoking Caesar in a Parisian salon, and startled society looks on while he sets the august shade to brush his boots; in another caricature he directs with a wave of his magic wand the operations of a number of detached hands that act as barbers and hairdressers to the company. In a third, the wizard is packing to quit Paris. A number of little imps stand meekly around, waiting their turn to be popped into the box where their fellows are already imprisoned; but the master goblin of the party, a fiend with the most imposing of tails and horns, is on his knees before the magician, begging for a longer stay. "Ah, my dear master," remonstrates the poor demon, "If you would but consider how much I like Paris, and how perfectly the society suits me here?"

The pictures that caricaturists drew in sport presented themselves to the imagination of the excellent Père de Ravignan in grim earnest. In his eyes the spirits were demons, and he who communed with them was a lost soul. Again and again he had assured Home that these evil beings would not be permitted to return to him; that the spirits must perforce keep their distance now he was a son of the Roman Church and specially blessed by the Pope. The night of February 10th falsified his prediction; but in spite of this proof that the invisibles actually could approach a son of the Church, though specially fortified by the Papal blessing, Père de Ravignan clung stubbornly to the belief that the forces at work were those of evil. The morning after the first visit to the Tuileries, Home called on him to tell him of the séance there.

"He expressed great dissatisfaction at my being the subject of such visitations; and said that he would not give me absolution unless I should at once return to my room, shut myself up there, and not listen to any rappings, or pay the slightest attention to whatever phenomena might occur in my presence."

Home attempted to reason with his confessor. He represented that the strain on his nervous system of the solitary confinement prescribed to him would be too great for endurance. As for paying no attention to the phenomena.

"How can I help it?" said Home. "If I were to strike on this table with my hand, could you avoid hearing?

"Yes," said the Father, stubbornly faithful to the traditions of his order: "I only hear when I wish to hear, and see when I wish to see."

"But, my Father, if you would listen to reason."

"You have no right to reason with me," replied the priest. "Do as I bid you, or bear the consequences."

"I left him," writes Home, "in great distress of mind. On reaching my room, I found there a very dear and valued friend, the Count de K (de Komar).

"He observed my agitation, and questioned me as to the cause. I told him all, and he said, 'There is but one thing to do; come home with me, and we will send for the Abbé de C, and consult him.'"

(Abbé Deguery of the Madeleine; murdered by the Communists in 1871.) "The Abbé came; and, after hearing my story, he said, 'That they might as well put me in my grave alive as to try to carry out what had been ordered;' adding, 'I would like very much to witness some of these wonderful things' Most fortunately my emotion had not destroyed the power, as is usually the case when I am agitated, for while we were together several interesting phenomena occurred. His words were: 'Let this power be what it will, it is in no way of your making.' He recommended me to seek another spiritual adviser, and added, 'I myself would gladly be your adviser, but, as it would be known, I should only be persecuted.' He gave me the name of one of the most eloquent preachers of the day, and I introduced myself to him, and remained under his guidance during the few weeks of my stay in Paris, previous to my going to America to bring back my sister."

There was great curiosity in Paris to find out Mr. Home's new confessor.

"The Countess L.—"(Lubinski), he writes, "having heard that he was a distinguished man, called upon several of the most noted in Paris; and after a short conversation, she abruptly said to each, ' So you are Mr. Home's confessor.' Most naturally, on one such occasion she chanced to find the right one, and his look of surprise betrayed him."

"M. Deguery," said Mr. Home in a letter published many years afterwards, "was ever a very kind friend to me, and he did not believe the manifestations to come from an evil source." As for Père de Ravignan, Home always cherished an affectionate memory of him; and that the good father had felt a more than common interest in Home, is sufficiently shown by his letters written before the return of the power caused the rupture of their relations. The following was one of the last that Home received from him:

"Mon bien cher enfant, Etes-vous malade? Faites-le moi savoir. J'irai pres de vous; car il y a trop longtemps que je ne vous ai vu. Vous savez que je vous aime tendrement en N. S. X. De Ravignan, S. J.

"Paris, 28 Janvier, 1857."

Six weeks after the return of his power, Home sailed for America. Of the séances that he had held in the interval, several were at the Tuileries; and though no details of these had been made public, a thousand partially or wholly untrue narratives circulated in Parisian society. Here is the true description of the first séance.

Although Home sometimes sat with as few as one or two, or as many as twelve or fourteen people present, his preference was to fix the number of sitters at seven or eight, both to prevent confusion, and because he had found that the manifestations were of more frequent occurrence with a moderate sized circle. On his first visit to the Tuileries, he informed their French Majesties that he should be able to admit to the séance eight persons at the most. The Empress was very vexed at this, having intended to bring her whole suite to the table with her; and declared that if Mr. Home persisted in his intention she should refuse to be present. Knowing that the presence of so many sitters would probably spoil the séance, Home could only express his profound regret that it was impossible for him to accept the conditions her Majesty insisted on. The Empress adhered to her resolve, and withdrew in displeasure; but the Emperor remained.

"I consent to your proposition, Mr. Home," said Napoleon. "Is there any other condition that you wish to be observed?"

"None, Sire," said Home, "and with your permission we will take our places at any table that your Majesty may indicate. I promise nothing, for I have no power over the manifestations; but should any occur, the first party of sitters may be replaced whenever your Majesty chooses by an equal number of other persons. I make this suggestion to prove my great desire to comply as far as possible with the wish of the Empress, although it is always a pity to interrupt a good séance."

Five personages of the Court were selected by the Emperor, and with his Majesty and Home took their places at the table, which, although large and massive, soon began to vibrate and tremble under the hands placed on it, then to move, and presently to be lifted from the ground. At last came raps on the table, and on the alphabet being called over, responses were given, not only to the spoken queries of the Emperor, but to questions he put mentally. Napoleon followed every manifestation with keen and sceptical attention, and satisfied himself by the closest scrutiny that neither deception nor delusion was possible. The replies to the Emperor's unspoken thoughts completed the impression made on him; and it was with a marked affability that he now addressed himself to Mr. Home, saying:

"I should very much like the Empress to see something of this. Will you consent to my going myself to seek her?"

"Certainly, Sire," said Home; "and if you desire, we will change the circle."

"No, no," said the Emperor, "I am much too anxious to see all that is possible of the manifestations, and will follow your counsels in every particular."

With these words Napoleon rose, and went to seek the Empress, who accompanied him on his return; but in taking her place in the circle, her Majesty said to Home, with a half-annoyed air, "I am only here on condition that next time all my party shall be present too; (toute ma clique y sera)." The manifestations were not long in recommencing; and Home once more desired the Emperor to investigate as closely as his Majesty pleased. Napoleon, extremely sceptical by nature, readily complied; looking under the table himself when raps came on it, and watching Home with the keenest scrutiny.

The Empress, in her turn, received through the rappings a reply to her unspoken thought; and presently feeling her robe pulled, started, and uttered a slight cry. Mr. Home sought to calm her agitation; and at his request she consented to place her hand below the table, Home saying, "If a hand takes that of your Majesty, I am confident that the touch will cause you no alarm." The Emperor and the other sitters looked on, Home's hands resting on the table. Immediately the look of the Empress took an expression of joy, but at the same time tears trembled in her eyes. When the Emperor asked the cause, she replied, "I felt the hand of my father in mine."

"How could you distinguish it?" asked the Emperor, incredulous.

"I would distinguish it among a thousand," answered the Empress, "from a defect in one of the fingers just as it was in life. As it lay in mine, I satisfied myself of this defect." The Emperor, in his turn, was touched by the hand, and verified the fact of the defect referred to by the Empress.

When the séance ended, her Majesty, still much moved, held out her hand to Home. "You will never again have reason to complain of me," she said; "and from this moment there shall only be present the number of sitters you prefer, and always the same persons."

Mr. Home quitted the Tuileries, leaving on the mind of the Empress an impression very different from that which he had produced before the séance.

Four personages of the Court were selected by their Majesties to be present at the second séance; the Duchess de Bassano and the Duchess de Montebello, with Count Tascher de la Pagerie and the Marquis de Belmont, Chamberlains of the Emperor. The evidences of the presence of an invisible but not the less real power caused a lively emotion to those who took part in the séance. The table rose to a height of several feet; then, to the astonishment of the beholders, descended gently and settled in its place again, light as a feather falling to the ground. An unseen force shook the apartment, till the crystal pendants of the lustre suspended in the middle rattled loudly against each other. A bell placed on the table was lifted by invisible hands and carried some distance; and a handkerchief that the Empress held in her hand was softly taken from her by invisible means and seen to rise and float in the air.

While the hands of all present rested on the table, other hands appeared. One of these, the small hand of a child, approached the Duchess de Montebello, who started back from it. The Empress was seated next to her. No longer susceptible of similar terror since she had held in hers the hand she recognized, she cried, "For my part, I am not afraid! (Moi, je n'ai pas peur!)" and caught the little hand in hers, where she felt it gradually melt back into air.

At this second séance at the Tuileries, the phenomenon of a massive table becoming light or heavy at desire exhibited itself in a marked degree, and greatly interested the Emperor, who assured himself of the fact by repeated trials, one moment easily moving the table with a couple of fingers, and the next, on the expression of his wish that it should become heavy; trying in vain to stir it with his whole strength. As this is one of the phenomena that have been attributed to delusion, it may be well to refer here to the experiments of Mr. Crookes.

"I had seen on five separate occasions," he writes, "objects varying in weight from 25 to 100lbs. temporarily influenced in such a manner that I and others present could with difficulty lift them from the floor. Wishing to ascertain whether this was a physical fact, or merely due to a variation in the power of our own strength under the influence of imagination, I tested with a weighing machine the phenomenon on two subsequent occasions when I had an opportunity of meeting Mr. Home at the house of a friend. On the first occasion, the increase of weight was from 8lbs, normally, to 36lbs, 48lbs, and 46lbs, in three successive experiments tried under strict scrutiny. On the second occasion, tried about a fortnight after, in the presence of other observers, I found the increase of weight to be from 8lbs. to 23lbs, 43lbs, and 27lbs, in three successive trials, varying the conditions." (*Quarterly Journal of Science*, October 1871.)

In the Salon Louis Quinze, at one of the Tuileries séances (I believe, the third), the hand of a man appeared above the table, on which a sheet of paper and a pencil were lying, placed there that any communications received might be written down. The hand moved across the table, lifted the pencil, and wrote on the paper the single word, "Napoleon." The writing was the autograph of the Emperor Napoleon I; the hand small and beautifully formed, as his is recorded to have been.

The Empress, moved by the sight of this hand, requested permission to kiss it; and it placed itself to her lips, then to the lips of the Emperor. The hand was distinctly seen; this séance, like all others at the Tuileries, being held in a good light.

In accordance with the promise of the Empress to Home, the same persons were usually present at each séance but occasionally one or two of the number were changed. I am not sure, however, that the four personages selected to be present at the Imperial séances, whom I have already named, were varied in any way until after the return of Home from America. After (or before) that short absence of Mr. Home, the Duchess of Hamilton was present at séances, as was also Prince Murat, of whom I have an anecdote to relate, interesting in view of the assertion sometimes made that Napoleon III remained always sceptical concerning the manifestations.

Some years after the séances at the Tuileries, Home was in London; and there was a séance one evening at the house of Lady Dunsany. Mrs. A. Senior, sister-in-law of the late Nassau Senior, was present, and a witness, after the séance, of the following occurrence, which I leave her to relate.

"Just as we were seated round the supper tray," writes Mrs. Senior, "a loud ring sounded from the door bell; and a servant came to say that two gentlemen were in the hall asking for Mr. Home, who immediately stood up and begged Lady Dunsany's permission to go down to them, when she most kindly said: 'Pray bring them up: any friends of yours will be welcome.' He quickly returned, introducing Prince Murat and Lord Adare (now Lord Dunraven). They had called hoping to catch Mr. Home at the end of his séance. After some very agreeable chit-chat, Prince Murat asked Mr. Home whether he remembered the first evening he met him at the Tuileries, and how very ill he had behaved, going under the table and laying hold of his feet, and declaring" that he would 'find out his tricks.' 'Was I not a saucy dog?' he said, to which Mr. Home laughingly agreed; and we were all much amused by the Prince's lively tale, which ended by his saying, turning to Mr. Home, 'When you left the room, the Emperor leant forward, with his arms on the table, and said, in the most impressive manner: "Whoever says that Home is a charlatan is a liar." "This we felt was information from the fountainhead. "They say, Sire, you believe in these things," said the Duke de Morney to the Emperor one day, when the talk was of the séances with Home.

"Whoever has said so is much deceived," replied Napoleon III. "I was sure of it, Sire," said the Duke delighted; "and felt it my duty to contradict the report."

"Quite right," said the Emperor; "but you may add, when you speak on the subject again, that there is a difference between believing a thing and having proof of it, and that I am certain of what I have seen."

I have mentioned that the Duchess de Bassano was one of the four personages of the Court selected by their Majesties to assist habitually at the Tuileries séances. The Duchess arrived one evening, wearing on her fingers rings that had been blessed at Rome, and having divers other consecrated objects attached to her bracelets. Curious to see what would happen, she said nothing of these saintly influences; but took her place as usual in the circle. Her new fashion of jewellery made no difference; or, if any, it seemed to encourage the manifestations; for the séance was very successful. The Duchess, astonished, demanded of the spirits if the neighbourhood of these consecrated objects was not disagreeable to them. "Not in the least," was the reply; and as a proof of the fact several manifestations were addressed to her personally.

An empty chair, at this séance, was seen to advance slowly from the end of the apartment, and to stop before the seat of the Empress. She made a gesture of surprise; and the chair recoiled to a little distance; then, as it halted, a motion was communicated to it that made it sway backward and forward. The Empress, as she watched the movement, recollected that it had been a habit with her father to balance himself thus in his chair; and inquired of Home, if he, the seer, could perceive any figure in the apparently empty chair before her. "Yes," he replied, "it is that of a soldier." "Give me a description of him," demanded the Empress. Home obeyed, and drew the portrait of her Majesty's father, whom he had not known, and of whom there existed but a single portrait, which the Empress, in whose possession it was, knew that Home had never seen.

The departure of Home from Paris in March 1857, astonished the Parisian world; and the press was at once filled with absurd and scandalous stories, to some of which I have referred in another chapter. In one thing the authors of these different falsehoods were agreed: Mr. Home's departure was compulsory, and he would never be seen in France again. In the meantime the subject of these calumnies was crossing the Atlantic, his sole errand being to bring to France his young sister, whom the Empress had offered to take under her protection and educate at her expense. As solicitous for the welfare of those whom he loved as he was negligent of his own, Home had accepted with much gratitude the kind and gracious proposal by which her Majesty proved how deep was the interest she felt in him.

The day before he sailed a wonderful case of healing occurred through his means, of which particulars are given in the *Incidents*, Vol. 1. Supplying the names of the witnesses, which' Mr. Home indicated only by initials, I reprint the circumstances here.

"On the 19th of March, 1857, when I was residing at 13 Rue des Champs Elysees, I received a letter from a stranger to me, Madame A. de Cardonne, of 233 Rue St. Dominique, St. Germain, stating that she had had a dream, in which she had seen her own mother and mine, and that the latter had told her to seek me at once, in order that her son, who had been deaf for four years from the effects of typhoid fever, might be cured. This was so strongly impressed upon her mind that she wrote to me to say that she would call upon me with her son, the following morning at ten.

"Accordingly, the next morning she presented herself with her son at my rooms, there being present the Princess de B. (Princess de Beauveau), and Miss E. (Miss Ellice), who were with me previous to my leaving Paris that very day, to proceed on my voyage to America. I had been so overwhelmed by persons wishing to see me that I had uniformly refused such visits; but on this occasion I had been so much preoccupied by my engagements in preparing for my voyage, that I had not been able to acknowledge her letter. I therefore received her with considerable embarrassment, which was fully reciprocated on her part. It was indeed an embarrassing meeting for both of us, the mother yearning for her son's recovery, and I not knowing how I was expected to be instrumental in healing this long total deafness, the more so that operations had been performed on the boy, as I afterwards found, by eminent surgeons of Paris, who had said that it was impossible he should ever be restored to hearing.

She sat down on a chair near a sofa, I taking a seat on the sofa and beckoning the son to be seated on my left. He was in his fifteenth year, tall for his age, of a delicate complexion, with large dreamy blue eyes that looked as if they would supply the place of hearing with their deep, thoughtful inquiring gaze. The mother began her description of the boy's illness, commencing with the attack of the fever, and ending in the entire loss of hearing. During the recital, told with all the warmth and tenderness of a mother's heart, and describing the various surgical operations to which he had been subjected, my sympathies were deeply moved, and I had unwittingly thrown my left arm about the boy and drawn him towards me, so that the boy's head rested upon my shoulder.

Whilst in this position, and as Madame de Cardonne was telling some of the most painful particulars, I passed my band caressingly over the boy's head, upon which he, partly lifting his head, suddenly exclaimed in a voice trembling with emotion, 'Maman, je t'entends!' (Mamma, I hear you!) The mother fixed on him a look of astonishment, and said, 'Emile!' (the boy's name); and he at once replied, 'Quoi?' (What?). She then, seeing that the child had heard her question, fainted with emotion; and on her recovery the scene was a most thrilling one the poor mother asking continually questions for the mere pleasure of hearing her child reply. The boy was able to resume his studies, and has continued to hear perfectly up to the present time" (1863.)

It was characteristic of Home that, as soon as Madame de Cardonne had left him, he quietly finished his preparations and started for America, without troubling himself in the least to make public the particulars of this wonderful cure, or to obtain the attestations of the mother and the witnesses. It was not till his return from America with his sister that Madame de Cardonne could write to him the grateful letter from which I extract the following passages:

"May 30th, 1857.

"Let me add myself to the number of those who love you, and who welcome your return.

"Messenger of Divine Providence! I bless you, for you have wrought a miracle for my son. I have inspired in all around me a sentiment of veneration for you, whose mission enlarges from hour to hour (grandit d'heure en heure)."

Madame de Cardonne then asks permission to introduce to Mr. Home her friend M. Sardou a name that has since become well known in France. I find among Home's papers a letter from Sardou, of nearly the same date as that of Madame de Cardonne, and expressing a hope that Home will name a day for the writer to call on him. It may be presumed, therefore, that the celebrated dramatist, among other persons, is able to testify to the fact that neither Madame de Cardonne nor the strange and sudden restoration of her son's hearing is a myth.

The mother's letter ends: "My son joins himself to me in offering you his tenderest regards. The kind caresses you bestowed on my poor child have resulted in so much good to me that the sweet memory of them will never leave me."

Again, on June 17th, 1857, she wrote:

"Dear, very dear Mr. Home. My son, who never ceases to bless you, begs me every day to take him to see you. He is so happy to have recovered his hearing that' he cannot rest till he expresses to you his gratitude. Will you be able to receive me tomorrow, Thursday, between 10 and 12?

"I renew to you, my very dear sir, the assurance of a devotion that I shall carry with me to the grave.

"A. Mauvoisin de Cardonne."

During Mr. Home's absence from France, Madame de Cardonne, the Princess de Beauveau, and Miss Ellice had all spoken to their friends of the miraculous cure; and the history was soon well known in Paris and eagerly discussed there. Many doubted, others credited; numbers carried their enthusiasm so far as to visit the house in the Rue des Champs Elysées, and entreat to see the chamber where the wonderful event had taken place. Some of these persons wrote to Home in a manner that was, of the many misconceptions concerning his mission, the most vexatious and intolerable to him. They addressed him in a language of worship, and exalted him to the height of a supernatural being. Home carried his repugnance to all such adulation, and his wish to be regarded as merely the instrument of the manifestations, to such a length that, after his séances, he was accustomed to reject even a simple expression of thanks from the persons present. "How can we thank you enough, Mr. Home, for the opportunity of witnessing such wonderful things!" was a frequent cry; and the invariable response was, "You will have thanked me sufficiently in not thanking me at all."

Neither angel, demon, nor charlatan, he wished it to be clearly understood that, apart from his extraordinary gift, he was a man like other men.

The restoration of hearing to the son of Madame de Cardonne was not the only extraordinary cure performed in France through the instrumentality of Mr. Home. I have selected it as one of the best known and best accredited instances of healing; but among his correspondence are preserved letters that testify to other cures wrought through him. Of similar manifestations in America and England, I have given details under the date of their occurrence.

When Home returned from America with his sister, the Empress graciously redeemed her promise by placing Christine Home in the celebrated convent of the Sacred Heart, where the daughters of the noblest families of France were educated. The Court was then at Fontainebleau; and Home was speedily summoned there, as a royal visitor had delayed his departure expressly that he might have the opportunity of seeing something of the phenomena on Home's return. This was the old King of Bavaria, predecessor of the sovereign whose melancholy fate is fresh in the recollection of the world. The séance was a successful one; and the Bavarian monarch, being new to the manifestations, was not only interested but startled by them; and overwhelmed Home with questions, much to the amusement of their French Majesties.

As several of the manifestations at Fontainebleau were of the same description as those witnessed at the Tuileries, I pass over them. A striking incident of the evening was the following:

An accordion was brought to Home that one of the Court servants had been sent to buy in the first shop in Fontainebleau. It was perfectly new, and Home had not even seen it before the séance. He held it in one hand, and it played; then Home withdrew his hand, and the instrument, without mortal fingers touching it, executed a charming air, which voices were distinctly heard accompanying. All present listened spellbound; and little by little these aerial voices seemed to recede into the distance, and were heard more faintly, till, as the music ceased, they died away, too, like an echo.

The next day was a Sunday. There was no séance in the morning, but in the midst of a conversation raps were heard. One of the ladies of the Court touched in succession the letters of a written alphabet, while another wrote down the letters the raps indicated. In this way the message "etlam" was received, a word incomprehensible to all present. The rappings began again, and added the letters "es" but "etlames" was as unintelligible as the first communication. A third time raps were heard, and gave the key to the enigma by the addition of the letters "se," "Et la messe?" was the hour for attending mass; but every one had forgotten the fact, until reminded of their religious duties by some invisible who perhaps wished to remove the fear always lurking in some minds that the phenomena were the work of the Evil One.

The same afternoon, there was an excursion on the lake at Fontainebleau. Their Imperial Majesties had the King of Bavaria with them in their boat, and invited Home to be the fourth in the party. Arriving at a little isle on which there was a kiosk, the three crowned heads and Home landed. There was no thought of a séance; but as they entered the kiosk raps sounded loudly; and on the alphabet being called over, a communication was addressed to the Empress.

Such were a few of the manifestations witnessed at the Tuileries and Fontainebleau. I have omitted various details, where the phenomena resembled those already described; and undoubtedly much occurred in the presence of the Emperor and Empress of the French of which I have no knowledge, and therefore cannot record.

Home returned from Fontainbleau to Paris in the Imperial train, and in the same carriage with their Majesties. During the journey various phenomena were witnessed and their unexpected occurrence greatly startled the King of Bavaria, who fairly fled from one moving object when he saw it advance towards him in broad daylight, untouched.

Home now remained in Paris till July 1857, and held many séances. He was in great power at this time; and extraordinary manifestations were witnessed, not only in fashionable salons, but by sitters of every class in life. Had he complied with half of the requests pressed on him for séances in Paris in the summer of 1857, and on his return there the winter following, he would have needed to sit for the whole of the twenty-four hours, and change the sitters every hour. Had he allowed himself to be tempted by the demon of cupidity into selling a gift, which was beyond price, he could have rapidly piled up a splendid fortune always supposing that his power had not abandoned him the moment he began to traffic in it. Again and again large sums were offered to him for séances by persons whose eager curiosity his refusal to sit had disappointed, and they were invariably offered in vain. I will cite but a single instance.

There was in Paris a society of certain of the *jeunesse dorée*, called the Union Club, among whose members there had been much talk of Home and his séances. It was known that he had repeatedly refused large offers of money; but the club probably thought, like the English Sir Robert Walpole, that every man has his price, and if Home had not yet been tempted, it was because his was an exorbitant one. They talked the matter over, and determined to bid high. Home was offered 50,000 francs for a single séance, and astonished the club by returning a prompt and decided refusal.

These facts were made known to the De Komar family, whose guest Home was at the time, by the younger of the two Counts de Komar, who happened to be a member of the Union Club. Friends of Count Branicka, with whom Home came to Paris in 1856, the De Komars speedily became the most prized and intimate of all his friends in France. There were two brothers, Alexander and Waldimir, the former much the elder of the two; and with them and their sisters, the Princess de Beauveau and the Countess Potocka, Home had many remarkable séances.

Long afterwards, Mr. Home happened to meet one evening in society the son-in-law of Count Alexander de Komar, who recalled to him the offer in Paris of £2,000 for a séance, and the surprise of the bidders when their proposal was rejected as an insult. Home at once took out a pencil, and sought a sheet of paper. "I have told that story, my dear Bodiska," he said, "and have had it treated as a fable put down your attestation of the fact on the spot. As justice is very seldom done to me, and the falsehood is constantly repeated that I am paid for my séances, it will probably be said of me, when I leave this world, that I accepted the 50,000 francs offered me for this séance or perhaps even double the amount." Bodiska complied; and added other incidents concerning Home that came within his knowledge. I have the paper before me at this moment, and will give it in the English of the writer, who was son of the Russian consul at New York:

"I first met Mr. D. Dunglas Home at the Hotel de Vouillemont, Paris, where my father-in-law, Count Alexander Komar, resided.

He resided in the family of my father-in-law; and I myself had ample opportunity of studying his private life and character, as well as the extraordinary phenomena occurring in his presence; and I can frankly state that nothing in natural principles can explain what others and I witnessed, not only once but surely a hundred of times. There was never any mercenary motive to incite him to call attention to his wonderful gift, for to my knowledge he refused many proposals, amongst which was one from the Union Club, that offered him francs 50,000, for a séance. A relative of my wife even offered him adoption, and to settle a life annuity on him, which likewise he refused. "B. Bodiska."

One of the celebrities who sought and made Home's acquaintance at Paris in 1857 was Madame Grisi, another was Mario, and a third was Francis Mahoney ("Father Prout"). A letter from Grisi to Home, dated December 8, 1857, is sufficiently interesting to translate here:

"Your extraordinary and mysterious power has continued during the whole night to exercise its influence over my astonished imagination. I am charmed to be able to express to you all the pleasure I have found in making your acquaintance; and I hope to see you again on my return from England. M. Mario desires me to present his best compliments to you, and he will be delighted to have a call from you. Receive &c., "Giulia Grisi."

Another celebrated person who made Home's acquaintance at this time was Marchioness de Boissy, who, thirty years earlier, as the Countess Guiccioli, had published her recollections of Byron. Madame de Boissy was present in 1857, and again in 1865, at several séances with Home, and beheld phenomena that deeply impressed her. There are several letters from her among Home's correspondence; but they give no details of the manifestations witnessed by her.

If only half of those who believed had had the courage of their belief! If they had published their testimony to their experiences; or, too timid for that, had at least written it down, and left it to be made public when they were beyond the reach of incredulity. But the silence they have preserved, the secrecy in which they have enshrouded their knowledge of the facts, are so many unspoken falsehoods that hinder the progress of a consoling verity.

Believers, no less than scoffers, look first of all to their own interests in these days, when all that remain of Christianity are its temples and its ceremonies. Each is for himself, and all are for the world.

When Home passed from earth, the press proved how much the intellect may be degraded by the moral nature associated with it, and hatred availed itself of the silence of death to exhaust itself in invectives accompanied by the insinuations that are worse than out-spoken calumnies. Invective is the natural weapon to which such enemies have recourse when proofs are wanting to them. But the name of Home is pronounced with respect by all whose opinion deserves attention and who have had means of forming it; and as for the honours or the reproaches that the mob decree to us, they ought to be regarded with equal indifference the one should cause no joy and the other no sorrow. He who had so many friends could not fail to have enemies even without knowing of them; for one may justly apply to Home these lines of Victor Hugo:

"Ces ennemis qu'il a s'il faut qu'il s'en souvienne, Lui viennent de leur haine, et non pas de la sienne."

CHAPTER 4

France and Russia

Meetings with the King of Wurtemberg and the Emperor William of Germany. Remark of the latter at Versailles. The Duke of Parma and the vision. Séance with the Queen of Holland. Adventures in Russia. Anecdotes of Alexandre Dumas. Spiritism and Spiritualism. Second loss of his powers. Marriage in St. Petersburg. Strange cure. His critics. Wild theories as to his powers.

HOME GUIDED HIMSELF in numerous actions of life by spirit-counsels; and, influenced by these, he took a resolution in 1857 to visit Turkey. Among his acquaintances in Paris was Lord Howden, for some years British Minister at Madrid. Lord Howden, attracted by simple curiosity, came to a séance, and was startled by the phenomena he witnessed out of his preconceived notions concerning them. He saw a great deal of Home during the next few weeks, inviting him frequently to dinner and taking every opportunity of being present at séances; and when Home was on the point of starting for the East, Lord Howden furnished him with introductions to the British Ambassadors at Vienna and Constantinople. I quote the letter that enclosed them:

"Rue d'Antin, Monday.

"My dear Home, Here are letters for our ambassadors at Vienna and Constantinople. If I can do anything else for you in the limited circle of my capabilities, freely command me. Will you come and eat a bad dinner at my Hotel at 7 o'clock on Saturday next, with only our friend Denys and my attaché Middleton?

"If you feel inclined afterwards, and will accompany me to Passy, to my friends the Delesserts and her sister, Madame Odier, you will please me, please them, and, I hope, please yourself, for they have a sympathy for you, as I have but do not consider yourself the least bound to me on this head.

"Yours with truth, Howden."

At the very moment of departure, Home's journey to Vienna and the East was abandoned as suddenly as it had been resolved upon. "My trunks were packed," he writes, "my passport sent for visa.

"I was making a farewell call on the Duchess d' A, and while in conversation with her, the drawing-room seemed filled with rappings, the alphabet was called for, and I was told that my journey must be postponed, as some political troubles were just about to occur. Instead, therefore, of going to Turkey, I went to Baden-Baden."

The "Duchess d'A" was the Duchess of Hamilton, daughter of the Grand Duke of Baden, and the incognito "d'A" was probably suggested to Home by the fact that the occurrence took place in the Hotel d'Albe, where the Duchess was then residing.

Home was at Baden during August and part of September 1857. His health was again failing; and his power, as was ordinarily the case when his health failed, had grown weaker. "I met, however," he writes, "the King of Wurtemberg and the then Prince, now King of Prussia, both of whom investigated the phenomena."

A letter with an almost illegible signature throws some light on the circumstances of Home's introduction to the King of Wurtemberg. It is addressed to him at the Hotel d'Angleterre, Baden, and was written by the physician to the King, Dr. Guggert. Other letters identify this correspondent with a physician who had been present in France at some of Home's séances, and whose obstinate scepticism was conquered by what he witnessed.

"My dear Mr. Home, I spoke yesterday to H. M. the King of Wurtemberg of your good disposition, and of your extraordinary and miraculous qualities. His Majesty would like to see you at noon today, as he will probably leave to-morrow morning for Stuttgart. If you should be disposed to accept the high invitation, you must be kind enough to call on me at twelve o'clock, and I will take you with me."

Home has himself described, in a letter published in 1883, his meeting at Baden-Baden with the then Prince Regent of Prussia, the late Emperor of Germany, and with his Majesty's son, the present Emperor. "My first meeting with the Prince of Prussia," he wrote, "was at once amusing and interesting. The Emperor William of today, then Prince Regent, sent one of his aides-de-camp to ask me to call on him. I went as desired, and on entering the drawing room, I was received by a gentleman whose commanding presence agreeably impressed me; but as he began a series of questions more or less personal and pointed, I became reticent, and replied rather coldly. It was a relief when the door opened, and the Prince Regent came in. I was taken aback when he laughingly said; 'I see that I do not require to present you to my son, for you already know him.'" Three séances with the Prince Regent of Prussia followed this interview.

Thirteen years later, at Versailles, Mr. Home again saw the King of Prussia, not yet crowned Emperor. Home was with a party of Prussian officers and English newspaper correspondents; and one of the latter, Mr. Kingston, correspondent of the *Daily Telegraph*, thus described the incident, in a letter published in that journal, October 31st, 1870:

"A staff-officer put his head in at the door, and exclaimed, 'The King! The King!' disappearing as he uttered the words. We hurried after him; and, sure enough, there in the dining room stood the venerable monarch, who had improvised a visit to the château during his afternoon drive, surrounded by the members of his personal staff. I never saw the King in better health or spirits. Among our party was an American General, with whom his Majesty conversed for some time. Another was Mr. Daniel Home, the celebrated Spiritualist, whom the King promptly recognized and addressed very kindly reminding him of the wonders that he (Mr. Home) had been the means of imparting to him, and inquiring about 'the spirits' in by no means a sceptical tone."

As the *Daily Telegraph* correspondent, an almost total stranger to Home, is an unexceptionable witness to the fact of this conversation, I have preferred to cite his account of it, although somewhat meagre. He might have added that the exact words King William addressed to Home were: "Ah, Mr. Home, when I relate the strange things I witnessed in your presence, they laugh at me; but the facts are true for all that."

It was late in August or early in September 1857 that Mr.

Home's presence at Baden afforded the late Emperor of Germany the opportunity of investigating the phenomena, an investigation renewed by his Majesty in subsequent years. Another séance at Baden was with the Prince of Nassau, whose interest had been excited by the account that the Princess had written to him of a séance with Home at Paris a few weeks before, at which her Highness and the Princess Mentchikoff were present.

The Court of France was at Biarritz in September 1857; and an Imperial invitation telegraphed to Mr. Home at Baden cut short his stay there. He had hardly arrived at Biarritz when his health failed him still more; and, hearing of his illness, various priests made persevering attempts to penetrate to his sick room. The Church had not yet lost hope of reclaiming the wanderer from her fold, and setting on his wonderful life the seal of the monastery.

In parting with the year 1857, I may add to the particulars already given the remark that I have named only a very few of the persons of intellectual and social distinction who were present at séances given by Mr. Home in France. Many names are unknown to me; for Home kept no record of the persons present at séances, and destroyed nine-tenths of the countless letters he received. As for the correspondence that remains, it is not always dated; and the higher the rank of the writer, the more common this omission. Several of these undated letters evidently belong to the year 1857, but to what month it is impossible to say. Among these correspondents are celebrities of every description, the aristocracy of talent as well as that of birth. There are letters from Princess Murat, Princess Orloff, Lacordaire (brother of the celebrated preacher), Madame de Balzac (widow of the great novelist and a life-long friend of Home), the Prince and Princess Metternich, Count de Sancillon, Count de Villiers, Madame de Girardin, the Duchess de Tascher, the Turkish Ambassador at Paris, the Duchess de Medina-Celi, the Countess de Lourmel, the Princess de Montleart, the Count de Riancourt, the Marquis Duplanri, the Marquis Strachan de Salza, the Duchess de Valmy, Baron de Retz, Baron de Stakelberg, Dossini the composer, and Hebert the painter. A note written by this last-named celebrated artist after a séance deserves quotation:

"Grand Home, Mes félicitations et mes remerciements les plus chaudes pour les hautes emotions que je vous dois.

"E. Hebert."

I have omitted from the above list the name of one of the most remarkable personages with whom Mr. Home became acquainted in France in 1857. I speak of the last Duke of Parma, who had abdicated some time previously, and was living at Paris in 1857 under the incognito of Count de Villafranca. The strange circumstances attending the commencement of the Duke's friendship with Home are related without names in the *Incidents*. Briefly summarized, the story is as follows:

In the early summer of 1857, the Count de Villafranca, a stranger to Home, called on him one morning and sent up a pressing request to see him:

"He advanced to where I stood," writes Mr. Home, "and, taking me kindly by the hand, he said to me, 'I have been sent to you, and you will yet know the reason why, though you do not even know who I am. 'I live at No. 4, Rue, and you will be obliged to come to me.' I shook my head at this incredulously, and told him my time was so taken up that I had scarcely time even to call on my friends. He smiled, and said, 'You will see, you will see.' The conversation then changed; and he left me after having written his address."

Home dined the same evening with the Baroness de Meyendorf, and, on entering the drawing room, saw a young man standing there. "I was surprised at this," he writes, "expecting to have met no stranger. With his eyes fixed upon me, he said, 'I am glad you have come, for we will go together to see my father;' and he then suddenly disappeared. I had thought till then he was a guest, so real was the vision."

Later in the evening the apparition again presented himself; and Home then delayed no longer, but went to the residence of his visitor of the morning. "On reaching No. 4, Rue, I was directed to the rooms of the Count; and his valet told me that his master was preparing to retire, and in all probability could not see me. Again the voice told me to announce myself; and at that very moment a door was opened, and the Count came towards me, and said, 'I have been waiting for you I knew you would come.' I described to him the young man I had seen, and all that had happened; and he at once recognized him as his son. He showed me a portrait of him, which exactly corresponded with my vision of him."

The tragic story of the death of the Duke of Parma's son need not be related here. It is enough to add that the Count or, rather, the Duke told Home in what manner he had been impressed to seek him; and that the morning visit and evening vision were the commencement of a friendship that Home valued greatly. The Duke of Parma, a brother of the celebrated Duchess of Berry, was one of the most finished and noble representatives of manners and traditions that are almost extinct in Europe. He had outlived his world and resigned his duchy; but he preserved that union of perfect simplicity with perfect dignity which constitutes the true grand seigneur. The exquisite charm of such manner is seldom felt now; but it will be remembered by all who were honoured with the society of the Count de Villafranca.

In his journey to Holland in January 1858, Mr. Home was accompanied by his friend Mons. Tiedemann, a Dutch gentleman then residing at the Château de Cergay, not far from Paris, where, two years later, Home's remarkable preservation from death occurred. I have no details of the séances at The Hague; but a circumstance connected with them left a profound impression on the mind of the Queen of Holland. The first took place in one of the grand apartments of the palace, among surroundings of a somewhat cheerless and sombre magnificence; and little or nothing occurred. On the occasion of the following séance, the Queen invited Home to choose for himself the room in which he would prefer to hold it; and her emotion was great on seeing him, after having traversed the whole length of the state apartments, pause in front of a locked door. None entered this chamber save the Queen. It was the chamber of her child, whose loss she had) never ceased lamenting. The manifestations that took place there left in the mind of this gifted and amiable sovereign a vivid remembrance, that was attested by the action of her Majesty. On the eve of Home's departure from The Hague, she drew from her finger a ring of which the chief value consisted in the fact that she had long worn it, and sent it to him with the following holograph note:

"February 4th, 1858.

"I send you a grateful (reconnaissant) souvenir of our séances."

"Sophie."

At the wish of Mons. Tiedemann, Home accompanied him from The Hague to Amsterdam, and held there a séance with a party of very pronounced sceptics, the proprietors and staff of a Dutch journal. His power was now weakening, and a few days later wholly left him. He returned to Paris suffering from the effects of a severe chill he had taken in Holland; and was ordered by his doctor to leave for Italy.

While he was living quietly in Italy, Paris and the Parisian journals were lending ready credence to an infamous falsehood concerning him. He had not left Paris, after all, ran this new slander. He had been arrested on the scandal-mongers knew not what charge, and was in the prison of Mazas. "Persons in official positions even told my friends that they had seen and spoken to me in that prison; and one, an officer, went so far as to state that he had accompanied me there in the carriage" (*Incidents in My Life, vol. I.*, p. 106).

Home, without knowing anything of the slanders that were in circulation, had already written from Rome to several friends in Paris. The recipient of one of his letters, the well-known author, Henri Delaage, showed it to the Paris correspondent of *Le Nord*, who, on March 17th, wrote to that journal: "Allow me to begin by a good action; it is to free an honourable man from calumnies, arising from what source I know not, but which for the past few days have been rapidly spreading. I speak of Mr. Home, who is for the moment in Italy, whereas it is whispered both secretly and openly that he is in the prison of Mazas, for we know not what crimes. The letter here given, dated Rome, 7th of March, was received yesterday by M. Henri Delaage, an intimate friend of Mr. Home. The letter is there before me with the postal mark."

On the publication of this paragraph in *Le Nord*, accompanied by Home's letter from Rome to Delaage, the spread of the Mazas slander was stopped. It had already travelled from Paris into Belgium and Holland; a delay of a week or two more in disproving it, and the lie would no doubt have made the round of the civilized world.

There was at Rome, in March 1858, a young Russian nobleman, Count Koucheleff-Besborodka, who, as well as the Countess his wife, so celebrated for her beauty, had a lively curiosity concerning Home and a great desire to make his acquaintance. As he refused all invitations to go into Roman society, the Koucheleffs ended by pressing into their service one of the few friends he saw, who promised to gratify their wish for an introduction, and arranged the matter in the fashion related by Mr. Home in the *Incidents*:

"He mentioned one afternoon, while we were walking together on the Pincian, the name of a Russian family of distinction then in Rome, and added that they were anxious to make my acquaintance. I excused myself on the ground of my health. At this moment a carriage was passing us and stopped; and my friend, before I was aware of what he was doing, introduced me to the Countess de Koucheleff, who asked me to come and sup with them that evening, adding that they kept very late hours."

The evening was destined to be a memorable one in Home's life. "I went about ten," he writes, "and found a large party assembled. At twelve, as we entered the supper-room, the Countess introduced to me a young lady, whom I then observed for the first time, as her sister. A strange impression came over me at once, and I knew she was to be my wife. When we were seated at table, the young lady turned to me, and laughingly said, 'Mr. Home, you will be married before the year is ended.' I asked her why she said so; and she replied that there was such a superstition in Russia when a person was at table between two sisters. I made no reply. It was true. In twelve days we were partially engaged, and waiting only the consent of her mother."

"Home had lost the power of making himself feared, but had preserved that of making himself loved," wrote Alexander Dumas in allusion to the fact that his friend's power had not yet returned to him. Mademoiselle de Kroll had seen nothing whatever of the phenomena, and was incredulous as to the possibility of communications with another world, at the time of her engagement to Home.

"The evening of the day of our engagement," continues Home in the *Incidents*, "a small party had assembled, and were dancing.

I was seated on a sofa by my fiancée, when she turned to me and said abruptly: 'Do tell me all about spirit-rapping, for you know I don't believe in it.' I said to her 'Mademoiselle, I trust you will ever bear in mind that I have a mission in trusted to me. It is a great and holy one. I cannot speak with you about a thing which you have not seen, and therefore cannot understand. I can only say that it is a great truth.' The tears came welling into her eyes; and laying her hand in mine, she said, 'If your mission can bring comfort to those less happy than ourselves, or be in any way a consolation to mankind, you will ever find me ready and willing to do all I can to aid you in it.' She was true to this noble sentiment till the last moment of her short life; and she is still my great comfort and sustainer since we have separated in this earthly sphere."

The acquaintance of the Koucheleffs with Dumas resulted in an invitation to 'the author of Monte Cristo to accompany them to Russia, and be present at the marriage of Home. Dumas accepted; and in the month of June the party left for St. Petersburg. On the eve of Home's departure, a banquet was given to him by his friends in Paris to celebrate his marriage; and a distinguished and numerous company of various nationalities assembled, including many of the names mentioned a few pages back, all, or nearly all, of them men who had been present at séances with Home.

Dumas insisted, like almost every other Frenchman, on regarding Home as a magician. At his pressing request, Home had given him a sketch of his life up to the year 1858, and this Dumas reproduced in his work, but could not resist the temptation to re-touch it. There are natures to which veracity is impossible, and history as treated by Dumas becomes fiction, biography becomes romance. Home, who had expected nothing else, laughed heartily over his metamorphosed biography when he read it; and Dumas responded to his laugh by another, that seemed to say, "Does the world ever take me seriously?"

Probably not; but the Paris correspondent of the *Daily News* would seem to have done so, when, in June, 1886, she sent to that journal her ridiculous biographical sketch of Home.

Count Koucheieff-Besborodka possessed a fine estate in the

neighbourhood of St. Petersburg that had been bestowed on his grandfather by Catherine II. Here the festivities took place that accompanied the marriage of Home; and here, on arriving in Russia, Dumas enjoyed the lavish hospitality of the Count. Within a few days of Home's arrival, the Emperor Alexander II. sent to request that he would present himself at Peterhoff, the summer residence of the Court. Dumas was something more than disappointed at not receiving a similar invitation; but affected to consider that the loss was the Emperor's not his. "There are many crowned heads in Europe," he grandiosely remarked; "but there is only one Alexander Dumas."

At the marriage of Home, it was necessary for Dumas to give his name; and on being asked for it, he responded briefly, "Dumas." The official repeated the question.

"Dumas!" replied the illustrious owner of that name, more loudly than before.

"But your Christian name, Monsieur Dumas?"

"Alexander! Is there another Alexander Dumas in the world?" demanded the outraged author.

A dozen such anecdotes might be told of Dumas in Russia. He was certainly one of the vainest of men; but his vanity was so naive in its display that it amused much more than offended. So long as sufficient incense was burnt in his honour, Dumas was the pleasantest companion in the world, and as entertaining as one of his own novels; but he lived in purgatory when he saw another excite more interest than himself. If he hardly did justice in Russia to his reputation of "bon enfant" it was because of his ill humour at attracting less attention than he had anticipated.

Dumas, who never took life seriously, could not accept the manifestations as matter for serious consideration. This truly French fashion of looking at the subject was more disagreeable to Home than any scepticism, and explains the statement made by Dumas that Home accused him of putting the spirits to flight.

A Paris anecdote of 1857 deserves a passing mention. It may or not be true but at least it is *ben trovato*. A Parisian journalist, so the story runs, came to a séance; and on seeing a heavy table rise to the ceiling when no person was touching it, was so startled that he rushed out of the house without his hat. "Frightened!"

said the witty fugitive, when joked with on his escapade;" no, not at all. Why did I leave my hat, then? What did I want with a hat when I had lost my head? "Dumas relates how at Polonstrava, the residence of Count Koucheleff-Besborodka, a spirit entered into a round table. In his fantastic narrative, the table is no longer a table; it has become an intelligence itself, instead of being merely the means of communication between one intelligence and another. In this confusion of things material with things spiritual, Dumas was a type of his nation. When, as so often happened at the séances of Home, a piece of furniture was seen to move without any person touching it, the French mind commonly grasped at the explanation that the spirit had entered into the table or chair, and animated it. In other countries, the belief of an invisible force acting from without on a visible object might be understood and accepted; but the French mind was seldom able to separate the spirits from the chairs and tables. In the pages of one of the many writers who have charged their own aberrations on the world of spirits, Count Theobald Walsh, we even find tables, footstools, and baskets animated at his bidding with the various passions of humanity, and representing anger, gluttony, pride, etc.

In no country were more extraordinary requests addressed to Home than in France. He received, for instance, a letter from a French officer quartered at Algiers, who was possessed with the belief that treasure had been buried somewhere under an old Moorish dwelling there, and was ready to share it with Home, if the wizard would tell him the exact spot. Another writer cherishes the memory of a friendship formed with Home during a previous existence in some other planet than the earth, and longs to know if on Home's part a similar recollection has been preserved.

Spiritualism does not exist in France; its place has been taken by Spiritism, a very different thing. The fundamental conceptions of Spiritualism are the individual immortality of the soul, and the reality of the invisible world. Home proved that death is a second birth. The facts collected in this volume show that there is no interruption in the existence of those who have passed from earth. What can be more comforting than such a belief? The certitude of immortality transfigures lives that were formerly filled with despair and the shadow of death, and inspires us with a keener sentiment of submission and gratitude to the Creator. There is nothing in this antagonistic to the Christian faith; but "Spiritism" (as its inventor named it) professes to be an anti-Christian religion taught by spirits if the name "religion" can be applied to so gross a superstition. It is not even a new heresy; it is merely a nineteenth-century application of the very ancient superstition of the transmigration of spirits. Revel, who first taught the doctrines of Spiritism in France, took the name of "Allan Kardec," asserting himself to have borne it in a former existence as a Breton Druid. Those who accept this doctrine do so entirely on the faith of pretended revelations made by spirits. Reason is set aside, and proofs of identity are replaced by the flights of an imagination more conspicuous for incoherence than for grandeur. If this superstition attracts in France and only in France people of no intellect or education, it does not include a single intellectual celebrity among its adepts.

When Home, at St. Petersburg, received the Imperial command so much envied him by Dumas, his power had been absent for nearly three months; and he replied to the invitation by acquainting the Emperor with the fact, and added that, at the earliest indication of its return, he would hold himself entirely at the disposition of his Majesty.

The marriage of Mr. Home and Mademoiselle Alexandrina de Kroll, sister of the Countess Koucheleff, took place on the 1st of August, 1858, new style, or the 20th of July by the Russian calendar. The ceremony was first performed according to the rites of the Greek Church in the private chapel of Count Koucheleff, and again in the Church of St. Catherine by a priest of the Roman Catholic Church. Three days before the marriage, the Emperor Alexander II sent to the bridegroom the wedding-gift of which I have spoken in a previous chapter. It was transmitted to Mr. Home by Count Schouvaloff, together with the following letter:

"Peterhof le 17/29 juillet, 1858.

"Monsieur, Le Ministre de la Maison de l'Empereur m'a fait parvenir une bague enrichie de diamants que Sa Majesty vous a destinée comme une marque de Sa bienveillance.

"Ayant l'honneur de vous la transmettre ci-joint, je vous

prie, Monsieur, de recevoir l'assurance de ma consideration très distinguée.

"Schouvaloff."

A comparison of the date of Count Schouvaloff's letter with that of Mr. Home's marriage would alone sufficiently establish the fact that the Emperor's gracious token of his interest in the bridegroom took the form of a wedding-gift.

Besides the letter just given, several others from Count Schouvaloff have been preserved. They convey, for the most part, the Imperial invitations to Mr. Home; but in one of those written in July the Count gladly accepts Home's offer to give him a special séance. "Discretion prevented me asking you," he writes, "but since you have the kindness to propose it to me, I will be with you any day and any hour that you can receive me."

Leaving St. Petersburg shortly after their marriage, Mr. Home and his bride spent the autumn in visits to the various estates of their brother-in-law, Count Koucheleff, some of which were situated in the farthest south of Russia; and it was November before they were back in St. Petersburg. On his return, Home, as the letters of Count Schouvaloff and Count Bobrinsky show, was several times summoned to the Palace of Tsarskoe-Selo, where the Emperor was just then residing. The social consideration that Mr. Home enjoyed in Russia does not need attesting, but such letters as the following sufficiently establish it:

"S. M. l'Empereur désire, cher Home, vous voir a Tsarskoe, lundi soir. Veuillez avoir la bonté de m'informer par le porteur si on peut compter sur vous ce jour-la. Une voiture vous attendra à la gare de Tsarskoe. Tout à vous, "Count A. Bobrinsky."

In January, 1859, Home fell ill, and was soon in great danger. The malady that had attacked him baffled his physicians, but was expelled in the manner he has narrated in the *Incidents*:

"The dangerous symptoms were greatly increased by my usual nervous debility. Friction was recommended, but the extreme pain it caused precluded its use. I was in this state when one evening my wife and a friend, the Baron de M (Baron de Meyendorff), were present, and my hands were suddenly seized by spirit-influence, and I was made to beat them with extreme violence upon the part which was so extremely sensitive and tender.

My wife was frightened, and would have endeavoured to hold my hands; but my friend, who had sufficient knowledge of spirit-manifestations, prevented her. I felt no pain, though the violence of the blows that I continued giving myself made the bed and the whole room shake in an hour I was in a quiet sleep; and on awaking the next morning, I found the disease had left me, and only a weakness remained. The expression of the doctor's face baffles my description, when he visited me early that morning, expecting to have found me worse, and felt my pulse and saw that a great change must have occurred, beyond his skill to account for."

In all countries but especially in France and America the number of persons who claimed Home's acquaintance without ever having met him was legion. He had several amusing *rencontres* with imaginative beings of this class, and often told in his own inimitable fashion the story of these meetings. One of the most amusing took place in a railway-carriage in which he was traveling to Fontainebleau, in May 1857.

In early summer there are few pleasanter places in France than Fontainebleau; and under the Empire that was the time of year usually selected for an Imperial visit to the beautiful old forest and château. The Court was there in May 1857; and on the 23rd, a few days after his return from America, Home received a telegram conveying an invitation from the Empress to present himself at the château, and left Paris by the evening train. Three gentlemen, all strangers to him, were his companions on the journey; and their talk fell on the news of the day.

"Home is back with us, it seems," said one. "I am told that the fact is he had never left Paris."

"So far from that being the case," replied oracle number two, "he will never be seen in Paris again. The journals may announce what they like; but, take my word for it, Home is far enough from Paris at this moment."

"Is it true, then, that the Emperor had him sent away?"

"Quite true. The Empress was so alarmed by what she saw at a certain séance I have my information from those who ought to know that the Emperor determined to allow no more of these diabolical scenes; and our sorcerer was ordered to leave France the next day."

"It is said he had received enormous sums."

"He was paid at the rate of a million francs a year," replied the other, with the air of a man who knows of what he speaks.

Home joined in the conversation at this point, and his gay and pleasant manner soon put him on the best of terms with his three travelling companions. A number of interesting particulars in his own history, all quite novel to him, were communicated by one or the other; and in the midst of these piquant anecdotes the train reached Fontainebleau. There was a servant in the Imperial livery on the platform, and Home beckoned to him.

"You are waiting for –?" "For Mr. Home, sir." "I am Mr. Home." Home stepped from the carriage, and took the politest of farewells of the blank and silent three within. They were neither the first nor the last of the Munchausen tribe in whose company he had the amusement of travelling incognito, and of listening to imaginary incidents in his history, sometimes recounted by romancers who claimed to know him personally. The same year, 1857, he happened to be the third occupant of a coupe on a French railway, the other two being an elderly man and a young man. The former mentioned the name of Home, and the young man at once claimed it as that of an acquaintance. "Not that I know him well," he explained; "but I have met him occasionally at the house of my friend, the Princess de Beauveau, who amuses herself sometimes by witnessing his feats of legerdemain." "They are well managed?" asked Home. "Oh, very clever!" "But Madame la Princesse has the reputation of believing in his spiritual claims." "If one believes all one hears! She has no more faith in them than I have myself, and recognizes Home for what he is." Home took a letter from his pocket. "You have interested me in mentioning a name very well known to me," he said; "since the Princess de Beauveau is a lady who honours me with her friendship. I have heard her speak of Mr. Home, but not as a charlatan."

"Pardon, monsieur; but I can affirm that such is her opinion of him." "You have seen him and would, of course, recognize him, if you were to meet him again," Home continued. "Without doubt." "And this letter," said Home, drawing it from the envelope and holding it out; "do you know the writing?"

No, the young Frenchman did not. "It is, however, from the

Princess de Beauveau to me. Will you do me the favour of reading it? You will find that she has considerable faith in the spiritual pretensions of Mr. Home."

But the young man, much embarrassed, declined to take the letter, and protested that he quite accepted the speaker's word.

"At least do me the favour to look at the envelope," said Home, presenting it, "that you may see to whom the letter is addressed."

The other did so; and said not another word, but at the next station he hurriedly left the carriage.

His exit was not so dramatic as that which another French railway companion of Mr. Home proposed for himself. This gentleman, equally unconscious to whom he was speaking, confided to Home his terror of Home. "I have never seen him I should be afraid to see him. If I were to meet him near a cemetery at midnight, it would cause me I cannot describe the feeling it would cause me."

"They say there is nothing very frightful in his appearance. If you were to meet him out of a cemetery in the day-time, you might take a liking to him," said Home.

"Impossible."

The journey was long, and the two had become excellent friends before it ended. As Home drew near the station where he was to alight, he said to his companion: "So you have never seen Home. What if I were to present him to you?"

"I would jump out of the window."

"Bon voyage," said Home, lowering it.

But the other, though he realized the situation with French quickness, did not jump.

These men were types of the greater portion of the world that had heard of Home without having seen him. The most outrageous falsehoods were told of him by one class of calumniators, the most absurd and fantastic legends invented by those who believed him a necromancer. A romancer who chose for a subject either of the two imaginary Homes would be spared the trouble of inventing; he would only have to collect enough falsehoods to fill his volumes, and arrange them with an eye to effect.

A very common report about Home in Paris was that he

carried in his pocket a tame, trained monkey, which was let out during a séance to twitch dresses and shake hands. As for the raps, he had "an electrical quality that he could throw off at command of the will." A method of explanation much favoured by scientists and pseudo-scientists was to alter the facts of séances in accordance with their preconceived theories; and then, on such basis of omission and addition, to proceed to demonstrate the theories in question. This disingenuous and unscientific method was largely employed, as a subsequent chapter of this work will show, by Dr W. B. Carpenter, V.P.R.S.

Medical men have been found who could gravely conjecture that Home administered "a thimble-full of chloroform" to each of the sitters before the séance began. Others declared that he magnetized or biologized his audience; and the things that they said they saw the poor mesmerized dupes only imagined they had seen. Mr. Crookes, F.R.S employed instruments to record the phenomena, and again and again the instruments recorded them. It seemed a bold theory to suggest that Mr. Crookes' instruments were capable of being mesmerized; but, since the biological explanation was advanced as a triumphant disproof of his experiments, it must be concluded that they were, and that Home somehow found out the fact, and turned it to account.

Of all phenomena, that of rising in the air has had the most ridiculous explanations adduced concerning it. The mesmeric theory is naturally a favourite here; and when the present Earl of Crawford, for instance, saw Home, in full light, rise from the ground, he was of course biologized. Some theorists have conjectured that Home carried with him a magic lantern truly deserving of the name!

The one really simple, scientific, and satisfactory explanation ever advanced to account for the phenomena from a non-spiritual point of view was that of an old woman in America. Asked if she could explain what she had seen, she replied, "Lor', sirs, it's easy enough! He only rubs himself all over with a gold pencil first."

"A general belief," writes Mr. Home in the *Incidents*, "is that I bribe the servants at whatever house I visit, that they may assist me in concealing my machinery. The intelligence displayed in obtaining names, dates, and other circumstances is previously communicated to me, either by my own inquiry from servants, or by visiting the tombstones of the relatives, or even by a body of secret police who are in my pay."

'"If such statements are circulated during my lifetime," wrote Home in 1883, "I often wonder what will be said of me when I shall have passed to spirit-life."

CHAPTER 5
England

Second English campaign. Faraday's dictum. Conversion of Dr. Elliottson. Stir in London Society. The Cornhill Article. Thackeray's position. Robert Chambers. His remarkable conversion. Convincing evidence to Mrs. Senior. Conversion of Lady Shelley, and of Dr. Lockhart Robertson, the alienist. Opinion of Professor Challis.

THE SECOND RESIDENCE OF Mr. Home in England lasted from November 1859, until the last week of July 1860. He returned a third time in the following winter, and was in England during the whole of 1861.

Coming events often cast their prophetic shadows on the mind of Home; but when he brought his young wife to London in the winter of 1859, and introduced her to his English friends, he had as yet received no impression of the parting that was already so near at hand. She was destined; it might have been reasonably thought, to outlive her husband, whose hold on life had more than once seemed so frail. Apart from the messages conveyed through him and the impressions granted to him, Home was no more capable of looking into the future than other men; nor could he command those messages and impressions at will; they were communicated or withheld as other intelligences than his own saw fit. He exercised no more volition in the matter than a wire, designed to convey the electric current, exercises with regard to the messages that travel over it.

The year 1860 was remarkable for the number of séances that Home gave, and for the variety of persons who investigated the phenomena. His power had returned to him very strongly, and was especially great during the early summer of 1860, when many very remarkable séances took place. I say "power," in default of a better word by which to describe Home's gift. His part was to be a passive agent; and the more he could detach his mind from the subject, the better were the results. Home's gift appeared to obey somewhat the same laws as the inspirations of a great poet or painter, concerning which the artist only knows that he cannot compel his power into his service, and that his inspiration is often absent when he would most desire its presence. No great writer or painter was ever yet able to declare with certainty in commencing a work that it would be a masterpiece; and Home, the manifestations of whose strange power were more capricious, as they were more wonderful, than the inspiration of any poet or painter, could never foretell at the commencement of a séance what would happen, or whether anything would happen at all. Yet such is the temper of the nineteenth century, that men distinguished for their intelligence and attainments considered Home's declaration of his inability to obtain manifestations at will a sufficient reason for declining to investigate the subject.

Among the letters of the English acquaintances of Mr. Home is one that throws an amusing light on the spirit in which some leaders of public opinion approached the question of Spiritualism, when they consented to approach it at all. A well-known scientific man had been pressed by Mrs. Parkes, the widow of an Indian judge, to come to a séance at her house with Mr. Home, and had ended by accepting the invitation. He duly appeared on the evening appointed; but demanded, as an indispensable preliminary to sitting, that he should be furnished with "a programme of the séance." It was in vain that his hostess represented to him that séances had no programmes, and there were no earthly means of arranging beforehand what should happen; he only replied that he was determined not to investigate at all, unless he knew exactly what he was investigating; and, refusing to sit, departed in much ill-humour.

His attitude was a caricature of that of Faraday, at whose feet he had probably sat. Faraday is deservedly a great name; but he was emphatically a thinker of the nineteenth century, and the thinkers of the nineteenth century are specialists, not philosophers. England is little likely ever to produce another Bacon, to take all knowledge for his province; or another Newton, whose great intellect, dimly apprehending the secrets of the universe and its own ignorance of them, could humbly compare its discoveries to the action of a child who walks on the sea-shore, and brings away a few shells and pebbles as indications of the treasures of the ocean. The modern scientist has no such overwhelming conviction of the vastness of that ocean, and of his own inability to penetrate its depths. He is a child who picks up one particular pebble, and, after close inspection of it, declares that the sea has nothing in it but pebbles, and they are all like his.

Faraday wrote, with reference to the phenomena of Spiritualism: "Before we proceed to consider any questions involving physical principles, we should set out with clear ideas of the naturally possible and impossible." He forgot that even the nineteenth century is not omniscient, that its ideas of the naturally possible and impossible are not those of the eighteenth, and will not be those of the twentieth. Man's knowledge of the possible never was and never will be final; though in every age humanity has repeated Faraday's mistake of supposing it to be so. The scientific critics of Stephenson had very clear ideas of the naturally possible when they proceeded to the consideration of the physical principles involved in the question of the locomotive; and their ideas led them to declare that it was impossible to run engines at the rate of thirty miles an hour. If we could resuscitate the Royal Society of 1787, and submit to its consideration inventions like the telegraph and the telephone, the ideas of a hundred years ago concerning the naturally possible would lead the Society to ridicule as chimerical such propositions for annihilating distance. Human conceptions of what is possible and impossible have been subjected to a thousand corrections since this world began, and are likely to be subjected to many more before it ends.

As Mr. A. R. Wallace ably wrote, in criticizing Faraday's dictum: "No man can be sure that, however 'clear' his ideas may be in this matter, they will be equally true ones. It was very 'clearly impossible' to the minds of the philosophers at Pisa that a great and a small weight could fall from the top of the tower in the same time; and if this principle (Faraday's) is of any use, they were right in disbelieving the evidence of their senses, which assured them that they did; and Galileo, who accepted that evidence, was, to use the words of the same eminent authority, not only ignorant as respects the education of the judgment, but ignorant of his ignorance."

De Morgan, the celebrated mathematician, answered Faraday, and pointed out, with equal truth and force, that the object of all investigation is to arrive at those very same "clear ideas," on the possession of which Faraday insisted as a preliminary. "Set out in physical investigation with a clear idea of the naturally possible and impossible!" exclaimed De Morgan, repeating his contemporary's words. "We thought the world had struggled forward to the knowledge that a clear idea of this was the last attainment of study and reflection, combined with observation; not the possession of our intellect at starting."

De Morgan's own opinion concerning Spiritualism had been "the last attainment of study and reflection, combined with observation." After investigating the subject for many years, he wrote in 1869: "I retain my suspense as to what the phenomena mean, but I am as fully persuaded as ever of their reality."

Mr. Faraday's dictum, if it meant anything with regard to Spiritualism, meant that the subject was to be dismissed without investigation, on the plea that it conflicted with existing ideas of the possible. This frame of mind, however, did not prevent Faraday from investigating the phenomenon (if it deserve the name) of table-tilting; and he was easily able to show that tables were often tilted, consciously or unconsciously, by the sitters themselves. Mr. Home was the last person to doubt the fact, and in the *Lights and Shadows of Spiritualism* has declared his conviction of the accuracy of Faraday's observations.

None of Faraday's experiments had been made with Home; and it was obvious to all men who knew anything of the séances of the latter, and were not blinded by prejudice, that here Faraday's theory of "involuntary muscular action" would not apply. Accordingly, in 1861, Sir Emerson Tennant endeavoured, with the help of Mr. Robert Bell, to bring about a meeting between Home and Faraday. Sir Emerson acted on his own responsibility, and without any authority from Mr. Home, who, as the *Morning Star* had the candour to admit when discussing the incident some years later, "did not appear to have been particularly consulted in the matter at all." As the writer in the *Morning Star*

(May 12th, 1868) was hostile to Home and friendly to Faraday, his description of the attitude assumed by the man of science will carry more weight than any words of mine would: and I will therefore give it:

"He" (Faraday,) "prescribed certain conditions which it would have been utterly impossible for Mr. Home, whether that gentleman be the apostle of a new science or a mere pretender and humbug, to accept. In fact, Mr. Home was invited, as a condition precedent to Faraday's entering on the investigation, to acknowledge that the phenomena, however produced, were ridiculous and contemptible." Faraday may have been right as regards what he had seen, but to judge before examining it of what he had not seen implied a confidence in his own infallibility as conceited, as it was dogmatic.

Faraday's second condition, of open and complete examination, Home would as readily have accepted as he afterwards did in the case of Crookes; but was it conceivable he should accept this? Mr. Robert Bell was so assured he would not, that he did not think it worth while even to transmit to Mr. Home a proposal so insulting; and accordingly the negotiations between Bell, Sir Emerson, and Faraday were dropped and never resumed.

Seven years later, at the close of the Lyon suit, Professor Tyndall published a letter in which he intimated his willingness to be present at a séance with Mr. Home, but expressly declared that he made the offer "in the spirit of Faraday's letter." In putting forth such a challenge, Professor Tyndall was only making a cheap vaunt of his prejudices. What did it matter to Home, who never sought to impose his own principles on anyone, whether Tyndall were of Faraday's opinion or not?

There is one aspect of the manifestations that probably even Professor Tyndall would approach in a serious mood, and would abstain from qualifying with such adjectives as "ridiculous "and "contemptible;" however emphatically he might express his denial and disbelief. I refer to the evidence afforded in the séances of Mr. Home of the identity of the beings communicating. It is only to those who have been fully convinced of that identity that Spiritualism can ever be Spiritualism.

If gratitude and the courage of one's convictions were virtues common among men, the recipients of incontrovertible proofs of identity would have more frequently placed their testimony on record. Unhappily, there are few who can face abuse, fewer still who do not fear ridicule; and the knowledge of what awaited them if they spoke outweighed with the majority every other consideration, and caused them to remain silent. Home never complained of this conduct; on the contrary, he was only too unselfishly ready to excuse it; and in *Incidents in My Life* (vol. I. p. 204), he even constituted himself the apologist of the timid many, and stated with generous candour the best defence that can be offered for their discreditable silence:

"I am sorry that in so many instances I am obliged to conceal the names of my friends who have witnessed wonderful things," he wrote; "but if the reader is disposed to complain of this, let him remember the reason, and take the greater part of the blame on himself. No sooner is the name of some honest and courageous person given, in obedience to the call for testimony, than it becomes a target for all the ridicule, jests, and abuse of the unscrupulous, the sceptical, the orthodox, and the scientific; in fact, of all who are not wise enough to think and observe, and weigh and judge before they decide. There is small encouragement for men, and still less for ladies, to come forward and stand in front of all this obloquy. If an example be needed of the truth of this, if it be not an obvious fact already in this uncharitable day, let my adventurous friends watch the extent to which I shall be abused, and called bad names, and given to the devil, for simply and truthfully writing in this little book a few of the incidents of my life, with the production of which I have had nothing to do".

Many of those who had wonderful and convincing experiences at the séances of Mr. Home in England have quitted the world, and have carried their knowledge with them. As for the survivors, it may readily be conceived that few of those who shrank from publicity when the impression made on them was fresh and vivid are inclined to come forward now. I am the more thankful that there are a courageous minority who have not feared to speak. Some of these, too, are now in another life, but their witness remains; others are still on earth, and I gratefully acknowledge the assistance they have afforded me. The life of Home and its marvellous phenomena are sufficient to prove that God rendered worthy of this gift, the man on whom it was bestowed.

All the facts I can give I shall give; my care is not to respect the scruples of the timorous, but to render justice to the truth. If the publication of names causes pain, I can only say that I am sorry; but that the timid portion of his friends must be content with having sacrificed him during his lifetime to their anxiety not to compromise themselves in the eyes of the world. I cannot imitate Mr. Home's generosity on this point; my duty forbids me, on account of the honour of a truth that was sacred to him, and for the future of which I write this book. I only regret that my want of full information must necessarily render my narrative incomplete, and that the history of many remarkable séances will never be known, unless such of the persons present at them as still survive will summon up courage enough to remember the duty they owe to the truth, and will put it in practice by giving the facts of those séances to the world.

During the years 1860 and 1861, the manifestations in England were, as I have said, of a very wonderful character. The mere list of the persons present at Mr. Home's séances would furnish sufficient testimony to the interest he excited in English society. He sought none of those persons; all his life his rule was to allow events to take their course with him; and his acquaintance extended itself without any efforts of his own.

On his arrival in England in November 1859, he received a warm welcome from the friends whom he had made during his visit in 1855; and various men of note who had then been present at his séances took the opportunity of renewing their acquaintance with him. Two of the earliest of these were Sir E. B. Lytton and Dr. Ashburner; the former of whom writes to Mr. Home, January 10, 1860, pressing him to pay a visit for two or three days to Knebworth. Home was unable to accept the invitation; but later in the year Lytton came to London, and then, and again in 1861, was present at various séances, of which I shall presently speak.

Dr. Ashburner had become a firm believer in Spiritualism; and his belief had estranged from him his old friend and colleague,

Dr. Elliottson, whose portrait Thackeray drew in Pendennis as Dr. Goodenough, and to whom the great writer affectionately dedicated that work. Elliottson and Ashburner had cooperated in investigating the phenomena of mesmerism; but after being present at one or two séances with so-called mediums, the former contemptuously refused to make further inquiry into Spiritualism, and lost all patience with what he regarded as his old friend's delusions on the subject. Elliottson was a man whose noble and upright character was worthy of all esteem; but, like many other great physiologists, he rejected absolutely the doctrine of a future life.

On Dr. Ashburner becoming an avowed Spiritualist, Elliottson broke off all intercourse with his old friend, and publicly charged him with worse than folly in assisting to promote the spread of so gross a delusion; nor did "Dr. Goodenough" hesitate to inveigh in unmeasured terms against Home, whom he had never seen. He was destined, however, to make Home's acquaintance, and under dramatic circumstances. The most tolerant of mankind, Home had never for a moment thought of resenting the conduct of Elliottson, whose prejudice he felt to be as honest as it was unreasoning and violent, and of whose estimable character he was well aware. The circumstances under which the two men at last met were related by Mr. Home in his second volume of *Incidents*, published after Dr. Elliottson's death, but during the lifetime of the lady who was the agent of the introduction.

"In the autumn of 1863, while at Dieppe," wrote Home, "I met my friend, Mrs. Milner Gibson, one afternoon on the parade there. In the course of conversation, she said: 'Do you know that Dr. Elliottson is in Dieppe at present?' 'Is he?' I replied; 'I should like to be introduced to him.' Mrs. Milner Gibson expressed surprise, but undertook to introduce me; and a few minutes afterwards we observed him on a seat. I was introduced to him, and said, 'Dr. Elliottson, you have said and written very hard things of me. Now, don't you think it was very wrong for an old man like you to make such accusations as you have done against me, and call a man an impostor of whom you know nothing whatever? If you like to know something of me, and to investigate the subject of Spiritualism, I shall be happy to see you at Mrs.

Milner Gibson's this evening, and to give you every opportunity of testing what you see.' He came; and saw so much that he was convinced of the truth of Spiritualism. The next day he called on me, and said: 'what I witnessed last evening was wonderful and convincing, but it is too much for me to change suddenly the convictions of seventy years. I must ask you to let me come again, and bring a young friend with me.' I agreed readily; and that evening he came accompanied by the two young Messrs. Symes. The fullest use was made by the three gentlemen of their power of observing and testing what they witnessed, and the result was that Dr. Elliottson was perfectly convinced."

On returning to London, Elliottson hastened to seek a reconciliation with his old friend, Dr. Ashburner, and during the few remaining years of his life made no secret of the change in his convictions, nor of the manner in which it had been wrought. Yet the old incredulity struggled at times to reassert itself, and to strengthen his new belief, he wished to obtain communications himself. He applied accordingly to Mrs. Milner Gibson for instructions as to the most favourable conditions under which to hold séances; and followed them carefully, but without effect. Disappointed by his failure, he wrote the following note to Mr. Home:

"Conduit St. 37, Oct. 30, 1863."

"My dear Sir, I have sat regularly accordingly to the instructions I received from Mrs. M. G., but with no result. When shall you be here? Yours sincerely, "J. Elliottson."

Elliottson was still only on the threshold of the subject. He Lad not yet learned that a gift of the nature of Home's can never be acquired. A man is born with or without it, and the vast majority without.

In the following year, 1864, Mr. B. Coleman, of Bayswater, received from Elliottson an account of the revolution wrought in his views by the séances with Home at Dieppe, and published it, with the full approval of the giver, in the *Spiritual Magazine*. This authorized version of the conclusion that Elliottson had arrived at is as follows:

'I am,' Dr. Elliottson said to me, and it is with his sanction that I make the announcement, 'now quite satisfied of the reality of the phenomena. I am not yet prepared to admit that they are produced by the agency of spirits. I do not deny this, as I am unable to satisfactorily account for what I have seen on any other hypothesis. The explanations which have been made to account for the phenomena do not 'satisfy me, but I desire to reserve my opinion on that point at present. I am free, however, to say that I regret the opportunity was not afforded me at an earlier period. What I have seen lately has made a deep impression on my mind; and the recognition of the reality of these manifestations, from whatever cause, is tending to revolutionize my thoughts and feelings on almost every subject."

Dr. Elliottson died in 1868. The *Morning Post* in the course of its obituary notice, related the story of his meeting with Mr. Home at Dieppe, which, it must be noted, Home had not yet published; and continued:

"He then spent some time in investigating the phenomena of Spiritualism, aided by the sons of his friend, Dr. Symes. The result was that he expressed his conviction of the truth of the phenomena, and became a sincere Christian, whose handbook henceforth was his Bible. Some time after this he said he had been living all his life in darkness, and had thought there was nothing in existence but the material; but he now had a firm hope which he trusted he would hold while on earth."

"In one of my latest interviews with him," a friend of Elliottson's wrote in 1870, "he expressed the great happiness his later convictions had brought him, and looked forward to the life hereafter with calm confidence. The leading characteristic of his mind, in addition to his high intellectual development, was the perfectly honest search after truth."

The same description might with equal justice be applied to Elliottson's friend Ashburner, who besides possessed a virtue that Eiliottson, with all his great qualities, lacked that of a well governed spirit. Ashburner's numerous letters to Home pleasantly illustrate the tranquil goodness of his character. I would like to relay a note by Mr. H. T. Humphreys: "It was to me that Dr. Elliottson made the remark quoted in the biography of him which I wrote for the *Morning Post*; and it was made at Mrs. Milner Gibson's, on the only occasion on which I had the pleasure of meeting him.

I try to give some of the pictures of a happy, religious, and tranquil old age these letters afford; but other demands on my space forbid it. Home had several séances with him, of which one that took place in May 1860 was perhaps the most remarkable.

No one in England saw more of the manifestations during the years 1860 and 1861 than the lady who introduced Mr. Home to Dr. Elliottson at Dieppe Mrs. Milner Gibson. She was almost as familiar a figure in French and Italian society as in English; and it was in Paris that Mr. Home first met her.

During Home's stay in London, it was customary for him to hold a séance once a week at Mrs. Gibson's residence in Hyde Park Place, a few doors from Dr. Ashburner. The lady's husband, a well known Member of Parliament, who, then or subsequently, held the position of President of the Board of Trade, uniformly declined to be present at these séances. Mr. Gibson was willing to extend a courteous tolerance to his wife's belief; but he did not share it, and did not wish to share it; not from any deep-rooted incredulity as to the verity of the facts, but from the fear that his presence at séances might tend to compromise that which was everything to such a man his political and social position.

At these séances in Hyde Park Place, and at others that Home held in London during 1860 and the years following, many of the best-known figures in English society were present. The effect on some was to convert them to a belief in the spiritual origin of the manifestations'; others preserved suspense of judgment as to their origin, while admitting the facts. In attempting to distinguish between these two classes, my chief, almost my only guide, has been the letters from English friends and acquaintances preserved by Mr. Home.

The witnesses whom letters to Mr. Home, or their published testimony, show to have not only recognized the manifestations as genuine but to have been convinced of their spiritual origin, included, between the years 1859 1866, the Duchess of Sutherland, Lady Shelley, Lady Gomm, Dr. Robert Chambers, Lady Ottway, Miss Catherine Sinclair, Mrs. Milner Gibson, Mr. and Mrs. William Howitt, Mrs. De Burgh, Dr. Gully of Malvern, Sir Charles Nicholson, Lady Dunsany, Sir Daniel Cooper, Mrs. Adelaide Senior, Mr. and Mrs. S. C. Hall, Mrs. Makdougall Gregory,

Miss Douglas, Mr. Pickersgill, R.A., Mr. E. L. Blanchard, and many others. No letters from Mr. Robert Bell remain; but his article, "Stranger than Fiction," in the *Cornhill Magazine*, constitutes sufficient proof that he is to be added to the list.

I am fully aware that I have named but a small number of the Englishmen and Englishwomen of high intellectual or social position who became convinced of the spiritual origin of the manifestations witnessed by them in presence of Mr. Home. The merit I claim for my list of believers is that, while very far from being exhaustive, it is of indisputable accuracy, as I have included in it only those present at the séances of Mr. Home, concerning whom I have written or printed evidence of the fact that they became Spiritualists. Some of them, as the Howitts and the Halls, had the courage to proclaim their belief openly; others shrank from such a course.

After the convinced, the half-convinced. I mean by this, that among the investigators present at séances of Mr. Home in England were certain distinguished persons, of whom I have warrant for stating that they acknowledged the phenomena they had witnessed at those séances to be inexplicable on the theory of imposture, but of whose beliefs or opinions if they formed any I cannot with certainty speak. I refer, among others, to Mr. Ruskin (one or two of whose letters to Mr. Home will be found in another chapter), Mr. Thackeray, Mr. John Bright, Lord Dufferin, Sir Edwin Arnold, Mr. Edmond Beales, Mr. Heaphy, Mr. Durham, the sculptor; Mr. Nassau Senior, the distinguished political economist, who secured the publication by Messrs. Longmans of Mr. Home's *Incidents*; Lord Lyndhurst, Mr. J. Hutchinson, ex-chairman of the Stock Exchange; Dr. Lockhart Robertson, & co. This short list, it will be observed, includes men whose habits of thought were as wide asunder as the poles; but on each the impression produced was the same that the theory of imposture was untenable. No man who impartially and honestly investigated the manifestations that occurred at the séances of Home ever failed to arrive at a similar opinion. The loudest declarations to the contrary have always proceeded from those who knew least of him, and their only importance has been to furnish an illustration of the hopeless incapacity of the mass of mankind to distinguish between prejudices and facts. A remarkable instance of this unhappy tendency of human nature to confound assertion with fact occurred in the year 1864, the details of which I shall briefly relate in an ensuing chapter.

Besides the Spiritualists and investigators already named, very many persons came to the séances of Mr. Home in London, of whom I know only this one fact that they were present at séances. The names of Mr. Buckle, Lord Clarence Paget, Lord Houghton, the Marchioness of Hastings, Lady Londonderry, Miss Geraldine Jewsbury, and Mr. Hain Friswell, author of *The Gentle Life*, may be of interest; but of the experiences and opinions of these inquirers I can say nothing with certainty; though it is evident from the letters of Lady Londonderry to Mr. Home that she was present at several séances, and that a considerable impression had been made on her.

During the early months of 1860 the circle of Mr. Home's English acquaintances continued to widen steadily, but as yet his name had not been brought prominently before the public. In August 1860, however, a startling impression was produced by the appearance of the article "Stranger than Fiction" in the *Cornhill Magazine*, then at the height of its popularity, and edited by Mr. Thackeray. As the article was unsigned, it lost the weight that the name of Mr. Robert Bell would otherwise have given to it; and Thackeray was bitterly attacked for having permitted the publication of statements, which his hasty and ignorant critics set down as pure invention.

To be reproached with over-credulity was the fate of every intelligent and honest inquirer into the phenomena of Spiritualism whose experiences conflicted with the prejudices of the public, but the accusation was especially unjust as regarded Thackeray, and must have galled him deeply. As the verses attributed to Dickens say of him, he was emphatically "the man, of all his time, who knew the most of men"; and that knowledge, combined with his great natural shrewdness, had rendered him the most wary and sceptical of mankind. He had had opportunities of testing the phenomena that occurred in Mr. Home's presence, and had availed himself of them in the most incredulous spirit. Many years afterwards a friend asked Home, "Who was the most sceptical inquirer you have ever met?" and Home, without any hesitation, answered, "Thackeray." Thackeray's first introduction to Home took place, I believe, during the great writer's lecturing tour in America. My reason for thinking so is that I well remember a description given by an American lady of a séance at which she was present in the States with Home, Thackeray being also present, and; of the amusements caused to her by Thackeray's minute examinations of floor, table, and everything in the room, in his persistent determination to unearth the trickery that he supposed to be at the bottom of the wonders he was witnessing. The character of a credulous dupe was the very last that would have been attributed to the author of *Vanity Fair* by any one who knew him intimately; and his honest and fearless action in publishing Bell's testimony was the more commendable because of the fact that he had himself been convinced entirely in spite of himself. I do not say that Thackeray ever got so far as to entertain the belief that the manifestations were produced by disembodied spirits. Most probably he did not; but when he published the *Cornhill* article, and vouched for his old friend Bell's good faith in an editorial note, he had certainly abandoned as incredible the supposition that they could be attributed to either delusion or imposture. I have only been able to identify one of the séances at which he was present in London with Home. It took place towards the end of December 1862, at the residence in Park Lane of (Mrs. or Miss?) M. G. Hope, the sister of Lady Home.

Robert Bell was less profoundly sceptical by nature than his friend Thackeray, but as frank and candid, and a close, intelligent, and dispassionate observer. No better account of the physical manifestations has ever been given than his lucid and unbiased narrative in the *Cornhill*, written by him with no other aim than to place on record, as befitted a candid inquirer, the results of a series of investigations conducted in a temper equally remote from unreasoning prejudice and foolish credulity. As for the reception accorded his testimony by the mass of the public, Bell had fully anticipated that storm of angry incredulity and ignorant derision. Quoting the reply of Dr. Treviranus to Coleridge, when the poet questioned the savant as to the reality of certain magnetic phenomena, Bell told his readers in the very first lines of his article: "I have seen what I would not have believed on your testimony, and what I cannot, therefore, expect you to believe upon mine."

"It is not to be expected," he writes, later on, "that any person who is a stranger to these phenomena, should read such a story as this with complacency. Yet here is a fact which undoubtedly took place, and which cannot be referred to any known physical or mechanical forces. It is not a satisfactory answer to those who have seen such things, to say that they are impossible; *since, in such cases, it is evident that the impossibility of a thing does not prevent it from happening.*"

In the words I have italicized, Robert Bell anticipated by eleven years the conclusion arrived at by Mr. Crookes after repeated and exhaustive experiments, and expressed by him in his reply to Sir Charles Wheatstone. Wheatstone had written, with regard to one of Crookes' experiments with Home: "It appears to me contrary to all analogy that a force acting according to physical laws should produce the motion of a lever by acting on its fulcrum." "In this," replied Mr. Crookes, "I entirely agree. I, too, cannot trace the analogy between the psychic force and a force acting according to known physical laws. Yet the facts recorded in my papers are true for all that."

In the presence of such experiences as those of Mr. Crookes and Mr. Bell, Science had but two courses open to it to carefully investigate the subject, or to deny its title to investigation. Science was content to adopt the latter course, as the easier and speedier way of arriving at a conclusion; but in so doing it ceased to be science.

I have not space to give in extenso Robert Bell's long and interesting narrative. In a former chapter I quoted his testimony concerning the detached hand that he seized, and that, without any effort at withdrawal, melted into air. His evidence as to another phenomenon repeatedly witnessed at the séances of Mr. Home, the playing of an instrument without the contact of mortal hand, is no less conclusive and emphatic:

"We heard the accordion beginning to play where it lay on the ground.

"Apart from the wonderful consideration of its being played

without hands no less wonderful was the fact of its being played in a narrow space which would not admit of its being drawn out with the requisite freedom to its full extent. We listened with suspended breath. The air was wild, and full of strange transitions, with a wail of the most pathetic sweetness running through it. The execution was no less remarkable for its delicacy than its power. When the notes swelled in some of the bold passages, the sound rolled through the room with an astounding reverberation; then gently subsiding, sank into a strain of divine tenderness.

"That an instrument should be played without hands is a proposition which nobody can be expected to accept. The whole story will be referred to one of the categories under, which the whole of these phenomena are consigned by 'common sense.' It will be discarded as a delusion or a fraud. Either we imagined we heard it, and really did not hear it, or there was some one under the table, or some mechanism was set in motion to produce the result.

"Upon the likelihood of delusion my testimony is obviously worth nothing. With respect to fraud I can speak more confidently. It is scarcely necessary to say that in so small a circle, occupied by so many persons who were inconveniently packed together, there was not room for a child of the size of a doll, or for the smallest piece of machinery to operate.

"But we need not speculate on what might be done by skillful contrivances in confines so narrow, since the question is removed out of the region of conjecture by the fact that, upon holding up the instrument myself in one hand, in the open room, with the full light upon it, similar strains were emitted, the regular action of the accordion going on without any visible agency. And I should add that, during the loud and vehement passages, it became so difficult to hold, in consequence of the extraordinary power with which it was played from below, that I was obliged to grasp the top with both hands. This experience was not a solitary one. I witnessed the same result on different occasions, when the instrument was held by others."

Bell was a sane man, and widely respected as an honest one. Did the accordion play in his hands under the circumstances he describes; or was he deliberately writing a falsehood, the only result of which, as he well knew, would be to bring upon him a storm of obloquy? Were the many other credible witnesses equally telling falsehoods, who have recorded a similar experience? The intellect that answers, "Yes" cannot be reasoned with; and unfortunately there are only too many who will answer "Yes."

In the *Morning Star*, in October 1860, appeared a letter from Dr. Gully, of Malvern, who had been present at the séance when the accordion was played, and who fully confirmed Bell's testimony.

"I held it myself for a short time," he wrote, "and had good reason to know that it was vehemently pulled at the other end, and not by Mr. Home's toes, as has been wisely surmised; unless that gentleman has legs three yards in length, with toes at the end of them quite as marvellous as any legion of spirits. For, be it stated, that such music as we heard was no ordinary strain; it was grand at times, at others pathetic, at others distant and long drawn, to a degree which no one can imagine who has not heard it. I have heard Blagrove repeatedly; but it is no libel on that master of the instrument to say that he never did produce such exquisite distant and echo notes as those which delighted our ears. The instrument played, too, at distant parts of the room, many yards away from Home and from all of us."

One of the phenomena at the same remarkable séance that most impressed and startled the persons present was the levitation of Mr. Home. The lights had then been put out, but the sitters were not in absolute darkness; they could still distinguish objects with the help of what light came through the windows from a gas-lamp outside, and of the fire that was dying in the grate.

"Mr. Home," writes Bell, "was seated next the window. Through the semi-darkness his head was dimly visible against the curtains, and his hands might be seen in a faint white heap before him. Presently he said in a quiet voice, 'my chair is moving I am off the ground don't notice me talk of something else;' or words to that effect." (In explanation of these words, it may be remarked that Home's experience of the phenomenon of levitation was that, until he had risen above the heads of the circle, any movement or excitement on the part of the persons present appeared to have the effect of checking the force at work to produce the manifestation.)

"It was very difficult," continues Bell, "to restrain the curiosity, not unmixed with a more serious feeling, which these few words awakened; but we talked, incoherently enough, upon some indifferent topic. I was sitting nearly opposite Mr. Home; and I saw his hands disappear from the table, and his head vanish into the deep shadow beyond. In a moment or two more he spoke again. This time his voice was in the air above our heads. He had risen from his chair to a height of four or five feet from the ground. As he ascended higher he described his position, which at first was perpendicular, and afterwards became horizontal. He said he felt as if he had been turned in the gentlest manner, as a child is turned in the arms of a nurse. In a moment or two more he told us that he was going to pass across the window, against the grey, silvery light of which he would be visible. We watched in profound stillness, and saw his figure pass from one side of the window to the other, feet foremost, lying horizontally in the air. He spoke to us as he passed, and told us that he would turn the reverse way and cross the window again, which he did. He hovered round the circle for several minutes, and passed this time perpendicularly over our heads."

As Home passed him, Bell touched his foot, and relates that it was "withdrawn quickly, with a palpable shudder. It was evidently not resting on the chair, but floating; and it sprang from the touch as a bird would."

"He now," ends Bell, "passed over to the farthest extremity of the room; and we could judge by his voice of the altitude and distance he had attained. He had reached the ceiling, upon which he made a slight mark, and soon afterwards descended and resumed his place at the table."

If nine hundred and ninety-nine men who had seen them united in testifying to such facts, would the thousandth man who had not seen believe their testimony? Probably not; but, in the words of Mr. Crookes, "the facts are true, for all that."

"You can have but a limited idea," wrote Mr. S. C. Hall to Mr.

Home, "of the sensation created by the article in the *Cornhill Magazine.* It was a bold, noble, and honest act in Robert Bell. Mrs. Hall wrote to thank him in our names. It was so well done so calmly yet so eloquently written; so judicious while so earnest; and so effectually redeeming your character of which the gaping crowd may have doubts, but which all who know you respect and esteem and regard you with something warmer than either respect or esteem.

"I need not add I have taken all opportunities to say I endorse (and so does Mrs. Hall) every sentence in the article."

The séance during which the accordion played without human hand touching it, and Mr. Home was lifted in the air, was the most remarkable of several séances at which Bell had been present; and a large portion of his article in the *Cornhill* is naturally devoted to a description of its various incidents. Besides Mr. Robert Bell and Dr. Gully, the sitters present on that occasion included a solicitor whom I have been unable positively to identify, and the well-known writer, Dr. Robert Chambers. Dr. Chambers had a remarkable experience in the course of the evening, which Dr. Gully related in his letter to the *Morning Star.*

"I may add," wrote Dr. Gully, "that the writer in the *Cornhill Magazine* omits to mention several curious phenomena which were witnessed that evening. Here is one of them. A distinguished litterateur who was present (Robert Chambers) asked the supposed spirit of his father whether he would play his favourite ballad for us; and addressing us, he added: 'The accordion was not invented at the time of my father's death, so I cannot conceive how it will be affected; but if his favourite air is not played. I pledge myself to tell you so.' Almost immediately the flute notes of the accordion (which was upon the floor) played through 'Ye banks and braes o' Bonnie Doon,' which the gentleman alluded to assured us was his father's favourite air, whilst the flute was his father's favourite instrument. He then asked for another favourite air of his father's 'which was not Scotch,' and 'The Last Rose of Summer' was played in the same note. This, the gentleman told us, was the air to which he had alluded."

Dr. Gully had been introduced to Mr. Home by Lady Shelley. He was not as yet a Spiritualist when he attended this séance. "I have endeavoured," he wrote in the same letter to the *Morning Star*, "to show that, as regards the principal and most wonderful phenomena, there could have been no contrivance by trick or machinery adequate to produce or account for their existence. How, then, were they produced? I know not; and I believe that we are very far from having accumulated facts enough upon which to frame any laws or build any theory regarding the agent at work in their production."

If ever a conversion to Spiritualism was remarkable, it was that of Robert Chambers. The fact that he was one of the most kindly and genial of men did not prevent him from being at the same time one of the hardest and most dogmatic of materialists; and he was known by his intimate friends to have been the joint-author, together with Leitch Ritchie, of a work that had startled the public by its outspoken scepticism, *The Vestiges of Creation*. Chambers published it anonymously, from a care of his reputation; and from the same motive he was unwilling, after becoming a Spiritualist, to let his name be mentioned in connection with Bell's *Cornhill* article, or to sign it to the Introduction and Appendix which he kindly wrote in 1863 for Mr. Home's first volume of autobiography. It was not until 1867 that Robert Chambers abandoned this attitude of reserve. In that year he was asked by Home to give an affidavit in connection with the Lyon lawsuit, and honourably consented.

Robert Chambers did not become a Spiritualist in a day, but in the end he did become one. His acquaintance with Home began in 1859, and was continued in 1860 and the years following. It is much to be regretted that he never had the courage to publish the experiences that were the means of converting him; for few men could have borne more remarkable testimony on the subject of identity, as established by the knowledge displayed, on the part of the intelligences communicating, of matters that Chambers was well assured were unknown to Home.

The first conviction at which intelligent and impartial observers present at the séances of Home arrived was that imposture had no part in the manifestations; the second fact demonstrated to them was that those manifestations were governed by intelligence. But by what intelligence? Was it that of Home or of the other persons present, acting in an unexplained manner and under unknown conditions? Or were the intelligences that produced the phenomena separate entities from the human beings present; and, if so, were they disembodied spirits?

What amount of proof could answer the last question in the affirmative? Each inquirer had to decide for himself; but it was obvious that only one class of proofs could be conclusive. If we find that an intelligence communicating with ours claims to be that of a friend whom death has separated from us, we may reasonably expect the spirit to remember something of the facts of his life on earth.

In the case of one investigator present at the séances of Home, messages from lost friends would be frequent, and the most remarkable proofs of identity would be given: another person might be present at séance after séance, and never receive a message of the kind. Why not? The question was often asked; and the reply the spirits gave was that the life beyond is, like our own, subject to conditions and restraints, differing indeed from earthly restraints and conditions, but often debarring spirits from communicating, just as we are often unable to carry out our wishes here below.

Robert Chambers was one of the former and more fortunate class of investigators, the recipients of evidences of identity that were conclusive to them. "Evidences that may be accounted for by the theory of thought-reading," some objectors will answer. If that theory be held sufficient to account for the knowledge shown at the *Cornhill* séance of the two airs that Chambers was thinking of when he put his question, it still remains to be demonstrated how an accordion that Home was not touching could be induced to play those airs. But can thought read thought at a distance of four hundred miles?

In the latter part of 1866, Dr. Robert Chambers was in Scotland, and Mr. Home in London. One day, at the rooms of the Spiritual Athenaeum in Sloane Street, where Mr. S. C. Hall, Mr. Humphreys, Mr. Jencken, Mr. Perdicaris, and Mr. Home had met for the discussion of some matters of business, a message was rapped out that claimed to emanate from a daughter of Dr. Chambers. Her name was given; and Mr. S. C. Hall, who had been for many years acquainted with the family, declared his disbelief that Dr. Chambers had ever had a daughter of that name. For the sequel of the incident, my authority is Mr. Hall himself, together with letters written by Dr Chambers on the subject, and quoted from by Mr. Home in his second volume of *Incidents*.

Mr. Hall relates that, as the message received had reference to certain very private matters, he was most reluctant to communicate it to Chambers under the circumstances; and, although he unwillingly undertook to write to the latter, neglected to fulfill his promise. Some weeks passed; and one evening, at a séance at the residence of Mr. and Mrs. Hall, in Essex Villas, Campden Hill, another message was received, declaring the regret of the spirit that Dr. Chambers had not been communicated with. She described herself as being accompanied on this occasion by the spirit of a sister who had died at an early age; and in reply to Mr. Hall's request for some token of identity that he might furnish to Dr. Chambers, the words, "Tell him, Pa, love," were spelt out.

Mr. Hall sent this message to Dr. Chambers, with a letter explaining the circumstances under which it had been received, and added that he thought it best to withhold the former communication made, until he had obtained Chambers' opinion of the test of identity. Dr. Chambers wrote back that it was a most remarkable one. "The whole of the communications," said his letter to Mr. Hall, "accord with actual facts. The words, 'Pa, love,' were the last words she pronounced in life."

Mr. Hall had now no scruple in forwarding the other message, which related to private affairs of the Chambers' family and entreated Dr. Chambers to adopt a particular course of action with reference to certain family matters. Chambers did as the spirit advised; and in a letter that he wrote to Home a short time afterwards he related the result of his action; adding, "You see, she was right about the imminence of that step, of which I Knew nothing."

I have dwelt on this incident at some length, because the theory of thought reading is clearly quite inapplicable here. In the narrative I am now about to give, such an explanation is, to say the least, very far-fetched, for it is evident that the recipient of the communication was not at the moment thinking of the person it referred to.

One of the friends of Dr. Chambers was the late Miss Catherine Sinclair, a well-known writer in her day, and a lady much beloved for the beauty and amiability of her character. She, like Chambers, became a Spiritualist; and one of the experiences that were the means of convincing her is thus narrated by Mrs. Adelaide Senior, sister-in-law of the late Nassau Senior. The séance in question took place in the summer of 1861; and Mrs. Senior, who was present at it, writes:

"We were all assembled in the summer twilight in a large drawing-room in one of those immense houses in the Regent's Park, where Mr. and Mrs. Home were staying with the widow of an Indian judge. Miss Catherine Sinclair was seated next me; we were not at a table, nor in a circle. Mr. Home went into a trance; and coming up suddenly to Miss Sinclair, he said in that peculiar trance voice 'You knew James Ferguson,' when she actually bounded up from her chair, and said, 'Yes, I did!' He went on in the same voice: 'He was called Sir James in life he wishes to communicate with you, but cannot do so you are so surrounded by your friends;' and she answered bitterly, 'Aye, I daresay!' Upon which I conjured up a love story in my mind, and I believe that I was perfectly right. Mr. Home meanwhile went on, 'He wants you to do something for him.' 'Oh! What is it?' she interrupted; 'there is nothing that I would not do for him.'"

Mrs. Senior then narrates a communication that was made relative to a son of Sir James Ferguson, to whom Miss Sinclair was requested to write; and continues:

A Note by Mr. H. T. Humphreys: "I was also present at the séance at Essex Villas, Campden Hill, where Mary Edwards (formerly Chambers) came accompanied by her little sister, and recollect how the window curtains were moved into something like a canopy on the occasion. We asked for an explanation of 'Pa, love,' and were told it was a test."

"'But I do not know where he is,' Miss Sinclair answered; 'can you tell me?' Mr. Home paused a moment, and said, 'I will try and find out.' When he turned to walk away from us, I saw a bright star glittering in the centre of his forehead, and said impulsively, 'Oh, look at the star!' but no one saw it except myself. He walked to the other end of the room, 18 to 20 feet, where there were folding doors, leading to another room; they were closed, and he began to walk up and down in front of them like a sentry on his post; and, as he did so, we all saw seven stars sparkling round his head, as they do in the sky on a frosty night. In a few minutes Mr. Home came over to us again, and walking close to me, said, 'No one saw the first star in my forehead but you that was Henry's star.' Then, turning to Miss Sinclair, he mentioned some foreign baths Baden-Baden, I think, and I afterwards saw a notice of the death of Sir J. Ferguson's son at the same place.

"I ought to have mentioned that when Mr. Home walked away from us in the first instance, Miss Sinclair turned to me, and said, in the lowest whisper: 'How very wonderful! He has been dead these thirty years,' when Mr. Home instantly called out in a tone that thrilled us: 'Don't say dead nothing kills but sin kills through the devil; but those who live in Christ never die.' This was said from the far side of the room, where no human ears could have heard Miss Sinclair's words.

"I had never met her before, nor did I ever see her again; but on that night we had a great deal of talk, and hoped to meet again. I have often wondered whether Miss Sinclair had left any record of her experience. She seemed very much impressed, and to believe fully all she heard and saw."

When he was thrown into the trance-condition referred to by Mrs. Senior, Home's identity became merged in that of the intelligences communicating, and he described the spirits he saw, and spoke in their words; but, on awaking from the vision, remembered nothing of what had passed. I shall write more fully on this subject in another chapter.

From one of the letters of Robert Chambers, it appears that he was in London late in April or early in May 1860; this, therefore, must have been the visit during which Chambers was present at the séance described a few months later in the *Cornhill*.

If any further evidence be asked that Chambers in the last years of his life was a Spiritualist in the full sense of the term, I may cite some words of his with reference to a pamphlet on the subject of Spiritualism, of which his friend Miss Douglas (another of Home's converts) was the author. "These twenty-four pages," he wrote, "in my opinion contain the germ of the greatest discovery and the greatest revolution of human thought that the world has witnessed." The same recognition of the spiritual origin of the manifestations is apparent in the following extract from a letter written by Dr. Chambers to Mrs. S. C. Hall, on hearing of Mr. Home's adoption by Mrs. Lyon:

"I need not say how delighted I am, in common with all his well-wishers, with the good fortune that has befallen him. Such is my opinion of him that not only do I think him deserving of it but that he will make good use of it. We may, I think, trust to see him propagating Spiritualism from the independent point he has reached, with power only bounded by the needful regard to his health."

Several of the letters of Dr. Robert Chambers and Miss Sinclair were printed by Mr. Home in his second volume of *Incidents*. A passage from one of Miss Sinclair's may be quoted here, as indicative of her convictions:

"The message of last night was most marvellous. I live with those who have heard, from my near relative Mrs. Hope Johnstone, a very detailed account of her experience and also Mr. Grant's of the *Advertiser*; but people cannot long resist conviction, seconded by manifestations so pleasing and elevating as those of last night. I merely relate what I have myself witnessed, and all become at once desirous to share in such revelations."

In an unpublished letter from Miss Sinclair to Mr. Home, I find the following grateful reference to her experiences:

"My brother and I would much like to be present at the séance, if you could obtain Mrs. Edgeworth's leave to allow us to accompany Lady Hesketh. I hear from Mr. S. C. Hall that you are now in great power; and I am so deeply interested in the subject of Spiritualism, and have had such experience of its truth and usefulness, that it interests me of all things. I have never forgotten the beautiful manifestations we had at your house in Sloane Street."

The séance, at which Miss Sinclair was so startled by hearing the name of Sir James Ferguson, was the second that the narrator of the incident, Mrs. A. Senior, had ever attended. Her own experiences on that and the previous occasion were still more impressive than those she relates in connection with Miss

Sinclair. I give them in Mrs. Senior's own words, written in 1862, and published under the initial "S "in Mr. Home's first volume of *Incidents*:

"I first attended a séance of Mr. Home's in the summer of 1861, when I was in very deep affliction. I had never seen anything of Spiritualism before, but had heard a good deal of it from a dear old friend who introduced me to Mr. Home. My own experiences that night were far more wonderful than anything I had ever heard or read of, and were to me most convincing. After many raps, movements of the table, &c., Mr. Home fell into a trance, and described my dear husband most accurately, said how noble he was in mind and body, and how he should have loved him had he known him in life; and then said, 'But who is that Mary standing by his side? What a noble woman, and how she loves him and how happy they are together and how they both love you; you were his star in life. But what was that misery about his watch? You forgot to wind his watch, and how miserable it made you.' Now this was a fact known to no living being but myself. I had wound the watch the night I lost my husband, and resolved never to let it go down again; but more than a month afterwards, when I returned to our old home, I forgot to wind it one night; and my agony was great when I discovered it in the morning, but I never mentioned it even to my husband's sister, who was in the house with me. "A month later I attended a second séance. Some remarkable things were told by Mr. Home, who was in a state of trance, to a lady present (Miss Sinclair) of her departed friend. Mr. Home came soon afterwards to me; and said that my dear husband and his mother the Mary spoken of before were behind my chair, and that both longed to comfort me. He then went on to say that I had had a conversation with my husband eight months before, and that he blessed me for that conversation now; that we were sitting in our drawing-room at home, he in his armchair and I in mine, with the little round table between us, and that I had just been reading a chapter in the New Testament. I remember perfectly the conversation alluded to, and it was a very remarkable one. " These are facts for which I can vouch. To me the comfort has been unspeakable."

"I do hope," wrote Mrs. Senior to Mr. Home in November

1866, with reference to one of her friends, "that Spiritualism may be the same comfort to her that it has been to me – more I cannot wish her."

For one who has had, like Mrs. Senior, the courage to speak, a hundred have been silent concerning their experiences with Mr. Home. Their letters often make allusions to wonderful séances at which the writers had been present, but the story of those séances remains untold. For instance, a lady who was a distinguished ornament of English society a quarter of a century ago, Mrs. G. Cowper, saw a great deal of the manifestations in 1861. "I was up till very late, thinking over and writing an account of the wonders of the evening," she tells Mr. Home in a letter written in the summer of that year but if Mrs. Cowper's account ever found its way into print, it did so anonymously, and cannot now be identified.

Again, there are several letters from Miss Sophia Hope-Vere. A very interesting one, written in 1860, describes the impression made on the writer by the first séance at which she was present.

"20 Park Lane, July 17th.

"Dear Mr. Home, Ere you leave London; I feel it due to you to thank you for admitting me to your séance. I feel I cannot, and never shall, forget what I have felt and heard. I am thankful for the opportunity I had of witnessing what I must honestly own I not only doubted but scouted. I fear, at the outset of anything so strange and mysterious, to express all I feel for I know not how far my present feelings on the subject may last. I shall ever hail with joy an opportunity of another such meeting. I am happy to say that what I narrated to my family has not been sceptically received. I prefaced my communications to them by saying: 'I do not give you my views or ideas in what I am about to tell I confine myself to facts; draw your own impressions, and make what comments you like.' They have paid me the compliment of not doubting one word of what I told them; and one and all are anxious to have a séance. I saw Lady P. yesterday; her feelings are quite in unison with mine on the point. Sincerely yours,

"Sophia J. Hope-Vere."

What were the experiences that drew from one who "not only doubted but scouted" the manifestations, such a letter as the above, after a single séance? What did the writer witness at the séances she subsequently attended? I cannot say: her letters are eloquent of the effect produced on her; but the history of the experiences that converted her scorn into belief is unwritten, and must remain unwritten.

The same blank exists in the case of Lady Shelley, who was present at numbers of Mr. Home's séances in London, including several at Mrs. Milner Gibson's; and who, with her husband, frequently invited him to Boscombe. I have no materials for writing the narrative of her conversion to Spiritualism; but of the fact that Lady Shelley became a Spiritualist her letters leave no question.

"We have been thinking and talking of you for many days past," she writes to Mr. Home in 1863. "All the world has read your book; and it has, I believe, done much good. The next best thing, you know, to seeing you was to hear from you, and to know that your heart yearns towards our little, dark, foggy island. The idea that you might have really been established at the cottage this winter, had we not pulled it down, is tantalizing; but you must let me know as soon as you return to England, and Sir Percy joins with me in hoping that you will come and spend a fortnight with us. We are in all the confusion at Boscombe of building new kitchens and offices, but we shall always be able nevertheless to give you a mutton chop.

"You know I am always living in hopes that some day my husband will have all the comfort from Spiritualism that I have had myself and if that knowledge is to come to him, it will certainly be through you.

"Direct to Boscombe, and say that we are to see you there before long."

The letters of Lady Shelley convey the impression of a nature at once intellectual and amiable. I may cite, as an instance, a letter written by her in 1862, on learning of the death of Mrs. Home:

"Boscombe, July 17th.

"Dear Mr. Home, Just before leaving town, I received from our friend Mrs. Milner Gibson the sad news of your loss. Accept my warmest and most heartfelt sympathy for whenever this parting comes, it must be a sorrow for a time; though to us Spiritualists, who know that our beloved ones are not separated from us, but have merely put off the earth-worn garment to enter into a more glorious life, it is indeed a far different sorrow to that which sees nothing beyond the grave. I trust you will not deem these few lines an intrusion at such a time but the warm interest I must ever take in all that concerns you must plead my excuse."

This chapter has already grown to such length that I had intended to close it here; but another name suggests itself in connection with Mr. Home and the year 1860, that I cannot pass without remark. Dr. Lockhart Robertson, long editor of the *Journal of Mental Science*, had been one of the most derisive critics of the new belief. When Mr. Rymer published a pamphlet on the sittings with Mr. Home at Baling, this distinguished physician replied to it with an essay of thirty-six pages, wherein he demonstrated according to the most approved logical methods the inherent impossibility of the asserted facts. His witticisms on Mr. Home and the believers in Mr. Home would have done honour to the Saturday Review. Dr. Robertson declared himself especially anxious that Mr. Rymer should "catch a sense of the pitying scorn with which those nurtured on the strong meat of the inductive philosophy within the very courts and halls that Newton trod, view these sickly Spiritualist dreamers, thus drunk with the new wine of folly and credulity."

These words were written in 1857. In 1860, Dr. Robertson was a convert. Of the spiritual origin of the phenomena he remained unconvinced; but the very manifestations that he had declared to be impossible, investigation compelled him to accept as facts; and he very honestly published his recantations of former denials in the *Spiritual Magazine* for April and August, 1860. He had the courage to wish to append his name to his testimony; but the editor strongly dissuaded him from doing so, on the ground that injury, and possibly ruin, to his professional reputation would be the result. Some years later, however, on the occasion of the inquiry by the Dialectical Society into Spiritualism, Dr. Robertson came publicly forward to re-state his experiences.

His testimony is that the most remarkable phenomena he witnessed were at a séance with Mr. Home, eight persons in all being present.

"The raps came on the table on the floor about the room the whole floor vibrated with a tremor," wrote Dr. Lockhart Robertson in the *Spiritual Magazine*. "The table was then lifted from the ground about two feet, all our hands being placed on the surface, we standing the while; and one of the circle knelt on the ground, and saw it so suspended. The accordion played the most beautiful music in the hand of Mr. Home, and also while suspended alone, as verified by one of the circle, under the table. I never heard anything more wondrous or unearthly than that music.

"During all these phenomena six wax lights were burning in the room.

"It was then intimated by raps that the lights were to be put out, and the table moved into the window. There was the light of a summer night mixed with the street gas, and enough to enable us distinctly to distinguish objects in the room, each other's faces, & c.

"In a few minutes X and I both distinctly twice saw, as did every one else present, a hand like that of a dark mulatto woman's rise up to the level of the table, in the open, unoccupied space between the table and the window, and take up a pencil laid on a piece of paper, and draw on it what afterwards we found to be a leaf and an eagle's head. I am most positive, and so is X., that this hand belonged to no one in the room, that it could not by any possibility so belong. Whether owned by angel, spirit, or demon I know not."

The silliest of many things said concerning Mr. Home was the frequently-repeated assertion that he avoided meeting sceptics, that wonders only happened in the presence of Spiritualists, and so on. Except Dr. Ashburner, not one of the persons whose experiences are described or referred to in the present chapter: Dr. Elliottson, Dr. Robert Chambers, Mr. Robert Bell, Dr. Gully, Miss C. Sinclair, Mrs. Senior, Miss Hope-Vere, Dr. Lockhart Robertson, etc., was a Spiritualist at the time of his or her first séance with Mr. Home. Certainly wonders happened in their presence after they became believers; but what had induced their belief? The wonders they witnessed and tested in Home's presence while they were still sceptics. I will quote a portion of the testimony of one more sceptic concerning his first séance with

Mr. Home. This was a Mr. Pears, a friend of Mr. Cox of Jermyn Street, who came to a séance in the early part of 1860, and whose letter to a friend on the subject was published, with its writer's permission, in the first volume of the *Incidents*:

"I said, half laughing, which you might expect from my scepticism," wrote Mr. Pears, "that I should not wonder if there were some one for me also. Immediately there were raps under my hand, strong enough to shake the table. Perhaps I looked dubiously at a phenomenon so unexpected; for Mr. Home said, 'I should like Mr. Pears to be convinced that we do not make these sounds; perhaps he would get under the table and observe.' I did so; and while I saw that they were not produced by any visible agency beneath, they were sounding as vigorously as ever; Mrs. P. being witness to their not being produced by the hands, or any visible means aboveboard.

"There was one part of the séance which forcibly struck me, and which I must relate." Having explained that the raps under his hand "purported to come" from his grandfather's spirit, Mr. Pears continues:

"Mr. Home soon after passed into a singular state half-unconscious as it were and said: 'Here's a tall, old, upright, Quaker-like man, yet not a Quaker'; then he seemed to take on the manner and gesture, as closely as a young man can, of those of an old one held out his hand to me, and grasped mine in a way that further reminded me of my grandfather, and addressed me in words somewhat characteristic of him; and went on to speak of one whom he had held very dear, but from whom he had long been separated, to his great grief; but that they had happily met in the other world, and were reconciled. All upon this point was said in a broken way, but with gestures and allusions which were intelligible solely to myself; as the person and events so alluded to touched closely upon my grandfather's history in conjunction with my own. My astonishment was increased when from Mr. Home's lips fell the name of her to whom the allusion had been made; my grandfather's daughter. Both died when Mr. Home must have been a boy in America. Long as I have known you, friend Dixon, I think I never told you that my grandfather was of a Quaker family, which was the case.

"I was by this incident astonished beyond expression; and acknowledged to Mr. Cox that the history which had been sketched, and the reflections upon it, were just what I should have expected might have been made by my grandfather. I have not yet found a place in my system for these phenomena, but that they are genuine phenomena is settled in my mind."

That a single observer, however acute and sceptical, might be deceived is very possible. That a dozen such observers, whose investigations were independently conducted, should all be deceived is highly improbable. That hundreds nay, thousands of sane and able investigators, of every country and condition of life, who had never seen each other, and whose habits of thought were as diverse as nationalities, should have, one and all, been deluded by a single man into the conviction that they witnessed phenomena which never took place is impossible. Were it possible, there would be an end of the value of human testimony; and the only reasonable being in the world would be the sceptic who endorsed unconditionally the Psalmist's hasty declaration, "All men are liars," and was even prepared to include himself, if his senses testified to facts that his prejudices rejected.

To the rash denials of those who have not seen, those who have seen cam only respond in the words which Mr. Weld, in his Last Winter in Rome, tells us were uttered by Thackeray shortly after the publication of Bell's article, "Stranger than Fiction." On being reproached, at a dinner in London, for having permitted such an article to appear in the *Cornhill Magazine*, Thackeray, says Mr. Weld, tranquilly listened to all that his critics had to say; and then replied: "It is all very well for you, who have probably never seen any spiritual manifestations, to talk as you do; but had you seen what I have witnessed, you would hold a different opinion."

Professor Chain's, the Plumierian Professor of Astronomy at Cambridge, had never been present at a séance; but a careful and unprejudiced examination of the evidence given by those who had, compelled him to write in 1862: "In short, the testimony has been so abundant and consentaneous, that either the facts must be admitted to be such as are reported, or the possibility of certifying facts by human testimony must be given up."

CHAPTER 6

England

Experiences of Count Tolstoy. Mrs. Milner Gibson. Miraculous Escape of D. D. Home. Evidence of Dr. Hoefer. Evidence of the Ex-Chairman, London Stock Exchange. Lord Lytton as Nicodemus. Home's Sunny Nature. Death of Mrs. Home.

FRIENDS IN RUSSIA had been urging Mr. Home to revisit them; but finding that there was no immediate prospect of his making the journey, two of their number, Count Alexis Tolstoy and Count Steinbock-Fermor, determined to go to him instead; and he had accordingly the pleasure of welcoming them to London about the middle of June, 1860. These accomplished gentlemen spoke English remarkably well; and were soon at home in English society. In the case of Tolstoy, his letters to Home are as often written in English as in French.

Mr. Home's weekly séance at Mrs. Milner Gibson's was often supplemented by others; and in June 1860, he was holding two, three, and sometimes four séances in the week at Hyde Park Place. The requests for invitations were more than numerous; and the eagerness of well-known personages in London society to be present was only equalled by the timidity with which they insisted on concealing their experiences from the world. Tolstoy's letters to his wife contain the description of two séances, both at Mrs. Milner Gibson's. The first was given to himself and Fermor, and to a third Russian, an entire sceptic, who had accompanied them to England; at the other the investigators present comprised Lord Dufferin and Lord Clarence Paget, neither of whom had previously seen anything of the phenomena. The first séance was the more remarkable of the two; and Botkine, the materialist companion of Fermor and Tolstoy, who had come to it incredulous, went away convinced. I translate the interesting record of the evening preserved in Count Tolstoy's first letter from London to his wife.

"June 17th, 1860.

"It is two o'clock in the morning; I have just left Home; and in spite of the pain it gives me to be away from you I don't regret my journey to London, for this séance has been overwhelming (cette séance a été renversante). Botkine brother of the doctor is converted; and wishes to shut himself up tomorrow and stay the whole day indoors, to meditate over what he has seen. Nicholas the donkey being rather unwell, did not choose to be present at the séance. There were myself, Botkine, Mrs. Home, Mrs. Milner Gibson (wife of the President of the Board of Trade), Count Alexander Steinbock-Fermor, and a dame de compagnie. First there occurred all the manifestations you have witnessed; then, on the light being reduced, every article of furniture in the room took to moving of its own accord. A table placed itself on another table; a sofa moved into the middle of the room; a bell rose in the air and went all round the apartment, ringing as it floated.

"Finally the remaining lights were put out, and we sat almost in darkness; there was only the faint light that came through the window from a gas-lamp outside. The piano played with no one near it; a bracelet unclasped itself from the arm of Mrs. Milner Gibson, and fell on the table, where it lay surrounded by a luminous appearance. Home was raised from the ground; and I clasped his feet while he floated in the air above our heads. Hands touched my knees and laid themselves in my hands; and when I sought to retain one it dissolved in my grasp. There were paper and pencils on the table. A sheet of paper came thrusting itself into my hand, and through the alphabet I was told to give it to Home. There was written upon it, 'Love her always. N. Kroll.' The writing exactly resembled that of the mother of Mrs. Home; we have compared it with that of her letters. A very faint voice was heard accompanying the piano while it played. Raps as loud as if made with a hammer were struck on the table under the hands of Botkine.

"What would have, above all, convinced me, were I a sceptic, are the hands I have felt, which were placed in mine and melted when I tried to retain them. A cold wind passed round the circle very distinctly, and perfumes were wafted to us. After the séance Home's hands were burning hot, and the tears were in his eyes.

His wife and he saw constantly a star on one of the chairs, but I did not see it. The curtains of the windows were drawn back, and hands were visible passing before the window faintly lit by the gas outside. Mrs. Milner Gibson made me promise to come to-morrow evening to a fresh séance, but unfortunately Botkine this time was not invited, as there will be so many without him."

Two days later another letter was written to the Countess Tolstoy by her husband to describe the second séance:

"London, 19th June, 1860.

"I had a headache of the worst sort yesterday; however, I put on my dress-coat and white tie, and went to the séance at Mrs. Milner Gibson's. I would have gone a thousand leagues to see these things. There were present Lord and Lady Clarence Paget, Lord Dufferin, Lord de Tablet, Dr. Ashburner, a celebrated physician; Miss Alice, daughter of Mrs. Milner Gibson; her brother, a very nice boy of the age of George, and Mrs. Home. The two children and Mrs. Home were in the room, but not at the table, where there was not room enough for every one. The séance was by no means so good as the first, but there was a new phenomenon. I saw the accordion play without being held; and after each note there was an echo very distant, but very distinct and agreeable which repeated it. Lord Clarence, feeling his knee clasped, wished me to touch the hand that was holding it; and when I placed my hand on his knee without finding anything, he still felt, besides my hand, another that was touching him. This time Home did not float in the air in my presence. The three lords were present at a séance for the first time; and did not fail, at the invitation of Home, to make a search under the table, while the rest of us were observing what went on above."

Count Tolstoy's words "in my presence," are explained by a note added by Mr. Home:

The apartment was lighted by two lamps and several wax candles; and when the séance was over, the company passed into another room, except Lord and Lady Clarence Paget and myself, who stayed behind conversing. Suddenly, I felt myself raised from the ground; and said so to Lord Clarence, who knelt down and passed his hands between my feet and the carpet, to satisfy himself of the fact."

Tolstoy and Home did not meet again till the year 1865, when, to the great joy of the Count, his friend at last consented to pay a second visit to Russia. The former had never written without a pressing invitation; and on arriving from America in the spring of 1865, Home found a charming kind of round-robin from the members of the Tolstoy family awaiting him at Cox's Hotel, and intended to second the following letter from the Count. If there are flaws in the English of the writer, there were none in his good heart.

"16th December, 1864.

"My dear friend Daniel, I am afraid you have not received my letter from Poustineka, which I sent to you three months ago. I, and all the persons living with me, required your presence, and expected that you would perhaps agree with our desire, and come here to pass the winter with us. ... Now I write you again, and tell you once more how happy I, my wife, and we all would be if you come to visit us and remain with us till summer. Come, my dear friend, it will be a good distraction for your sorrows."

To enforce the invitation, every member of the household has penned a few words. "I hope we shall see you, dear Mr. Daniel," writes the Countess. "Please come we shall be so glad to see you again," another of the family adds. "Come come," write friends four, five, and six; and "Venez, Mon Cher Home," is the concluding appeal addressed to him by a correspondent who has no English. It was impossible not to yield; and Home started for Russia forthwith.

Count Steinbock-Fermor must either have remained in London in 1860 after Tolstoy's departure, or have returned the following year; for I find him present at a séance in 1861, at 7, Cornwall Terrace, Regent's Park, the residence of a Mrs. Parkes, with whom Mr. and Mrs. Home were then staying. Besides Count Steinbock-Fermor, the circle included Mr. and Mrs. William Howitt (the well-known authors), and Mr. and Mrs. W. M. Wilkinson. The phenomena of this séance were described in the *Incidents* (vol. I.) both by Mr. Howitt and Mr. Wilkinson.

"Mr. Home," wrote the letter, "now held the accordion in his right hand beside his chair, and it at once began to play. He held it by the bottom, the keys being on the top, and therefore out of his reach. It was impossible that he could touch them. I carefully examined the instrument, opening the slide beneath the keys, and I found it to be a common instrument with only the usual mechanism of the keys. There was nothing inside it. I looked steadily at it, and at the hand and fingers with which he held it. There it was, being pulled up and down, and discoursing sweet sounds whilst his hand was stationary and his fingers motionless. I could see above and beneath the instrument, but there was no visible cause for its motion, nor for the opening and shutting of the keys which caused the music.

"When it ceased, my wife asked if it could not be played in her hand and immediately the instrument emitted three sounds, which we took to mean that it would have much pleasure in trying. It was accordingly given to her, and whilst in her right hand it began to play. She felt it distinctly lifted up and drawn forcibly down; and she did not and could not touch the keys, which however, must necessarily have been touched and opened to make the sounds. ... I have once had an accordion play in my own hand, when I know that I did not do it. I also know that Lord Lyndhurst and many other public men whom I could name have had a similar experience." 'There were, besides Mrs. Howitt and myself," writes Mr. William Howitt of the same séance, "a Russian, Count Steinbeck, and several others. We had beautiful music played on the accordion, when held in one hand by Mr. Home, who cannot play a note; and the same when held by a lady "(Mrs. W. M. Wilkinson). Flowers were taken from a bouquet on a chiffonier at a distance, and handed to each of us. I saw a spirit hand as distinctly as I ever saw my own. I touched one several times."

The Howitts were at this time living near Hampstead; and their house was the resort of half the authors and artists of London. Several of Mr. Home's séances were held there in 1861 and subsequent years; and he met a number of new investigators on these occasions.

The letters of Count Steinbock-Fermor to his friend are numerous and interesting. One of them, belonging to the year 1861, discusses the philosophy of Spiritualism as the writer viewed it, and is annotated with a few remarks by Mr. Home some endorsing, others rejecting the propositions it contains. I give part of this long letter, bracketing Home's annotations with the statements they refer to:

"Spirits," writes Steinbock-Fermor, "never wholly cease to be linked with matter." (Certainly not.) "In continually progressing, they put more distance or, more correctly, difference between them and their first state of being." (Through refinement.) "They attain a nearer resemblance to the One Spirit who is God; but it is comparable to geometrical proportion, which removes farther and farther from I without approaching infinitude." (Yes.) "Spirits can advance until they at last attain to their perfection the perfection of the created." (We can never arrive at absolute perfection, and there is no arbitrary limit set.)

In the months of May and June 1860, hardly a day passed without a séance; and the constant drain on his vital force had most injurious effects on Home's health. The experience of years had taught him that, in the words of Mr. Crookes, "the evolution of psychic force is accompanied by a corresponding drain on vital force;" and he well knew that after a séance he required a period of repose during which his exceptional organization might recruit its exhausted energies, and that the interval of a day only was not long enough. While holding daily séances, he saw his health grow rapidly worse; but all that others regarded was their eager desire to see as much as possible of the manifestations. Had he remained a few months longer in London, he would probably have prostrated himself utterly; for he could not say "No" to a friend who pressed him to sit, and believers, inquirers and sceptics by the hundred were besieging him for séances. There was nothing for it but to escape from his surroundings for a time; and towards the end of July 1860, Mr. and Mrs. Home went on a visit to friends in France.

Mr. Wason was invited by Mrs. Milner Gibson to a séance, at which, among numerous manifestations, an accordion played in his own hand. He also witnessed on this occasion the phenomenon of Home's levitation, the room being faintly lit from the outside in the manner already described by Count Tolstoy.

"Mr. Home crossed the table over the heads of the persons sitting around it," said Mr. Wason. "By standing and stretching upwards I was enabled to reach his hand, about seven feet distant from the floor; and laying hold and keeping hold of his hand, I moved along with him five or six paces as he floated above me in the air, and I only let go his hand when I stumbled against a stool. ... I saw his body eclipse two lines of light of issuing from between the top of a door and its architrave such door leading into an adjoining room that was brilliantly lighted.

"I make no comments on the above, and advance no theory or hypothesis: I have confined myself simply to facts," adds Mr. Wason, who was at this time a sceptic, but, as the result of continued investigation with Mr. Home, became a Spiritualist, and was subsequently Home's hast at Liverpool.

Mrs. Milner Gibson had narrated to numbers of her friends the wonderful phenomena of the séances in Hyde Park Place; and as Mrs. Gibson, in society phrase, "knew every one worth knowing," the natural consequence of the curiosity excited was that her letters to Mr. Home are filled with well-known names, the owners of which were pressing her for invitations to a séance. She gives a long list on one occasion of those who had been invited by her and were waiting their turn; including Lord Dufferin, Sir Emerson Tennant, Lady Trelawney, Mdlle. Tietjens, Mr. Lawrence Oliphant, Sir Fitzroy Kelly, Mrs. Grote, Mr. Stirling, Mr. Higgins, and Mr. Hayward. "Fancy my joy on Saturday night at Lady Palmerston's," writes Mrs. Gibson, "when Higgins (Jacob Omnium) and Hayward both asked me to be permitted to come to a séance. I told Robert Chambers, who called on Sunday, and he was greatly astonished and pleased. I had a conversation with Lord Dufferin, and promised to let him know as soon as you return."

Mrs. Milner Gibson went often to Dieppe. "There is a ludicrous story here about you and Le Père Ravignan," she tells Mr. Home during one of her visits; "how the Father persuaded you to give up Spiritualism, and the Evil One seized you and threw you down, and forced you to continue! I was very amused."

In November, 1862, when Mr. Home was preparing his first volume of *Incidents* for publication, he discussed with a friend of Mrs. Milner Gibson's the propriety of asking that lady to write a narrative of some of the séances at Hyde Park Place, and authenticate it with her name. On hearing of this, Mrs. Gibson, who was abroad at the time, wrote to him to say that her testimony was at his service; all she asked was that a declaration of her religious views should accompany the publication of the fact that she was a Spiritualist. I copy her letter:

"November 15th.

"Dear Daniel, I have just received a letter from Witch, wherein she says that you want an account of the séance in which you placed your head on the fire and took up a burning coal in your hand. I regret to say that I have no detailed account of that séance, though I have of many others. I think Robert Bell was present; and I can, of course, give my testimony. Witch says that you mentioned something about my name. My name is quite at your service you have never found me shirk from declaring the truth, and all who know me know that I am a Spiritualist. There is only one point which I wish to be clear upon, and that is a religious one. I attack no one's creed: I sit with all creeds: I go side by side with many who hold different opinions from mine; but I am very firm in my opinions, and very anxious that it should be distinctly understood that I am wholly and entirely apart from those who in any way question the New Testament. I see with fear and horror that some Spiritualists are making a weapon of Spiritualism to attack what is divine, instead of upholding it. I abominate discussion, and never enter into it; I therefore rarely mention my fears, unless I see danger of being supposed to belong to those who deny the Divinity of our Saviour. Therefore, my dear friend, I give you my credo."

In spite of the generous readiness of Milner Gibson to give her name, Mr. Home, with equal generosity, finally determined to omit it from his book. Not only did he shrink from allowing so dear a friend to expose herself to the ridicule and insult that she was willing to brave, but the delicacy of the situation was increased by the fact that her husband did not share her beliefs, and was nervously anxious to shun all appearance of identifying himself with them. I have already said that Mr. Milner Gibson had never been present at a séance; and it may be added that he took every opportunity of making that fact as public as possible. None the less, many people annoyed him by insisting on associating his name with Spiritualism; and in 1864, when Mr. Roebuck brought the question of Mr. Home's expulsion from Rome before Parliament, an appeal that he addressed to Mr. Milner Gibson, under the misconception of his being a Spiritualist fairly drove the President of the Board of Trade out of the House.

Mrs. Gibson was no less provoked, and writes to Home:

"I suppose in this stupid country they so idiotically mix up husband and wife that they seem never to dream of or allow a woman to hold independent ideas; and as I am well known to be a Spiritualist, I fancy that they torment the poor man out of his mind by asking him about the manifestations thinking that he must believe or that I should never have dared to do so. How Roebuck made the blunder of fancying him one I cannot conceive; you see it drove him out of the House. He says he denies loudly to all that he knows anything about it; and we must excuse the irritation caused by their stupidity.

He said to M. that he had nothing to say against you, that you might be an angel all he wanted was to be able to say that he knew nothing of Spiritualism."

When Mr. Home's book appeared, it did not contain the name of Mrs. Milner Gibson, though one, and probably more, of the anonymous records of séances included in it was written by her. Anonymous evidence is no evidence, as Home well knew; and in commenting on his book, a portion of the press even delicately insinuated that such narratives as were unsigned were fictitious, and had been written by Home himself to fill his pages. I hope I have made it clear by the evidence of Mrs. Milner Gibson's letters (which I need hardly say are in my possession) that Mr. Home had the full permission of that lady to publish her name, and was only deterred from doing so by motives which all will admit to have been as unselfish as honourable.

Leaving London towards the end of July 1860, Mr. and Mrs. Home went to stay at the Château de Cergay near Paris, the residence of Mons. Tiedemann, who has been already mentioned in connection with séances in Holland. At his beautiful French country-seat, on the 16th of September, Home's life was wonderfully preserved in the manner he has described in the *Incidents*:

"Being recommended to take much out-door exercise during my stay at the Château de Cergay," he writes, "I used to take with me my gun more that it might be said I was out shooting than for any great attraction the sport has for me. The Château de Cergay, distant half an hour by railway from Paris, stands in a beautiful old park. Some of the trees are of very great height; one of the largest, a northern poplar, stands a quarter of a mile from the Château at an angle of the park, where it is separated from the outer grounds by a hedge. To this spot, when there was much shooting going on in the neighbourhood, the game used to come for shelter; and I, who am but an indifferent marksman, could get easy shots by planting myself by the hedge.

"I had been walking with my friend, Mons. T (Tiedemann), and on his leaving me I bent my steps to this favourite corner, wishing to take home a partridge. As I neared the hedge, I stooped and advanced cautiously. When close up to it, I was raising my head to look for my game; when, on my right, I heard some one call out, 'Here, here!' My only feeling was surprise at being thus suddenly addressed in English. The desire to have a good look out for my game overruled my curiosity as to whom the exclamation had come from; and I was continuing to raise my head to the level of the hedge, when suddenly I was seized by the collar of my coat and vest, and lifted off the ground. At the same instant I heard a crashing sound, and then all was quiet. I felt neither fear nor wonder. My first thought was that by some accident my gun had exploded, and that I was in the spirit-land; but looking about I saw that I was still in the material world, and there was the gun still in my hands. My attention was then drawn to what appeared to be a tree immediately before me, where no tree had been. On examination, this proved to be the fallen limb of the high tree under which I was standing. I then saw that I had been drawn aside from this fallen limb a distance of six or seven feet. I ran, in my excitement, as fast as I could to the château. "The limb which had thus fallen measured sixteen yards and a half in, length, and where it had broken from the trunk it was one yard in circumference. It fell from a height of forty-five feet. The part of the limb which struck the very spot where I had been standing measured twenty-four inches in circumference, and penetrated the earth at least a foot. The next day a friend made a sketch of the tree and branch. We speculated as to how it could have happened.

The tree is not a dead one, nor was the branch at all decayed; and there was scarcely wind enough to stir the leaves. The branch was so clearly separated from the trunk that one might think at first it had been sawn off, and the bark was not in the least torn about it. I have been informed since that such accidents are not uncommon with trees of this species of poplar, and that there are trees of a similar quality in Australia, under which settlers will not remain for fear of such sudden breakages." A day or two later the well-known Dr. Hoefer, editor of the *Biographic Generate* and a complete sceptic as to the manifestations, paid a visit to Mons. Tiedemann, and asked for a séance. The séance was held; and the sequel to it is best related in the published words of one of the persons present, Mons. Pierart:

"Dr. Hoefer declared himself satisfied with the answers, and wished to continue the conversation; but the spirits proposed that all should now proceed to the tree where Mr. Home had escaped being 'crushed.' Dr. Hoefer still urged his questions; but there being no response, we agreed to proceed to the tree. The arm still remained as it had fallen, one end resting against the trunk, the other imbedded in the earth, so that to detach it from its place would have required all the strength of a man's two arms. Moved by some secret impulse, Dr. Hoefer proposed that Mr. Home should touch with a finger the end of one of the small branches. He did so; and immediately the enormous arm, 13 metres in length and 95 centimetres in circumference, moved from its point of support and fell. I had had only the testimony of Mr. Home himself as to the previous occurrence at this spot; but this strengthened it, and showed the operation of something beyond chance."

Dr. Hoefer remained some days at the Château de Cergay, and took part in other séances there. "Will you not pay another visit soon to your friends in France?" he writes to Home the following year. "All my leisure moments are devoted to meditating on the immensity of the horizon of which those wonderful evenings at Cergay gave me a glimpse (m'ont laissé entre-voir). I try all I can to lift a corner of the veil that hides such great mysteries from us; perhaps I shall succeed one day, especially if the intelligent powers that surround us are kind enough to aid me."

The winter of 1860 was quietly passed in London. Mrs. Home's health was very delicate; and she and her husband did not go so much into society as during their previous visit.

I find among the letters of this period one giving news to Home in London of his friends at Florence, and written to him by a celebrity of the day, whose acquaintance he had made a few years previously, the musician Blumenthal. Blumenthal, who subsequently came to stay with Home in Sloane Street, was an ardent Spiritualist twenty-five years ago but on that point I may leave his letter to speak for itself. Like Mons. Tiedemann with whom, by the way, he was acquainted Blumenthal writes in English, and writes it well.

"Florence, December, 1860.

"My dear Dan, We are both very anxious to have some news of you and dear Sacha (Mrs. Home). I had written you some time ago a little letter through Mr. Tiedemann; but as I have not heard from you, I suppose it has never reached you. I send this one to Cox's Hotel, as you told me once that they always knew your address. In a letter from England, which I received a few days ago, there was even a rumour as if you were there yourself. If you are not there now, I hope, at all events, you will come there in spring, when we return. We want to know all you have done since we saw you, as well as some particulars as to the manifestations at Tiedemann 's in presence of Mr. Hoeffer. Was Mr. Hoeffer convinced, and what did he say?" As for us, we have settled for the winter in Florence. You must not think that we forget for a moment Spiritualism; and as you are in our eyes its personification, we think and talk a great deal about you. There is much occasion for it here, as you have so long lived here and we see often people who have known you at the Crossmans', the Trollopes', &c. Your dear portrait is always on our drawing-room table, and I wish we had Sacha's as well. I wish you were all here wouldn't we enjoy it? However, one must not be egotistical; and I suppose you can do more good for the promotion of spiritual ideas where you are than you could here. The other day we tried to sit with Miss Grossman and Mrs. Baker round a table, but with no result. I wish I could be a medium of some sort or other some day.

"If you are in London, I suppose you have resumed your

Monday sittings at Mrs. Milner Gibson's tell me when something particular happens. If you were here, we could see each other much oftener than in London, where life is too busy for friends. Good-bye, dear Dan, and don't forget your affectionate J. Blumenthal."

Another acquaintance of this period was Herzen, the banished Russian political writer whose wild theories had inflamed so many minds. Home met him in London early in 1861, an old man, but still as enthusiastic in labouring to disseminate his insane ideas as he had been in youth. Herzen seems to have established a printing press in London for their propagation; for he writes to Home in April, "We make a fete and illuminate the printing-office on the 10th to celebrate the Emancipation" (of the serfs); "come in the evening and take a look at us."

Still another Russian acquaintance made in London (I forget in what year) was Turgenieff – a nature that attracted Home; for in the famous writer there was much of the naive, child-like joyousness, beneath which lay sadness, that characterized his own temperament. Turgenieff would seem to have also resembled him in taking delight in the society of children, and was in the habit of spending a good deal of his time in playing with Home's baby son, of whom the great novelist made a great pet, as did also another literary giant of Home's acquaintance Thackeray.

In January 1861, Mr. James Hutchinson, for many years Chairman of the London Stock Exchange, was present at a séance with Mr. Home, and wrote and published an account of it. Having heard from friends of what they had witnessed, says Mr. Hutchinson, and being unable to believe what he heard, he determined to see for himself. "I feel it a duty," he wrote, January 26, 1861, "to openly bear my testimony to the facts, leaving others to theorize on the causes and tendency of these remarkable phenomena." Recently introduced by a friend to Mr. D. D. Home, a séance was arranged for the 23rd instant; and, together with Mr. and Mrs. Coleman, Mr. G. S. Clarke, Mr. T. Clarke, Mr. Gilbert Davidson, and another lady and gentleman unknown to me, we formed a party of nine. Shortly after sitting down, we all felt a tremulous motion in our chairs and in the table, which was a very heavy circular drawing-room table.

"The rapping sounds on the table and floor were constant; the heavy table was raised up repeatedly; and these manifestations were continued whilst my friend, Mr. Clarke, and another were seated, at the request of Mr. Home, under the table.

"Two hand-bells, one weighing at least a pound and a half, were passed from one to another of the party by unseen agencies. All of us in turn felt the touch and pressure of a soft and fleshy life-like hand. I saw the full-formed hand as it rested on my knee. The accordion, whilst held by Mr. Home in one hand, discoursed most eloquent music; and then, to our great astonishment, it was taken from him, and whilst both his hands, and those of all the party, were visibly imposed on the surface of the table, the accordion, suspended from the centre of the table, gave out an exquisite air, no human hand touching it!

"These, and many other incidents of a seriously impressive but private character, of which I do not hesitate to speak among my friends, occupied about four hours of what I must admit to be one of the most interesting evenings I have ever spent. Contrary to the assertions constantly made, that the manifestations are always in the dark, the whole of the phenomena of which I have spoken were manifested in a room lighted with gas, and a bright fire burning. "J. A. S. Hutchinson."

Mr. Hutchinson, it will be seen from a passage in his letter, was one of the many who kept to themselves the tokens of spirit identity that were communicated to them. The Mr. B. Coleman who was present with him at the above séance, gave evidence in 1869 before a committee of the Dialectical Society concerning similar tokens received by him at his own first séance with Mr. Home in the year 1855.

"At the first séance which I attended," stated Mr. Coleman, "there were fourteen persons in the room, seated round a long dinner-table. Mr. Home sat at one end, and I at the other. Through the rapping sounds several messages were given to different individuals of the party. One purported to be from the spirit of an aunt of mine, who gave me her name as Elizabeth; and another spirit, also an aunt of mine, gave the name of Hannah. I did not recognize the names I had never known of any aunts of those names; but subsequently I wrote to my mother, and asked whether she recognized them as family names; and she then told me what was quite new to me, that two sisters of my father were named Elizabeth and Hannah, who died before I was born."

Confronted with evidence of this kind, the ingenious philosophers who trim the facts of Home's life into accordance with their pet theories of "thought-reading," "unconscious cerebration," and so forth, have but one course open to them to declare boldly that they do not believe the witness, and would not believe ten thousand witnesses if they swore to similar occurrences.

The letters of Mrs. Milner Gibson to Mr. Home in the spring of 1861 show that the séances at Hyde Park Place had been resumed; and among the new names mentioned in connection with them is that of Mrs. F. C. Parkes, of 7, Cornwall Terrace, Regent's Park, a lady who had been long resident in India. Her introduction to Home and Spiritualism was made through Mrs. Milner Gibson in December 1860. "I returned home from this my first séance with Mr. Home," she noted in her journal, "convinced of the truth of our being permitted to hold intercourse with those who have passed to the spirit-land."

Mr. and Mrs. Home were for some time the guests of Mrs. Parkes; and before and during their visit numerous séances were held at 7, Cornwall Terrace. A diary of the manifestations witnessed was kept by Mrs. Parkes; and having been placed by her at the disposal of Mr. Home, he published large portions in the *Incidents* (vol. I.), the identity of the writer being veiled, at her desire, under the initial, "Mrs. P."

Sir E. B. Lytton was a good deal in London in 1861; and besides séances at his house in Park Lane when Home dined there (Mrs. Milner Gibson being sometimes one of the party), the distinguished litterateur frequently came to séances at Mrs. Gibson's and with Mrs. Parkes in Cornwall Terrace. I find in one of Mrs. Milner Gibson's letters an interesting account of attempts made by Lytton and herself to obtain manifestations at Nice in 1865, at a time when Home was in London. "There was not much," she adds.

Lytton was a typical example of the weak man who, above all things, fears ridicule. In public he was an investigator of Spiritualism, in private a believer. Not long before his death he wrote to Mr. S. C. Hall to inquire if the latter could give him the name of "some reliable medium" in London, with whom he might put a friend of his in communication who had just lost a near and dear relative; a strange thing to do, if he were quite candid in his published declaration: "So far as my experience goes, the phenomena, when freed from the impostures with which their exhibition abounds, and examined rationally, are traceable to material influences of the nature of which we are ignorant. They require certain physical organizations or temperaments to produce them, and vary according to those organizations and temperaments." (Letters of Lord Lytton to the secretary, of the Dialectical Society, February 1869).

From a man so timid and so sensitive to ridicule, even this cautiously weighed testimony is remarkable. Lytton refers to the abundant impostures that simulate the phenomena; but he admits that his experiences have satisfied him of the existence of the phenomena themselves. It was the least he could honestly do, after the remarkable séances at which he had been present with Home; and if his numerous letters to Home are of no great interest in themselves, they at least demonstrate by their friendly tone that their writer did not do his correspondent the injustice of classing him with the charlatans of whose trickery Lord Lytton had only too abundant evidence. It was his own fault that he received so many proofs of it. The wonderful things he had seen with Home had excited in him, as in many others, an eager desire for more and more wonders; and, like subsequent inquirers whom I could name, he sought out persons calling themselves "mediums," with the result, in his case as in theirs, that where he had hoped to see marvels he ended by detecting imposture. Such disappointments taught at least one lesson to those who encountered them how more than rare was the marvellous gift of Home.

That Lord Lytton should never have publicly declared his knowledge of the genuineness of that gift was only to be expected from him. All the days of his life he was constantly giving proofs of his excessive sensitiveness to ridicule; and what could have brought more ridicule on him than a fearless, candid statement of the convictions impressed on him by his investigations of Spiritualism with Mr. Home in London, and on occasions when the latter was his guest at Knebworth, Lytton's intimate friends knew the truth; but the public who wish to arrive at the real sentiments of this talented man with regard to Home and Spiritualism must read between the lines. It is for that reason I pause here to say a few words concerning the fragments in my possession of Lord Lytton's correspondence with his frequent guest, Mr. Home.

The letters range from 1855 over a period of ten years subsequent. As, during those ten years, Lytton's tone is unchanged and cordial as he is constantly pressing Home with invitations to dine in Park Lane or run down for a few days to Knebworth the obvious inference is that, whatever his reasons for associating imposture with the word "Spiritualism," he had never seen cause to associate imposture with the name of Home. A man of Lytton's position and celebrity would not have continued year after year on intimate terms with another who had given him reasons for even a suspicion of charlatanism.

Mrs. Home passed away from earth on the 3rd of July 1862; and Lytton writes to Home from Spa towards the end of the same month:

"I condole with you most sincerely on the sad loss of your amiable and interesting wife. The intelligence pained me much. It is indeed a consolation to you to know that she looked so serenely on quitting this world, and with so intense a faith in that happier world which was familiar to her thoughts.

"I certainly did not think her dying when I saw her, nor was she so then. It affected me greatly to receive her touching remembrances from you, and I shall mournfully treasure the photograph you so kindly promise.

"Perhaps I, too, may winter in Italy. I find no climate worth the winter change except Nice and Naples. Wishing you a complete restoration to health, and assuring you of my sympathy in your bereavement, believe me, truly yours, "E. B. Lytton."

I have said that Lord Lytton was probably present at 7, Cornwall Terrace when Mrs. Home's approaching departure from earth was referred to in the touching and beautiful words already quoted. That Lytton had been one of the five persons who formed the circle of the previous evening, June 2nd, 1861, I know from the testimony of the single survivor of the five, Mr. S. C. Hall, whose recollections have enabled me to identify the séance in question among those recorded in the diary of Mrs. Parkes.

The five sitters present that evening were Mr. and Mrs. Home, Mrs. Parkes, Sir E. B. Lytton, and Mr. S. C. Hall. Mr. Hall relates that he had brought with him to Cornwall Terrace a large hand-bell, which he placed on the centre of the table to try if it would be rung there, and that he distinctly saw a hand appear above the table, grasp the bell, and ring it violently; Mr. Home's hands resting quietly on the table the while in full view, and the light being quite sufficient to enable Sir E. B. Lytton and Mr. Hall to satisfy themselves that no machinery of any kind was connected with the apparition of the mysterious hand. Mr. Hall adds that he perfectly remembers the impression produced on Lytton and himself by the noisy displacement of the idols in the Hindu shrine at the end of the large drawing-room, while all five persons present were quietly seated in the summer twilight at the table.

The diary of Mrs. Parkes contains an account of the same séance, written by her at the time.

"June 2nd," she writes. "A séance of five persons. As twilight came on, a pleasant dimness fell over the room. The spirits moved the table with violence up to the window, near the Hindu shrine; and the accordion, no human hand touching it, played in the most charming manner, exquisitely and with great power. There was much noise at the Hindu shrine; the images of Vishnu and the Holy Bull were brought, and put on the top of the table; then a large hand, which appeared dark, being between us and the light, put up the accordion entirely above the top of the table. Another hand took a bell off the table, and rang it. Mr. Home was raised from his chair erect into the air. Then he was drawn to the other end of the room, and raised in the air until his hand was on the top of the door; thence he floated "horizontally forward, and descended. I saw a bright star constantly flashing forth; the raps died away in the distance, and the séance ended." (Extracts from the diary of Mrs. P: *Incidents in My Life Vol 1.* Lord Lytton had many séances with Mr. Home more remarkable than the above; but I have preferred to narrate this one, because I have the attestation of Mr. Hall to the fact that Lytton and himself were both present and witnessed the phenomena described.

It is not generally known that, when Lytton commenced that wildest of all his romances, *A Strange Story* (which was written, I believe, in 1859 or 1860), he had intended making an attempt to portray Home in its pages; but speedily abandoned the design, and substituted for it the fantastic conception of Margrave. So, at least, Lytton told Home; adding that the original plan of *A Strange Story* differed almost as materially from the course the story actually took, as Home's portrait would have differed from that of Margrave. "Of all I have written," said the celebrated romancer, "*A Strange Story* satisfies me the least."

In forsaking his design of attempting to picture Home, Lytton took from him a single hint not for the character of Margrave, but for the impression that abnormal being is represented as making on the ordinary mortals who encountered him. All who knew Home were struck by the joyousness of his nature, and the gaiety and sweetness of a temper that no wrong could embitter and no sufferings sour. In his happy moments of freedom from pain he had the bright cheerfulness of a child, and that keen joy in living which charms us in young children, and makes us look back regretfully with Wordsworth to the lost days when

"The earth and every common sight
To us did seem Apparelled in celestial light,
The glory and the freshness of a dream."

Home's gaiety and cheerfulness in his moments of respite from suffering exercised an irresistible spell on all around him, that won for him in Russia and France the sobriquet of "Le Charmeur." Lytton, like others, had remarked this trait; and he attached it to the outward man of Margrave in *A Strange Story*, exaggerating it somewhat in his description, as it was the habit of Bulwer Lytton to exaggerate.

As I probably shall not again have occasion to allude to Lord Lytton in these pages, I will give here two letters written by him to Mr. Home in the year 1864. They are not of very great importance; but they show that his relations with Home and interest in Spiritualism remained unchanged; and the second contains, in as explicit a manner as could be expected from so timid a

Spiritualist, Lytton's recognition of the fact that Home was a man phenomenally gifted.

Both letters are addressed from 21 Park Lane, and the earlier is dated April 27th, 1864. "I hear you are in town how long do you stay?" Lytton asks. "I am still suffering under a severe attack of bronchitis, and unable as yet to call on any one or see any one here. But my doctor promises me I shall be much better the moment the weather becomes more genial, and in that case I shall hope for the pleasure of seeing you."

The second note dated July 18th, 1864. Is still shorter, but of more interest. "Let me introduce to you my eldest brother, Mr. Bulwer," Lytton writes. "He is seriously interested in the extraordinary phenomena which are elicited by your powers and you will thank me for presenting to you so intelligent and unprejudiced an examiner."

Not much; but at least evidence from Lytton himself that an acquaintance extending over nine years had left unchanged or, rather, had confirmed the conviction impressed on him in 1855 of the extraordinary nature of the phenomena "elicited" (to put it in his own phrase) "by the powers of Home."

Till the middle of July 1861, Mr. and Mrs. Home remained in London. "During our stay," writes the former in the *Incidents*, "I had a séance almost every night, my wife feeling that they did her good, both physically and spiritually." The fatal malady had not yet developed itself sufficiently to prostrate the sufferer; and so long as his wife could be present at séances and took joy at being present, Home was happy to hold them. A few months later she had become too ill to sit, and her husband's every thought was absorbed in caring for her. At the same time his power had left him, or nearly so; but it was by reason of his wife's illness, even more than of his weakened power, that he declined to hold séances, and in so doing gave great offence, both to Spiritualists and inquiring sceptics.

A well-known Spiritualist, whose name I naturally withhold, was anxious that some friends should witness the manifestations; and pressed Home for a séance, which was refused. More than a year later, and some months after Mrs. Home had passed away, Home wrote to his acquaintance to express a hope that the other had got over the annoyance his refusal to sit had caused; and received a reply from which I extract a few lines:

"My dear Mr. Home, I am sorry you continue to think of the little contretemps of some time ago. I was certainly very much vexed at the time; however, I have long ceased to think of it I can only hope the good angels will in future do their best to arrange matters between séances and sick-beds."

Such was the feeling and considerate manner in which some who called, and perhaps thought themselves his friends, behaved to Home. It was nothing to the writer of these almost brutal words a man very estimable in many respects that Home had refused him a séance because he was absorbed in attendance on a dying wife: all lie could think of was that his sceptical friends had been disappointed of their séance; and, from the tone of his letter, he evidently felt that he had just ground for complaint against Home and the "good angels" both.

I have already given in the words of Mr. W. Howitt, Mr. Wilkinson, and Mrs. Parkes, their description of manifestations witnessed at the residence of the latter in the summer of 1861. The portions of the diary of Mrs. Parkes that are published in the *Incidents* narrate the events of more than twenty séances; and a brief extract or two may be of interest.

"On July 7th," writes Mrs. Parkes, "we (four persons) were sitting at the centre window in the front drawing-room, talking together, when the spirits began to rap on the floor. ... It was a fine summer evening, and the room was perfectly light. Mr. Home fell back in his chair, and went into the deep sleep for some time; then he walked about the room, led apparently by a spirit; a very large bright star shone on his forehead, several clustered on his hair and on the tips of his fingers. Mr. Home passed in front of a very large mirror a sea of glass. I saw a form leading him, over the head of which was thrown a tinted robe flowing to the ground, marking the shape of the head and shoulders. He followed close upon it: I saw them both in the mirror; his features, face, and hair perfectly distinct; but the features of the form that led him were not visible beneath the dark, blue-tinted robe that covered them. They passed from before the glass; and then we all saw a female figure with a white veil thrown over her head which fell to the ground; at the same time, but rather higher, the form of a man in Oriental costume. The startling vision faded away; and the great mirror remained with only the light from the window, which streamed in upon it."

"July 12th. En séance six persons. Stars appeared above Mrs. Home's head; and a light was seen, with fingers passing over it as it floated above our heads. It was the Veiled Spirit. I saw the hand that held the veil, which was spangled with stars; and the fingers moved distinctly as it floated just in front of us."

The note appended by Mr. Home to the extracts from Mrs. Parkes' diary furnishes a clue to the probable origin of a mendacious story published in America by a certain Celia Logan, who untruly asserted Home to have stated that his wife changed visibly into an angel as she died.

"In this diary," wrote Home, "there are several remarkable manifestations, and amongst them that of the presence of the veiled spirit, who thenceforth was frequently seen by my wife and by me, as will be read in the beautiful memoir of my wife written by that most estimable type of womanhood, Mrs. Mary Howitt. The veil of that spirit kept gradually being raised through the successive stages of my dear wife's painful illness, and became almost an index of the insidious advances of her disease."

The silver cord was loosed on July 3rd, 1862. There was no priest of her own Russian Church within many miles of Château Laroche; and the last consolations of religion were received by Mrs. Home at the hands of the Catholic prelate whose visits had been so kind and constant. Mrs. Howitt, in the pages already quoted from, gives an exact and touching account of the emotions her beautiful resignation stirred in him:

"The last sacraments were administered to her by the Bishop of Perigueux, who wept like a child, and who remarked that, 'though he had been present at many a death-bed for Heaven, he had never seen one equal to hers."

"At her funeral," continues Mrs. Howitt, "four of the men servants of her sister asked each to lead a horse of the hearse to the burial ground, saying that they could not allow hired persons to be near the dead body of her who had ever had a kind word and a loving look for all. The peasantry, instead of, as is customary, throwing earth upon the coffin, first covered it with flowers fittest for her last garment, and fittest for the expression of their love."

Soon after the parting, Mr. Home returned to London. There, many tokens of the nearness of the spirit that had just departed were received, one of the most remarkable being given at a séance at Bannow Lodge, West Brompton, then the residence of Mr. and Mrs. S. C. Hall. It is related by Mrs. Hall in her memories of Mrs. Home, published the following year, 1863, with those of Mrs. Howitt, in the *Incidents.*

"More than the usual manifestations came that night," writes Mrs. Hall;' "not only the table, but our chairs and the very room shook, and the 'raps' were everywhere around us. ... A very eminent sculptor, whose engagements on public works are unceasing, had been rising before day to finish a bust of Sacha (Mrs. Home), which he desired to present to her husband this fact was not even known in his own household. He received a message thus: 'Thanks for your early morning labour: I have often been near you.'"

The eminent sculptor of whom Mrs. Hall speaks and to whom frequent references are made in her letters to Mr. Home was Mr. Durham.

CHAPTER 7

England, Rome and Paris

Breakdown of Home's Health and Powers. "Incidents in My Life." Works as a Sculptor. Expulsion from the Papal States. Investigation by Mr. Ruskin. By John Bright. False Accusations and Apologies. The "Evil Spirit" Hypothesis. Conversion of Varley the Electrician. Dr. Carpenter's Blunder.

ALL WHO HAD KNOWN the spirit now gone from earth had loved her; and the letters in which friends spoke of their affection for her and mourned her loss were treasured as precious by Mr. Home. Out of many that lie before me, I select one or two passages the first from the letter of a friend to whom she had been very dear, Mrs. Milner Gibson.

"We have received the news. Our darling Sacha is happy now. May He permit me so to live here that I may meet the dear child in that happier state. We weep for you and with you, but yet with a feeling of gladness that she is happy very, very happy, I know."

"Robert Bell came to see me today," says Mrs. Gibson in another letter. "He will have written to you, and told you that poor Mrs. Bell knows nothing of your sorrow; for her husband had carefully hidden it from her, fearing the shock for her in her delicate state of health. Grattan, I too, came, with tears in his eyes, begging me, of all people, to write a short notice of dear Sacha. I, who have never written for the press and cannot write of her for I feel too much to write."

In a former chapter some of the early Spiritual experiences are given of one who became a very dear friend of Mr. Home Mrs. Adelaide Senior. "I am so pleased," she now wrote, "to think that your sweet wife spoke of me before her departure and so very grateful to her for wishing me to have her picture, which I shall indeed beyond price. I have the unspeakable comfort of knowing of comfort in knowing that your darling is watching over you it is indeed beyond price. I have the unspeakable comfort of knowing that my darling husband is ever near me. I feel that is so; and I am so very grateful to God that He has, through you, given me this comfort."

A touching letter is that of Mrs. De Burgh, a friend of Mrs. Milner Gibson, who had been present at many of the séances in Hyde Park Place:

"My dear Daniel, Mrs. Milner Gibson has told me that the blow so long pending over you has fallen, and that you are left alone. I must write, although you will probably not read my letter; but I feel so truly and so deeply for you in your heavy sorrow that I cannot resist writing. She was so charming and irresistibly attractive that all who knew her loved her, and many, many will mourn sincerely for her. I never heard anyone speak of her but with the warmest interest and affection. She was so winning so bright and loving I can hardly realize that she is gone.

"Mr. Colley Grattan, M. P."

"I am writing strange comfort, but I feel there is none for such sorrow as yours at least, none that any friend can offer. But you will not give way to sorrow, as one who mourns without hope; for Spiritualism will suffer, if it is found to fail you now in your strong need. You must think of this, and prove that the practical good it supplies takes the sting from death, and enables the one left to rejoice in its consolations. I pray that that blessed spirit may be permitted soon to communicate, and thus make you share her happiness.

"You soothed her months of trial, and were the tenderest and best of nurses you must now take care of your shattered health for the sake of her child."

Mr. Home's health was indeed shattered by the racking anxiety and limitless devotion of the many months during which he had watched so lovingly and constantly over her who was gone. How much his most sensitive nature had suffered in seeing her suffer, none but himself could know; but the strength which unselfish affection bestows had never failed him, and he had soothed and tended her to the last. It was not till his cares were no more needed that strength and! Cheerfulness both forsook him, and breaking down terribly, he paid the penalty of an overtaxed nervous system and week after week passed almost without food or sleep.

I will not dwell on these dark and bitter moments of a life that was filled with trial. As soon as some return of health permitted, Home occupied himself in the completion of his first volume of autobiography, which he had begun writing nearly three years before. In January, 1863, he paid a short visit to his friend Waldimir de Komar, at Paris; held séances at the Tuileries, in obedience to a summons) from the Empress; and then, returning to London, prepared for the press, with the kind assistance of Dr. Robert Chambers, his now completed work. It was published, under the title of *Incidents in My Life*, in the spring of 1863, the introduction and concluding chapter being from the pen of Robert Chambers.

Through Mrs. Senior, Home had made the acquaintance of her brother-in-law, Nassau Senior, the noted political economist, twice Professor of Political Economy in the University of Oxford. Mr. Nassau Senior investigated the phenomena at various séances with Mr. Home, was convinced of the impossibility of attributing them to imposture; and on the completion of the *Incidents*, obtained the publication of the work by Messrs. Longmans and Co.

An early copy of the work was sent by Mr. Home to the Empress of the French. I find among his papers a letter from the Secretary to the Empress, conveying her acknowledgments, and translate it:

"12th March, 1863.

"Sir, I hastened to place in the hands of the Empress the work that you did me the honour of entrusting to my care.

"Her Majesty has charged me to thank you for your attention" 'and' to say to you that she will read this work with interest. Receive, etc., Damas Hinard,

"Le Secretaire des Commandements."

The *Incidents* attracted widespread notice; and were criticized in every spirit, from fair and unprejudiced inquiry to dishonest misrepresentation and ignorant abuse. True to the traditions of a certain class of journalism, some critics reviewed the book without reading it; described Mrs. Home as "an ardent Spiritualist and medium" when Home first met her, and turned her husband into an American, although the first words of his first chapter were, "I was born near Edinburgh."

"I had no reason to complain of the neglect of the press," wrote Mr. Home; "for several journals fell foul of me with commendable speed. I have; however, to thank some of those who reviewed my book for the fair and candid tone in which they treated the subject. The *Spectator*, the *Times*, and the *Morning Herald* call for special mention in this respect."

The *Times* review I have not seen. Those of the other two journals named certainly deserve the character of "fair and candid" that Mr. Home bestows on them. I quote a portion of the remarks of the writers in the *Morning Herald*:

"The more a man learns, the more wary he is as to this word 'impossible.' Mr. Grove shows us in his book on the *Correlation of Forces* how little we know as to physical laws; on the relations of matter and spirit we know hardly anything. All we can say is, that these manifestations appear to us to be in the highest degree improbable. But here we are met by evidence that, improbable or not, they have taken place. We are narrowed to the alternative, that either Mr. Home is an impostor, or that Spiritualism is true.

"Now as to imposture. Assuredly Mr. Home is very different from the ordinary type of an impostor. When only eighteen years old, he began his career of mediumship by doing, or appearing to do, things so difficult as to involve almost a certainty of the early detection of any sort of deceit. In 1852, Mr. Bryant, the American poet, joined with three others in a declaration that closed by saying, 'We know that we were not imposed upon nor deceived.' Again, we cannot but remark that the manifestations are not now more elaborate than they were twelve years ago. We might expect a successful impostor to use his advantages of experiences and wealth to produce new and stronger effects; but this has not been the case with Mr. Home. The spirit hands (by far the most difficult manifestation for an impostor to produce) are said to have been seen at a very early period of his mediumship. Again, an impostor always tries to weave his deceptions into a system; generally to form some sort of sect. Now, Mr.

Home, with every temptation to do this, in that he has persuaded so many of the truth of the manifestations, not only does not try to establish any great position for himself as the high priest of Spiritualism, but he constantly denies that he has any power in the matter. Mr. Home speaks of his book as a collection of facts, which are worthy of investigation, and may be found useful in revealing some of the yet hidden laws of creation.

"We must note also the strangeness of the fact that Mr. Home has never been detected, if indeed he is an impostor. To move heavy tables, to raise himself to a horizontal position near the ceiling, to play tunes upon guitars etc, would require elaborate machinery. But these things have been done in palaces and in private houses, in every part of Europe."

In July, 1863, the *Quarterly Review* noticed the book; and after commenting on the a priori improbability of the narratives contained in it continued: "But on the other hand we are bound in justice to Mr. Home, to admit that this internal evidence against his statements has to be weighed against a very respectable amount of external evidence in their favour; that his own character, so far as we have been able to ascertain, offers no ground for suspecting his integrity; and that the authorities whom he brings forward, both as vouchers for his own trustworthiness and as eye-witnesses of the marvels which he exhibits, are such as would probably be sufficient to ensure belief in any story less intrinsically incredible."

The *Quarterly* reviewer (evidently not Dr. Carpenter) deserves credit for having had the fairness to deal with the names given, instead of following the unfair line adopted by some other writers; who confined their attention to the fact that many names of witnesses were suppressed, and pretended to disbelieve Home's statement that he withheld those names from consideration for their owners, who feared the ridicule and obloquy that awaited them if they came forward to bear witness. Certainly, his consideration for timid friends was carried to the verge of Quixotism; but if a mistake, it was a very unselfish and generous one. In these pages I have filled in the blanks he left as far as lies in my power, and will cite now the testimony of two other English witnesses of the phenomena called forth by the publication of the

Incidents. Both of these gentlemen had been present at numerous séances with Mr. Home in London, in the years immediately preceding 1863.

The first was the Hon. Colonel Wilbraham, who had the courage to allow his letter to Mr. Home to be published. It was as follows:

"46, Brook Street, April 11th, 1863.

"My dear Mr. Home, I have much pleasure in stating that 1 have attended several séances, in your presence, at the houses of two of my intimate friends and at my own when I have witnessed phenomena similar to those described in your book which I feel certain could not have been produced by any trick or collusion whatever. The rooms in which) they occurred were always perfectly lighted; and it was impossible for me to disbelieve the evidence of my own senses. Believe me, yours very truly, E. B. Wilbraham."

The second witness to facts recounted in *Incidents in My Life* was not as courageous as Colonel Wilbraham; and his letter to Mr. Home now sees the light for the first time. Its writer had been present at some very remarkable séances at Mrs. Milner Gibson's:

"46, Sussex Gardens, Hyde Park, W., April 9th, 1863.

"My dear Mr. Home, I have just finished reading your book, and have been very much interested in it. Having witnessed so much of what you and others have narrated, every page brought back to me those evenings which never can be forgotten.

"I very much like the quiet manner in which you have mentioned scenes and events which, almost word for word, I perfectly remember witnessing and hearing; and I think you hare given much value to your book by keeping so well and clearly to the original incidents.

"I hope you are better in health. Blumenthal and Madame Loeser come over from Paris at the end of this week to pay a visit to us. Mrs. Kater unites with me in kind remembrances; and believe me, yours faithfully,

"Edward Kater."

As Mr. Kater justly remarks, the great value of the book consists in its fidelity to facts. Nothing is added, nothing taken away;

Home relates the events of his life exactly as they occurred, and leaves the final judgment on them to be passed by future ages. That of his own generation was the verdict of the blind and deaf on a man who could see and hear.

The unpretentious candour of the *Incidents* impressed many besides Mr. Kater among them that gifted writer and charming woman, Mrs. S. C. Hall. "I do not know which most to admire in your book," she writes to Mr. Home; "its simplicity, so perfectly free from every taint of self glorification, or the facts that speak trumpet-tongued." Then, referring to that prudent timidity of friends for which Mr. Home had so Quixotic a consideration, Mrs. Hall, who had courageously allowed her name to appear in the *Incidents*, continues: "I only wish that more names had been given Robert Chambers', for instance, and Sir Edward Lytton's, and Mr. Bell's. I have no patience with the cowardice that withholds testimony from truth."

A month or two after the appearance of the *Incidents*, and) when the first edition was nearly exhausted, the publishers were threatened with an action for libel. In the portion of his book where he dealt with the Brewster controversy, Home had brought forward the published evidence of Dr. Carpenter, F.R.S and Messrs. Stevenson, to show that Sir David Brewster had treated certain of his scientific contemporaries even worse than he had treated Home. Brewster now threatened (June, 1863) a libel action; and Messrs. Longmans, alarmed, terminated their connection with the work.

Home promptly sought another publisher and a few months later a second edition of his book appeared. Not a word was erased or changed of the chapter dealing with Brewster; on the contrary, Home wrote a preface for the new edition, in which he added *Arago, the Edinburgh* Review, and the *Westminster Review* to his list of the authorities that had exposed Brewster's mendacity.

"It appears," said Home, "that, in addition to his other claims, Sir David Brewster sets up a claim that he alone is gifted with the power of feeling. To me he denies all feeling, and has coarsely and untruly held me up to the public as a cheat and an impostor. But when I prove by documents and independent witnesses his true character, he actually feels it, and complains."

Sir David Brewster did not bring a libel action. Perhaps he felt the force of Home's remark, when, after citing the authorities for his statements, he added: "It is a great pity that Sir David Brewster did not bring actions to vindicate his character against the authors of some of these books, or against Dr. Carpenter, against whom he made an abortive threat, instead of attacking me."

This preface to the second edition was written at Rome in December 1863, where Mr. Home had gone to study art. For some months past the longing had possessed him to attempt turning to account the keen artistic perceptions he possessed; and the career in which he believed himself most likely to succeed was that of the sculptor. It was in vain that friends, especially medical friends, remonstrated with him, and warned him that such a career was of all others most unsuited to him, who had twice already been at the point of death from affections of the lungs. Home was determined to gratify his longing; the more so that pecuniary difficulties were threatening him, as his right to the inheritance of his wife's little fortune was very unjustly disputed by her relatives. He had made the acquaintance in London of some eminent sculptors, Mr. Durham, Mr. Boehm, and others; and before going to Rome; he consulted with some of these, and took lessons in the art.

In the year 1863 he was often a visitor at two houses where artists of every description congregated those of Mr. and Mrs. Howitt and Mr. and Mrs. Hall. I need not bring forward evidence of the faith of the Halls and the Howitts in Spiritualism all four declared it publicly; and all four, be it marked, had commenced the investigation of the subject as absolute sceptics. "I laughed," wrote Mrs. S. C. Hall, "at the idea of a spirit giving a message by raps on a table. I did worse, I became angry." Her husband has borne equally emphatic testimony to his original incredulity.

How Mr. and Mrs. William Howitt were led to investigate I do not know, but by the year 1861 they had both become zealous Spiritualists.

Mr. Home's acquaintance with Mr. and Mrs. S. C. Hall commenced in 1860. Among the various inquirers, more honest and candid than Brewster, who were present in 1855 at séances with Home at Baling, were Mr. and Mrs. Newton Crossland. They became firm Spiritualists, declared their convictions; and Mr. Crossland suffered much loss and persecution in consequence. They were acquainted with S. C. Hall, then a sceptic concerning the manifestations. He only laughed at his friends' accounts of what they had seen at Baling and elsewhere; but on making in his turn the acquaintance of Mr. Home, the incredulity of a lifetime was vanquished.

Mr. Hall has frequently related to his friends one of his earliest experiences with Mr. Home; and in 1884 he made the incident public. I copy his narrative:

"In 1860, sitting with Daniel Home (some persons of distinction being present), the spirit of my father came to us. When the name 'Robert Hall' was announced, I asked if he were my father or my brother the answer being, 'Your father, Colonel Hall.' I requested some test to make me sure. The answer given was this (it excited laughter among the party, by whom it was not understood; but I knew that a more conclusive and convincing test could not have been given to me): 'The last time we met in Cork you pulled my tail.' Like all military officers of his time, he wore the queue; he wore it, indeed, up to his death, and was buried in it. Few persons living can remember the queue: the hair behind was suffered to grow long, and was tied with black ribbon up to nearly the end."

All who knew Mrs. S. C. Hall remember her as one of the most gifted, charming, and warm-hearted of women. It was a privilege to call her friend; and Home was one of her dearest friends; the difference in their ages enabling her to counsel and encourage him in something of the spirit of a mother speaking to a son. Letters from very dear friends, Mr. Home carefully preserved; and there remain hundreds of Mrs. Hall's extending over a period of twenty years, and as interesting as they are outspoken and affectionate.

The letters of the years 1863 and 4 show Mrs. Hall as interesting herself cordially in Home's project of becoming a sculptor.

"I received your letter late on Saturday," she writes on first learning of that project; "and wrote at once to Mr. Durham. I am sure you have the corner in his heart, and will have one in his studio, if there is one to spare."

It seems that there was not; and so Mr. Home's first essays in the art were made at Dieppe in the autumn of 1863. It was there and then that the angry incredulity of Dr. Elliottson was shattered in the manner already described; Mrs. Milner Gibson being one of the witnesses of the wonderful change wrought in his sentiments by his two séances with Home. A letter of February 1864 shows Mrs. S. C. Hall to have also been at Dieppe when Elliottson was there:

"Mr. Dallas of the *Times* was opposite me at dinner at Mr. Warde's yesterday," writes Mrs. Hall. "He said across the table, 'Dr. Elliottson is attending me do you know he is almost a believer in Spiritualism?' 'Almost!' I repeated; 'he was altogether so, when I saw him at Dieppe.'"

In November 1863, the intending sculptor went to Rome to study his art. For six weeks he quietly pursued it among the artist colony there, with several of whom he was acquainted; but on the 2nd of January, 1864, he received a proof that the Papal Government had neither forgotten nor forgiven his refusal, eight years before, to let the monastery gates close upon him. He was summoned before the chief of the Roman police, subjected to a long interrogatory, and finally ordered, on the ground of sorcery, to quit Rome within three days.

Mr. Home at once claimed the protection of the English Consul; the result of whose intervention, joined with that of a distinguished personage friendly to Horn, was somewhat incorrectly related by the *Times* correspondent in writing to that journal:

"On Monday morning," said the correspondent, "the British Consul saw Monsignor Matteucci, the Governor of Rome, and complained that any British subject should be interfered with in consequence of his opinions. He stated that Mr. Home had conducted himself during his residence in Rome in a strictly legal and gentlemanly manner; and demanded that the obnoxious order should be rescinded. Monsignor spoke of dangerous powers of fascination, of the prohibition by the Government of all the practices of the black art; and finally assented to Mr. Home's remaining, on condition of his entering into an engagement, through Mr. Severn, that he would desist from all communications with the spiritual world during his stay in Rome."

Mr. Home entered into no such engagement. He could not. Nothing was more common with him than for manifestations to occur unexpectedly, and he could do nothing to prevent their happening. The actual written promise that he gave, at the request of the Governor of Rome, was word for word as follows:

"I give my word as a gentleman that during my stay in Rome I will have no séance, and that I will avoid, as much as possible, all conversations upon Spiritualism."

No séance was held; but behind the Governor of Rome there were higher powers still, who were determined that, séances or no séances, Home should leave the city. The British Consul was falsely informed that Home had broken his promise, and Home himself was once more ordered to quit the Papal territory, the excuse made being that, since he could only promise to hold no séance, and was unable to say that manifestations would not occur in spite of such abstention, it was impossible to allow him to remain. It deserves to be added, as characteristic of the methods of the defunct Papal Government, that for the four weeks preceding the expulsion none of Home's letters had been delivered to him, the authorities retaining them to study their contents at leisure.

"Is there anything against Mr. Home's character?" asked a high personage who interviewed the Governor of Rome on his behalf. "No," replied Monsignor Matteucci, "nothing. During the two months he has been in Rome we have had him watched, and we believe that his character is without blemish. But he is a sorcerer, and cannot be permitted in Rome; and he must go."

Home left for Naples; and was escorted to the railway station by a number of his friends in Rome, as a mark of sympathy and a public protest against his expulsion. The present King of Italy, then Prince Humbert, was at Naples at the time; and by his Highness's command Mr. Home was presented to him, and favoured with an invitation to a Court ball. A short but pleasant stay in Naples was followed by a few weeks at Nice, where Mrs. Milner Gibson was then among the winter residents, as was also, it would seem, Sir E. B. Lytton. Several séances were held at Nice;

and about the beginning of April 1864, Home returned to London. He addressed the Foreign Secretary on the subject of his expulsion from Rome; and on Earl Russell declining to make any representations to the Papal Government; Mr. Home brought the matter before the House of Commons, through the instrumentality of Mr. Roebuck. He did this in no expectation of obtaining redress, but it concerned him to make as widely known as possible that the reasons of his expulsion from Rome in no way affected his character.

It was on this occasion that Mr. Milner Gibson was driven out of the House by the jocose appeal of Mr. Roebuck to the President of the Board of Trade, whom Roebuck mistakenly assumed to be a Spiritualist. Nothing came of the question in the House of Commons beyond the discussion that ensued; but the correct facts concerning Mr. Home's expulsion from Rome were reported next morning in the leading English journals, which was all that he had expected or sought.

Between his departure from Nice and return to London he had spent a week or two in Paris, where the Empress commanded his presence at the Tuileries. Among the celebrities then in Paris was Nubar Pasha. The Egyptian statesman was present at one or more séances, was greatly impressed and startled by the manifestations; and on writing to express his sentiments to Mr. Home, he sent him a souvenir in the form of a small chain a trifle that it would have been ungracious to refuse.

The letter that accompanied the chain is dated March 22nd, 1864.

"You are leaving today," writes Nubar Pasha; "and I expect to have quitted Paris myself before your return from London.

"I take the liberty of sending you a small chain; it is a souvenir, a memento; for truly I should be happy to know that you will think of me occasionally. As for me, you may believe me I carry away a recollection of you that will never be effaced. Your very devoted servant and friend,

"M. Nubar."

In writing the narrative of a life so full of incident as that of Home, I find myself compelled sometimes to group together the events of different years. Were I to preserve strict chronological sequence, and to accompany Mr. Home step by step in his thousand and one journeys, these chapters would read rather like a record of travel than a biography.

I am now about to group together the incidents of the years 1863 and 1864 so far as they relate to London. Home was much in the English Metropolis during those two years, and held frequent séances. At these various English celebrities were present, including Mr. John Bright, Mr. Ruskin, Sir Charles Nicholson, and Sir Daniel Cooper. All four were deeply impressed by the manifestations they witnessed; of Mr. Ruskin and Sir Charles Nicholson I have reasons for saying that the effect on them was to render them unavowed Spiritualists reasons that I shall presently put before the reader. Sir D. Cooper made no scruple among his friends of avowing his belief, but he shrank from proclaiming it to the world.

In Mr. Home's second volume of *Incidents*, published in 1872, he passes over that interesting period of his life, the early summer of 1864, with the brief remark, "I returned to England, and then crossed the Atlantic, to revisit my old friends in America." Consideration for the feelings of timid inquirers could hardly be carried to a higher pitch.

It was through Mr. and Mrs. S. C. Hall that Mr. Ruskin, Mr. Bright, and Sir D. Cooper made the acquaintance of Mr. Home. The letters of Mrs. S. C. Hall during the years 1861, 2, 3, and 4, are fortunately very numerous; and they have materially assisted me in arriving at the facts of that portion of Mr. Home's English experiences I am now dealing with.

Before speaking of Mr. Bright and Mr. Ruskin, I may take the opportunity those letters give me to say a few words of a man less intellectually distinguished, but who was, I believe, in some sort a social, artistic, and literary celebrity in London a quarter of a century ago; Mr. Heaphy. To begin with, he is the hero of an amusing anecdote related by Mrs. Hall. "Mr. Heaphy looked in on Sunday evening," she writes in February, 1864; "and we are so amused Old Lady P., we hear, has been carried up to the ceiling and has written on it she told this to Mr. Heaphy, saying, 'Do you know, I am a floater!' Now Mr. Heaphy's deafness played him a bad trick, and he thought she had said, 'Do you know, I am a bloater!' So Mr. Heaphy went about telling how Spiritualism had changed poor Lady P. into a Yarmouth bloater."

A cool-headed, clever man of the world, Heaphy could joke at a Spiritualist like "old Lady P.," but he was very differently impressed by the mysterious gift of Home. "Mr. Heaphy called here last night," writes Mrs. Hall in 1861; "and I do rejoice at the change wrought in his mind through your means. Sometimes, even now, his spirit rises against conviction; and then again it is brought right by the wonders he has seen, the marvellous information you gave him. He tells me darling Sacha's portrait is greatly improved. It is such a blessing he has been brought to you."

As a reference in Mrs. Hall's letter indicates, Mr. Heaphy, whose genius was of a versatile order, painted a portrait of Mrs. Home. He had never the courage to make his convictions public; but in private he showed himself an attached and sincere friend; and when Home formed the design of studying sculpture at Rome, it was Heaphy who sent him an introduction to one of the most eminent of the artist colony there, the sculptor Gibson.

"My dear Dan," writes Heaphy, "I am glad for many reasons that you are back in the old place at last; though I could have wished that you were at Paris instead, that I might have a better chance of coming to see you. My wife tells me you wish for an introduction to Gibson; I enclose one.

"You will find many of our London friends at Rome, Edward Stirling among the number. Possibly I may be in Rome by the Holy week. Adieu! When you have an opportunity let us hear how you are getting on. Yours ever truly, "Thos. Heaphy."

Mr. Ruskin's investigations of Spiritualism appear to have commenced in the year 1863, when he accepted the invitation of a well known English, or, rather, Scottish Spiritualist, Mrs. MacDougall Gregory, widow of Professor Gregory, to be present at a séance. The medium was not Mr. Home, who was at the time absent from England; and a letter of Mrs. S. C. Hall's declares the distinguished investigator to have been very unfavourably impressed.

Some little time afterwards, Mr. Ruskin was one evening at the house of a Mr. Bertolacci, who was a Spiritualist, and an acquaintance of Mr. Home. The topic of Spiritualism came up for discussion; and Mr. Ruskin appears to have said something of the unfavourable impression made on him by the mediums pretended or real that he had seen.

"Mr. Bertolacci told him," writes Mrs. Hall, "that he ought to see your mediumship. He asked if you were a true man to be depended on as a man; and added, 'Of your wonderful gifts there could be no doubt.' Upon this, the whole family burst out into their belief in all your goodness that we (Mr. and Mrs. Hall) knew you so well, etc., etc. And then the rest came about."

The "rest" to which Mrs. Hall refers was the fact that Mr. Ruskin had ended by expressing a desire to meet Mr. Home at a séance. The Bertolaccis communicated his wish to Mrs. S. C. Hall; and, delighted with the hope of so eminent a convert to Spiritualism, she at once penned the letter to Home just quoted from. He willingly promised the séance; and the Halls, who had been on the point of starting for Ireland, deferred their journey for a few days to be present. In her next letter Mrs. Hall writes:

"My dear friend, Mr. Ruskin comes on Monday evening he asks if he may bring a friend who is coming to stay with ham a clergyman: 'that is,' he adds, 'if his friend wishes it.' There will be you, the three Bertolacci's, our two selves, Mr. R. and his friend; that is all we have thought about exactly eight."

Either the Halls were finally obliged to leave for Ireland on the eve of the séance, or it was followed by a second séance that they could not wait for; for on the 14th of June, 1864, Mrs. Hall writes: "We greatly regret leaving town just now. I am so interested about Mr. Ruskin do let me know if anything to catch hold of his apathetic yet energetic nature occurs to-morrow evening; and do, dear friend, go to him in his own home."

What occurred? The Halls were in Ireland most of the summer; Mr. Ruskin has never spoken. I do not know if he had two séances with Mr. Home or twenty; but that, whatever their number, those séances had, in Mrs. Hall's phrase, "caught hold" of him, the friendly, and even affectionate tone of his subsequent letters to Home sufficiently demonstrates. "Only fancy Ruskin being convinced!" Mrs. Hall writes some months later, when Home had again left England. "But he does not wish it talked about," she adds, underlining the words emphatically. In the early autumn of 1864, Mr. Home sailed for America. Evidently he had written to Mr. Ruskin on the eve of his departure, and the subjoined letter from which I omit some confidences of Mr. Ruskin concerning himself was the answer to his own:

"Denmark Hill, 4th September, 1864.

"Dear Mr. Home, It is so nice of you to like me! I believe you are truly doing me the greatest service and help that one human being can do another in trusting me in this way, and indeed I hope I so far deserve your trust, that I can understand noble and right feeling and affection though I have myself little feeling or affection left, being worn out with indignation as far as regards the general world.

"Till March is long to wait and it really isn't all my fault. I did not write that week for I was not sure if I could get into town for you on Monday but you never told me you were going away before Monday, and I thought my Saturday's letter quite safe.

"Well do, please, write me a line to say you are safe in America. And come to see me the moment you come back. I shall be every way, I hope, then more at leisure and peace. May you be preserved in that wild country, [1] and brought back to us better in health and happier. Ever affectionately yours, "J. Ruskin."

In this pleasant letter, Mr. Ruskin would seem to say in effect: "Do not expect too much from a man worn out by his warfare with the spirit of the time, but as far as I have feeling and affection left, I feel for and sympathize with you, my new friend." Sympathy and liking were precious to Home, than whose nature none was ever more sensitive, and who all his life stood as a target for the shafts of abuse and calumny loosed against him by men who knew nothing of him but his name. Mr. Home returned from America in May 1865, but spent only a day or two in London, before leaving for France and Russia. It seems to have been at this time that the following undated letter of Mrs. Hall's was written.

"Saturday Night.

"Dear friend, I have just received such a charming note from Mr. Ruskin. I cannot even 'lend you the loan' of it for a single look, I am so proud of it but I can quote: 'I'm coming at one o'clock on

Monday to take possession of Mr. Home, to drive him over to Denmark Hill; and so we shall have all the drive time besides so please tell him this, and hold him fast on Monday morning till I come.' I have written to Mr. Ruskin to say that you have escaped that I write by tonight's post to catch you at Cox's Hotel that I am sure you would forego any engagement to spend a few hours with him (who would not?) and, well, that was all I could say. Nothing can exceed the cordiality of his letter."

The winter of 1865 brought Home back from Russia to England, and while on a visit to Dr. Gully at Malvern, he received a letter written by Mr. Ruskin by way of New Year's greeting:

"Denmark Hill, 29th December, 1865.

"Dear Mr. Home, This is only to thank you for your kind letter, and to wish you a happy new year. Your letter from America stayed by me reproachfully day by day it was the deep summer time, and I was out all day long, and came in at night too tired to write, and at last it was too late. But now I hope I may soon see you. Please say that I may, and believe me affectionately yours,

"J. Ruskin."

As Mr. Home was much in London during 1866, Mr. Ruskin's desire that he might soon meet again was probably gratified; but on this point I have no means of speaking positively. Passing over nine months, I find, from, a letter of Mrs. Hall, dated October 16th, 1866, that Mr. Ruskin was then wishing for a séance on a friend's account:

"My dear Daniel, All the town is ringing with the story giving it, of course, various readings but all your old friends are full of rejoicing.

"Mr. Ruskin called here today. Carter desires me to enclose you a note he received from him. I wish, my dear Daniel, you could fix an evening to receive his friend. If you could meet him here or at the Athenaeum? (the Spiritual Athenaeum in Sloane Street), only please do attend to it, and write to me and to Mr. Ruskin. He rejoiced for you but, oh! He is looking so worn and ill. We had such a long talk on Spiritualism."

As I am unable to give the particulars of that talk or of the séances that had preceded it, I have printed here instead the indirect, but none the less conclusive testimony that such letters from Mr. Ruskin as have been preserved afford of the deep and favourable impression made on him by his experiences with Mr. Home; and leave it now to the judgment of the reader, together with the corroborative evidence of Mrs. Hall. Other portions of her letters also refer to Mr. Ruskin in connection with Spiritualism; but as the statements are hearsay, I have confined myself to the passages where she speaks from personal knowledge.

Mr. John Bright's introduction to Mr. Home also took place through the Halls, and at an earlier date than that of Mr. Ruskin. The Mr. Wason, of Liverpool, whose description of his first séance has already been given, was an intimate friend of a once-noted politician, Mr. E. Beales; and his relation of the wonderful phenomena he had witnessed excited the interest and curiosity of Mr. Beales, who, through Wason, obtained an introduction to Home. Mr. Beales, like his friend, was vividly impressed by the manifestations he beheld; and it was his influence that induced the *Morning Star* newspaper to open its columns to letters on the subject of Spiritualism. "As regards my having been instrumental in throwing open the columns of the Star to the discussion of Spiritualism," Mr. Beales writes to Mr. Home, October 16th, 1862, "I assure you that it was to my mind both a pleasure and a duty."

In his turn, Mr. Beales, by his narrative, of the séances at which he had been present, inspired his friend, Mr. John Bright, with the desire to witness and investigate the phenomena. Being an acquaintance and near neighbour of the Halls, with whom Home was holding frequent séances in the winter of 1862–3, Mr. Beales communicated Brights' wish to them, and a séance at their house was appointed. Mr. John Bright came accordingly, bringing with him Mr. Lucas, managing editor of the *Morning Star.* Among the other sitters present was a lady whose narrative of her own early experiences with Mr. Home has already been given, Mrs. Adelaide Senior. The little I know of the occurrences of the evening is from her.

"In November, 1862," writes Mrs. Senior, "I was present at one of Mr. D. D. Home's séances in the house of Mr. S. C. Hall, to which Mr. John Bright had been invited, he having expressed a strong wish to see something of Spiritualism. On the day of the séance, Mr. Hall received a note from Mr. Bright, asking to be allowed to bring a friend, Mr. Lucas, editor of the *Star* newspaper."

Mrs. Senior describes the manifestations of the evening as numerous and remarkable, and gives the following narrative of one of the early incidents of the séance:

"Not many minutes after we were seated at the large, heavy round table, knocks were given for the alphabet, and the words given were: 'You are trying to prevent our raising the table.' Mr. Hall asked, 'Who is trying?' and pointed to each in succession, when three knocks for 'Yes' were given in front of Mr. Lucas, who at once said, 'Yes, I was putting my whole weight upon it.' I, sitting next but one to him, then asked, 'Do you think that right?' 'Oh, yes,' he answered, 'I came here to investigate.' 'Certainly,' I said; 'but neither to assist nor retard the movements.' A message then came, desiring Mr. to sit upon the table; this was a stout gentleman who was present. The desire was complied with; and instantly the table was not only raised, but tossed up, as you would toss a baby in your arms saying, as plainly as words could have done, 'You tried to prevent our raising the table with nothing upon it, and we will prove to you that we can do it with this additional weight."

Laughable as this incident may seem to some sceptical readers, it could not but impress the two shrewd and incredulous inquirers present that evening. The room was fully lighted; Mr. Bright and Mr. Lucas had satisfied themselves that no machinery was concealed under the table or connected with it. There sat Mr. Home, his fingers lightly resting on the table; and again and again the heavy table rose clear of the ground, with the weight of a heavy man upon it in addition.

As Mrs. Senior cannot furnish me a precise account of the numerous other phenomena of the séance, I refrain from describing them.

"I asked Mr. Bright, on his leaving," says Mr. S. C. Hall, "what he thought of the manifestations he had witnessed that evening. 'They are very wonderful,' he replied; adding, ' I know, Mr. Hall, you would not lend yourself to any trickery. It is very remarkable." "Mr. Beales is just gone," wrote Mrs. Hall a day or two after the séance to Mr. Home. "I am most thankful for the impression which he assured me had been made both on Mr. Lucas and John Bright. Both are most wishful to meet you again." An invitation to a second séance was given and accepted; but on the eve of the day appointed Mrs. Hall writes: "Carter has had a most melancholy note from Bright, saying he cannot come on Friday. He goes out of town, but hopes the week or so after next to be fortunate. He is evidently deeply impressed." Probably Mr. Bright was ultimately present at a second séance. I find the following letter from him to Mr. S. C. Hall among Mr. Home's papers:

"4, Hanover Street, May 6, '64.

"My dear Mr. Hall, Would Wednesday next, the 11th inst., suit you for another sitting with Mr. Home? Mr. Tite, M.P whom I think you know, "has several times expressed to me his great wish to be present on an occasion when manifestations may be expected; and it would gratify him very much if he could come.

"Wednesday will suit me best, but if some other evening, Saturday excepted, can only be set apart for it, I will try to come.

"I hope you will not think me troublesome. You were kind enough to ask me to come again, and to propose a day. I hope you may be able to arrange with Mr. Home, and that he will not think me intrusive. Very truly yours,

"John Bright."

I believe Mr. Bright has never made public any account of his experiences with Mr. Home; but in conversing on the subject, the testimony of Mr. Hall and that of Mr. Beales, as reported by Mrs. Hall, showed that he declared freely the impression made on him. I have the evidence of another person to add to theirs. Mr. J. M. Peebles, a United States consul, was in England about this time, and had a talk with Mr. Bright on Spiritualism. Lecturing in America, September 3, 1870, on his travels in Europe, Mr. Peebles stated:

"While in England I dined with John Bright, when transpired quite an earnest conversation upon the subject of Spiritualism. He said he had witnessed some of D. D. Home's manifestations. They were wonderful. He could attribute them to no cause except it be the one alleged, that of intelligent, disembodied spirits. 'But,' he added, with due caution, 'I do not say that this is so; but if it be true, it is the strongest tangible proof we have of immortality.'"

Sir Charles Nicholson, to whom I have referred a few pages back, seems to have been a very amiable man, and, like many amiable men, a very timid one. He had been present at a number of séances with Home, was entirely convinced of the genuineness of the manifestations and probably satisfied of their spiritual origin; but he could not summon up courage to make his convictions public. In 1864, after Mr. Home's expulsion from Rome, some of his English friends planned an address to him that should be at once a declaration of sympathy and a testimony of their belief in Spiritualism. The wish of the promoters of the address naturally was to obtain the signatures of various distinguished Englishmen who had privately expressed their conviction of the genuineness of the phenomena witnessed by them in Home's presence; but it was found that nearly all were too timid to let their names go forth to the world.

"Of course I am ready to be a witness either in private or in public," wrote Mr. S. C. Hall to Mr. Home; "but will others will Robert Chambers, Sir E. B. Lytton, Sir Charles Nicholson and others be both?"

It was found that they would not, and the testimonial ultimately took a private, instead of a public form. But if timorous of publishing his faith to the world, Sir Charles Nicholson would seem to have declared it freely to his friends.

"At dinner at the Larnocks in Kensington Palace Gardens," writes Mrs. S. C. Hall to Mr. Home, "Sir Charles Nicholson began about Spiritualism he is now a perfect believer. Carter and he fought it out bravely with the Larnocks."

And again, writing to Mr. Home in America, March, 1865: "Sir Charles Nicholson told Mr. Durham that he had been informed you had renounced Spiritualism. Both friends were in great anxiety and distress at such a report; so I sent Sir Charles your last letter, and had such a very nice reply. I think he is a very sincere Spiritualist."

Sincere in secret, that is. Of what avail to any cause is such sincerity?

Sir Charles Nicholson's letters to Mr. Home are hardly of

sufficient interest to print here, except perhaps the following, which slightly bears on the testimony of Mrs. Hall concerning his convictions:

"My dear Mr. Home, Many thanks for your kind note. Be assured that the pleasure of cultivating social intercourse, and of enjoying your society, will always be regarded as a privilege by me, irrespective of curiosity regarding the wonderful phenomena, which I may have an opportunity of witnessing in your presence. Ever most faithfully yours, "Charles Nicholson."

That Sir C. Nicholson had séances at his own residence with Mr. Home, I learn from a letter written by Sir Daniel Cooper:

"20, Prince's Gardens, 9th July, 1864.

"My dear Home, Lady Cooper desires me to say that we shall be very happy to see your friend, Captain Pemberton, at 3 past 8 o'clock. Our party will consist of Mr. and Mrs. Witt, Admiral and Mrs. Denham, Dr. Barrett, and our two selves. Admiral Denham has met you at Sir Chas. Nicholson's the others have never seen any manifestations, and are very anxious to see you at a séance. Lady Cooper joins me in kind regards. Believe me, yours very faithfully, "Daniel Cooper."

I do not know that Sir D. Cooper, any more than Sir Charles Nicholson, ever made his convictions public; but in private both Lady Cooper and himself were converts.

"I heard last night," writes Mrs. S. C. Hall, "that Sir D. Cooper was ill, so I called there en route to Mrs. Milner Gibson's, and found him better. Lady C. said, 'I fear your maid never gave Sir Daniel's card to Mr. Home I left it for him expressly, and hoped he might have called here before his return to Paris.' 'Paris!' I repeated; 'he is in London.' I wish you had seen the expression of pleasure that lit up her serious face. Then she told me of the battles she and Sir Daniel had fought, both here and at Brussels, about Spiritualism since that séance how deeply they are impressed, how impossible they find it to reconcile the manifestations they saw with any human power, and how eager they are to see more. Do, dear friend, call on them. Sarah says she gave you Sir D.'s card, but I dare say you forgot all about it. In their quiet way they are as much impressed as Pickersgill. I had no idea they were so deeply impressed."

The above letter was written early in 1863, and, during that and the following year, fresh séances with Home deepened and strengthened the Spiritual convictions of Sir Daniel and Lady Cooper. I understand that some of the manifestations were described in the *Spiritual Magazine*; but if so, the testimony was of that anonymous kind which timid friends of Home were so fond of furnishing, and consequently valueless.

If friends were timid of telling the truth they knew of him, foes were always ready to make reckless statements based on hearsay or sheer malice. I have remarked in another chapter that a striking illustration of the tendency of human nature to confound assertion with fact was given in the year 1864.

A Captain Noble, a scientific man of some small note, wrote a letter to the *Sussex Advertiser* in March 1864, on the subject of Spiritualism, with especial reference to the séances of Mr. Home. He had never been present at one; but the unimportant fact that he had no materials for arriving at a judgment did not prevent him from forming one; and he summed it up in the words: "Home is as rank an impostor, I verily believe, as ever lived."

A few weeks later Mr. Home arrived in England; and his attention was called to the letter in the *Sussex Advertiser.* He at once gave instructions on the subject to his solicitors, who wrote to Captain Noble:

"Mr. Home is astonished at this public and gratuitous attack which you have made upon his personal character, and he is determined to have a public investigation, in which you will have an opportunity if you can of proving your charge against him. We are therefore instructed to ask "&c.

Captain Noble responded to the application for the name of his solicitor by writing as follows to Mr. Home:

"44 Forest Lodge, Maresfield, 14th April 1864.

"Sir, My attention having just been directed to a passage in a long letter addressed by me to the *Sussex Advertiser*, reflecting strongly on your character, I take the earliest opportunity of withdrawing the charge therein implied, and of offering you, with all frankness and unreserve, the fullest apology for having made what a moment's reflection tells me to have been an unjustifiable assertion on my part.

"In affirming the grounds of my disbelief and in attributing Spiritual manifestations to natural causes, I was inadvertently led to make the allusion to yourself which I so much regret. You will, I feel assured, acquit me of having entertained an) malevolent feeling against one of whom I had no personal knowledge, and will readily perceive that I spoke only from general conclusions hastily, and, I freely admit, unfairly formed. Under these circumstances, I feel it alike due to you and to myself to offer you every apology which one gentleman is entitled to from another; and, inasmuch as my attack was a public one, I now express my readiness to make my retraction equally public, and shall with pleasure clothe it in any appropriate form which you may deem satisfactory to your own honour."

In making this amend honorable, it does not seem to have occurred to the writer that the want of all knowledge of Mr. Home to which he confesses, instead of being, as he implies, a mitigation of his offence, greatly aggravated it. It was the way of the world, however, to fling random slanders at Home; and probably nine-tenths of his maligners, if brought to book, would have hastened to plead, like this Sussex country gentleman, that they had acted more in heedlessness than in malice. Then and always the most tolerant of mankind, Home, whose desire was to vindicate himself, not to punish others, very readily accepted the reparation offered; and the incident was terminated by Captain Noble publishing in the journal that had contained the libel an unreserved withdrawal of his statements and apology for having made them.

I forget what celebrity described himself, or was described, as the best abused man of his day. Mr. Home was unquestionably the best (or worst) calumniated of his. The most harmless and meaningless word dropped by one of his acquaintances was enough: some listening ear picked it up, and in twenty-four hours the most astonishing fictions had been built upon it. For instance, the distinguished sculptor Mr. J. E. Boehm pointed out in a statuette made by him of Mr. Home the well-formed hands and feet. Some one present repeated the compliment with distortions; and in a few days the most extraordinary stories were circulated in London of what the sculptor had said. Home wrote to inform him of these wild fables, and Mr. Boehm wrote in return:

"Dear Mr. Home, with astonishment I received your letter yesterday, and hasten to reply. I cannot understand who can possibly be ill-natured enough to spread such reports, and though I try to remember what could have given cause to the origin of it, I cannot think that it was anything else but my pointing out on your statuette your delicately formed hands, feet, and limbs in general. If such remarks raise such interpretations, I may as well give up priding myself in that which I consider the only merit in my humble works viz., that I pay just as much attention to the characteristics of the tip of the fingers as the tip of the nose. I need not say more, as I know that these things occur often to you, and that you would not really attach any importance to them; and I beg you to believe me, dear Mr. Home, truly yours,

"J. E. Boehm."

The most sensitive of all men, past or present, Home could not but sometimes feel the annoyance of the untruthful and malignant chatter of the world, heartily though he despised it. On the ears of all who really knew him it fell unheeded a fact well pointed out in the following letter to him, which needs no other comment:

"Hotel de Rome, 12th Dec., '63.

Dear Sir, I cannot conceive why you give the slightest attention to the circumstances you mentioned to me this morning.

"Your numerous friends in England, France, and Russia will certainly not be influenced by idle gossip, and a man who holds so prominent a position in European society as you do is inevitably exposed to attacks of all kinds. Believe me, dear sir, yours truly,

"Odo Russell."

About the time when he accepted Captain Noble's apology, Mr. Home received a letter that took the form of a solemn warning to cease dealing with familiar spirits. Its writer was especially earnest in counselling him to read his Bible. Here again, as in Captain Noble's case, a total lack of information is apparent; for few men have ever searched the Scriptures more attentively and constantly than Home.

Evidently the writer of this letter was actuated by the belief, so common among pious, narrow-minded people, that the phenomena of Spiritualism were the work of the Arch-Fiend. Home often met with such persons: he met with some of them in this same year, 1864.

He had made the acquaintance of a Captain Chawner, and went on a visit to him for a few days at Newton Vallence, Hampshire. Several people were staying in the house; and on Home's coming séances were held, of which a startling account was subsequently circulated. It was said that the Fiend himself had visibly appeared in the form of a radiant angel, but had been put to flight at once by the exorcisms of a lady who was present.

This story was so frequently repeated in society that some friends of Home ended by trying to trace it to its source, and had the fortune to arrive at the facts on which it was based. They found that at one of the séances with the Chawner family a lady had been present who believed the manifestations to be the work of demons. She came to the séance accordingly with the Lord's Prayer and various texts written on small slips of paper, that she had placed inside her rings and within the pockets of her dress. None the less, manifestations occurred; and some of them were addressed particularly to her. If I interpret correctly the narrative of the séance furnished by one of the Chawner family, Mr. Home, in the trance state, was controlled by a lost friend of the believer in demon-wrought miracles, who gave striking tokens of his identity. With this explanation, I may leave the following extract from a letter written in March 1866, to speak for itself:

"My dear Miss Cameron, I am very much obliged to you for telling me of Mr. Home's answer to my story. The lady who told it is the wife of General Brounker, who has just got an appointment of consequence in India. I will try to get the relation of the séance written down it took place when Mr. Home was staying with the Chawner family at Newton, near Selbourne, in Hampshire.

"There can be no doubt as to the reality of the phenomena in the minds of those who have fairly inquired into them. I believe the true difficulty to be that the whole of the religious world, of every denomination, is strongly opposed to Spiritualism the scientific opposition is nothing in comparison. Very truly yours, "Jane Alexander."

The writer of the above letter obtained from a member of the Chawner family a written narrative of the séance at which Mrs. Brounker had been present, and had it forwarded to Mr. Home. I extract a portion:

"The manifestations were not prevented from continuing with the general circle; only, as Mrs. Brounker supposed, the bad spirits could not come to her. She had texts and the Lord's Prayer about her, and inside her rings, written on a tiny piece of paper, was the Lord's Prayer, slipped between her rings and her fingers. Several things about one who was dear to her came out at this séance. Indeed, he appeared himself; and this brings me to the real point of Mrs. B.'s ideas on the subject. She and her sister feel convinced that, though, to all appearance it was this gentleman – there was even his peculiar shake of the hand, also a phrase quite peculiar to himself was used – yet, with all this, they feel convinced that it was not he himself, but an Evil Spirit personating him with his peculiarities. I said, 'Why should an evil spirit know his ways and phrases, &c.?' She answered, 'that is the argument used, but very easily met. The Arch Fiend knows all about us and all our peculiarities, and makes use of that knowledge in his temptations and so, for his purpose, he can tell all his emissaries. I believe, in every case, it is an evil spirit that personates our dear lost friends.'"

Of such reasoning, one can only remark that it is curious how much stronger a faith very orthodox people seem, as a rule, to have in the power of Satan than in that of God. Such being their faith, it is inevitable that, of all prejudices hostile to Spiritualism, that which sees in every manifestation a deceit of the Fiend should be the most inveterate. What token of identity can convince a person who meets every proof with the objection: "Yes, yes, to others that may seem convincing, but not to me, who know that the Evil One is omniscient and omnipotent."

I have not space to do more than allude to various persons who investigated the phenomena in the years from which I am now passing. Among them was George, Prince of Solms, who was converted to Spiritualism by his séances with Mr. Home at

Ryde, in 1862, and tried, on his return to Hanover, to convert the King. I quote a portion of one of his numerous letters in the English of the writer:

"My dear Mr. Home I can give you good news, because I found an occasion to speak with my dear King of all I know about Spiritualism. He was very interested, but has still an objection if we are right to communicate in this way with spirits in the other world. He only believes a part of that which I believe, but I am yet happy that he has got an interest, and that is enough for me I am not so alone in Hanover as I expected."

No allusion to the séances at Ryde with the Prince of Solms was made by Mr. Home in the *Incidents*. The following extract from a. letter that the Prince wrote to him in 1862 will explain why:

"I beg of you not to speak of my knowledge of Spiritualism and interest in you, because it might be bad for my King. My relations, to whom I told about this, asked me not to speak of it, because I was so near to the royal family, that if the people knew the King had a Spiritualist in his house, they would profit of it to speak against him. My dear Mr. Home, promise me your discretion, and I will never forget you. Believe me, for ever, yours very truly, George, Prince of Solms."

Two other inquirers the date of whose experiences I can only fix as antecedent to 1864 were the Marchioness of Hastings and Lady Combermere. In a letter written after her first séance, the former tells Mr. Home that she "was so surprised and startled by what she saw as to feel it impossible to come to any conclusion, till she had seen it several times."

In 1864, the distinguished electrician, Cromwell Varley, F.R.S had a séance in his own house at Beckenham with Mr. Home. In his letter to Professor Tyndall (May 12th, 1868) on the subject of spiritual manifestations, Mr. Varley describes phenomena (the movements of a table, a large sofa, &c., untouched by any person present) that took place while the room was brilliantly lit. "Deception," he wrote, "was impossible."

The introduction of Cromwell Varley to the phenomena of Spiritualism took place in 1860, at a séance with Home. The manifestations he witnessed that evening were described by him in his letter to Tyndall, and again in his evidence given before the Dialectical Society in 1869.

Varley, who, before seeing anything of the manifestations, seems to have been inclined to attribute them to known forces, presented himself to Mr. Home in the spring of 1860. "I am," he said to Home, "the electrician of the International and Atlantic Telegraph Companies; and, therefore, have considerable knowledge of electricity, magnetism, and other physical forces. I have heard peak of the extraordinary phenomena which are produced in your presence, and am very desirous to see them and search into their cause. Are you willing to allow me to be a witness of these phenomena?"

"With great pleasure," replied Home; and after warning his new acquaintance that he could not promise him manifestations would take place, and that sometimes several séances in succession were held without anything particular happening, he invited Mr. Varley to come to a séance and bring his wife with him.

Varley minutely describes the occurrences of that séance. The room, he told Professor Tyndall and the Dialectical Society, was lighted by four gas burners; and when raps began to sound on the table he carefully searched beneath it, while Mrs. Varley kept watch above. Later in the séance the sitters felt themselves touched. Varley mentally asked that his coat-collar might be pulled on the left side, and had hardly shaped the thought in his mind when three pulls were given to the collar, on the side he desired, by an invisible hand. He then mentally requested that his right knee might be touched three times, and instantly the unuttered wish was complied with.

"Now my left knee," desired Varley, still without speaking. It was touched three times without an instant's delay.

"My right shoulder," continued the investigator always mentally.

"On the instant it was touched," he writes, "without my being able to see anything." Varley adds that, as he had neither spoken nor stirred, no one present had any idea of what had taken place until he informed them.

As for the conjecture of Mr. Home having been able to read his guest's thoughts and produce the touches that responded to them, Varley disposes of it by stating the two facts that the room was brightly lit, and that a lady whom he designates as "Mrs. A." was seated between himself and Home.

But, remarkable as was the séance, it was destined to be followed by an incident that impressed Varley with more decisive conviction than all the wonders that had gone before. He lived, he relates, some five or six miles from the scene of the séance, and reached home that night between twelve and one. I copy from the published report of the evidence that he gave before the Dialectical Society his account of what ensued:

"These," said Mr. Varley, "were the first physical phenomena I saw, and they impressed me; but still I was too much astonished to be able to feel satisfied. Fortunately, when I got home, a circumstance occurred which got rid of the element of doubt. While alone in the drawing room, thinking intently on what I had witnessed, there were raps. The next morning I received a letter from Mr. Home, in which he said. 'When alone in your room last night, you heard sounds. I am so pleased.' He stated the spirits had told him they followed me, and were enabled to produce sounds. I have the letter in my possession now, to show that imagination had nothing to do with the matter."

Here again is testimony so decisive that it can only be attacked by impugning the sanity or the credibility of the witness. But it was never so much as hinted by Mr. Varley's bitterest critics that he was insane; and those scientific brethren who passed to the other side of the way from him when he declared himself a Spiritualist never ventured to impugn his honesty. Of his scientific ability there can be no doubt; though, in October, 1871, Dr. Carpenter assured the readers of the *Quarterly Review* that there were grave doubts of it, and that these misgivings of the learned world had kept Mr. Varley out of the Royal Society. "His scientific attainments," said the reviewer amiably, "are so cheaply estimated by those who are best qualified to judge of them, that he has never been admitted to the Royal Society." Unfortunately for Dr. Carpenter, Mr. Varley had been more than three months a Fellow of the Royal Society when this *Quarterly* article was published. Yet its inaccurate and pretentious author, who could blunder so grossly and spitefully about a fact that ought to have been well within his knowledge, is supposed by some simple people to have been an impartial and painstaking investigator of Spiritualism!

CHAPTER 8

America, Russia and England

Invitation to Cambridge. Recitations in America. Home's Personal Appearance. Second Visit to the French Court. Lecture in London. Baseless Attacks. Fraudulent Imitators. The Spiritual Atheneum. The Lyon Case. A Perjured Plaintiff. A Legal Dilemma. Robert Chambers' Affidavit. A Miscarriage of Justice. Moral Victory of Home. Posthumous Libels in the "Times" and "Daily News".

AMONG MR. HOME'S correspondence are many letters hinting at remarkable experiences the writers have had with him, but giving no details. For instance, in the year 1864, a Mr. J. M. Bellew, writing from Portsdown Gardens, Maida Hill, is anxious that his friend Mr. Frith, R.A., should be impressed as he himself has been. Again, there are numerous letters in the same year from a Mr. Jermyn Cowell, establishing two facts first, that their writer had seen at séances with Home sufficient to impress and interest him deeply; secondly, that Mr. Cowell was well acquainted with distinguished men at Cambridge Professor Sidgwick amongst others and was very desirous to have Home make a visit to some of his friends at the University. Another correspondent associated with Cambridge is a clergyman, the Rev. A. W. Hobson, who writes in May, 1864, that his friend, the famous astronomer Adams, is very much interested by what he, Mr. Hobson, has had to tell him, and would like to meet Mr. Home, if the latter could conveniently come to Cambridge.

Probably Home was unable to accept the invitation, or there would remain some record of the visit. It is evident, however, from their letters that Messrs. Bellew, Cowell, and Hobson all belonged to the too-numerous class of inquirers who had seen enough to convince them that the phenomena could not be accounted for by the easy hypothesis of imposture, but who shrank from making their convictions public.

The testimony given and letters quoted from in preceding chapters sufficiently indicate how varied and extensive would be the full list of the English investigators present at séances with Mr. Home. A full list I could not give; for many names are unknown to me, and others I have omitted because I had no particulars of the experiences connected with those names; but the incomplete record these passes contain will at least dispose of the untrue statement so frequently made, that miracles were to be seen only by the faithful, and that Home avoided meeting sceptics. On the contrary, he seldom held a séance in England at which there were not one or more sceptics present, and often the sitters wholly consisted of disbelievers in the phenomena. That many of these sceptics became Spiritualists through their séances with him is true, but surely that fact will not be urged in disproof of the manifestations!

Sailing for America in the early autumn of 1864, Mr. Home remained six or seven months in the States, renewing his acquaintance with all the old friends of ten years earlier who were still on earth, and adding new friends to their number. Among the latter was Mrs. Sarah Helen Whitman, herself a poetess of some merit, but more celebrated from having charmed the fancy of that strangest of beings and weirdest of geniuses, Edgar Poe, who addressed to her some of his most exquisite verses. Mrs. Whitman was present at séances with Home; and it was she who wrote to the editor of an American journal, apropos of Browning's doggerel on Spiritualism: "If you will take the trouble to read the poem of Mr. Browning to which I have referred, you will understand why it is regarded by some of Mr. Browning's warmest admirers as 'a blot on the 'scutcheon.'"

The name of Henry Howard Brownell is almost unknown in England. It is that of a young American of rare gifts who wrote two poems, "The River Fight" and "The Bay Fight," in which he described two of the most stirring naval operations of the Civil War Farragut's dash past the forts at the mouth of the Mississippi and capture of New Orleans, and secondly, the defeat by the same commander of the Confederate squadron in Mobile Bay, when wooden Federal vessels surrounded and captured a

Southern ironclad. Brownell, who died young, was present at both engagements; being, I think, secretary to Admiral Farragut; and the battle-fever has surely never been more wonderfully breathed into words than in a verse of "The Bay Fight:"

Fear! A forgotten form:
Death! A dream of the eyes: We were atoms in God's
great storm that roared through the angry skies.

Both poems were favourites with Home, and none who heard his magnificent and fiery rendering of them will ever forget it. It was during this visit to America that he first gave public expression to his genius as a reader; and he several times recited the two poems of Brownell, who had recently made his acquaintance. A notice of one of these readings from the pen of Mrs. Whitman, records that Admiral Farragut was among the audience, and was delighted with Home's "masterly and daringly original rendering of the Bay Fight."

At a private party in New York just after the close of the war, Home read the same poem; and on this occasion a strange tribute to the author's genius and his own was paid. One of the most telling portions of the "Bay Fight "describes the action of the commander of the Confederate ironclad, when his consorts had fled or were taken, and nothing remained to him but the choice between sinking and surrender:

Haughty, cruel, and cold, He ever was strong and bold:
Shall he shrink from a wooden stem.' He will think
of that brave band He sank in the Cumberland:
Aye! He will sink like them.
"Nothing left but to fight Boldly his last sea-fight: Can he strike?
By heaven! 'Tis true, Down comes the traitor blue, And..

The verse was never finished; Home's voice and play of feature had put such life into the stinging words, that, at the reference to the "traitor blue," a young Southerner present was maddened out of all self-control, and sprang at the reader like a wild beast. He was mastered before he could do any mischief; but this dramatic incident abruptly terminated the reading. The occurrence was noticed in American papers of the time.

Brownell, in whom Home felt a deep interest, became a Spiritualist. He gave his friend a copy of his poems; and Home in return sent him a copy of the *Incidents*, after reading which Brownell writes to him: "I have read your book with the greatest interest. Heretofore, I had only known you as a vehicle for the most wonderful communications which we have had with the next world; but now I am beginning to be acquainted with you mentally and morally. I can only say that this acquaintance gives me high pleasure, and that I hope to improve it personally at some future time."

"I had heard of the great sensation produced by your reading in Paris," he says in another letter, "and feel indebted to you for presenting my poem so nobly." Then, in words that have a pathetic interest in view of the early death of their writer, Brownell adds: "If I live, I will devote something of my poor verses to advocating the truths of Spiritualism."

At Norwich, Connecticut, Mr. Home gave a reading for the benefit of the Soldiers' Aid Society. On the announcement of this charitable intention in the local journal, a young clergyman wrote to the latter, "craving permission, as a Christian man, to say a few words to the Christians in Norwich." It was kind and courteous of Mr. Home, he admitted, to assent to the request of the Soldiers' Aid Society that he would give a reading on its behalf.

"I have no doubt he is sincere in his spiritualistic belief. I have no quarrel with him. But are the Christian men and women of Norwich reduced to such extremities that they must resort to a representative and exponent of Spiritualism for aid in their Christian and patriotic work? Is it seemly that Christians should patronize such an entertainment?"

And so on, through half a column of the Norwich Bulletin. Mr. Home and some of his friends replied, pointing out to this curious bigot that charity is of no creed, and that it must require a very Jesuitical eye to detect the wickedness of allowing Home by his genius as a reader to benefit the victims of the Civil War. Had he been a wounded soldier in need of aid, the justice of this reasoning would probably have commended itself to the Rev. Mr. Lewis; but as he was only a very young clergyman aping the authority of a Pope, he replied, as hotly as inconsequently:

"My own private opinion of Spiritualism is that it is of the devil from beginning to end." Then, with a triumphant effort of charity: "It does not necessarily follow that every one who professes Spiritualism is consciously in league with the devil. And I gave Mr. H. the benefit of the doubt when I said that I conceded his honesty and sincerity."

Much to the mortification of the reverend casuist, his appeal only served to advertise the reading more widely; and the room was crowded with an enthusiastic audience, from whose numbers the Soldiers' Aid Fund reaped substantial benefit. "Possibly," wrote a correspondent of the *Bulletin*, "the author of this last encyclical, with deep insight into human nature, may have seen that in no other way could he ensure so large an attendance upon the occasion of Mr. Home's reading, as by an apparent effort to dragoon the public away from the reading. Looked at in that light, the letter has been a grand success."

It was not only by Ms reading at Norwich that Home gave practical proofs of his sympathy with those victims of the Civil War, who, in 1864 and 5, were so numerous in every town and village of the Union. Out of his small means very small at that time, he contributed freely to funds for the relief of such sufferers; and at Philadelphia, which city was just then crowded with human wrecks that the war had made, he brightened the wards of the hospitals by giving readings there, "to the great delight of the sick and wounded soldiers," says the Philadelphia newspaper which informs me of the fact. He, whose own life was so full of suffering, had the keenest sympathy with the pain of others a practical sympathy that found expression in deeds; and in America in 1864-5, and again in France in 1870, the sight of the terrible suffering caused by war stirred him to do many acts of kindness and devotion of which the world never heard, nor did he wish that it should hear.

Mr. Home gave several readings, public and private, in New York; and among his clippings from newspapers of that date, I find the following description of the first by some reporter present a lady, if one may judge by the writer's eye for personal advantages:

"I really have had a sensation. I have heard Home, the great medium, read. The programme did not appear attractive, and I had made every preparation to be disappointed. When Home entered the room, a change came o'er the spirit of my dream, for Home's personality alone is sufficient to absorb a physiognomist's attention for hours. Fancy, my dear Republican, the most distinguished man you have seen for years, and then you will not have reached the plane on which Home stands. His figure is singularly fine and graceful, his hands and feet beautiful, the former being the embodiment of artistic genius. 'Show me a man's hand, and I will tell you what he is.' Then Home's head, excellently shaped, is marvellous in expression. He is of the blonde type, with beautiful hair, fine teeth, a good mouth, and eyes that really look as though they saw things in heaven and earth not dreamed of in our philosophy.

"And now, how does he read? Beautifully, wonderfully. His pathos is exquisite, his humour perfect. Why the audience did not go frantic with delight is because the audience did not appreciate the genius of the reader. His rendering of Brownell's stirring poem, 'On the Hartford in Mobile Bay,' was superb. Home would make a great actor. He is grace itself; his manner is thoroughly refined, his voice rich and of large compass, his facial expression unequalled. Home is a marvel. He is one of those gifted creatures that nature makes every now and then, to show what she can do when in the mood."

And such Home was. It was impossible to be long in his society without yielding to its spell. Prejudices the most inveterate melted away before that irresistible charm of manner, coupled with, his joyousness of nature and kindliness of heart. It was always those who knew least of him who libelled him most flagrantly, the outer man no less than the inner. No portraits could bear less resemblance to the original than those drawn from time to time in pen and ink of Home. Were it worthwhile a dozen such flights of journalistic fancy might be cited here. Those who took their notion of Horns from pictures so unlike him had a wide choice offered them every possible colour of eyes, hair, and complexion, a figure now tall, now short, at one time slender at another robust; in short every variety of counterfeit, the two opposed extremes of which were the haggard spectre invented by *All the Year Round* in 1866 and the "dark-complexioned person, with quick, shifting eyes, curly black hair, and a nose which seemed to vouch for a purely Caucasian descent of Echoes from the Clubs, April 29th, 1868."

Robert Bell sketched slightly the actual Home in his *Cornhill* article, the Home of 1860:

"The expression of his face in repose is that of physical suffering; but it quickly lights up when you address him, and his natural cheerfulness colours his whole manner. There is more kindliness and gentleness than vigour in the character of his features; and the same easy-natured disposition may be traced in his unrestrained intercourse. He is yet so young, that the playfulness of boyhood has not passed away, and he never seems so thoroughly at ease with himself and others as when he is enjoying some light and temperate amusement."

Bell thus refers to the emphatic disclaimer by Home of that power of evocation foolishly attributed to him:

"Mr. Home's supernatural power is a current topic in all circles where these phenomena are talked of by people who have never witnessed them. But the truth is, he neither possesses such power nor pretends to it. ... He not only cannot call up spirits, as we hear on all sides, but he will tell you that he considers such invocations to be blasphemous."

As a pendant to Robert Bell's sketch of Home, I translate from "Le Monde Elégant à Nice" a description written seventeen years later by M. Fabre des Essarts:

"I must tell you frankly that Home was not at all like what I had imagined he would be. To begin with, he is a perfect man of the world, with .a most refined and winning aspect. Then, there is absolutely nothing in his appearance to suggest the necromancer.

"Instead of that bat's claw, which certain English reporters give him, he held out to me with perfect affability a hand quite aristocratic. One of those Olympian foreheads, which seem to have been moulded by Nature as the temple of thought: an eye of an intense blue, that looks as if formed to sound the depths of the unknown; such are the details that complete this noble and intelligent figure."

Saddened as it as by the sight of the widespread and terrible suffering caused by war, the visit to America that ended in May, 1865, could not have been a very happy time to Home, in spite of the numerous friends who welcomed him. On his return to London, he stayed there only two or three days; and then left for Paris to take charge of the young sister who had grown up to womanhood under the gracious protection of the Empress of the French.

It has been frequently asserted, in print and out of it, that long before 1865 Mr. Home had lost the favour he formerly enjoyed at the Court of France. He never took the trouble to disprove this falsehood, which he might easily have done by publishing half a dozen letters in his possession, such as the following:

"4th July, 1864.

"My dear Mr. Home, I lose no time in answering your letter, as I am sure that you are awaiting with anxiety the result of my communication with the Empress" (a communication respecting Miss C. Home). "I was at Fontainebleau on Saturday, and have the most gracious acquiescence in your request. So that you may make your arrangements accordingly, yours truly,

"Caroline, Princess Murat."

"June 10th, 1865.

"My dear Mr. Home, The Empress told me last night to write to you and say that she would receive you tomorrow at half-past three. Yours truly, "Caroline, Princess Murat."

July saw Mr. Home in Russia, he having at last yielded to the repeated invitations that Tolstoy and other friends there had been pressing on him for years.

After a pleasant visit to one of the country-seats of his friend, Count Alexis Tolstoy, Home returned to St. Petersburg, and from there went to London where he passed the winter of 1865–6, a dreary winter to him, for ill-health was aggravated by anxiety about the future. Had he sought to profit by the exercise of his wonderful gift, that anxiety would soon have been at an end; but then, as ever, he preferred the care and struggles of poverty. He had other gifts, however, that he could honourably turn to account; and after taking counsel with his friends in London; he conquered the repugnance he had felt to appear on an English platform, and decided to become a public reader.

Before carrying out the resolve, he gave a lecture upon Spiritualism, at Willis's Rooms, in February, 1866; a portion of which I quote:

"There is in Spiritualism," said Home, "a wide field for profitable research, if only it be conducted in the true spirit of inquiry the spirit that is willing to study and learn of facts, however strange they may seem, however counter to the prejudices of philosophy; for philosophy, as well as ignorance, has its prejudices, and sometimes those of philosophy are the most inveterate.

"I would not have you think for a moment that I am not aware of the many abuses which may arise from this contact with the spirit world. But God gives to every man the power of reason, and this it is in no way the province of Spiritualism to supersede. If a spirit were to give advice which our reason told us should not be followed, why should we pay more attention to him, now that he is freed from the body, than if he were still moving among us on earth, as formerly?"

Speaking of the many imposters who counterfeit the genuine phenomena of Spiritualism, and trade in pretended wonders for a living, he said:

"I have known of the most gross impostures being carried on, and in every case have exposed them; and, God being my helper, ever will do so. Of course, in cases like these, I have much to contend with, even from my best friends. They say, 'It is not your place; let others do it.' I feel it to be my place; and when I see the pure and glorious truths I advocate drawn down and made a mockery of by the mob, I will lift up my voice and say, 'This is not Spiritualism?' If they will prove it to be so, then I wish to have nothing to do with it; for it is a dark and damning error, and the sooner pure truth-seekers leave it, the better. But there is no doctrine which is without its abuses, and which is not abused by outsiders."

After rebutting the assertion that insanity is a frequent consequence of the belief, Mr. Home adverted to the various "explanations" of the phenomena.

"When in Russia this autumn, on a visit to his Majesty, it was told for a fact that I had a great number of cats to sleep with me, and by this means became so charged with electricity that the rappings were heard in my presence. Another story was that I held my feet a long time in ice water, and then ran and sat by the Emperor, putting my feet in his hands; and so he thought he touched a corpse-like hand. It is currently reported that my feet are like monkeys' feet, and that I can do as I please with them. Some of my friends have even asked to see my feet without shoes or stockings, that they might contradict this. These, and many other fantastic, far-fetched, and inadequate explanations, which in turn need explaining, have been from time to time put forth; each new hypothesis unkindly exploding its predecessors, and being in its turn exploded "Those tyros who, with little or no knowledge of the subject, think themselves justified in denouncing the whole thing as imposture, ought surely (if not wholly deficient in modesty and common-sense) to be arrested by the circumstance that scientific and learned men, sceptical as themselves as to the supra-mundane origin of the facts, have yet, after the fullest investigation, been constrained to concede their reality and genuineness."

The distinguished and numerous company that had assembled to listen to the lecture were derided by a writer as "fools." They might, in view of the untruths and misstatements of fact that abounded in his article, have replied that there are much worse things than a fool in the world, if the fool is only honest.

Mr. S. C. Hall wrote to the editor of *All the Year Round* to contradict from his personal knowledge two of the many untrue statements concerning Mr. Home that the article contained: "In reference to the first of these two untruths," wrote Mr. Hall, "I can only give you now my own assurance that Home distributed no bills, having none to distribute. In regard to the second falsehood, I sent you a copy of the only circular he issued. You will see for yourself how dishonourable and disgraceful has been the change of a word to give a totally different meaning to the sentence. The writer of that article, be he who he may, is a dishonest man, to say the least."

As the editor of *All the Year Round* had nothing to say in

defence of his contributor he returned no answer. It is needless to add that he did not publish Mr. Hall's letter in his columns.

Wonderful and beautiful manifestations were witnessed at the residence of Mr. and Mrs. S. C. Hall on Easter Eve, 1866. Five persons composed the circle, the host and hostess, Lady Dunsany, Mrs. Adelaide Senior, and Mr. Home. A narrative of the occurrence was drawn up a few days later by Mrs. Senior, was submitted in turn to Mr. and Mrs. Hall and Lady Dunsany for their endorsement, and subsequently, with the consent of all four witnesses, was published by Mr. Home in his second volume of *Incidents.*

After naming the persons present at the séance Mrs. Senior writes:

"When Mr. Home arrived he was pale and worn, and we feared that we should have few manifestations. He sat down to the piano, and played and sang for some time; and on his beginning a little Russian air, a favourite of his late wife's, a chair which was at some distance from the piano slid up and placed itself beside him. I was sitting close to the piano on the other side, and I first saw the chair move.

"We sat down at the table, which at once began to vibrate and tremble, and was raised off the floor to a considerable height. Very loud and heavy knocks were heard on the table, the floor, and the furniture round the room; presently the accordion was touched, the alphabet was asked for, and it was spelt out 'We will play the earth-life of One Who was not of earth.'

"First we had simple, sweet, soft music for some minutes; then it became intensely sad; then the tramp, tramp, as of a body of men marching mingled with the music, and I exclaimed, 'The march to Calvary!' Then three times the tap-tapping sound of a hammer on a nail (like two metals meeting). A crash, and a burst of wailing which seemed to fill the room, followed; then there came a burst of glorious triumphal music, more grand than any of us had ever listened to, and we exclaimed, 'The Resurrection!' It thrilled to all our hearts."

Thus far the manifestations, including that wonderful music played by no earthly hands, had taken place in a brilliantly lit room. The circle kept their places at the table for a while longer;

but with the last thrilling chords of the triumphal harmony that had symbolized the Resurrection all manifestations ceased.

"Nothing more was done for some time," writes Mrs. Senior, "and we decided upon putting out the lights in the rooms, so as only to have that from the outside which came through the conservatory" (from a hanging lamp there, explains Mr. Hall). ... "Soon after this, we observed the face of Mr. S. C. Hall shining as if covered with silver light; we all remarked it and commented upon it. The accordion was carried round the circle, playing beautifully; it rested on the head of our host, then on my shoulder, and then went on to Mrs. Hall, who was next to me." ("Mr. Home's hand never being near the instrument," adds Mrs. Senior in a subsequent letter.) "Mr. Home was then raised up to the ceiling, which he touched, and regretted not having a pencil to make a mark there. When he came down, Mr. Hall gave him one, hoping that he might be again raised; and in five minutes after he was so, and left a cross on the ceiling. Just before this took place we saw his whole face and chest covered with the same silvery light which we had observed on our host's face. We had been sitting all this time at the table; and soon after our hands were touched and patted by other hands, and our brows touched by loved hands whose touch we knew. Shortly afterwards we heard the knocks and sounds die away in the distance out of doors, and we felt that it was all over. That burst of music was still thrilling on our hearts. Nothing of mortal composition could equal it, and its sound was that of a fine organ. We greatly regretted that no one in the room could take down the notes. The wondrous effect of the sound of feet, and the sound of the hammer and nails running like a thread through the music, it is impossible that those who have not listened to it could understand; in the music itself also there was a mixture of tones out of my power to describe."

Lady Dunsany, who was present with Mrs. Senior at this séance, will be remembered for her amiable and charming disposition by all who knew her. She was already advanced in years in 1866, and, I believe, passed from earth no long time afterwards; but her letters to Mr. Home show that to her last day she preserved an esteem and affection for him, and was a steadfast Spiritualist.

Like all other years, 1865 and 6 offer for my inspection letters written by persons who had evidently had numerous opportunities of investigating the phenomena, but whose experiences appear never to have been published. Some of the writers are Spiritualists, others form extraordinary theories to account for the manifestations, others again express no theory at all, but content themselves with admitting the reality of the facts. I select a letter from a correspondent of the later class:

"7, Prince of Wales Terrace, Kensington, 26th December 1865.

"It was a real pleasure, my dear Daniel, to see your 'fist' again. I thought you had quite given me up as an unbeliever, because, while admitting the extraordinary character of the phenomena that occur when you are present, I never could feel convinced that they emanated from the volition of the spirits of those who had once enjoyed, or rather passed through, the life of this earth. I have, I fancy, examined you more closely than many of those who have no doubt at all, than many of those who say, 'its all humbug; and he must have some secret machinery or electrical apparatus about him.' The result has been what I told you the last time we met I believe you, but as to your theory, I am as yet, so far as I know it, a doubter. It is quite possible that a man with a wonderful attribute may not know exactly whence his peculiar quality springs.

"There! I don't pretend to be a philosopher; but I do pretend to be a friend, and I shall be very glad to see you here. There are a great many things and a great many persons I want to talk to you about, besides hearing all your travels and experiences. I beg to ask you to dine here the first Sunday you come to London. Are you aware that I am now an underpaid, overworked Government official, and not any longer, like O'Connell's Ireland, 'great, glorious, and free'? Yours very truly,

"W. H. Ashurst."

The letter is valuable for the evidence it affords that Home was tolerant of honest doubt of the spiritual origin of the phenomena, however obstinate. As for the long silence on which the writer had placed the mistaken interpretation that was removed by the receipt of Home's letter, Mr. Ashurst, like hundreds of other people, had forgotten to consider that probably no man ever lived who had so extensive an acquaintance as Home. It was easy for his friends to write to him, but the vast mass of his correspondence rendered it sometimes simply impossible for him to answer their letters. His whole time would have been swallowed up in the task, and often half his means in paper and postage.

"Do find time to send me a few lines," writes from Vichy in June 1866, a lady signing herself "P. M. Lockhart." "I have had no direct communication with you since we had the pleasure of seeing you in town in January last. Mrs. Anfrere has felt greatly interested and bewildered ever since she saw those comparatively slight manifestations in London; and I unluckily should never have confidence in any medium but you, so how can I persuade her to see Spiritualism in any other form?"

This declaration that the séances of Home alone brought conviction is explicit in many letters, and implied in others; and in the later years of his life Mr. Home frequently received assurances from has friends from Mr. William Howitt and Mr. Crookes, for example that, had it not been for their recollection of séances with him, disgust with the impostures that usurped the name of Spiritualism would have utterly shattered their belief.

"Lady Helena Newenham," writes from 14, Wilton Place, S.W. in December, 1864, a correspondent whose signature, if I decipher it correctly, is G. M. Edgeworth, spent ten days here, and she often spoke of you and the comfort which she had derived from the séances which she and her husband had had with you. I wish much you were near us all now, and that your good influence was in the atmosphere. I am so disgusted by amateur would-be Spiritualists, who pretend to be mediums. When I say that I see people kicking the tables and lifting them, they are so angry, and wish to put it down that I believe nothing. I say, 'Yes, I do: I believe in Dan, and I do believe he has wonderful power' . . . Your affectionate friend,

"G. M. Edgeworth."

In February 1866, some long-past scenes of Home's life were unexpectedly recalled to his mind. Twelve or thirteen years before, he had been the guest of Mr. Ogden, a resident of Long Island, U.S. one of whose daughters had subsequently lost her husband, and her fortune before him; and with brave spirit had then set herself to turn to account the great talent for the stage with which she, was endowed. As an actress, Mrs. Cora Mowatt Ritchie will be better remembered in America than England, where she only took up her residence, I think, on retiring from the boards; but in both countries she was endeared to her friends by her attractive and lovable qualities as a woman. It happened, in February 1866, that a lady very intimate with her was seeking a séance with Mr. Home; and this fact led to the two old acquaintances meeting again. Mutual liking and esteem soon grew into friendship; and during the few years that remained to her on earth, Mrs. Ritchie was a Spiritualist, and one of the most prized and cordial of Home's friends. When the Lyon lawsuit closed, she instantly took steps for furnishing to American newspapers the true facts of the case, before any garbled account should have reached the States,

During the whole of 1866, Mr. Home's health was very feeble. The anxieties of the mind were reacting on the body. In the summer of that year an alternative to the reader's platform was suggested. It had occurred to various English Spiritualists and inquirers that the establishment of a kind of headquarters in London would be of great advantage to the movement. Some of their number interested themselves in carrying out the suggestion, which, it must be noted, did not in any way originate with Mr. Home. Premises were taken in Sloane Street; and, under the name of "The Spiritual Athenaeum," an institution was opened there, intended, as the circular of the promoters stated, to be "a rallying point for Spiritualists and their friends." The post of resident secretary was offered to Mr. Home, and accepted by him. In the list of the Council of the Spiritual Athenaeum occurs the name of Dr. Elliottson; a fact that bears convincing testimony of the great change the Dieppe séances had wrought in his views. Among the remaining members were Captain Drayson, R.A., and the popular writer on natural history, the Rev. J. G. Wood. The former had been present at several séances with Mr. Home. Of Mr. Wood's experiences in Spiritualism I am ignorant.

Hardly had the Athenaeum been brought into working order, when increasing ill health and the circumstances connected with his temporary change of name and fortune compelled Mr. Home to resign his appointment as secretary. With him the life of the institution went; and after languishing a short time, the Spiritual Athenaeum died a very natural death.

The story of the Lyon lawsuit has often been told by writers whose object was to cast a slur on Mr. Home. It served the purpose of these dishonest controversialists to affect credence of the numberless perjuries sworn to by the plaintiff in that suit a person of whom even so prejudiced a critic of Spiritualism and Spiritualists as Vice-Chancellor Giffard said, when delivering judgment against Mr. Home (I quote from the report of the Vice Chancellor's judgment in the *Pall Mall Gazette*): "The expenses" (of the suit) "have been very seriously increased, first by the unwarrantable attack in the plaintiff's affidavits on Mr. Wilkinson; and, secondly, by her innumerable misstatements in many important particulars misstatements on oath so perversely untrue that they have embarrassed the Court to a great degree and quite discredited the plaintiff's testimony."

"You are of course pained, my dear Daniel," wrote Mrs. S. C. Hall to Mr. Home, "that the Vice-Chancellor did not clear you by a few words from all suspicion of fraud as a Spiritualist but how would you have felt if he had blasted your character, as he has that of Mrs. Lyon, by being the first to accuse her of perjury?"

On what grounds, then, the reader unfamiliar with English law will ask, did the Vice-Chancellor order the restitution of Mrs. Lyon's gifts, when he so emphatically declared that her story of the circumstances under which those gifts were made had been utterly discredited? On two grounds, the one of law the other of prejudice. In a suit like that of Lyon v. Home English law throws the onus of proof on the defendant. It mattered nothing that Mrs. Lyon had signally Tailed in seeking to show that the gifts were made in consequence of communications claimed to be from her deceased husband, and had established only her own total disregard of truth by the "innumerable and perversely untrue misstatements on oath" to which the Vice Chancellor referred in such severe terms. English law, as interpreted and no doubt correctly interpreted by Vice Chancellor Giffard, did not require the plaintiff to prove the affirmative, that influence had been exercised on her mind. It required the defendant to prove the negative, that he had exercised no influence over the mind of Mrs. Lyon. Clean as were the hands of Mr. Home in this matter, how was he to establish his uprightness to the satisfaction of a judge who shared the common prejudices against Spiritualism to such an extent that he travelled out of his way to denounce that belief as "mischievous nonsense, well calculated on the one hand to delude the vain, the weak, the foolish, and the superstitious, and on the other to assist the projects of the needy and of the adventurer?" To put the matter in a nutshell, Vice Chancellor Giffard propounded to the unfortunate defendant the following dilemma: "If you are to retain these gifts, you must prove to my satisfaction that you exercised no influence over the plaintiff when she made them; but no amount of evidence you can bring forward will satisfy me that you are innocent of having exercised such influence."

Lest I be suspected of misstating the grounds of the Vice-Chancellor's decision, I extract from the "Equity Series of the Law Reports" a portion of the note summarizing the suit of Lyon v. Home

"Held, that the relation proved to have existed between them implied the exercise of dominion and influence by B. over A.'s mind, and consequently that, as B. had failed to prove that these voluntary gifts were the pure, voluntary, well-understood acts of A.'s mind, they must be set aside."

Coming from law to justice a very different matter an impartial critic will be of opinion that, if Mr. Home failed to prove to the satisfaction of the judge that the gifts were voluntary it was simply because no amount of proof to that effect would have convinced the Vice Chancellor of the defendant's uprightness. "Be thou pure as snow, thou shalt not 'scape calumny if thou art a Spiritualist."

Except as complicated by the false witness of the plaintiff, the facts relating to Mr. Home's adoption by Mrs. Lyon were sufficiently simple. She was an old and rich widow, and a believer in Spiritualism long before she sought the acquaintance of Mr. Home. Not only was she a believer long before she met him, but, according to her own account, a seer, who communed in vision with the world of spirits. After her adoption of Mr. Home, she told many persons that on first meeting him she had immediately recognized him as the figure that she had often seen in vision, and that her own visions, and not spirit communications made through Mr. Home, had inspired the thought of adopting him. Witness, for instance, the late Dr. Robert Chambers, from whose affidavit I shall presently quote.

Happening to hear of the *Spiritual Athenaeum* and its secretary Mr. Home, "I wrote on the 30th of September, 1866," says Mrs. Lyon in her affidavit, "that I was anxious to become a subscriber, and asking for a prospectus and particulars. Not having received any reply from the said defendant, I called, and asked to see him.

I had never before seen the said defendant."

At this visit, Mrs. Lyon, an absolute stranger to Mr. Home, entered into conversation with him concerning his work, *Incidents in My Life*, which she declared herself to have read with much interest. She informed him that she had been a believer in the occurrence of spiritual manifestations from her childhood, and that she was herself a medium and saw visions. Her chief interest, however, appeared to be centred in the royal and aristocratic personages mentioned in the *Incidents in My Life*, and she asked Mr. Home many questions concerning them and his intimacy with them. A day or two afterwards she made a gift of £30 to the funds of the Athenaeum, and followed this act by astounding Mr. Home with the declaration that she had taken a great fancy to him, and was determined to adopt him as her son, and settle a handsome fortune upon him. She was rich, she explained, was without children or relatives of her own, and her husband's relatives she detested. He would add her name of Lyon to his own; they would keep house together as mother and son; and two people would be made happy, he in becoming rich through her means, she in being introduced through has to the fashionable world. "She told me," said Mr. Home in his affidavit, "that she was the illegitimate daughter of a tradesman in Newcastle, that her late husband was of good family, and his family always held aloof from herself and husband." This passed at his second interview with Mrs. Lyon.

Bewildered by an incident so extraordinary even in a life that had been full of facts stranger than any fictions, Mr. Home at first treated her offer of adoption as a jest, but finding that she was perfectly serious, began to think that she could not be in her right mind. Yet to all appearance she was a sane, shrewd woman. Uncertain how to regard the affair, he did not call on her again for some days. When he at last went, she greeted him most warmly and affectionately, repeated that she had made up her mind to adopt him, and inquired if he had acted on her wish that he should consult a lawyer about the adoption. Mr. Home replied that he had not, and did not like her to act so hastily in a matter of such importance. She again assured him that her mind was fully made up, and added: "Whether you will or not, I shall settle a fortune on you, and you will be obliged to accept it. You are a gentleman, and have friends in the best society. I shall go out with you, and your friends will come to us; and my old age will become a joy instead of a burden."

He told her that he feared she sought him for the strange gift he possessed. Her answer, as given in his affidavit, was: "Why, you foolish fellow, I've seen nothing of your strange gift, as you call it; and though it is through your being celebrated for that that I first heard of you, now that I know you I love you for yourself, and should not care if you never had anything singular occur to you again." As no third person was present at the interview, it was impossible for Mr. Home to demonstrate that Mrs. Lyon's subsequent denial of having spoken these words was but one more addition to the many false oaths which the Vice Chancellor declared her to stand convicted of having taken.

He took twenty-four hours more to consider the proposed adoption, and then called on Mrs. Lyon and told her that he was unable to accept her proffered kindness. She urged him earnestly to reconsider his determination, and repeated her entreaties at a subsequent interview. Finally, he consented to take counsel with his friends, and began with Mr. S. C. Hall, who called by his request on Mrs. Lyon, Home not accompanying him.

After the visit, Mr. Hall related to Mr. Home what had passed. Mrs. Lyon said nothing on the subject of Spiritualism, but declared her intention of adopting Mr. Home, and asked her visitor what he thought she should settle on him. "I suggested," said Mr. Hall, "that two or three hundred a year would suffice," on which she said, "Oh, that's not enough."

"Finding from Mr. Hall's conversation," says Mr. Home in his affidavit, "that he thought her not only sane and in her right mind, but a very sharp business woman, who gave efficient reasons for what she had contemplated doing, I decided to accept what she offered me."

The day following, October 10th, Mr. Home and Mr. Hall called on Mrs. Lyon to suggest that she should delay executing her intention until she had considered it further. She refused, and said that she had determined to transfer at once to her adopted son a sum of £24,000. "When she said that she would give me £24,000, Mr. Hall said, 'Do, you good lady, take time and think this well over. Do not act so hastily.' And I joined with him in saying so; but she only said, 'What is £24,000 to me in comparison with having a son that I can love, and who will be kind to me?" (Affidavit of Mr. Home.)

On the day of this interview, but a few hours previous to it, Mrs. Lyon had written to Mr. Home naming £24,000 as the sum she intended to settle on ham. He found her letter waiting for him on IMS return as follows. The italics and small capitals represent the single and double underlinations of the writer.

"My dear Home, I have a desire to render you *independent* of the world, and having ample means for the purpose without abstracting from any needs or *comforts* of my own, I have the greatest satisfaction in now presenting you with and as an *entirely* FREE GIFT from me the sum of £24,000, and am, my dear sir, yours very truly and *respectfully*, "Jane Lyon."

Mr. Home accepted the gift of £24,000, and changed his name to Home-Lyon. In spite of the unanimous approval that his friends bestowed on the course he had taken, he sometimes doubted its wisdom. His advisers, one and all, looked on the impulsive action of Mrs. Lyon as a signal favour of Providence, that it would have been not only foolish but wrong to reject. But he could not forget that, in America, in Italy, and in France, offers of adoption had been made to him by persons who were all of them better bred and more amiable than Mrs. Lyon, and some of them as wealthy or wealthier; and that he had never regretted his grateful refusal of those offers. All his life he had studied to preserve an absolute independence of thought and action. He soon found reason to fear that, in becoming the adopted son of Mrs. Lyon, he had sacrificed that independence.

On becoming the possessor of the £24,000, his first thought was of others. The aunt who had adopted him as a child passed the last years of her life in the house her nephew bought for her.

In November, 1866, Mrs. Lyon unexpectedly asked her adopted son for the name of his solicitor; and a few days later Mr. Home was astonished to find that, without giving him any hint of her intention, she had ordered a will to be drawn up constituting him heir to her fortune.

The lawyer who received her instruction, Mr. W. M. Wilkinson, remonstrated strongly against them.

"I reminded her," he stated in his affidavit, "of what she had already done for Mr. Home, and that she might be disappointed with him, or he with her. ... I asked her in the most pointed way if what she was doing was in consequence of any spiritual control or orders, and she said it was not, but was her own unbiased wish and determination. She assured me in the most positive manner that in what she was doing she was not influenced by any such reasons, but that she had taken the greatest liking to Mr. Home, and found him all that she could wish; and it was a delight to her to find that she could make such a good use of her money. ... I told her that, as I was a friend of Mr. Home, it would be much more satisfactory to me if she would advise with some other solicitor; but she said she was perfectly satisfied with me and would not go to anyone else, that I had cautioned her in every way that anyone else could, and she quite understood what she was about, and was a good woman of business."

Dr. Hawksley and Mr. Rudall, two gentlemen of high standing and unimpeachable character, were the witnesses to the will. In their presence Mr. Wilkinson repeated all his former cautions to Mrs. Lyon. She again replied that she was influenced by no spirit communications, and insisted on signing the will.

Early in December 1866, Mr. Home formally assumed the

name of Home-Lyon. Without saying anything to him, Mrs. Lyon wrote on this occasion to the same solicitor:

"7th December, 1866."

"My dear Mr. Wilkinson, On the occasion of my adopted son taking the name of Lyon, I wish to give ham a little surprise. I intend to add six thousand pounds to the twenty-four I have already given him, making a sum total of thirty thousand. Yours very truly, "Jane Lyon."

Mr. Wilkinson in reply once more suggested that, as he had known Mr. Home long and intimately, she should employ another solicitor to transact the business. Mrs. Lyon refused. "I am perfectly satisfied with your legal advice," she wrote, "and wish for no other adviser;" and very soon afterwards informed him of her desire to transfer a further sum of £30,000 to Mr. Home.

The solicitor not only wrote but called on her to remonstrate. She explained that she wished to save legacy duty by transferring this large portion of her fortune to her adopted son during her lifetime.

"I told her," says Mr. Wilkinson in his affidavit, "that the mere question of saving legacy duty was not to be considered against the all important question of divesting herself of her property, and that it was impossible to say that she might not afterwards regret giving so large a sum to one whom she had known so short a time. She said she would do it, and desired me to have the deed made out in his name. I asked her if she were desirous of doing this in consequence of any spirit communications, for that, if so, I could have nothing to do with it on any such ground. She said that she was not influenced by anything but the intention of placing him in an independent position and saving the legacy duty, as she was satisfied she should never change her mind."

On Monday, January 7, 1867, Mr. Wilkinson again called on Mrs. Lyon.

"I saw her," he stated," and had a long conversation with her as to her intended gift to the defendant Home. She expressed the greatest affection for him, and said that she was determined to carry it out in the way proposed. I reiterated to her all the old arguments. I again warned her against being in any way influenced by any spirit-communications, or by anything but her unbiased reason, and she assured me that she was not. On this occasion she told me that she had received the same advice from Lady Dunsany, who had told her not to be guided in any worldly matters by any communications, and she did not intend to be. She said, whatever happened, she had more money than she could want, and she was only too glad to make Daniel independent after all the obloquy he had suffered."

The winter of 1866 was very severe in England, and Mr. Home's health grew worse and worse. Under the advice of his physicians, he tried frequent change of air, and visited Brighton, Malvern, Hastings, Torquay, and other health-resorts. All this while Mrs. Lyon remained in London, and he saw her only during his occasional residences there.

The will that Mrs. Lyon had made in favour of Mr. Home was far from being her first testament. He discovered that she had executed and revoked at least five wills, in favour of different persons.

He found her untruthful, ignorant, violent, capricious one day testifying the warmest affection for him, the next loading him with abuse. A feeling of aversion gradually began to contend with the affectionate gratitude that had at first been his only sentiment towards her. On her side, Mrs. Lyon wearied of her caprice as she had wearied of twenty others that had preceded it; and the more speedily because she found herself, in her own brutal phrase, "tied to a dying man." She had taken a violent dislike to Home's little son; and the thought that, if she and Mr. Home died, the boy would inherit her property made her talk of changing her will. She was grievously disappointed with her reception in the society where Home moved, and to which he had introduced her. His friends saw as little as possible of her, for she was as ignorant of the ways and habits of well bred people, as destitute of their breeding. With this disappointment working on her violent temper, and surrounded by persons who had sought her acquaintance in the hope of diverting her wealth from Mr. Home to themselves, she determined to recall a portion at least of her gifts; and in May, 1867, consulted a retired barrister who was acquainted both with Home and herself, as to the means she should adopt to recover the second sum of £30,000 that she had forced upon her adopted son. "She told him," says Mr. Home in his affidavit, "that she did not wish to disturb the gifts of £24,000 and £6000 to me, but thought she had been too lavish in bestowing on me the subsequent gift."

Home, who was at Malvern, knew nothing of these proceedings. He returned to London early in June; and his doctor having prescribed a visit to some of the German baths, he informed Mrs. Lyon of the fact, and invited her to accompany him. "I wish you would go with me," he wrote. "I have been out of London more than I wished, but I have ever asked you to join me."

"My dear Daniel," wrote Mrs. Lyon in reply: "I have this instant got a letter from you that you are packing up to go away. I perfectly approve of your determination. I think it will do you good; and be assured I wish you every enjoyment, and that of health in particular."

The letter closed with a request that Home would call on her. He went at once: and throwing aside the pretended affection of her letter, she demanded, in language of outrageous abuse and insult, the return of the trust-deed that had conveyed the second £30,000 to Mr. Home.

No situation could be more painful and perplexing than that in which he found himself suddenly placed. He knew that, if he surrendered the trust-deed thus insultingly demanded of him, the world would declare that he had yielded to Mrs. Lyon's threats because he feared to stand a lawsuit. He consulted his friends in London. One and all advised him not to give up the deed. In spite, however, of their opinion that he could both legally and honourably retain the whole £60,000 bestowed on him, Mr. Home finally determined to return that second £30,000 to which he supposed Mrs. Lyon's demand to be still limited; but only on condition that be received from her a written retraction of the charges she had made against his honesty and that of his friends. He wrote to make this offer. "I was wholly ignorant at the time," he explained in his affidavit, "that she had filed her Bill in Chancery, making charges against me and my friends. I was in very feeble health at the time, and required rest and freedom from anxiety. I had no ill feeling towards the plaintiff; and I wrote without taking advice of any one, and for the sake of peace and quiet. Had I been aware of such Bill having been filed, I most certainly would have scorned to make or accept any offer of compromise."

Dishonestly suppressing the facts that Mr. Home's intended journey to Germany was prescribed by his medical adviser, that he had requested her to accompany him, and that she had expressed entire approval of his intention, Mrs. Lyon obtained a writ of *Ne exeat regno*, upon which Mr. Home was arrested on the 18th of June, 1867. He was liberated the following day, on depositing in the Court of Chancery the deeds of gift relating to the £60,000; and from the moment of his arrest his friends Lord Adare and Lord Lindsay had never left him. Their generous sympathy and companionship lightened the trial of these twenty-four hours to Mr. Home; but coming at a time when he was already prostrated by illness, the shock to his sensitive nature had all but proved fatal. It was three months before he had sufficiently recovered to give any instructions to his legal advisers.

On adopting Mr. Home, Mrs. Lyon had taken possession of the jewellery, lace, & c., that had belonged to his wife. She retained them even after the close of the lawsuit, and some of the most valuable objects were never restored.

In April 1868, the case of "Lyon against Home" came on for hearing before Vice Chancellor Giffard without a jury. The plaintiff declared that she had been influenced to adopt Mr. Home as her son by communications which she had believed to proceed from the spirit of her late husband. She asserted that during her first visit to the Spiritual Athenaeum the following words were spelt out by rappings on the table: "My beloved Jane, I am Charles, your own beloved husband. I live to bless you." Yet by her own sworn statement, she was an entire stranger to Mr. Home when that interview took place, and he had no means of knowing that her husband's name had been Charles.

Here I may state a fact, known to others besides myself. When Mrs. Lyon first manifested the intention of reclaiming part of her gifts, Mr. Home was recommended by at least one of the friends whom he consulted to place the money where it would be out of the reach of any English Court, but has honourable nature rejected the advice.

The proof of *mens eonscia recti* that he craves in investing the whole of the fortune bestowed on him in English securities, puzzled even the most prejudiced and hostile of his critics. "It is difficult to understand," said the *Daily News* of May 2, 1868, "why the object of the widow's motherly bounty, and more than motherly affection, should have invested the large sums so prodigally cast at his feet in securities within the reach of a widow's second thoughts and of the Court of Chancery. These mysteries are beyond our ken."

In his answer to the plaintiff's affidavit, Mr. Home absolutely denied that any allusion to the late Charles Lyon had been made when Mrs. Lyon called on him at the *Spiritual Athenaeum*, or that any spiritual manifestations whatever took place. With regard to the second interview, he similarly swore that no spirit communications were received. At the third interview, and after she had declared her intention to adopt him, a manifestation took place which Mr. Home fully described in his affidavit. It did not refer to the proposed adoption.

Such are the prejudice and dishonesty of the world that the English press in general treated Mrs. Lyon's account of what passed on these occasions as if it had been worthy of credence conveniently ignoring the fact that the witnesses called by Mr. Home had convicted her of false swearing in very many other particulars of her evidence, and that the Vice Chancellor had declared it to be impossible to believe her on her oath. In order to fling a stone however muddy at Mr. Home, the press calmly assumed that, although the plaintiff stood convicted of falsehood in almost every other particular of her evidence, she was telling the truth as to those interviews at which only herself and the defendant had been present.

Mr. Home could call no witnesses to what had passed at interviews where no witnesses had been. All he could do, he did; he brought forward witness after witness to prove that she had never attributed her adoption of him to the communications she now pretended to have received, and had uniformly declared that she was influenced only by her affection for him in the course she had taken.

Take, for instance, the evidence of Mr. Home's lawyer, Mr. Wilkinson, a solicitor in large practice, whose bona -fides the

Vice-Chancellor held to be fully established, and whose costs he ordered Mrs. Lyon to pay as he ordered her to pay her own costs.

"So far as it relates to matters within my own knowledge," said Mr. Wilkinson in his affidavit, "the plaintiff's affidavit is almost wholly untrue, and is at variance with the facts, or with her own previous and repeated statements to me. ... I was the friend of the defendant Home, though I seldom saw him. I have always found him a person of honour and integrity; end when I heard that he had been adopted by the plaintiff, and that she had given him £24,000, I was very glad of it, as a compensation for the unmerited abuse to which he has been subjected. When, however, that munificent gift had been made to him, I thought it was enough for all purposes, and any further gifts I considered quite unnecessary. This made me very independent in advising her, and very determined that she should do nothing more for him upon my advice. I never told Mr. Home or any other person what I intended to do in the way of questioning her when I took her will, but I questioned her in the strictest way. ... If she had at the time she signed her will the conviction that she was influenced by any spiritual cause, she not only concealed it from me, but resolutely denied it, and gave as her reason that she did it out of her liking for Mr. Home, and to make him independent.

"She assured me repeatedly that she was not influenced in any way by spirit-communications, but only by her liking for him, and that if he were not a medium at all, she should have the same affection for him. If it were otherwise, she is alone to blame for concealing it from me and constantly denying it, but I spoke to her so often against being led away by communications that the subject got quite threadbare between us. ... I have given her the same advice, both when by ourselves and in the presence of the, defendant Home; and on such occasions he has always said the same to her. I could have done nothing more than I did, except refusing altogether to carry out her strict orders; and had I done so, and she had gone to another solicitor, and had told him the same as she told me, he would have had no alternative but to act on her instructions.

"The plaintiff has repeatedly told me that she acted altogether on her own judgment in what she was doing, and that it was the greatest pleasure to her to have made such a use of her money, and to have found one who was such a comfort to her."

How are these sworn statements of Mr. Wilkinson to be reconciled with the plaintiff's assertion that spirit-communications had led her to adopt Mr. Home?

What she had stated to Mr. Wilkinson concerning the motives of the adoption, she stated to many besides, some of whom came forward in Court to swear to the fact, while others, residing at a distance from London, sent affidavits. She had told Lady Dunsany, for instance, that she was not influenced by any spirit communications and did not intend to be. She had made declarations of a similar nature to Mr. Gerald Massey the poet and to numerous other persons whose names are not before me.

Among the papers in my possession that relate to the Lyon law suit is an affidavit made by Dr. Robert Chambers, whom, on one of his visits to London, Mr. Home had introduced to Mrs. Lyon. I copy this interesting document. It will be seen that Mrs. Lyon spoke to Dr. Chambers, as she had spoken to others, of her own visions previous to her acquaintance with Mr. Home, and added that he identified him with the person she had seen in those visions. A very different story this from the one she afterwards told in Court, when all mention of her visions was suppressed, and in their place imaginary communications made at her first interviews with Mr. Home were substituted.

"I, Robert Chambers, LL.D., make oath and say as follows: I was introduced by Mr. Home-Lyon to Mrs. Lyon, the plaintiff, at her house in Albert Terrace, on the 4th of December last. I congratulated her on her recent act of adopting Mr. Home as her son, as I knew him to be worthy of her affection, as well as the fortune she had conferred upon him. She entered into a recital of what had led her to do so. Mr. Home was a recent acquaintance, and on seeing him she had recognized him as the person pointed out by her husband in vision. Her motives had sprung solely from her own visions. Both on this occasion, and when I met Mrs. Lyon with her adopted son at the house of a lady of rank in Onslow Square (Lady Dunsany), Mrs. Lyon spoke of and to Mr. Home entirely as an affectionate mother.

"I have known Mr. Home for many years, and believe him to

be of irreproachable character. "Robert Chambers."

Sworn at St. Andrews, the fifth day of September, 1867."

In a letter written to Mr. Home shortly before making this affidavit, Dr. Chambers says: "She" (Mrs. Lyon) "mentioned a habit of visions from her youth." But surely for such a habit even English law could not hold Mr. Home responsible? It was his misfortune, not his fault that on seeing him Mrs. Lyon should have identified him with the figure seen in her visions, on whom her ancient affections were to be lavished.

The pleadings in the suit of Lyon v. Home closed on May 1st, 1868, and the Vice-Chancellor reserved judgment. The trial had, in his own words, "quite discredited the plaintiff's testimony;" and the one or two persons who in some degree supported her statements consisted of those very people who were most deeply interested in seeing her gifts to Mr. Home revoked. His testimony, on the other hand, was unshaken; and his witnesses consisted of persons of rank and character, unbiased by those interested motives of which the plaintiff's witnesses might very reasonably be suspected. At the close of the case, those of his friends who knew little of law and were sanguine enough to suppose that equity would rule a Court of Equity, even when Spiritualism was in question, predicted confidently that he would win. Their expectation was shared mirabile dictu! by an authority so learned in the law as the *Law Times*. In its issue of May 2nd 1868, that journal said:

"Does she" (Mrs. Lyon) "show that she was imposed upon by the defendant? Was it not rather that she imposed upon herself. This is not the common case of a weak mind enthralled by a strong one of advantage taken of ignorance. When feeling is put aside, and the strangeness of the Spiritualists' creed forgotten, and we look only at the fact, that a woman of more than common sagacity gave to a man, whom she believed to possess certain miraculous powers, a large sum of money, from a desire, then sincerely entertained by her, to benefit the object of her admiration, we shall probably come to the conclusion that no sufficient case has been shown for the interference of the law to undo the act of benevolence, now that her feelings towards the object of it have changed, and she repents of her generosity. Such a principle so established would be applicable to cases far beyond the range of Spiritualism. It would affect many religious and not a few charitable gifts."

On the other hand, Mr. Home's counsel, Mr. Henry Matthews, Q.C had warned him to be prepared for an adverse judgment; and one of his friends, a medical man in large practice, wrote to him:

"B. Said last autumn to me, 'they will give it against Home, whatever the evidence be.' Sir W. Bovill told me a week ago, 'The precedents are against Home, though the evidence is for him.' Lawyers go all by precedent, I find."

Delivered towards the end of May, 1868, the Vice Chancellor's judgment was adverse to Mr. Home on the grounds I have already stated: that the proved false swearing of the plaintiff was immaterial, and that English law in a suit like this reversed the ordinary maxims of jurisprudence, and held a defendant guilty unless he could prove himself innocent. But, to the mind of every unprejudiced critic the evidence called for Mr. Home had established his innocence. The Vice-Chancellor seems to have felt that awkward fact, or why, besides ordering Mrs. Lyon to pay her own costs, did he seek to give a colour of reason to his judgment by denouncing Spiritualism in general terms, as "well calculated to delude the vain, the weak, the foolish, and the superstitious." Had his candour been equal to his prejudices, Vice Chancellor Giffard would have said in so many words: "The law requires the defendant to prove that he did not exercise undue influence over the plaintiff. He has called evidence to show that he did not, and the evidence is undisproved. Nevertheless, I decide against him; for, as I hold Spiritualism to be a delusion, I must necessarily hold the plaintiff to be the victim of a delusion, and no amount of evidence will convince me to the contrary."

The reductio ad absurdum of the Vice Chancellor's reasoning was wittily set forth in the *Malvern News* of June 6th, 1868:

"We do not see how poor Mr. Home is henceforth ever to retain a bequest or gift from anyone with whom he has ever sat at a table, for that may be construed into a séance, and that again into an influence destructive of the validity of the gift."

"The woman Lyon," says the same article in the *Malvern News*, "again and again stated that she had believed in Spiritualism long before she knew of Home's existence. She swore that he persuaded her to give the money, but offered not a little of evidence to rebut the mass of written and oral evidence that he had never attempted to persuade her."

From beginning to end of the trial there was not a particle of evidence to show that Home had used direct influence, based on spirit communication, to cause the old woman to give her money in the deliberate yet speedy way in which she did. Even the judge admitted that there was no such evidence."

Mr. Home was subsequently taunted by the multitude of his prejudiced critics with not having prosecuted an appeal against the judgment. Why should he have done so? His object in defending the suit had been to vindicate his character, and that he had done in the eyes of all whose opinion he valued. His friends did not fall from him; on the contrary, they crowded the court during the ten days the suit lasted, welcomed him when he entered and left the building; and both before and after the judgment was delivered, those friends, who included persons of the highest standing in English society, gave generous and open testimony that their esteem for him remained unchanged, because in the evidence given during the suit of Lyon v. Home there was nothing that should cause him to forfeit it.

English law being what it was, and popular prejudices against Spiritualism what they were, it would have been useless for Mr. Home to appeal. Any fresh judges before whom the suit came would almost certainly have shared the prejudices of the Vice-Chancellor against Spiritualism; and sharing his prejudices, they would have confirmed his judgment. Against a foregone conclusion facts fight in vain.

The brief and imperfect outline of the suit Lyon v. Home that I have given in the foregoing pages will prove to any impartial reader that, if Mr. Home lost his case, he vindicated his character. As to what passed during his first two or three interviews with the plaintiff, he could but set his oath against hers; and her oath, on the declaration of the Vice-Chancellor himself, was that of a person who could not be believed. She pretended that on those occasions messages had been rapped out in which she was told to adopt him as her son. Mr. Home conclusively established that at the time of the adoption, and for several months afterwards, not only had she made no mention of such messages she had, times without number, emphatically denied being influenced by any spirit-communications. On that head, the evidence of Mr. Wilkinson would alone be conclusive, but it was confirmed by a number of other witnesses.

When Home passed from earth, various leading English journals in their notices of his death grossly misstated the grounds on which judgment was delivered against him in the suit of Lyon v. Home. Vice Chancellor Giffard, with all his prejudices, had gone no further than to declare that putting the plaintiff's evidence aside as worthless the defendant had failed to show to the Vice Chancellor's satisfaction that the gifts of Mrs. Lyon were the well-understood acts of a reasonable being. Yet the *Times* of June 24, 1886, could state: "By 'messages' which were rapped out on tables, she was induced to execute deeds of gift to him covering sums of money amounting in all to about thirty thousand pounds." Had the writer of these words taken the trouble to consult the records of the Chancery suit, he would have found that the only evidence as to these pretended messages was contained in the statements of the plaintiff, and that her testimony was discredited as perjured by the judge.

"Mr. Home," said a discreditable article in the *Daily News* of the same date as the *Times* leader, "explained the meaning of this utterance from another world to be that twenty four thousand pounds' worth of stock should be invested for him in the Bank of England. Soon afterwards he declared it to be the spirit's will that Mrs. Lyon should leave him everything she possessed."

Compare these statements not with the actual facts on record but simply with the less garbled account published by the same journal in May, 1868, immediately after the Vice Chancellor had delivered judgment. "Mrs. Lyon," said the *Daily News* of that earlier date, "proposed to be Mr. Home's mother. She insisted on his acceptance of £30,000 as a free and absolute gift and of an equal sum in reversion, subject to her life interest. Mr. Home had the necessary deeds prepared with no undue haste, and with reasonable caution."

How to account for this extraordinary difference between

two versions of the Lyon lawsuit published at different times by the same journal? Probably by the fact that when the first version was published Mr. Home was still within the protection of the law of libel. English law, I am told, does not account it any offence to libel those who have passed from earth.

"There is no such thing as fair play in this world," says Mr. Serjeant Cox in one of his letters to Mr. Home; "at least, I have never met with it." Home might justly have echoed the words after the Lyon lawsuit. I will only add that the resignation with which Home supported every trial of has life is perhaps an even rarer virtue than fair play and justice.

CHAPTER 9

England

Evidence of the Earl of Dunraven and Lord Adare. The Dialectical Society. Evidential séances. Insensibility to heat. The effects of faith. Light and dark mediumship. Spirit music. "A hundred instances of levitation." The Levitation at Ashley House. Dr. Carpenter's misstatement. Captain Wynne's evidence. Dr. Carpenter as a Universal Spiritualist.

COMPARATIVELY FULL records have been preserved of séances with Mr. Home during the years 1867-9. The phenomena witnessed were remarkable both for their nature and their variety. One of their frequent investigators at this time was the present Earl of Crawford, then Lord Lindsay, whose scientific attainments might have been expected to secure for his evidence the impartial consideration of the scientific world; but the reception accorded to it only demonstrated how very timid, prejudiced, and unfair that world can be.

A record of eighty séances with Mr. Home was preserved by the Earl of Dunraven and his son, then Lord Adare, in a volume printed for private circulation. In the preface the writers relate that the occurrences of each day were noted down at the time, that when both had been present at a séance both drew up an account of the manifestations, and insured accuracy by comparing them; and that, still further to test the correctness of the narrative, the record of every séance was sent to the remaining persons who had been present, with the request that they would state whether it coincided with their own recollections. Every answer was in the affirmative. It is added that, while nothing had been inserted that did not occur, or had been exaggerated that did, it was found necessary to omit a great deal a very important fact to bear in mind. In all such narratives it is precisely the most vital part of the tale that is left untold, the communication of private matters to the persons present at the séance, and unknown to Home.

"Even in the original letters to my father," said Lord Adare, "I was obliged to omit a few circumstances of great interest; in some cases on account of their having reference to persons who did not wish those circumstances to be mentioned."

It was always so, or almost always. Sometimes the witness would not speak, because the communications he had received so intimately concerned himself; sometimes he could not, because the startling facts with which he was conversant had reference to other persons, who declined to make them public to the world. It is thus that much remarkable evidence received and verified at séances with Home and the late Earl of Crawford and Balcarres has been lost to the world. There are very few who, like Lords Lindsay and Dunraven, have placed the history of their investigations on record.

An inquiry into the phenomena of Spiritualism was conducted by the Dialectical Society in 1869; evidence, both oral and written, being received, while various sub-committees were appointed to hold séances. The committee appointed to meet Mr. Home contained some of the most incredulous members of the Society, among others Mr. Bradlaugh and Dr. Edmonds. Lord Adare and Lord Lindsay attended the séances, which, to the number of four, were held in a fully lit room. The manifestations did not extend beyond slight raps and movements of the table; and the illness of Mr. Home preventing an extension of the inquiry, the committee were only able to report that nothing material had occurred; adding that "during the inquiry Mr. Home afforded every facility for examination."

It is a pity that circumstances prevented the Society's committee from holding fourteen or twenty séances with Mr. Home instead of four. In such a case numerous séances might be necessary to enable the spirits to establish conditions rendering manifestations possible. In what the difficulty of establishing such conditions consisted it would be impossible to say, but that the mere fact of scepticism did not constitute it was a hundred times proved. No scepticism could have been more thorough or aggressive than that of Dr. Elliottson when he came to his first séance with Home at Dieppe, but the invisible forces went to work at once. Similarly, Thackeray,

Chambers, Mr. John Bright, Mr. Crookes, Dr. Huggins, and very many others that I might name for instance, the Emperors of Russia, France, and Germany were completely incredulous concerning the phenomena when they first sat with Mr. Home; but in none of these cases did the scepticism of the investigator paralyse the manifestations. When Mr. Home sat with the Dialectical Society's committee, either his variable power was almost absent at the time, or his state of health was such that the power, although present, could not venture to manifest itself.

It is curious to notice with what ardour certain zealots of disbelief maintain that the negative results of one or two séances constitute an affirmative of their incredulity. If men of science are forced to avow how little they comprehend of the nature of the visible universe what must be their ignorance of the nature of a gift so mysterious as that of Home, which passed the limits of human experience, and whose source was connected with the origin and mysteries of our spiritual being.

In a previous chapter I have collected instances of the proofs of identity received at the séances of Home. The smallness of their number, as I have already explained, is not due to the fact that these convincing tokens were seldom forthcoming; on the contrary, they were the invariable characteristics of his séances, and referred constantly to matters of the most intimate and remarkable nature. In the present chapter I shall deal chiefly with physical manifestations; but first I am enabled to add one or two interesting items to the facts establishing identity that have been already given. Several of the séances described by Lord Adare took place at the house of Mrs. Hennings, a lady residing in Thicket Road, Anerley, who became a dearly valued friend of Mr. Home. She has very kindly written for me a narrative of some of the experiences that made her a Spiritualist, from which I extract the following details:

"At a séance in 1869, Mrs. Jencken, senior, Lord Adare, Mrs. Scott Russell, and Mr. Bergheim being also present, Mr. Home fell into the trance condition, rose from his seat, paced the room, and then knelt down by me, saying, 'George is here' (meaning my nephew, whom he had never met, and who had recently passed away, in consequence of being thrown from his horse. He had held a high legal position, and was employed against Mr. Home in the Lyon trial). 'He wants to say something, but will not say it through me, from prejudice; therefore I have it from other spirits.'

"Home then said to me: 'Do you remember that George, as a boy, had an accident at your house in Dulwich, where, having teased a dog, the animal flew at him, threw him down, and bit him severely in the groin?' I did remember the occurrence perfectly, though it had occurred many years before; for the severe nature of the wound had caused us great alarm." Of another communication Mrs. Hennings writes: "As a proof of recognized identity this case stands unrivalled." Her narrative of the incident is as follows:

"Séance of October 26th, 1867. Present, Mrs. Jencken, senior, Mrs. Hennings, and Mr. Percival. The second of the séances especially addressed to me, for the purpose of establishing the identity of communicant spirit friends. The following circumstances occurred:

"D. D. Home fell into the trance state; and after giving a few words to each of the party from, or relating to, departed spirit friends, drew a chair close to me, took both my hands in his, and addressed me in the following words:

'The night before your father passed away, you played whist with him. When it was his turn to play, he hesitated, and looked upwards with a smile, as if entranced – that was the first glimpse he had of the spirit sphere. With the dawn, he passed away without pain.

'He had previously communicated with Mr. Hennings, who told him "that he had taken care of Mary," in consequence of which your father left you but little in comparison with the others. Now, through me, he wishes to assure you this did not arise from any want of affection, but only from a misapprehension of the state of affairs.'

"Home then returned to his former seat; but, looking across the room, his face became radiant with smiles, as he repeated: 'He is so pleased so pleased.'

"Mr. Home had never seen my father, nor heard anything about him; and most wonderful to me was this detail of such long-past events, known only to myself. "M. Hennings."

Mrs. Scott Russell, who was one of the circle when Mrs. Hennings received the remarkable proof of her nephew's identity narrated by her above, was the wife of the eminent engineer of that name. She was present at numerous séances with Mr. Home, and the communications she received entirely convinced her of the reality of spirit communion. When he was about to bring out his second volume of autobiography, Home consulted Mrs. Russell with regard to the publication of her name as a witness to some of the facts narrated, and received the following reply:

"Westwood Lodge, Sydenham.

"My dear friend, Certainly I have no objection to my name being inserted as present at your séances. I thank God for it, and shall always gratefully bear witness to what I have been permitted to see. Always affectionately yours,

"Harriette Scott Russell."

In spite of this kind and brave permission, Mr. Home, with his invariable delicate consideration for his friends, omitted Mrs. Scott Russell's name from his book. "I never forget," writes Mrs. Scott Russell to Mr. Home in 1880, "my deep debt of gratitude to you for the faith which I believe I never should have received through any other channel." A number of English ladies and gentlemen who had been present at séances with Mr. Home gave evidence of their experiences before the committee of the Dialectical Society. Among them was a much esteemed friend, Mrs. Honywood, who, like Mrs. Hennings, had been present at several of the séances recorded by Lord Adare, including some of the most remarkable. I have received narratives of manifestations witnessed at the séances in question from two or three of the most frequent sitters, and have compared them with the records contained in Lord Dunraven's book. In every case the various accounts agree perfectly; and therefore in describing the manifestations that Mrs. Honywood, Mrs. Hennings, Mr. and Mrs. S. C. Hall, the Earls of Dunraven and Crawford, Captain C. Wynne, and some fifty or sixty other persons witnessed during the years of 1867–9, I shall generally be enabled to do so on the authority of more than one of the beholders who were present. Sometimes I have two or three records by different sitters of the phenomena of the same séance. It is obvious that, within the limits of a single volume intended to include the whole range of Mr. Home's life on earth, I cannot print them all textually.

In their evidence given before the Dialectical Society, Mrs. Honywood and the Earl of Crawford described the very startling phenomena that occurred at a séance held on the 17th of March 1869, at the residence of a Mrs. E., who did not permit her name to be published.

I extract some of the most interesting particulars.

There were present Mrs. Honywood, Mrs. E, the Earl of Crawford (then Lord Lindsay), Captain Gerard Smith, of the Scots Fusilier Guards, and Mr. Home. The room was well lighted all the time of the séance:

"Mr. Home," deposed Mrs. Honywood and Lord Lindsay, "passed into a trance, and went to the table, on which stood a moderator lamp. Taking off the globe, he placed it on the table, and deliberately clasped the chimney of the lamp with both hands; then, advancing to the lady of the house, he asked her to touch it; but she refused, knowing it was hot. Mr. Home said, 'Have you no faith? Will you not trust in Dan if he says it is cool?' She replied, 'Certainly;' and, placing her fingers on the glass, exclaimed, 'Oh, it is not at all hot!' This was corroborated by Lord Lindsay and myself, who, in turn, laid our finger on the glass several times, to test it. Holding it towards Mr.–, Mr. Home turned, apparently addressing someone, and said: 'It is necessary, to confirm the faith of others, that it should be made hot for him.' Mr. now touched it; and exclaimed, 'You have indeed made it hot!' shaking his hand and showing me a red mark. So hot was the glass when the fourth person touched it, that it raised a blister, which I saw some days subsequently peeling."

The "Mr.–" who suffered to confirm the faith of others was Captain Smith, of the Scots Fusilier Guards. A letter from Mrs. Honywood to me relates this remarkable incident as follows. Mr. Home, be it remembered, was holding all the while, in a well-lighted room, the large glass chimney that Mrs. Honywood and Lord Lindsay had just touched and found cool:

"I placed my finger on the top part of the glass several times to test it. Each time the heat appeared to recede like a wave of the sea. I cannot describe the sensation in any other words, but the heat seemed to be withdrawn each time. Mr. Home then laughed, and said, turning to Captain S., 'We will make it hot for you!' Turning his head, he appeared to listen, and his expression changed; then, speaking in a sad tone of voice, he said: 'It is necessary, to confirm the faith of others, that the glass should be made hot for you.' Captain Smith now touched it, and cried out, 'By Jove! you have,' shaking his finger, and showing a red mark. He had a blister which lasted several days."

I resume the joint narrative of Mrs. Honywood and Lord Lindsay:

"Mr. Home then walked to the fireplace, and thrust the chimney among the red-hot coals, where he left it for four or five minutes, then took it in both hands. He went to the table, took a lucifer match from a box, and, handing it to the lady of the house, desired her to touch the glass with it. The match instantly ignited; and having called our attention to this fact, he observed: 'The tongue and lips are the most sensitive parts of the body,' and thrust the heated glass into his mouth, applying especially his tongue to it. ...

"Going to the fire, Mr. Home moved the red embers about with his hand, and selected a small red-hot coal, which he placed in the glass chimney. He approached Mrs. E.; and saying, 'I have a present for you,' shook it out on her white muslin dress. Catching up the coal in dismay, Mrs. E. tossed it to Lord Lindsay, who, unable to retain it in his hand, threw it from palm to palm, till he reached the grate and flung it in. While we were all looking at the white muslin dress and wondering that it was not singed or soiled, Mr. Home approached, and, in a hurt tone of voice, said: 'No, no, you will not find a mark. Did you think that we would injure your dress?'

This wonderful phenomenon of preservation from fire was repeated with a spray of white flowers, taken from a vase on the table, which flowers were held by Mr. Home in the fire of the grate and then in the smoke rising from the coals, without their being injured or their pure white colour so much as dimmed. Shortly afterwards Mr. Home awoke from his trance, and the séance closed.

Again and again was the phenomenon of the instantaneous

withdrawal of intense heat from burning coals and other objects, and its equally instantaneous restoration, witnessed at séances with Home. I could fill many pages with the names and narratives of those who beheld and tested the facts; but must limit myself to two or three extracts from the mass of testimony. In the narrative just given, it will be observed that the intensely hot lamp-glass was handled without harm by Mrs. Honywood and Lord Lindsay, as well as by Mr. Home; and the same innocuous contact with an intense heat was experienced by persons whose testimony is equally above suspicion, on each of the occasions about to be described. In all these cases it was declared by the spirits that, to prevent harm from happening, it was necessary for the person experimenting to have a perfect faith that no injury would be received.

The present Earl of Dunraven, while Lord Adare, was among those who had the opportunity of personally satisfying themselves that the invisibles at work could so deal with fire that it would not burn. In the winter of 1868, there was a séance at Mrs. Hennings' house at Anerley. The sitters consisted of Mrs. Hennings, Mrs. Jencken, senior, Lord Adare, Mr. Jencken, Mr. Saal, Mr. Hurt, and Mr. Home. A full relation of the séance was written by Lord Adare, and the most remarkable manifestation of the evening was also described by Mr. Jencken in one of the Spiritualist journals.

Mr. Home, in the trance-state, went to the fire, and with his hand stirred the red embers into flame. "Then, kneeling down," records Lord Adare, "he placed his face right among the burning coals, moving it about as though bathing it in water."

"He placed his hands and then his face in the flames and on the burning coals," says Mr. Jencken. "I had the amplest opportunity of watching the exact movements, and quite satisfied myself of the fact that Mr. Home touched the burning coals."

Taking from the fire a burning ember, "about twice the size of an orange," Mr. Home carried it to the sitters.

"Home held it within four or five inches of Mr. Saal's and Mr. Hurt's hands," relates Lord Adare. "They could not endure the heat. He came to me, and said: 'Now, if you are not afraid, hold out your hand.' I did so; and having made two rapid passes over my hand, he placed the coal in it. I must have held it for half a minute, long enough to have burned my hand fearfully: the coal felt scarcely warm. Home then took it away, laughed, and seemed much pleased."

At some of the séances at Anerley with Mrs. Hennings and her neighbours, the Jencken family, there was present Mr. J. H. Simpson, of 10, Campden Grove, Kensington, a gentleman of considerable scientific attainments and a total disbeliever in Spiritualism. I do not know that Mr. Simpson ever succeeded in convincing himself of the spiritual origin of the manifestations; but, after having submitted the phenomena witnessed by him at Anerley to every test he could contrive, he was compelled to admit that they were real and occurred independently of Mr. Home. That Mr. Simpson was a very keen and sceptical inquirer, the following fact may help to attest. He went to a "dark séance" in January 1868, with a "medium" who need not be named here; and, in spite of the obscurity, succeeded in demonstrating so plainly both the fact of fraud and the modus operandi that the proceedings came to an abrupt end. The letter to Mr. Home in which he narrates the whole occurrence concludes with the following words:

"There could be no greater contrast than that of the disgusting dark affair of last night with the beautiful, light-loving series of phenomena which I had the privilege of witnessing the previous night, thanks to yourself. Your sincerely obliged, J. H. Simpson."

In a paper read before the Dialectical Society in July 1869, Lord Lindsay thus narrates his night vision at Norwood and the proof afforded next morning that the form he had seen was no creation of his fancy:

"I first met Mr. Home at the house of a friend of his and mine, Mrs. Gregory; and when we left the party I asked him to come into my rooms in Grosvenor Square to smoke a cigar. I heard a shower of raps run along a beam that crosses the ceiling. This was the first thing of the sort I had ever heard; and naturally I was interested, and wished for more, but in vain: nothing more happened; and soon after he went away.

"On the Sunday following, I was asked by Mr. Jencken to

come to his house in Norwood to dine, and afterwards to have a séance. I went, and that evening I missed the last train to Crystal Palace, and had to stay at Norwood. I got a shakedown on a sofa in Home's room. I was just going to sleep, when I was roused by feeling my pillow slipping from under my head, and I could also feel what seemed to be a hand under it, which was pulling it away. Soon after this ceased.

"Then I saw at the foot of my sofa a female figure standing in profile to me, and asked Home if he saw anything. He answered, 'A woman, looking at me.' Our beds were at right angles to one another, and about twelve feet apart. I saw the features perfectly, and impressed them upon my memory. She seemed to be dressed in a long wrap, going down from the shoulders, and not gathered in at the waist. Home then said: 'It is my wife; she often comes to me.' And then she seemed to fade away.

"The next morning, before I went to London, I was looking at some photographs, and I recognized the face I had seen in the room upstairs overnight. I asked Mrs. Jencken who it was, and she said it was Home's wife."

Lord Lindsay also described in his paper various phenomena that he beheld after the disappearance of the figure, the following being one of the most striking:

"I saw on my knee a flame of fire about nine inches high. I passed my hand through it, bat it burnt on, above and below. The flame, which had been flitting about me, now left me, and crossed the room about four feet from the ground, and reached the curtains of Home's bed. These proved no obstruction; for the light went right through them, settled on his head, and then went out."

Lord Lindsay was another of the numerous witnesses whose experiences enabled them to testify that they had not only seen Mr. Home expose himself for minutes at a time to the contact of fire without being burned, but had experienced a similar protection in their own persons. "Eight times," he told the Dialectical Society, "I myself have held a red-hot coal in my hands without injury, when it scorched my face on raising my hand. Once I wished to see if they really would burn; and I said so, and touched a coal with the middle finger of my right hand. I got a blister as large as a sixpence. I instantly asked Home to give me the coal; and I held the part that had burnt me for three or four minutes in the middle of my hand without the least inconvenience."

Both Lord Lindsay and Lord Adare witnessed more than once the strange phenomenon of the alternate elongation and shrinking of the form of Mr. Home. It is my belief that this manifestation did great physical harm to him; fortunately, it was of rare occurrence. One of the most remarkable instances was witnessed in the year 1868 at the house of Mr. and Mrs. Hall. Among the persons present at the time was Mr. H. T. Humphreys, a journalist, who subsequently published an account of the occurrence, as follows:

"I formed one of a party of nine or ten. We sat in a room well lit with gas. Mr. Home was seen by all of us to increase in height to the extent of some eight or ten inches, and then sank to some six or eight inches below his normal stature. Having returned to his usual height, he took Lord Adare (now the Earl of Dunraven) and the Master of Lindsay (now the Earl of Crawford and Balcarres), and, placing one beside each post of the folding doors, lay down on the floor, touching the feet of one with his head and the feet of the other with his feet. He was then again elongated, and pushed both Lord Adare and the Master of Lindsay backward along the floor with his head and feet as he was stretched out, his arms and hands remaining motionless by his side."

Mr. S. C. Hall says that he measured the extent of this elongation, and found that Lord Lindsay and Lord Adare were pushed to a distance of more than seven feet apart, Mr. Home's head still touching the one, his feet the other.

The form seen by Lord Lindsay at Norwood, when he shared Home's room, was again seen on the evening of February 7th, 1869, by Viscount Adare, Captain Gerard Smith, and Dr. Gully, of Malvern, at the rooms of the first-named in London. The three were sitting with Mr. Home in a small room, the objects in which were dimly visible by the faint light that came in from the window, when Home was impressed to rise and place himself near the latter. Another form slowly revealed itself beside his that of Mrs. Home.

"Her form," wrote Lord Adare the next day, "gradually became apparent to us; she moved close to Home and kissed him. She stood beside him against the window, intercepting the light as a solid body, and appeared fully as material as Home himself; no one could have told which was the mortal body and which the spirit. It was too dark, however, to distinguish features. I could see that she had her full face turned towards us, and either that her hair was parted in the middle and flowed down over her shoulders, or that she had on what appeared to be a veil."

This was witnessed; be it noted, in Lord Adare's own rooms in London. At his request, Captain Gerard Smith wrote to him attesting the fact that he had equally beheld the form, and furnished his observations of the apparition in the following words:

"Home rose, and stood at the window with his right arm extended; and the spirit seemed to sweep down until it rested both hands on his outstretched arm, looking up into his face. From the position in which I sat the profile of the face was perfectly visible to me, and when the two faces approached each other to kiss, there was no apparent difference in the density of the two figures."

Apparitions of other persons than Mrs. Home are also related by Lord Adare to have been seen by him at different times. In August 1868, he beheld a luminous form standing at the foot of Home's bed; and at Adare Manor, in March 1869; a figure that was white and slightly luminous appeared to him. He approached it, and it vanished.

Mr. Home spent some weeks at Adare Manor in the early spring of 1869.

On the night of the 4th of March, Lord Dunraven, Lord Adare, Captain C. Wynne, and Mr. Home visited the ruins of the Abbey of Adare, and startling phenomena occurred. On March 12th, a remarkable séance was held at Garinish, a cottage of Lord Dunraven's on the Kerry coast. There were present Lord Dunraven, Lord Adare, Major Blackburn, and Mr. Home. After twice forming a circle without result, the sitters were about to give up the hope of manifestations for that evening, when Lord Adare felt the cold air blowing over him, the presence of which always heralded further phenomena. Manifestations sometimes occurred at séances when no such chill current had been noticed to pass round the circle; but I do not think there was ever an instance of its presence being remarked when it was not the precursor of other phenomena.

On this night at Garinish it heralded a séance full of interest. Home went into a trance, arranged the position of the chairs and tables in the room, as if for unseen guests, placed the miniature portrait of Mrs. Home on one table, and on another the photograph of a little friend of his who had lately passed away; all the while, says Lord Adare, appearing to consult with some presence invisible to the other sitters. He then put out the candles, leaving the little room (all the rooms at Garinish are very small) illuminated by the glow of the firelight; and taking his seat with the rest of the party, arranged two vases of flowers on the table, in such a way as to make with Pressensé's *Life of Christ*, which he had placed between them, the figure of a cross. Almost immediately afterwards he awoke from his trance.

Currents of cold air then blew round the circle very strongly, the table vibrated, rose clear of the ground, and remained for some time poised in the air. A hand formed itself above one of the vases of flowers placed on the small table round which the party of four were grouped, and carried a flower to Lord Dunraven. Lord Adare and Mr. Home saw the hand; the other two sitters only the flower moving through the air; whereupon Lord Dunraven remarked that he was very desirous also to see a hand. Presently one became distinctly visible to him just above the vase of flowers. The miniature of Mrs. Home was now brought from the other table. None but Home saw the hand that held it they could see only the miniature approach them and place itself gently upon Home's hands, as they rested on the table in full view. The photograph above referred to was next carried to the sitters in the same way; but this time Lord Adare distinctly saw a hand holding it, and soon afterwards a whole hand and arm, white and slightly luminous, that hovered in the air between the sitters and the window.

Again flowers were carried to the sitters; but the recipients saw no hand holding them, only the blossoms moving through the air. A book that lay on the other table, six or eight feet away from the circle, rose, floated through the air, and placed itself on the séance table. Hands were again seen, and the flowers that remained in the vases were stirred; then the round table from which Mrs. Home's miniature had been brought rose into the air, no one touching it and none of the sitters being near it, and placed itself gently on the larger oblong table at which the four persons present were seated. Immediately afterwards loud sounds like high pitched voices were heard at a little distance. The suspicion of ventriloquism was impossible; for Lord Adare relates that Mr. Home continued speaking during the whole time that these voices were heard, and that the louder he spoke the louder the sounds became. A lady who had retired to rest in the room beneath Mrs. Blackburn, told the others of the party at Garinish the next day, that she had heard a strange sound, and imitated them so well, that, says Lord Dunraven, we at once recognized that she had really heard the voices. No articulate words were distinguished, but the effect is described as having been most weird.

Manifestations similar to the wonderful phenomenon recorded at Garinish of spirit voices sounding in the air, while Mr. Home, by talking incessantly, negated the theory of ventriloquism, were not very rare occurrence. In August 1868, Lord Adare and Mr. Home were about to start for the Continent together; and on the eve of their departure Home came to stay at his friend's rooms in London. They had just retired for the night when a phenomenon attracted their attention, of which, to obviate any suspicion of exaggeration, I will cite Lord Adare's own description, written at the time:

"We both heard music, much the same as at Norwood, but more powerful and distinct. Home said that the music formed words; that, in fact, it was a voice speaking, and not instrumental music. I could hear nothing but the chords like an organ or harmonium played at a distance. Home became quite excited because I could not distinguish the words, thinking that, if I could not hear them, it must have been his imagination. He asked the spirits, if possible, to make the words sufficiently clear for me also to hear them. They said 'Yes' (by raps); and the music became louder and louder, until I distinctly heard the words, 'Hallelujah, praise the Lord, praise the Lord God Almighty.' It was no imagination, or the result of anxiety on my part to hear the same as Home did. Every now and then I could not distinguish words, although he said he could; but I repeatedly heard the words above mentioned as plainly as possible. I cannot in the least explain to you how the voice articulated; the words were not separately spoken, neither did it resemble a human voice. The sound was slightly reedy and metallic, not very unlike the vox humana on an organ. If you can imagine an organ pipe of some rather reedy stop speaking to you, it will be as near it as anything I can describe."

Of a similar, but less remarkable manifestation, that occurred during the third séance at which he was present, Lord Adare says:

"During the time the sounds were heard Home was talking, which I was glad of, as I wished to feel sure the sounds were not the result of ventriloquism on his part."

As already mentioned, the records of séances made by Lord Adare, Lord Lindsay, and others are chiefly confined to the physical manifestations witnessed. These embraced every variety of phenomena. Tables were raised in the air when neither Home nor any other person was touching them; chairs and sofas moved across the floor in full light when no one was near them; flowers, books, and other objects were carried to the sitters by hands that they sometimes saw distinctly, and that on other occasions were invisible to them; music was played without the touch of any mortal hand on the instrument, and was frequently heard when no instrument of any sort was there. It need hardly be remarked that at those séances to which accordions were brought to see if they would be played upon, it was always one or more of the sitters who brought the accordions, and never Mr. Home. At Malvern, for instance, in November, 1867 (present an American lady, Mrs. Thayer, Lord Adare, whose first séance it was; and a total disbeliever in Spiritualism, Mr. Earl), Mrs. Thayer sent out a servant to borrow an accordion from a friend, and it played, first an air resembling a voluntary on the organ, and then an air asked for by Mr. Earl. At Adare Manor, on March 4th, 1869, Captain Wynne fetched an accordion. It played very beautifully, both while held by Mr. Home with one hand and when his hand was withdrawn. The air, "Oft in the Stilly Night," was softly played; and the late Earl of Dunraven, who was one of the sitters, records that this air had many years before been one of his greatest favourites. The room in which the séance was held was lighted by one candle and a fire.

No séance with Mr. Home was ever held in total darkness; but occasionally messages were rapped out, desiring the lights to be momentarily extinguished, in order that the phenomenon of the production of other lights by the spirits might be witnessed to advantage. These evanescent, but wonderful manifestations, were of a very varied character. Sometimes a white, pure light would fill the room, rendering every object distinctly visible; sometimes vivid meteors darted through the air, or rested on the heads and hands of the sitters. The ridiculous theories thrown out by persons who were never present at a séance with Mr. Home did not suggest themselves to the minds of the investigators who beheld and were impressed by these strange phenomena. "I have taken precautions to avoid being imposed upon by phosphorized oil, or other means," wrote Mr. Crookes, in the *Quarterly Journal of Science* for January 1874. "Moreover, many of these lights are such as I have tried to imitate artificially, but cannot." Yet Mr. Crookes, who could not in his laboratory imitate these lights that were beheld in the houses of a hundred different people during séances with Mr. Home, is one of the most distinguished of modern chemists. The notes of Mr. Crookes on *Luminous Appearances* refer principally, but not entirely, to his experiences with Mr. Home. The following describe phenomena witnessed at séances with Home.

"I have seen," says Mr. Crookes, "luminous points of light darting about and settling on the heads of different persons; I have had questions answered by the flashing of a bright light a desired number of times in front of my face. I have had an alphabetic communication given by luminous flashes occurring before me in the air, whilst my hand was moving about amongst them. In the light, I have seen a luminous cloud hover over a heliotrope on a side table, break a sprig off, and carry the sprig to a lady."

These luminous appearances were sometimes perceptible to the touch as well as to the sight. On November 24th, 1868, Lord

Lindsay and Mr. Home returned from Norwood about 11 pm to the rooms of Lord Adare in London; and, together with the latter, sat down at a table, the room being nearly dark. It may be noted here that the few séances that Mr. Home held in a dim light (never in total darkness) were with friends who had already seen much of the phenomena in strong light, and were convinced of their reality. On this occasion a variety of manifestations occurred, one of which was that luminous bodies, described by Lord Adare as "balls of light," flitted about the room, and sometimes touched the sitters, feeling to the latter "like a material substance and highly electrical."

Lord Adare, Lord Lindsay, &c., were frequently witnesses of that singular manifestation described in an early chapter, the retention on the surface of a table inclined at an angle not far from the perpendicular of the various objects that had been lying there before the table was tilted. During a séance at Mrs. Hennings' house at Anerley, Home, in a trance, brought a book to Lord Adare, and placed the hand of the latter flat upon the cover that was uppermost. Raps came on the volume; and Home then withdrew his own hand from it, leaving the book suspended in air beneath Lord Adare's open hand. "My fingers," says Lord Adare, "were not near the edges, my hand was extended flat upon the cover. I could not have grasped and retained the book in any way; it simply adhered to my hand. The book felt to me as though supported from beneath by a cushion or column of air."

The most startling of the hundred or more recorded instances of the levitation of Mr. Home was witnessed by Lord Lindsay, Lord Adare, and Captain C. Wynne. Before turning to it, I may add to the numerous instances already given of the more frequent physical phenomena, the following narrative of a séance in London. Mrs. Honywood, who was present, has kindly furnished it to me from her notes made at the time.

"On the 23rd of June, 1869," writes Mrs. Honywood, "I was invited by Mr. and Mrs. S. C. Hall to meet Mr. Home for a séance. We sat at a heavy round table, seven in number; Mr. and Mrs. Hall, Mrs. Senior, Lord Louth, Mr. Musgrave, Mr. Home, and myself. After quietly talking for a little while, raps were heard and vibrations felt in the table and floor. Before a séance Mr.

Home always took off all his rings, lest inadvertently they might make any sound.

Mr. Home held the accordion in one hand, and notes were sounded upon the instrument to indicate the letters of the alphabet in various messages given. The air 'Auld Lang Syne' was then most beautifully and touchingly played.

"A small, but very solid table upon castors, with a heavy stereoscope resting on it, containing 50 glass slides, moved across the floor from the window where it stood, and placed itself between Mr. Home and myself, having glided about six or seven feet. Mr. Home requested Lord Louth to come and place his hand on this table. Raps sounded distinctly on it, and the vibration was felt very strongly by Lord L. We all heard a strange noise inside the camera, and thought the slides were breaking; but, although shaken violently, none were cracked or broken.

"A chair now moved up between Mr. Home and Mr. Hall, a second chair followed, a third, and then a fourth, also a very large arm-chair. A small chair rose from the floor, and moved up and down close to Mr. Hall, appearing to float in the air.

"After the séance, Lord Louth measured the distance each chair had traversed, and found it to range from six to nine feet. The little table had moved seven feet from the window to Mr. Home. This was the first séance at which Lord Louth had ever been present."

Of the many wonderful phenomena witnessed in connection with Mr. Home, none has been the subject of more discussion than that of his levitation, and none is established by more conclusive testimony. After having carefully considered that testimony, Mr. Crookes wrote, in the *Quarterly Journal of Science* for January 1874:

"There are at least a hundred recorded instances of Mr. Home's rising from the ground, in the presence of as many separate persons; and I have heard from the lips of the three witnesses to the most striking occurrence of this kind the Earl of Dunraven, Lord Lindsay, and Captain C. Wynne their own most minute accounts of what took place. To reject the recorded evidence on this subject is to reject all human testimony whatever; for no fact in sacred or profane history is supported by a stronger array of proofs.

"The accumulated testimony establishing Mr. Home's levitations is overwhelming. It is greatly to be desired that some person, whose evidence would be accepted as conclusive by the scientific world if indeed there lives a person whose testimony in favour of such phenomena would be taken would seriously and patiently examine these alleged facts."

The desire expressed by Mr. Crookes was not responded to by his scientific brethren.

Mr. Crookes was enabled by his séances with Mr. Home to add his own testimony to that already in existence concerning the phenomenon of levitation. "On three separate occasions," he writes, "have I seen Mr. Home raised completely from the floor of the room. Once sitting on an easy chair, once kneeling on his chair, and once standing up. On each occasion I had full opportunity of watching the occurrence as it was taking place." (*Notes of an Inquiry into the Phenomena called Spiritual.*)

The present Earl of Crawford, when giving his testimony before the Dialectical Society concerning the strange things he had seen in Home's presence, was questioned as to the possibility of explaining the phenomena by contrivance. "The more I studied them," he answered, "the more satisfied was I that they could not be explained by mere mechanical trick. I have had the fullest opportunity for investigation."

It was asked if the phenomenon of levitation did not invariably occur in semi-darkness. "No," replied Lord Crawford (then Lord Lindsay), "I once saw Home in full light standing in the air seventeen inches from the ground."

In November, 1868, Lord Adare and Lord Lindsay saw Mr. Home raised in the air about four or five feet. On December 20th of the same year, Lords Adare and Lindsay, Captain C. Wynne, and Mr. Arthur Smith Barry were present when he again rose from the ground. During the manifestations in the ruined abbey at Adare, Home was seen by Lord Dunraven, Lord Adare, and Captain Wynne to float above the ground for a distance of ten or twelve yards at a height that carried him over a broken wall two feet high. He passed close by the three watchers during this aerial journey.

Of another instance of levitation Lord Lindsay gave the

following description: "Home floated round the room, pushing the pictures out of their places as he passed along the walls. They were far beyond the reach of a person standing on the ground. The light was sufficient to enable me to see clearly." (Evidence given before the Dialectical Society.)

But the most striking of the many occasions on which Home was seen to float in the air was that to which Mr. Crookes so particularly alludes in the passage I have quoted from him. This event occurred in London, on December 16th 1868, in the presence of three unimpeachable witnesses, Lord Lindsay, Lord Adare, and Captain Charles Wynne, a cousin of the latter.

A séance was in progress; and Home, who had been in the trance state for some time, began to walk about uneasily, and finally went into the adjoining room. At that moment a startling communication was made to Lord Lindsay. "I heard," he related in his evidence before the Dialectical Society, "a voice whisper in my ear, 'He will go out of one window and in at another.' I was alarmed and shocked at the thought of so dangerous an experiment. I told the company what I had heard, and we then waited for Home's return."

Mr. Home was at the moment in the room adjoining that where the three sitters waited. Besides his evidence given before the Dialectical Society, Lord Lindsay published a second and more minute description of the levitation, in which he thus narrated the events that immediately followed the spirit-intimation he had received, and had communicated to Lord Adare and Captain Wynne: "We heard," writes Lord Lindsay, "the window in the next room lifted up, and almost immediately afterwards we saw Home floating in the air outside our window.

"The moon was shining full into the room. My back was to the light; and I saw the shadow on the wall of the window sill, and Home's feet about six inches above it. He remained in this position for a few seconds, then raised the window and glided into the room feet foremost, and sat down.

"Lord Adare then went into the next room to look at the window from which he had been carried. It was raised about eighteen inches, and he expressed his wonder how Mr. Home had been taken through so narrow an aperture.

"Home said (still in a trance), 'I will show you' and then, with his back to the window, he leaned back and was shot out of the aperture head first, with the body rigid, and then returned quite quietly.

"The window is about seventy feet from the ground. I very much doubt whether any skillful rope dancer would like to attempt a feat of this description, where the only means of crossing would be a perilous leap.

"The distance between the windows was about seven feet six inches, and there was not more than a twelve-inch projection to each window, which served as a ledge to put flowers on."

One of the other two witnesses of the scene, Lord Adare, had the distances between the windows and other details measured, and included them in the record written by him of the occurrence. Lord Adare's testimony is as follows:

"Wynne and I went over to Ashley House after dinner. There we found Home and the Master of Lindsay. Home proposed a sitting. We accordingly sat round a table in the small room. There was no light in the room, but the light from the window was sufficient to enable us to distinguish each other, and to see the different articles of furniture. Home went into a trance.

"Lindsay suddenly said: 'Oh, good heavens! I know what he is going to do; it is too fearful.'

"Adare: 'What is it?'

"Lindsay: 'I cannot tell you; it is too horrible. A spirit says that I must tell you. He is going out of the window in the other room, and coming in at this window.'

"We heard Home go into the next room, heard the window thrown up, and presently Home appeared standing upright outside our window. He opened the window, and walked in quite coolly. 'Ah,' he said, 'you were good this time'; referring to our having sat still and not wished to prevent him. 'Adare, shut the window in the next room.'

"I got up, shut the window, and in coming back remarked that the window was not raised a foot, and that I could not think how he had managed to squeeze through. He arose, and said, 'Come and see.' I went with him: he told me to open the window as it was before. I did so: he told me to stand a little distance off; he then went through the open space, head first, quite rapidly, his body being nearly horizontal and apparently rigid. He came in again, feet foremost; and we returned to the other room. It was so dark I could not see clearly how he was supported outside. He did not appear to grasp, or rest upon, the balustrade, but rather to be swung out and in. Outside each window is a small balcony or ledge, nineteen inches deep, bounded by stone balustrades, eighteen inches high. The balustrades of the two windows are seven feet four inches apart, measuring from the nearest point. A string-course, four inches wide, runs between the windows at the level of the bottom of the balustrade; another, three inches wide, at the level of the top. Between the window at which Home went out and that at which he came in the wall recedes six inches. The rooms are on the third floor.

"I asked Lindsay how the spirit had spoken to him. He could scarcely explain; but said it did not sound like an audible human voice, but rather as if the tones were whispered or impressed inside his ear. When Home awoke, he was much agitated; he said he felt as if he had gone through some fearful peril, and that he had a most horrible desire to throw himself out of window. He remained in a very nervous condition for a short time, then gradually became quiet.

"We now had a series of very curious manifestations. Lindsay and Wynne saw tongues or jets or flames proceeding from Home's head. We then all distinctly heard, as it were, a bird flying round the room, whistling and chirping, but saw nothing; except Lindsay, who perceived an indistinct form resembling a bird. There then came a sound as of a great wind rushing through the room; we also felt the wind strongly: the moaning, rushing sound was the most weird thing I ever heard."

It will be seen that the testimony of the two observers is in perfect agreement. Lord Adare's narrative was written quite independently of that of Lord Lindsay, but precisely the same facts are recorded in each. It is clearly established that Lord Lindsay, as Home left the room, received an intimation of what was about to happen, and communicated it to his two companions, that Mr. Home was carried out of one window and in at another, at a height of seventy feet from the ground; that, on Lord Adare expressing surprise at his having been carried through the aperture of a window only raised a foot, Home, before his eyes, was a second time floated through that opening into the space outside, and back again. As Lord Adare gives the measurements between the windows, &c., his figures are naturally more precise than those of Lord Lindsay, who judged by the eye. They establish that the ledges of the two windows were seven feet four inches apart, between the nearest points. Along the wall ran two string courses, the lower of these four inches wide, the upper three. It was obviously impracticable that anyone could walk along the lower of these two very narrow shelves, as the space between it and the upper ledge was only eighteen inches. The sceptic as to the phenomenon of levitation is reduced therefore to two alternatives either to accept the testimony of Lords Adare and Lindsay as an exact narrative of facts, or to suppose that Mr. Home chose to attempt, late at night, the impossible feat of walking along a ledge three inches wide, at a height of seventy feet from the ground, and successfully accomplished the impossible. Yet even this theory would not explain the second levitation of which Lord Adare was the witness, when Home, before his eyes, was floated out of the partly opened window into the empty air beyond.

Dr. W. B. Carpenter, V.P.R.S imagined, indeed, another theory, and communicated his imaginations to the public under circumstances more daring than honest. The narrative of Lord Lindsay informed him that there had been a third sitter present when the levitation occurred Captain Wynne, the cousin of Lord Adare. In the absence of any detailed testimony from this gentleman, Dr. Carpenter chose to assume that his evidence, if made public, would have contradicted that of Lords Lindsay and Adare. A little inquiry would have informed Dr. Carpenter that Captain Wynne had narrated to Mr. Crookes, Mr. S. C. Hall, and others what he saw, and that his evidence exactly corresponded with that of Lord Adare and Lord Lindsay. This trained man of science, this exact investigator, made no inquiry, however. He took his hypothesis concerning Captain Wynne for granted – singular conduct on the part of the very man who had always been loudest in accusing Spiritualists and inquirers into Spiritualism of basing their conclusions on insufficient evidence, but quite consistent with the whole method of Dr. Carpenter's warfare against Spiritualism. The temper in which he conducted his assaults was not that of a philosopher desirous to arrive at the truth and nothing but the truth, but of a theorist who thought no sacrifice of the truth too great to make in the interests of his favourite doctrine of "unconscious cerebration." To throw doubt on the phenomenon of the levitation of Mr. Home, he ventured on one of the boldest of those sacrifices. Knowing all the while that his assumption concerning Captain Wynne was sheer supposition; he deliberately stated it to the world as a fact. Of course, no names were mentioned; that would have been to court investigation, and Dr. Carpenter was aware that his statements would not bear it. It was sufficient for him to tell the public, in an article published in the *Contempary Review* of January 1867:

"The most diverse accounts of the facts of a séance will be given by a believer and a sceptic. ... A whole party of believers will affirm that they saw Mr. Home float out of one window and in at another, whilst a single honest sceptic declares that Mr. Home was sitting in his chair all the time. And in this last case we have an example of a fact, of which there is ample illustration, that, during the prevalence of an epidemic delusion, the honest testimony of any number of individuals, on one side, if given under a prepossession, is of no more weight than that of a single adverse witness if so much."

It seems to me that, written under the circumstances I have just detailed, nothing could well be more discreditable to Dr. Carpenter than this passage. Published in a widely circulated organ of opinion, it could not but leave, and was evidently intended to leave, on the minds of all who read it the impression that Dr. Carpenter's "honest sceptic" had actually been present with Lord Adare and Lindsay on the only occasion when Home ever floated out of one window and in at another, and had, to the knowledge of Dr. Carpenter, declared "that Mr. Home was quietly sitting in his chair all the while." If so, this "single adverse witness" could be no other than Captain Wynne. Only once had Mr. Home been seen to float out of a window and in at another in Ashley Place, S.W. on the 16th of December 1868. Three persons in all had observed the phenomenon: two of them, Lords Lindsay and Adare, had printed their testimony to the occurrence. They were, therefore, Dr. Carpenter's "party of believers" Lord Lindsay, who told the Dialectical Society, "I have no theory to explain these things;" and Lord Adare, who wrote: "I make no attempt to offer any explanation of the phenomena, or to build up any theory upon them; I only say that they have occurred as I have stated them." The third and last sitter present when Mr. Home was carried out of one window of Ashley House and in at another more than seven feet distant was Captain Charles Wynne. To him, therefore, Dr. Carpenter's statements concerning the "honest sceptic" referred. Every one understood them so to refer, Captain Wynne included; and his answer to them is contained in a letter written by him to Mr. Home under the following circumstances.

In or about the year 1876, an American of the name of Hammond published a foolish book wherein he gave Dr. Carpenter's fable of the "honest sceptic" a niche among numerous fables of his own concerning the experiments of Mr. Crookes; his ingenuous method or dealing with the latter being to pass over the most conclusive in silence, substitute for the remainder dummy experiments that in no way resembled them, and then proceed to triumphantly demolish the shams he had himself created. In retailing as fact the fictions of Dr. Carpenter, Dr. Hammond took occasion to find for those airy nothings "a local habitation and a name," and boldly stated that the levitation referred to was that in Ashley Place, and that Dr. Carpenter's "honest sceptic" was the cousin of Lord Dunraven. His book came under the notice of Mr. Home, who wrote to Captain Wynne as follows:

"Nice, January 5th, 1877.

"My dear Wynne, I have been reading a book intensely stupid and absurd called *Spiritualism and Nervous Derangement*: by W. A. Hammond, M.D. On page 81 of his book I found the following question regarding the very extraordinary manifestation you witnessed in Ashley Place, when I was brought in at a window eighty feet from the ground, in the presence of your cousin, Viscount Adare (now Earl of Dunraven), Lord Lindsay, and yourself:

'There were three gentlemen present in the room besides Mr. Home. Lord Adare, we may admit, accepts the account given by

Lord Lindsay. Indeed, he may be said to be the father of it. But why have we no word from the "cousin of his" who formed one of the company? There cannot be too much evidence on so important a point as this.'

"I would have paid no attention to this question, but on the same page I found the following reply, which perfectly suited this Dr. Hammond; and he has either arranged it so as to be a reply to the above question, or it may be that it is an arrangement of Dr. Carpenter's. I am sorry to say that Dr. Carpenter is not innocent, as regards these little arrangements to suit his own convenience. Hammond says:

'But as these lines are being written, the true (save the mark!) explanation comes to hand, showing that both Lord Lindsay and Lord Adare suffered from a hallucination. In an interesting paper, Dr. Carpenter, evidently referring to the account of Lord Lindsay, says, "A whole party of believers will affirm that they saw Mr. Home float out of one window and in at another, while a single honest sceptic declares that Mr. Home was sitting in his chair all the time." This "honest sceptic" is probably the cousin incidentally mentioned by Lord Lindsay. It is scarcely necessary to pursue the inquiry further.'

"Under ordinary circumstances, I would have paid no attention even to this, but in December, 1876, Dr. Carpenter, at the London Institution, made a statement so utterly at variance with the truth that it is just as well to remind him that, whatever his peculiar prejudices may be, he does wrong in stooping to falsehoods. I give you his words, as reported in the public prints: 'Mr. Crookes had admitted that . . . Mr. Home having exhibited marvels, Mr. Crookes afterwards devised scientific tests, but the marvels were no longer shown. That was Mr. Crookes' statement.' Mr. Crookes never made such a statement, and it is a most audacious and willful falsehood on the part of Dr. Carpenter to have said so.

"You will fully understand why I wish a reply to this. You have read the statement as given to the world by Lord Lindsay and Lord Adare. Is it, or is it not, a simple and concise statement of the facts just as they took place?

"I am well pleased that this question should have been asked while you were here to give your testimony. Else these would-be great men who condescend to untruthful statements might have found those capable of giving credence to their inventions. Ever yours, "D. D. Home."

Captain Wynne's reply to the above letter of Mr. Home is before me as I write. It will be observed from it that he had already publicly contradicted Dr. Carpenter's mendacious reference to him:

"Feb. 2, '77.

"Dear Dan, Your letter has just come before me. I remember that Dr. Carpenter wrote some nonsense about that trip of yours along the side of the house in Ashley Place. I wrote to the Medium to say that I was present and a witness. Now, I don't think that anyone who knows me would for one moment say that I was a victim to hallucination or any other humbug of the kind. The fact of your having gone out of the window and in at the other I can swear to; but what is the use of trying to convince men who won't believe anything not even if they see it. I don't care a straw whether Dr. Carpenter or Mr. Hammond believe me or not it does not prevent the fact having occurred. But this I will say, that if you are not to believe the corroborative evidence of three unimpeached witnesses, there would be an end to all justice and courts of law. Ever yours, "C. Wynne."

"P.S. Honest, but not a sceptic."

By which postscript Captain Wynne meant that, like Lord Adare and Lord Lindsay, he believed the testimony of his eyesight. He was precisely the kind of witness whose testimony Dr. Carpenter would have accepted with rapture, had it been unfavourable to Mr. Home a frank soldier and gentleman, with no bias towards Spiritualism, but who, happening to have been present with Lords Adare and Lindsay on the occasion of Home's remarkable levitation, candidly added his testimony to theirs.

In face of his letter, what becomes of the reputation of the Vice-President of the Royal Society for common candour? Dr. Carpenter had a perfect right, if he thought it consistent with his reputation as a man of intellect, to propound the astonishing dictum that, given a hundred persons equally honest, of whom ninety-nine testified that Mr. Home had risen in the air, while the hundredth declared he had not, the testimony of the one ought to outweigh that of the ninety-nine. But what of has conduct in inventing the "honest sceptic who declares that Mr. Home was sitting in his chair all the time," and his presentation of this fiction to the readers of the Contemporary Review as a fact, when all the while Dr. Carpenter was aware that the anonymous "honest sceptic," on whose authority he dismissed the evidence of Lords Lindsay and Adare as hallucination, was himself a hallucination, and the coinage of his own brain?

In parting with Dr. Carpenter, let me remark that the tone which unbounded egotism, and the eagerness of a timid man to stand well with the world, induced him to take publicly on the subject of Spiritualism and the phenomena associated with Mr. Home was some what modified in private. It will perhaps be news to those who have "read, marked, and inwardly digested" Dr. Carpenter's various onslaughts on Spiritualism in the *Quarterly Review*, the *Contemporary Review*, &c., to learn that he regarded Mr. Home as an honest man, and that he not only believed in the continued existence of the departed, but thought it possible nay, probable that spirits influence the minds of the dwellers on earth.

A letter has been sent to me that was written by Dr. Carpenter under the following circumstances. In November, 1877, a young journalist, who was acquainted with Mr. Home, wrote to Dr. Carpenter apropos of the lectures on "Spiritualism, Mesmerism, &c.," that the latter had recently republished in book form. Two or three letters followed; and finally, at the invitation of Dr. Carpenter, his correspondent called on him with a view to further discussion. He found Dr. Carpenter's private views somewhat inconsistent with his published utterances, as, indeed, had been already demonstrated to him by the letter he has placed in my possession. Mr. Home never saw this letter, and was wholly ignorant that any correspondence between Dr. Carpenter and its recipient had taken place. Dr. Carpenter writes as follows:

"56, Regent's Park Road, N.W. Nov. 27, 1877.

"Dear Sir, I am greatly obliged to you for your letter, and shall be very glad to communicate further with you on the subject of it. You will have observed that I do not anywhere call in question the continued existence of departed spirits, or their influence over living minds. This is a matter altogether distinct from that of the reality of the 'physical manifestations'; and there seems to me nothing inconsistent with possibility or even with probability in such spiritual influence. For, altho' Mr. Home and a great many other persons rank me as a Materialist, my philosophy (as my British Association Address would show) is much more like Priestley's a universal Spiritualism.

"I hold myself open to new evidence in favour of the existence in particular individuals of a power of direct communication of mind with mind, which would solve many difficulties and clear up many obscurities. But all my experience has led me to see such an amount of self-deception and unconscious fitting-together in such revelations, that I distrust all stories that I have not the power of myself verifying.

"I always used to regard Mr. Home as an honest man, believing in himself; but I must own that my faith was shaken by the Lyon trial. The publication of this book (*Lights and Shadows of Spiritualism*), on the other hand, has given me a more favourable opinion of him; and you will have remarked that the only thing I have said in depreciation of him has been in regard to the 'physical manifestations.'

"Should you be able to call upon me here on any morning this week before 11 am, I shall be glad to see you. Yours truly,

"William B. Carpenter."

Coming from the author of the bitter attack on Mr. Crookes and others that appeared in the *Quarterly Review* for October 1871, this letter is a very curious production. In public, Dr. Carpenter imputed the physical phenomena of Spiritualism to fraud, and explained the mental by his pet theory of "unconscious cerebration"; in private, he sees "nothing inconsistent with possibility or even with probability" in the exercise by the spirits of the departed of an influence over us who are still on earth.

In private, Dr. Carpenter "used always to regard Mr. Home as an honest man, believing in himself." It would be easy to collect from his published writings a dozen passages that impute or hint the contrary. On his own confession, then, Dr. Carpenter could think one thing and say another.

Not only does his letter contradict his published statements, but one part of it contradicts another. He holds Mr. Home honest, yet he considers the physical manifestations witnessed at Home's séances to have been imposture. It would seem, therefore, that Mr. Home was, in his opinion, an honest man who spent his life in deceiving others. It is fortunate for Dr. Carpenter's reputation that he went with the world of his day on the question of Spiritualism. Had he been a Spiritualist, what severe things would that world have said of him and of his muddled, illogical habits of thought!

As Dr. Carpenter never was present at a séance with Mr. Home, it is obvious that he was incapable of expressing an opinion of any value on the phenomena, whether mental or physical, that were witnessed at the séances of the latter. The intelligent reader who has impartially considered the facts I have here published, will perhaps share my conclusion that the opinions of such a thinker as Dr. Carpenter on such a subject as Spiritualism would have been of no great value in any case.

Mr. Home, who, in 1868, had readily engaged in controversy with such an antagonist as Professor Tyndall, never took the trouble to contradict publicly the false statements of Dr. W. B. Carpenter concerning the levitation in Ashley Place. He considered the inventor of the "honest sceptic" a foeman somewhat unworthy of his steel.

In concluding this chapter, let me ask the reader, sceptical or otherwise, what proof of a fact could be more complete than the proof here given that, on December 16th, 1868, Mr. Home was floated out of one window of Ashley House and in at another window nearly seven and a half feet distant? There were three witnesses of the occurrence Lord Adare, Lord Lindsay, and Captain Charles Wynne. I have printed here the testimony of all three in their own words. If, on comparing the evidence of these three unimpeachable witnesses and finding it identical, the reader still objects: "For all that, I decline to believe the impossible, I can only answer: The thing would have seemed equally impossible to Viscount Adare, the Master of Lindsay, and Captain Wynne, if their eyesight had not assured them that it was a fact."

CHAPTER 10

Public Readings – Scotland and France

Home as a public reader. Séance at Edinburgh. Mr. Alexander's narrative. Enormous correspondence. Home's benefactions. Franco-German War of 1870. His experience at Versailles. On the Battlefield. Saving a German officer. Story of the German Sergeant.

THERE IS NO BRANCH of the dramatic art in which failures are more numerous and triumph more difficult than the career of the public reader. In the theatre, scenery and costumes count for much of the effect produced on the spectator, and often render him indulgent to indifferent acting. The reader has no such ready-painted pictures to offer; and, as a consequence, he finds his audience colder and more exacting than that of the actor. When the curtain rises on the first scene of a play, the interest of the house is already evoked before a word has been spoken; but the platform-reader must speak, and speak to some purpose, if he is to carry his listeners with him. In nine cases out of ten he fails to do so. The number of readers who weary their listeners is legion, and, even of those who really succeed in interesting an audience, how few can carry that interest to the pitch that Home did. He could not only convulse his listeners with laughter by his fun and humour, but he had the much rarer faculty of touching them by his pathos so deeply as to call forth tears. None who heard them could readily forget his renderings of such pieces as The Vagabonds, Jane Conquest, The Death o' the Old Squire, and Mr. Hamilton Aide's Lost and Found. I may quote one or two of many press tributes to his powers of pathos: "His pathetic yet forcible rendering of The Death of the Old Squire won for the reciter the honour of a double recall," says the *Era* of March 20th, 1870. "Mr. D. D. Home, who is now established as one of our best readers, caused a marked sensation amongst the audience many of whom were melted to tears by his admirable recital of The Vagabond" (Court Circular, Aug. 14, 1869).

Besides his wonderful pathos and humour, he had a fire such as few readers possess, and his rendering of battle pieces was stirring to the last degree. The usual resource of the reader who attempts martial poetry is to stun his listeners by the noise he makes; with Home there was no noisy rendering, but the power and fire of the reader held his audience breathless. I have already related the singular tribute paid to his genius in New York, by the Southerner whose feelings his impassioned recitation of the Bay Fight had wrought beyond control. "I don't see how he could help flying at you," wrote an American friend to Home, on reading a notice of the incident in the newspapers;" for your rendering brings the scene to life. We see it with our eyes; and to that Southerner it must have been like going through it all again."

It was constantly remarked by his press critics sometimes with approbation, at other times with astonishment that Mr. Home's readings were "thoroughly natural." They could not be otherwise; for his good taste and his exquisite sense of the ludicrous gave him a horror of anything "stagy," and he would rather have missed an effect than have obtained it by the means some readers do not scruple to employ. It is, above all, the amateur of the Penny Reading who revels in a superabundance of such sham effect; and it was the fortune of Home on one occasion to be present at a recitation by one of the most melodramatic of the species. He added A Penny Reader's Charge of the Light Brigade to his repertory from that evening; and there are none of his humorous pieces over which his auditors have laughed more heartily.

It was a common thing for him to be made to deliver a reading twice, and even a third time. "Though only down in the programme three times, he had to appear on six occasions" (*Glasgow Herald*). "He was recalled every time he read; once he had to appear a third time" (*Ladies' Own Journal*). Home was fond of relating an incident that occurred to him in connection with Tennyson's Grandmother, a poem that was an especial favourite of his, and the homely pathos of which he rendered with inimitable effect. He read The Grandmother to a North of England audience, and was enthusiastically recalled. The poem is long, and the programme of the evening was long, too; and Home, having made his acknowledgments, was pleading the latter fact, when a man in one of the back seats jumped up. "The programme be," he interrupted, "cut all the rest of it out, and give us the old lady again."

A master of the pathetic, the humorous, and the stirring, Home was no less successful in the weird. His Raven was a memory to haunt for days those who listened breathless to his dialogue with the "grim, ungainly, ghastly" bird of Poe's conception; and the music of the same poet's Bells could not be more perfectly rendered than it was by Home. In his last illness he often passed hours in repeating the poems that had been his favourites; and only a day or two before the end came, has doctor, visiting him one morning, found him reciting The Bells, and rendering their melody with an effect as exquisite as any that had ever delighted the listeners of former years.

When in the vein, he improvised additions to a narrative with irresistible effect. The reading that lent itself the most readily to such treatment was The Widow Bedott, a rambling monologue that, I forget what American writer, has placed in the mouth of a Yankee Mrs. Gamp, as she sits by her fireside relating the history of her courtship to a neighbour, and wandering continually from her narrative to discuss matters and people that have no relation to it. When he had ceased to read in public, Home continued to charm his friends with his readings; and on such occasions it was his custom, when he impersonated The Widow Bedott, to make her introduce on the spur of the moment references to various of the party assembled. One evening his guests included a clergyman I will name him Smith who had never heard Widow Bedott before, and who, unluckily for both himself and the reader, was innocent of any sense of humour. Home did not know this, or the Widow would hardly have included the divine among those of her auditors of whom she had something to say; but, in the belief that he would see the joke, she presently wandered away from her narrative in his direction, with the remark: "Phineas," says I, "that reminds me of our parson. 'Mr. Smith,' says I to him the other day.

'Me!' said the worthy man, astonished. 'I beg Mr. Home's

pardon for interrupting him, but surely he must be mistaking me for some one else.'"

Home, much tempted to laugh, but thinking that this time, at any rate, the reverend gentleman would see the joke, answered, as Widow Bedott: "Ah, deary me! It's them learned men that have short memories. The many times I've listened to Mr. Smith telling us we're all poor sinners, and now he says to me– says he–"

But Mr. Smith, more bewildered than ever, had turned to his wife, who was sitting next him. "Have you any recollection, my dear, of hearing me say to Mr. Home that we are all poor sinners?" he asked, solemnly.

Widow Bedott got no further with her gossip that evening.

Even under the most favourable circumstances, the readings that Mr. Home gave during the years 1869 and 1870 in London, Edinburgh, Glasgow, Liverpool, and fifty other places in England and Scotland, would have been an exhausting drain on the energies of a nature so nervous and sensitive. To the last he retained a horror of the trying hurt that preceded his appearance and his successes; and those who saw him agitated by the fear of failure, and distrustful both of his ability and his memory, were astonished when, a few minutes later, he presented himself before the audience another being, and entered on the task before him with the happiest ease and self possession. But the emotions natural to his highly strung temperament were not all he had to contend against. The events of the year 1868 had not only injured his health, but had burdened him with heavy debts that he was anxious to discharge as speedily as possible. He had a young son to provide for; and there were numerous relatives and friends who looked to him for a continuation of the assistance he had generously afforded them, and was desirous still to give. Such anxieties would have preyed on any man; on Home they preyed tenfold, for he had been constituted to feel both sorrow and joy more keenly than his fellows. It was, therefore, under conditions the most discouraging that he commenced his career as a reader; and what efforts it cost him to present himself night after night to his audiences, and lavish all his rich resources of humour and pathos for their amusement, only he could know. But he always faced his trying task bravely, and went through it with brilliant success.

Among the letters of Mr. Home to Mr. and Mrs. S. C. Hall that have been placed at my disposal, there are several belonging to this trying time. Written with the perfect simplicity and openness that mark all his letters to his friends, they form a journal of his daily life that tells, better than any words of mine can, how full it was of care and struggle. A brief extract or two is all with which I shall supplement my narrative.

From Edinburgh, on January 30th, 1870, Home writes:

"Dear friends, The agent here was very unwilling to engage me, and told me that readings 'did not take' that 'Miss was a dead failure, and that had been hissed off the platform.' At last he engaged me for a merely nominal sum. ... Of course, knowing that others had been hissed off, I went on with fear and trembling. I had six or seven friends in the house, and I truly believe that these were the only ones who applauded when I came on. Oh, the silence was fearful! I began my piece 'Scotch Words,' and before it was half over I had round after round of applause, and such an encore. My every piece was encored, and at the termination of the last they would not have the singers, and I had to go on three times. I am curious to see what the papers will say to-morrow.

"I have just learnt such a poem! It is beautiful; above all where he speaks of the light from a burning ship as it enters the cottage-window in the dark night:

"It shone with a radiant glory on the face of the dying child, Like a fair first ray of the shadowless day in the land of the undefiled. I will not tell you the story, but I know the poem will deeply touch you. I am far from being well, but the result of last night has cheered me."

Either during this or a subsequent visit to Scotland for the purpose of giving public readings, Mr. Home became acquainted with a well-known Edinburgh medical man, a relative of Sir James Simpson. Dr. Doun was an entire sceptic on the subject of Spiritualism. Home had not intended to hold any séances in Edinburgh; he went there as a reader; but a train of circumstances too long to detail here led to his becoming the guest of Dr. Doun, and by the doctor's wish he held several séances in the doctor's house. The result was that the beliefs of the doctor were revolutionized in spite of himself; and he became convinced of the continued existence of the so-called dead, and of their ability under exceptional circumstances to hold communion with us.

I could have wished to narrate here some of the experiences that made the doctor a Spiritualist, were it in my power; but my knowledge of the facts is limited to the information contained in a small volume, entitled, *Spiritualism: A Narrative with a Discussion.* By Patrick Proctor Alexander, M.A., author of *Mill and Carlyle, Moral Causation,* &c. Edinburgh: W. P. Nirnrno: 1871. This little book is ably written, and evidently the work of a candid, clear headed man a sceptic, but a sceptic who investigated, instead of prejudging. Mr. Alexander, an old friend of Dr. Doun, attended a séance with Mr. Home at the doctor's house. He obtained permission to bring with him his friend, Dr. Findlater, as a fellow-observer. Neither had previously attended any séance; both were educated, intelligent, hard headed Scotchmen, entirely incredulous on the subject of Spiritualism, and much astonished that what they conceived to be hallucinations should have taken such hold of such a man.

"Jane Conquest."

"On an evening fixed," writes Mr. Alexander, "I presented myself at the house, taking with me (by permission) Dr. Findlater, a man very well known in Edinburgh intellectual circles not hitherto suspected by his friends of a tendency to undue credulity in any matter; a friend, and in some sense disciple, of Mr. John Stuart Mill; with a couple of good sharp eyes in his head, and perhaps as accurate notions as most men as to what may constitute Evidence, and the conditions of scientific inquiry. We found a small party assembled, and to Mr. Home we were, of course, introduced. His manners were simple and quiet, and very much those of a gentleman. There was no trace in him whatever of the charlatan; and, except for an occasional wildness in his eye so slight that I may have merely imagined it none of the Magus, or seer, accustomed to hold awful commune with spirits, either evil or good.

"I may premise that I cannot readily conceive conditions much more favourable to Dr. Findlater and myself, as regards the interest of truth, than those under which this little experiment was made more unfavourable to Mr. Home, presumed a mere juggler and impostor. Had Mr. Home advertised an entertainment to take place in a hired apartment of his own, I don't think I should have cared to go to see him, any more than I ever cared to go to see Professor Anderson bring puddings out of a hat, or pour liquors from his magic bottle. But the room was Mrs. Doun's drawing-room, and could scarce in any way have been prepared by Mr. Home without her or Dr. Doun's connivance a theory of the matter, in my own mind, and, I venture to say, that of every one who has ever had the pleasure of their acquaintance, disposed of as utterly inadmissible, in virtue of the known and high character of both. Further, it is certified to me beyond question, that the 'manifestations,' as they are termed, took place indifferently in any or every room in the house, and most particularly in Dr. Doun's bedroom, which could scarce have been tampered with by Mr. Home without his becoming aware of it. None of the company had any relations with Mr. Home, excepting as we ourselves had, per favour of our host and hostess; or could thus, any more than we, be suspected of complicity with Mr. Home. The drawing room was fully and brightly lit with gas; and the table, which was good enough to vouchsafe us intelligence from the Spirit-world, an old acquaintance, at which I had aforetime taken tea, dreaming of Mr. Home or of Spirits. If conditions more favourable can be suggested by any scientific gentleman, I shall be glad to have the benefit of his wisdom."

For a detailed description of the phenomena witnessed and searchingly investigated by Mr. Alexander and Dr. Findlater, I must refer the reader to the interesting brochure of the former. "Both of us were a good deal perplexed," says Mr. Alexander, "and remain so – as quite unable to suggest any plausible explanation of the wonders we witnessed. As to the obvious explanation of malafides and jugglery on Mr. Home's part, the only little objection to it is (and. perhaps may be thought but a little one), that, with our very best will and care to that effect, and the best opportunities for doing so, we utterly failed to detect any trace of these whatever."

The host and hostess (Dr. and Mrs. Doun), Mr. Alexander, Dr. Findlater, and other Edinburgh ladies and gentlemen to the number of nine, formed, with Mr. Home, a circle about "an ordinary round drawing-room tea-table, solidly built, and thus of considerable weight;" and waited some time without any manifestations occurring. "The first hint or fore shine we had of the 'phenomena,'" writes Mr. Alexander, "came in the form of certain tremors which began to pervade the apartment. These were of a somewhat peculiar kind; and they gradually increased till they became of considerable violence.

"Not only did the floor tremble, but the chair of each person, as distinct from it, was felt to rock and as we Scots say dirl under him."

Ice-cold blasts of air were felt by some of the sitters drifting across their hands. Mr. Alexander and Dr. Findlater did not experience this sensation so frequent a forerunner of other phenomena; but, in common with the remaining sitters, they heard the rappings that followed. "Presently, as to the ear it seemed, exactly in the centre of the table," says the former.

"Came a tap, tap, tapping, regular, continuous, and prolonged; on hearing which Mr. Home announced that he was now nearly sure we should have 'manifestations' of some sort; and, turning to me, he suggested that, a9 naturally I might wish to test the thing a little curiously, I had better go under the table, and satisfy myself as to whether there was anything there to account for what would probably take place. Accordingly though a little loth, as suspecting a slight degradation in it I performed what Mr. Darwin would call an act of 'reversion'; and, in the enthusiasm of scientific inquiry, was content, for the nonce, to relapse into the condition of an 'ape-like progenitor' or member of the genus Quadrumana. As such, I crept quietly under the table, and kept steady watch there for the space of ten minutes or so; Dr. Findlater, as an observer of the genus Homo, keeping the like steady watch above. I may remark that the light under the table, though necessarily dimmer than above, was yet amply sufficient for purposes of clear observation. For a good while nothing took place but raps, which flew about all over the table; and I could indicate, when desired by Mr. Home to do so, the precise locale upon the table of each rap as it occurred. Meantime, by anything beneath the table, the raps were entirely unaccounted for; and

Mr. Home, in particular, had his feet steadily at rest beneath his chair: his hands, as observed by Dr. Findlater, were quietly before him on the table."

Various movements of the table followed. During their occurrence, it was certified by Mr. Alexander that Mr. Home's feet were motionless beneath his chair, by Dr. Findlater that his hands were at rest above. The former resumed his seat; and the sitters proceeded to try if the table would become light and heavy at command. Mr. Alexander describes the result of the experiment:

"'Be light,' said the operator; and the table, when softly solicited, moved readily from beneath his fingers. 'Be heavy!' and the table seemed weighted to the floor with lead, and could only at all be moved by a great expenditure of force. Every one of the party in succession tried this: Dr. Findlater carefully twice, I twice, with scrupulous care, and invariably with the above results. On my trying the experiment the second time of course, if possible, with some additional care and scruple it actually seemed to me that the table sprang from under my fingers, almost before the initial touch could take the form of distinct pressure the difficulty of moving it afterwards being well-nigh, in proportion, great. These results certainly seemed curious, as to every one present quite unaccountable."

Five raps presently called for the alphabet; and various communications were spelt out, one of them being from a departed friend of certain of the sitters present. Other manifestations occurred, which I pass over, and quote Mr. Alexander's account of the phenomenon that seems to have impressed him the most:

"Two accordions," he writes, "were on the table, one of which Mr. Home selected. The instrument, he explained, was not his, but the property of Dr. G (a gentleman present I had not before met, but very well known to me by reputation), who had been good enough to bring it with him. This Dr. G confirmed; and it is to be in fairness supposed he could scarce be mistaken as to its being his own accordion. Taking the instrument in one hand by the end unfurnished with keys, Mr. Home put it under the table. It almost immediately began to emit sounds; and, having begun, went on to play pretty briskly. Guiding the instrument in his direction, Mr. Home then desired Dr. Findlater to go under the table, and, after careful examination, return and give an account of what he saw there. Dr. Findlater did so. He remained some little time under the table, the accordion the while continuing to sound as before; and then, resuming his chair, he reported that the instrument held motionless in Mr. Home's one hand his other hand being, of course, all the time on the table was moving and giving out sound, precisely as if it were worked by a hand at the other end of it; whilst, to account for this phenomenon, not to be questioned, except in so far as his eyesight might be, nothing whatever was visible. Going down to make strict examination, I came up in a little to report precisely as Dr. Findlater had before done. The accordion, held motionless in Mr. Home's one hand at an angle of about forty-five degrees, was moving backward and forward, and continuing to play, just as if a couple of hands had been manipulating it; and to account for this nothing was visible. Meantime there was no hint of a tune in the sounds produced; they made just such an aimless monotony as a child, let us say, might produce, amusing itself with the instrument."

It was at this instant that raps came again on the table, and the message already referred to was spelt out.

"It appeared," writes Mr. Alexander, "that this deceased Colin Campbell, a gentleman of Aberdeenshire, had been intimately known to two or three of the party. Almost instantly after, the five raps were again heard; 'He does not forget' was rapped out by the spirit of the faithful though defunct Colin; and odd as it may seem the accordion under the table, still held in Mr. Home's one hand, played distinctly 'Auld Lang Syne!' (the reader may laugh if he likes, as indeed to myself, had I not been present to witness it, such a thing must have seemed at once ludicrous and incredible). The tune was played distinctly, recognizably, and yet withal a little bunglingly; and then, as if Colin had suspected a certain deficiency in his own performance, it was played over again, this time in tones of exquisite modulation, which moved the admiration of all present."

Public readings and the séances that, wherever he went, he was pressed to hold, filled up Home's time so largely that he had less of it than ever to bestow on those thousands of voluminous correspondents who, by the number and merciless length of their letters, must have made the postman's knock a horror to him. "I am behind again with all my correspondence," he writes to a friend. "My head is in a whirl. This morning brought me in a mass of letters. One is from Mrs.–, who writes that 'the Dublin doctors are killing her,' and she sends me what she calls a statement of her case. You will imagine my feelings when I tell you it consists of sixty pages of letter paper crossed. Not being very well, I get so dreadfully nervous with these things that I know not what to do. G. declares that he will burn all my letter paper, and allow me to write only to you and a very few others."

"I know," writes Mr. Home another time to Mrs. Hall, "you will feel for me, and that in your prayers I shall not be forgotten. My sister is in a very delicate state of health her lungs are very weak. Does it not seem strange that I, who am young myself, should thus be called upon to see the nearest and dearest pass to the summer land before me?"

The Russian lawsuit still dragged on, and was likely to do so for several years more. With the utmost exertions and economy, Mr. Home could only pay off very slowly the sums he had borrowed to defray the heavy legal expenses that had been forced on him in England. Some of his friends advised him to sell his jewels, but he would not part with them. It was not their value or beauty that influenced him in this determination, but the associations connected with these stones. Every ring or other jewel was a testimony to the fact that the royal donor had learned to regard Home with goodwill and esteem. Whatever the original scepticism of these high personages and it is an idle fancy to suppose that their investigations of the phenomena were entered on in a credulous spirit they had ended by being convinced of the reality of the manifestations, and had also recognized that Mr. Home's other qualities worthily accorded with his wondrous gifts.

I have said enough to show that the years 1869 and 1870 were not among the happiest of a life that had more cloud than sunshine in it. But, whatever the accumulated cares and difficulties of his own existence, Home had always a heart to feel for others, and a brain and hand active to relieve their distresses. The world knew nothing of his many deeds of kindness; even those nearest and dearest to him often knew nothing; for it was his choice to do good unseen, and to keep silence afterwards concerning it. But among his papers I find many letters filled with expressions of gratitude and thankfulness. Now it is a young and unknown artist, for whose brush Home's generous efforts have found employment; now a distressed working man writes of his sick wife's life saved by comforts and medical help that Home had provided; now a mother thanks him for the start in life that he has secured for her son.

Home's charity was not the cheap kindness that begins and ends with the giving of money. That he gave freely of his scanty means, the letters before me show; but they bear witness also to many acts of a rarer and higher benevolence, they prove how much time and thought he devoted to helping others, when the circumstances of his life would have led most men to think only of their own needs and cares. There is, for instance, a letter written to Mr. Home about the date when his pressing difficulties led certain friends to recommend him to sell his jewels, and others to offer him aid that was gratefully declined. The first few words are all I need quote: "Dear Sir, You must allow me to express how exceedingly kind I feel it for you to take so much trouble in introducing my work." How many of the Brewsters and Brownings who misrepresented Home would have been capable of a benevolence so real, unpretending, and self sacrificing as this, in the midst of such depressing anxieties as then beset him?

I need hardly say that I have no thought of printing here the numerous letters in my possession that testify to the active and constant benevolence of Mr. Home. It would give pain to those of the writers who are still on earth; and He himself would be the last to desire that the details of kindness so modest should be vaunted before the world. These letters must remain in the same obscurity as the generous actions that led to their being written; but there is one written to him in the summer of 1870 from which I cannot help copying a few lines. Probably they will not seem so touching to the reader as to me, who know the circumstances that called them forth:

"Sir, I have learnt from day to day through my son in London with what fatherly goodness you have come to our rescue, and proved a saviour to my poor son, whose sad case is so distressing. No words of mine can convey sufficiently the gratitude which I feel I owe you for that pure goodness of heart alone which could have prompted you to it. The future of my poor son's life will be devoted to rewarding you; and time, I am sure, will prove that he is worthy of what you have done for him.

"Again I pray you accept the heartfelt gratitude of an afflicted father, who can never reward you for your charitable goodness, and but for which the poor boy could never have been rescued."

The writer of this letter was then ill in the country; and, I believe, passed from earth without ever having met his son's preserver. If I were to relate that son's story, it would furnish one proof more that the realities of Home's life were stranger than any fiction. But the fact has already been sufficiently demonstrated in these pages; and, except to illustrate it, the history could serve no useful purpose. I leave it untold, therefore, and pass to other events of the year to which it belongs 1870.

Very soon after a kindness beyond all price had been acknowledged in the touching letter to Mr. Home, of which I have quoted a part, he left England, in company with a friend, for the theatre of the Great War then raging. They reached the German headquarters within a few hours of the battle of Sedan; and next day Home went over the field. The sight would have tried any nerves; to a nature so sensitive and keenly compassionate of suffering as his it was agonizing. He was able, while he followed the operations of the German armies, to be of frequent service to victims of the war; but the months of September, October, and November 1870, did irreparable damage to his health. The spectator of a Great War needs a heart of steel and nerves of iron, and Home had neither.

He witnessed the investment of Paris and the greater part of the siege, including more than one of the sorties attempted by the garrison. During his stay at Versailles, he acted as correspondent of an English newspaper I believe of more than one; but my information on this head is scanty, and I have only in my possession one of the letters that he wrote the last of the series, dated November 23rd "We are told at least twenty times a day," it begins, "that we are about to witness one of the greatest events in history the capitulation of Paris; and for a few minutes we reconcile ourselves to this dreadful monotony. The very sight of these spiked helmets begins to weary one. I am half-inclined to think that there is a strong undercurrent of sympathy for France, at least in the outer circle; and though it would be akin to treason to repeat such a thought, yet I am convinced that the greater part of the men would be rejoiced to terminate this starving-out process.

"I send you the menu of a dinner given to an English diplomatist, to which I had the honour of being invited. When we sit down to a dinner like this, the thought of so many within a few miles of us, who are actually suffering for the necessities of life, rises like an unbidden Banquet to the feast. I know it does so in my own case, and am equally certain of its so doing with the rest of the guests."

The remainder of the long letter consists of anecdotes relating to the siege. The most interesting of them has often been narrated; how a German officer with his men visited a château on which they were not quartered; how they destroyed furniture and pictures, drank the best of the wine in the cellar and spilled the rest; and how finally the Prussian officer turned the mistress of the château out of her room, and occupied it; taking his leave afterwards with the explanation, "Madam, when I was a little boy, I have often heard my mother relate the cruel treatment she had to endure at the hands of a French officer and his men. I took an oath, even when a boy, that I would take revenge; and I have now done so. It is unfortunate that you should have been the victim, but so it had to; be." "Si non e vero e ben trovato," says Home, in telling the story.

Furnished with a safe-conduct from the German headquarters, Home came and went freely. I have related in an earlier chapter the circumstances of his meeting with King William (a few months later Emperor of Germany), at Versailles, in October, 1870; when, as the *Daily Telegraph* correspondent, who was present, wrote to that journal: "The King promptly recognized Mr. Home, and addressed him very kindly reminding him of the wonders that he (Mr. Home) had been the means of imparting to him, and inquiring about the spirits in by no means a sceptical tone." It was a dramatic incident, that few minutes' conversation of the crowned representative of force triumphant with the man who had been so wonderfully made the means of proving to his contemporaries that around them were forces of whose existence they had little dreamed.

On two occasions during the siege of Paris probably on more Home, found himself under fire. The second time, he went under the fire of the forts after a sortie to assist in removing the wounded. He came on a young German officer, who had received a bullet in the thigh and was in imminent danger of bleeding to death. Home bound up the wound to the best of his ability; and there being no assistance at hand, lifted the sufferer and carried him to the ambulance an exertion that threatened to have cost him his own life from the effect it had on his lungs, which just then were in a condition more than weak. His kindness did not end here. He visited his protégé constantly while the wounded man remained in hospital at Versailles, cheering him and alleviating his sufferings by every comfort in his power; and, finally, took a cordial leave of him when the young officer was included in a party of disabled Germans who were sent back to the Fatherland. The two never met again; but a year later Home received a long letter from Beirut in Syria, in which Lieutenant Sauer related all his fortunes since their parting. I append an exact translation of as much of this interesting document as I have space to quote:

"Beirut, Syria, November 21st, 1871.

"Honoured Sir, More than a year has passed since I left Versailles and saw you no more; and although I have so long remained silent to one who alleviated the most dreadful moments of my existence, I now offer my sincerest thanks for all the bountiful aid you rendered to a poor victim of war, who was on the point of perishing but for your assistance. Perhaps you will accuse me of ingratitude for not having written ere this, but sad events have transpired to hinder my good intentions. I trust, however, you will excuse my neglect when I relate the following events. You may remember the transport party to which I belonged left Versailles the 8th November 1870. Although fearful weather prevailed, five days later we arrived at Nanteuil, where our privations partially ceased. You can form some idea of the discomfort such a journey upon rough wagons would entail even upon healthy persons, how much more to those whose sad condition was aggravated by continual rain and snow, falling upon partially frozen limbs? Our joy was unbounded on reaching Nanteuil at finding a Wurtemberg train prepared for the comfortable reception of poor suffering creatures, who hailed the succour as just in time to save them.

"Towards Christmas I was able to walk with the support of a stick, although the ball could not be extracted from my leg; so I carry it even now in sad remembrance of that memorable day for us Germans. I must here remark that after a few days' sojourn in Gorlitz, I received the cross which his Majesty had hitherto only lent me.

"When I again sought my regiment, I heard from the doctor that I was totally unfitted for further duty, and applied for permission to quit the service. I could have wished to remain an officer, though no doubt my wound would have proved a serious obstacle to my progress. Upon casting aside my regimentals, it became necessary to seek some occupation for my future existence; and on application I received offers from Beirut, where I formerly resided. These I accepted; so at present I am surrounded by loving friends, who had anxiously followed my career on French territory.

"Should these lines reach you, be assured that one being on earth is indebted to you for his preservation, and only longs for an opportunity to prove his gratitude to one he must ever remember with intense thankfulness. May I ask you to complete your kindness by letting me know that these lines have reached you? Hoping some day to thank you personally, I remain, your ever grateful, "R. Sauer,

"Lieutenant of the Reserve, 1st Westphalian Grenadier Regiment."

The "memorable day for us Germans" of which the writer speaks was one of the struggles that took place in the direction of Bougival, when the besiegers of Paris were attacked by the besieged. In the same month October 1870 another sortie of the French led to an occurrence that Home could never speak of without emotion.

The morning of the sortie, he had left his lodging with his pocket filled with cigars, many hundreds of which he distributed at this time among the troops and the wounded, though I doubt if he ever smoked a cigar himself. As he passed along a boulevard where some French children were playing it was at Versailles he noticed a non-commissioned officer sitting on a bench near them, who seemed to be talking to one of the smallest. Home, interested by the scene, stopped as he came near; and was astonished and amused to hear the grizzled Prussian sergeant chatting away amicably to his small companion in the best of German.

"But, my friend," he said to the soldier, "the boy doesn't understand a word you're saying to him."

"Ja, ja," answered the Prussian seriously, "he understands me well enough;" and then, patting the child's head and smiling at Home's look of astonishment: "I have eight of them at home," he said simply, "the big and the little waiting for the old father to come back to them."

The words, and something in the way they were spoken, brought the tears to Home's eyes. He sat down and talked with the soldier; and when in a few minutes the veteran rose to go: "Stop," said Home, pulling out a handful of cigars; "here is something to help you to pass the time, sergeant."

The same day the besieged attacked the German positions near Buzenval. When the skirmish was over, and the French columns were retreating on Paris, Home joined a party that went out to seek the wounded. On the battlefield, they came on his acquaintance the sergeant again dead. The cigars were in his pocket still. But the hand that had placed them there was already cold; and as the searching party turned away to look for those who were not past help, Home thought of the bench where he had sat only a few hours before with the brave sergeant at Versailles, and seemed still to hear him speaking of his German home and the children who were waiting his return.

Of the many miseries of war that he witnessed during the great siege, there was none that he remembered with a sadder heart.

CHAPTER 11

England – Spiritualism and Science

The Investigation of Professor Crookes. Rigid tests. Wild theory of Professor Balfour Stewart. The evidence of recording instruments. Matter through matter. Materialized hands. A reversal of the law of gravity. Refusal of organized Science to investigate. Their mediaeval attitude. Dr. Higgins in public and in private. Sergeant Cox, O.C. Dr. Carpenter in the Quarterly Review.

"VIEWS OR OPINIONS I cannot be said to possess on a subject I do not pretend to understand."

Mr. W. Crookes, F.R.S published this declaration in July 1870, shortly after the announcement had been made in the Atheneceum that he was commencing a scientific investigation of Spiritualism. As nineteen-twentieths of mankind come by their opinions in the manner of the historic jury that proposed to return its verdict without hearing the evidence, the public naturally concluded that Mr. Crookes shared this common weakness of humanity, and he was deluged with letters inquiring what his opinions of Spiritualism were. By way of general response, he published a short article, "Spiritualism Viewed by the Light of Modern Science" that opens with the explanation above quoted.

"I consider it the duty of scientific men who have learnt exact modes of working," Mr. Crookes continued, "to examine phenomena which attract the attention of the public, in order to confirm their genuineness, or to explain, if possible, the delusions of the honest, and to expose the tricks of deceivers.

"In the present case, I prefer to enter upon the inquiry with no preconceived notions whatever as to what can or cannot be, but with all my senses alert and ready to convey information to the brain; believing, as I do, that we have by no means exhausted all human knowledge or fathomed the depths of all the physical forces.

"The modes of reasoning of scientific men appear to be generally misunderstood by Spiritualists with whom I have conversed; and the reluctance of the trained scientific mind to investigate this subject is frequently ascribed to unworthy motives. I think it will be of service if I illustrate the modes of thought current amongst those who investigate science, and say what kind of experimental proof science has a right to demand before admitting a new department of knowledge into her ranks. We must not mix up the exact and the inexact. The supremacy of accuracy must be absolute."

After passing some very severe reflections on "pseudo-scientific spiritualists," Mr. Crookes declares that: "In investigations which so completely baffle the ordinary observer, the thorough scientific man has a great advantage." The nature of that advantage he indicates as follows:

"The Spiritualist tells of bodies weighing 50 or 100lbs. being lifted up into the air without the intervention of any known force; but the scientific chemist is accustomed to use a balance which will render sensible a weight so small that it would take ten thousand of them to weigh one grain; he is therefore justified in asking that a power, professing to be guided by intelligence, which will toss a heavy body up to the ceiling, shall also cause his delicately poised balance to move under test conditions.

"The Spiritualist tells of tapping sounds which are produced in different parts of a room when two or more persons sit quietly round a table. The scientific experimenter is entitled to ask that these taps shall be produced on the stretched membrane of his phonautograph.

"The Spiritualist tells of rooms and houses being shaken, even to injury, by superhuman power. The man of science merely asks for a pendulum to be set vibrating when it is in a glass case and supported on solid masonry.

"The Spiritualist tells of heavy articles of furniture moving from one room to another without human agency. But the man of science has made instruments which will divide an inch into a million parts; and he is justified in doubting the accuracy of the former observations, if the same force is powerless to move the index of his instrument one poor degree."

I omit from my quotation the last of the tasks that Mr. Crookes, in the name of science, requested the spirits to perform an important exception. Later in this chapter I will explain what the demand was, and what the answer he received.

It will be by this time plain to the reader, I hope, that Mr. Crookes did not approach in anything like a credulous frame of mind an investigation which he states, in the same preliminary paper, to have been suggested to him "by eminent men exercising great influence on the thought of the country." His attitude towards Spiritualism was absolutely neutral and impartial an attitude that science ought surely to maintain in investigating any subject whatever, but that Faraday and Tyndall had failed to preserve. Of Dr. Carpenter's attitude towards Spiritualism I say nothing. I think I have already proved in these pages that he had at least two sets of opinions one for the public, another for himself but both of them contradictory and illogical.

An often-quoted passage from Lord Lytton's *Strange Story* seems to express exactly the temper in which Mr. Crookes began his inquiry. "I have no belief," Lytton makes the hero of his romance say. "True science has none. True science questions all things, takes nothing upon credit. It knows but three states of the mind denial, conviction, and that vast interval between the two, which is not belief, but suspense of judgment."

Mr. Crookes, then, until his investigations were completed, had suspended judgment. Like everybody else who had heard the subject of Spiritualism discussed, he had his impressions; but unlike the great body of the world especially of the scientific world he was able to distinguish those impressions from convictions, and to banish them from his mind in entering on his task. What they were, he has plainly stated in the paper from which I have already quoted: "Like other men who thought little of the matter and saw little, I believed that the whole affair was a superstition, or at least an unexplained trick." And that his expectation in July, 1870, was to be able to refer the phenomena to natural causes, and demonstrate those causes, the concluding words of the same paper prove: "The increased employment of scientific methods, will produce a race of observers who will drive the worthless residuum of spiritualism hence into the unknown limbo of magic and necromancy."

The announcement of Mr. Crookes' investigation, and his statement of its aim and methods, were received by the English press with high favour. At last the scientific St. George had stepped into the lists who was to slay the dragon of Spiritualism. The press was jubilant, and had nothing but compliments for Mr. Crookes. His proved ability and his high standing in the scientific world were loudly but a little too hastily extolled by writers who were confident that their accepted prophet would prophesy as they wished. One leading journal expressed "profound satisfaction that the subject was about to be investigated by a man so thoroughly qualified;" another was "gratified to learn that the matter was now receiving the attention of cool and clear-headed men of recognized position in science;" a third declared that "no one could doubt Mr. Crookes' ability to conduct the investigation with rigid philosophical impartiality;" and the proclamation of a fourth to its readers ran in these words: "If men like Mr. Crookes grapple with the subject, taking nothing for granted until it is proved, we shall soon know how much to believe."

The history of Balaam often repeats itself; but the world of our days is not so clear-sighted as the ass of the prophet, and has much to learn from her. Prolonged and rigid investigation compelled Mr. Crookes to bless where he should have cursed; and his late panegyrists united heartily in a chorus of invective when that eminently respectable authority, Dr. Carpenter, came forward to deride and calumniate Mr. Crookes and all who had shared his labours.

For the phenomena, it need hardly be said, had not been witnessed and tested by Mr. Crookes alone. Often the experiments were of such a character that at least two observers were necessary to ensure the scientific accuracy which the principal investigator desiderated. His chemical assistant took part in the researches; his brother, Mr. Walter Crookes, was also present at several séances; and from time to time Mr. Crookes invited several of his scientific brethren to witness his investigations and assist in them. The two secretaries of the Royal Society were asked by him to meet Mr. Home at his house. Both of them declined the invitation. It was quite within their right to do so; but really, after these and other refusals, the uncandid assertion that Mr.

Home shunned meeting scientific observers might with decency have been abandoned at least in England.

Of the various well known men who accepted the invitation of Mr. Crookes, two names came prominently before the public, those of Dr. Huggins, F.R.S the eminent physicist and astronomer, and Mr. Serjeant Cox. Both the distinguished man of science and the shrewd lawyer attested publicly the accuracy of a narrative contributed by Mr. Crookes to the *Quarterly Journal of Science* for July 1871.

This record dealt only with the phenomena witnessed and the tests applied at one particular séance. It was far from being the most remarkable of the series that took place at the house of Mr. Crookes; but he was influenced by weighty reasons in selecting it for publication. Not only had Dr. Huggins and Serjeant Cox been present, but Mr. Crookes had contrived for the occasion special apparatus to be employed in testing two of the most frequent physical phenomena, should they occur; the alteration in the weight of bodies and the playing of an accordion when no human hand was touching the keys. In the course of the evening both phenomena were searchingly and satisfactorily tested.

In dealing with the subject of Spiritualism, scientific critics repeatedly showed themselves as unfair and hasty as the rest of mankind. They did so on the publication of the results of this séance. Mr. Crookes had taken care to state that numerous other séances and experiments had preceded it; but his critics either did not notice the declaration or did not choose to notice it. They accused him of having rashly arrived at a conclusion on the strength of one or two experiments hastily performed. How thoroughly baseless was the charge even a sketch of Mr. Crookes' preceding investigations will show.

In July 1870, he published the explanation of the nature and aims of his inquiry from which I have quoted. Mr. Home returned from Russia at the end of March 1871; and immediately afterwards the series of experiments commenced that enabled Mr. Crookes "to affirm conclusively the existence of a new force."

The investigation had neither been avoided nor courted by Mr. Home. I repeat what I have already said, that he was indifferent whether Science concerned herself with his strange gift or not. He was perfectly ready to meet' scientific men if they wished it; but he was by no means disposed to admit that either Spiritualism or himself was honoured by their attentions, and considered that he best maintained the dignity of his cause by preserving an absolutely passive attitude in the matter, and neither seeking the notice of the scientific world nor shunning it. He rightly felt, too, that, if the manifestations were experimented upon, the experimenters ought to be men who showed themselves capable of approaching the subject in an unbiased and impartial manner. Faraday and Tyndall had prefaced their condescending intimation that they were willing to come to a séance by prejudging the question of the phenomena and insulting himself. I have in my possession a letter to Home written in the year 1868, at the time of his controversy with Professor Tyndall, the writer of which (Mr. Bertolacci) tells him that Tyndall had declared that "if his own senses were convinced of the reality of Spiritualism, he would deny his own senses." Was Mr. Home to go out of his way to court "with bated breath and whispering humbleness" the notice of such philosophy?

Unlike Professor Tyndall, Mr. Crookes had the courtesy to approach Mr. Home as one gentleman usually approaches another by obtaining an introduction. The acquaintance who gave it was Lady Burton, wife of the distinguished traveller and Orientalist. Home's absence at the scene of war, and afterwards in Russia, delayed the proposed series of experiments for some months, but on his return from St. Petersburg the sittings began.

In addition to this main series of experiments, Mr. Crookes investigated the pretensions of various persons claiming to be endowed with a gift akin to that of Home. With these researches I have no concern, nor am I called upon to offer an opinion as to their value. I am writing only of Mr. Home, on whom the gift that St. Paul terms "discerning of spirits," and that Serjeant Cox and Mr. Crookes termed "the development of psychic force," was conferred in greater measure than on any other man or woman of his time.

Home imposed no conditions whatever on the investigator, but placed himself unreservedly in the hands of Mr. Crookes.

The séances that ensued were held in a strong light. Here are the words of Mr. Crookes:

"Of all persons endowed with a powerful development of this Psychic Force, Mr. Daniel Dunglas Home is the most remarkable, and it is mainly owing to the many opportunities I have had of carrying on my investigation in his presence that I am enabled to affirm so conclusively the existence of this Force.

"It is a well-ascertained fact that when the force is weak a bright light exerts an interfering action on some of the phenomena. The power possessed by Mr. Home is sufficiently strong to withstand this antagonistic influence; consequently, he always objects to darkness at his séances. Except on two occasions, when, for some particular experiments of my own, light was excluded, everything which I have witnessed with him has taken place in the light.

"There is a wide difference between the tricks of a professional conjuror, surrounded by his apparatus and aided by any number of concealed assistants and confederates, deceiving the senses by clever sleight-of-hand on his own platform, and the phenomena occurring in the presence of Mr. Home, which take place in the light, in a private room that almost up to the commencement of the séance has been occupied as a living room, and surrounded by private friends of my own, who not only will not countenance the slightest deception, but who are watching narrowly everything that takes place. Moreover, Mr. Home has frequently been searched before and after the séances, and he always offers to allow it. During the most remarkable occurrences, I have occasionally held both his hands, and placed my feet on his feet. On no single occasion have I proposed a modification of arrangements for the purpose of rendering trickery less possible which he has not at once assented to, and frequently he has himself drawn attention to tests which might be tried." (*Quarterly Journal of Science*, 1871 and 1874.)

What could investigator ask more than to conduct his inquiry under circumstances so favourable to exact research? Here were no darkened cabinets, rendering necessary the invention of a phosphorus lamp to bring the eyesight into play at all. The room was always fully lighted; Mr. Home imposed no conditions, and objected to no tests. The séances were held in Mr. Crookes' house, the sitters were selected by himself. "With the exception of cases specially mentioned," he writes, "the occurrences have taken place in my own house, *in the light, and with only private friends present* besides the medium." (*Notes of an Enquiry into the Phenomena called Spiritual.*) The italics are Mr. Crookes' own.

Of the ability of Mr. Crookes to conduct an inquiry, especially scientific in its character, no fair-minded man could have a doubt. His scientific training had commenced before he was sixteen, and at the time of his séances with Mr. Home had continued during a quarter of a century. "My scientific education," he declared in his reply to the spiteful calumnies of Dr. Carpenter, "has been one continuous lesson in exactness of observation." His labours have extended over a wide field of science; and their valuable nature has been repeatedly recognized by various scientific bodies, including the Royal Society, of which he was elected a Fellow so long ago as 1863. Recent honours conferred upon him by that body will be fresh in the minds of English scientific readers. The reception accorded by the Royal Society to the papers in which he detailed some of his experiments with Mr. Home only demonstrated that scientific men in general are creatures of their age and share its prejudices.

Not till June 15th, 1871, did Mr. Crookes submit to the Royal Society a description of certain of the phenomena he had witnessed in Mr. Home's presence, and of the scientific tests he had applied to them. By that time a great number of séances had been held. Mr. Crookes had keenly scrutinized the phenomena witnessed, and had called in the help of other scientific men to aid him in scrutinizing them. Unsatisfied with the testimony of their senses and his own, he had proceeded to call in better witnesses still, witnesses that could not exaggerate or be mistaken. Much of the phenomena he had witnessed seemed to negative that cardinal article of scientific faith, the invariable action of the force of gravitation. Mr. Crookes accordingly proceeded to construct instruments capable of registering this fact, if a fact it were. Having perfected his apparatus, he employed it again and again; and on every occasion it recorded the fact that appeared so incredible to him. How incredible it had appeared, let his own words testify:

"The phenomena I am prepared to attest are so extraordinary, and so directly oppose the most firmly-rooted articles of scientific belief amongst others, the ubiquity and invariable action of the force of gravitation that, even now, on recalling the details of what I witnessed, there is an antagonism in my mind between reason, which pronounces it to be scientifically impossible, and the consciousness that my senses, both of touch and sight and these corroborated, as they were, by the senses of all who were present are not lying witnesses when they testify against my preconceptions."

Lying witnesses, however, some of the scientific brethren of Mr. Crookes insisted them to have been. Professor Balfour Stewart, for instance, hazarded the theory that Mr. Home was simply a man possessed of great "electro-biological power," by means of which he influenced those present at his séances in plain words that he was a mesmerizer who could mesmerize at once a whole room-full of people. In reply, Mr. Crookes pointed to the apparatus that he had invented and the results that it had recorded. "However susceptible the persons in the room might have been to that assumed influence," he wrote, "it will hardly be contended that Mr. Home biologized the recording instruments."

Probably Professor Stewart, if reduced to select between this hypothesis and a confession that the evidence adduced by Mr. Crookes could not be overset, would have boldly pronounced for the former, and have declared that he saw no reason why instruments might not be susceptible to mesmeric influences as well as human beings.

It is much to be regretted that Mr. Crookes has never published an exhaustive account of his experiences with Mr. Home. He had intended, he wrote in January 1874, to embody the results of his lengthy investigations of Spiritualism, or, as he preferred to term it, of "Psychic Force," in the form of one or two articles supplementary to those he had already published in the *Quarterly Journal of Science*. "However, on going over my notes," he adds, "I find such a wealth of facts, such a superabundance of evidence, so overwhelming a mass of testimony, all of which will have to be marshalled in order, that I could fill several numbers of the *Quarterly*. I must therefore be content on this occasion with an outline only of my labours."

It may be asked what origin Mr. Crookes attributed to the phenomena of which he so emphatically attested the existence. He hesitated to propound a theory at least to propound it publicly. "I have desired," he wrote in December 1871, "to examine the phenomena from a point of view as strictly physical as their nature will permit. I wish to ascertain the laws governing the appearance of very remarkable phenomena. That a hitherto unrecognized form of Force whether it be called psychic force or x force is of little consequence is involved in this occurrence, is not with me a matter of opinion, but of absolute knowledge; but the nature of that force, or the cause which immediately excites its activity, forms a subject on which I do not at present feel competent to offer an opinion."

And again, in January 1874: "It is obvious that a 'medium' possesses a something which is not possessed by an ordinary being. Give this something a name. Call it 'x' if you like. Mr. Serjeant Cox calls it 'Psychic Force.'"

This last passage occurs in a paper entitled *Notes of an Enquiry into the Phenomena called Spiritual*." By far the greater portion of the notes refer to phenomena observed at séances with Home. "I speak chiefly of Mr. Home," writes Mr. Crookes, "as he is so much more powerful than most of the other, mediums I have experimented with." A few extracts from these interesting and valuable notes will convey some idea of the number and variety of the phenomena witnessed and tested by Mr. Crookes in Mr. Home's presence during an inquiry extending over several months of 1871.

Mr. Crookes classifies the phenomena in question under thirteen different headings. The first treats of the movements of tables and other heavy bodies when the hands of the sitters were laid on them. This manifestation he dismisses with brief remark.

"It varies in degree," he writes, "from a quivering or vibration of the room and its contents, to the actual rising into the air of a heavy body when the hand is placed on it. The retort is obvious that if people are touching a thing when it moves, they push it, or pull it, or lift it; I have proved experimentally that this is not the case in numerous instances, but as a matter of evidence I attach little importance to this class of phenomena by itself, and only mention them as a preliminary to other movements of the same kind, but without contact."

More interesting to Mr. Crookes was the remarkable phenomenon that thousands before him had noted at séances with Mr. Home.

"These movements," he continues, "and, indeed, I may say the same of every kind of phenomenon, are generally preceded by a peculiar cold air, sometimes amounting to a decided wind. I have had sheets of paper blown about by it, and a thermometer lowered several degrees. On some occasions I have not detected any actual movements of the air, but the cold has been so intense that I could only compare it to that felt when the hand has been within a few inches of frozen mercury."

Passing to that means of communication with the sitters ordinarily employed by the intelligences at work, the manifestation popularly termed "rappings," and by Mr. Crookes "percussive and other allied sounds," he says: "The popular name of raps; conveys a very erroneous impression of this class of phenomena." I have quoted in an early chapter his description of their varied nature. "With a full knowledge," he adds, "of the numerous theories which have been started, chiefly in America, to explain these sounds, I have tested them in every way that I could devise, until there has been no escape from the conviction that they were true objective occurrences not produced by trickery or mechanical means."

Concerning the messages conveyed by means of these "percussive sounds," Mr. Crookes says very little. A discussion of this most important subject of all would have led him beyond the scope of his inquiry, which he wished to limit as much as possible to phenomena that he could make the subject of scientific experiment. In other words, he devoted has attention to the physical phenomena of Spiritualism, passing over the psychical with the remark:

"At a very early stage of the inquiry, it was seen that the power producing the phenomena was not merely a blind force, but was associated with or governed by intelligence: thus the sounds to which I have just alluded will be repeated a definite number of times, they will come loud or faint, and in different places at request; and, by a pre-arranged code of signals, questions are answered, and messages given with more or less accuracy. The intelligence is sometimes of such a character as to lead to the belief that it does not emanate from any person present."

Towards the close of his article, Mr. Crookes reverts to the question of the intelligence directing the phenomena, and narrates the following occurrence, among others, in support of his testimony that he had "observed some circumstances which seem conclusively to point to the agency of an outside intelligence, not belonging to any human being in the room":

"During a séance with Mr. Home, a small lath, which I have before mentioned, moved across the table to me, in the light, and delivered a message to me by tapping my hand; I repeating the alphabet, and the lath tapping me at the right letters. The other end of the lath was resting on the table, some distance from Mr. Home's hands.

"The taps were so sharp and clear, and the lath was evidently so well under control of the invisible power which was governing its movements, that I said, 'Can the intelligence governing the motion of this lath change the character of the movements, and give me a telegraphic message through the Morse alphabet by taps on my hand?' (I have every reason to believe that the Morse code was quite unknown to any other person present, and it was only imperfectly known to me.) Immediately I said this, the character of the taps changed, and the message was continued in the way I had requested. The letters were given too rapidly for me to do more than catch a word here and there, and consequently I lost the message; but I heard sufficient to convince me that there was a good Morse operator at the other end of the line, wherever that might be."

Under his third heading, Mr. Crookes deals with the alteration of the weight of bodies. For particulars he refers to former papers published by him, of which I shall presently speak, including the experiments witnessed by Dr. Muggins and Serjeant Cox.

The fourth and fifth sections treat of a phenomenon that has been witnessed on thousands of occasions at séances with Home, and that always startled those who observed it for the first time the movement of articles of furniture when no person was near them. Sometimes these bodies glided across the floor towards the sitters, at other times they rose clear of the ground; the one and the other manifestation, let it be remembered, taking place in full light.

"A chair," writes Mr. Crookes, "was seen by all present to move slowly up to the table from a far corner, when all were watching it; on another occasion an arm-chair moved to where we were sitting, and then moved slowly back again (a distance of about three feet) at my request. On three successive evenings a small table moved slowly across the room, under conditions which I had specially pre-arranged, so as to answer any objection which might be raised to the evidence. I have had several repetitions of the experiment considered by the Committee of the Dialectical Society to be conclusive, viz., the movement of a heavy table in full light, the chairs turned with their backs to the table about a foot off, and each person kneeling on his chair, with hands resting over the backs of the chairs, but not touching the table.

"On five separate occasions a heavy dining-table rose between a few inches and one and a half feet off the floor, under special circumstances, which rendered trickery impossible. On another occasion the table rose from the floor, not only when no person was touching it, but under conditions which I had pre-arranged so as to assure unquestionable proof of the fact.

"A remark," adds Mr. Crookes, "is generally made when occurrences of this kind are mentioned, why is it only tables and chairs which do these things? Why is this property peculiar to furniture? I might reply that I only observe and record facts, and do not profess to enter into the Why and Wherefore; but, indeed, it will be obvious that if a heavy inanimate body in an ordinary dining-room has to rise off the floor it cannot very well be anything else but a table or a chair. That this propensity is not specially attached to furniture, I have had abundant evidence; but, like other experimental demonstrators, the intelligence or power, whatever it may be, which produces these phenomena can only work with the materials which are available."

On three separate occasions Mr. Crookes saw Mr. Home in full light rise clear of the floor of the room and float in the air. I have already quoted his description of these levitations.

Besides the movements of heavy bodies, such as tables and chairs, at a distance from the sitters, Mr. Crookes witnessed similar phenomena in connection with smaller articles, the room being always fully lighted. "It is idle," he wrote, "to attribute these results to trickery, for I would again remind my readers that what I relate has not been accomplished at the house of a medium, but in my own house, where preparations have been quite impossible. A medium, walking into my dining-room, cannot, while seated in one part of the loom with a number of persons keenly watching him, by trickery make an accordion play in my own hand when I hold it keys downwards, or cause the same accordion to float about the room playing all the time. He cannot introduce machinery which will wave window-curtains or pull up Venetian blinds eight feet off, tie a knot in a handkerchief and place it in a far corner of the room, sound notes on a distant piano cause a fan to move about and fan the company, or set in motion a pendulum when enclosed in a glass case firmly cemented to the wall."

The last of these phenomena, it will be remembered, was among the demands that Mr. Crookes, in the name of science, had put forth in his preliminary paper. The remaining tests there indicated by him as satisfactory were all furnished to him at one time or another during his séances with Home, with the exception of the last. I designedly omitted that concluding demand in quoting the others: it was as follows:

"The Spiritualist," wrote Mr. Crookes in July 1870, "tells of flowers with the fresh dew on them, of fruit, and living objects being carried through closed windows, and even solid brick-walls. The scientific investigator naturally asks that an additional weight (if it be only the 1000th part of a grain) be deposited on one pan of his balance when the case is locked. And the chemist asks for the 1000th part of a grain of arsenic to be carried through the sides of a glass tube in which pure water is hermetically sealed."

No "flowers with the dew on them," &c., had ever been brought through closed windows or solid brick walls at séances with Home. Such phenomena generally occur only in absolute darkness. That answer made by the spirits to the last of Mr. Crookes' demands was that the passage of matter through matter was impossible; and some manifestations having occurred at his house that seemed to contradict this statement, it was affirmed in the following manner:

"The circumstance I will relate," says Mr. Crookes, "occurred in the light one Sunday evening, only Mr. Home and members of my family being present. My wife and I had been spending the day in the country, and had brought home a few flowers we had gathered. On reaching home we gave them to a servant to put in water. Mr. Home came soon after; and we at once proceeded to the dining room. As we were sitting down, a servant brought in the flowers, which she had arranged in a vase. I placed it in the centre of the dining table, which was without a cloth. This was the first time Mr. Home had seen these flowers.

"After several phenomena had occurred, the conversation turned upon some circumstances which seemed only explicable on the assumption that matter had actually passed through a solid substance. Thereupon a message was given by means of the alphabet: 'It is impossible for matter to pass through matter, but we will show you what we can do.' We waited in silence. Presently a luminous appearance was seen hovering over the bouquet of flowers, and then in full view of all present, a piece of china-grass, 15 inches long, which formed the centre ornament of the bouquet, slowly rose from the other flowers, and then descended to the table in front of the vase between it and Mr. Home. It did not stop on reaching the table, but went straight through it, and we all watched it till it had entirely passed through. Immediately on the disappearance of the grass, my wife, who was sitting near Mr. Home, saw a hand come up from under the table between them, holding the piece of grass. It tapped her on the shoulder two or three times with a sound audible to all, then laid the grass on the floor, and disappeared. Only two persons saw the hand, but all in the room saw the piece of grass moving about as I have described. During the time this was taking place, Mr. Home's hands were seen by all to be quietly resting on the table in front of him. The place where the grass disappeared was 18 inches from his hands. The table was a telescope dining table, opening with a screw; there was no leaf in it, and the junction of the two sides formed a narrow crack down the middle. The grass had passed through this chink, which I measured, and found to be barely 1/8th inch wide. The stem of the piece of grass was far too thick to enable me to force it through this crack without injuring it, yet we had all seen it pass through quietly and smoothly; and, on examination, it did not show the slightest signs of pressure or abrasion."

With such phenomena and others still more marvellous constantly occurring under the circumstances that he, Mr. Home, had arranged, it was impossible for Mr. Crookes to resist conviction. And I cannot too often repeat, for the benefit of the reader who is accustomed to associate Spiritualism with the idea of darkness, that Mr. Crookes carried on his investigations with Mr. Home in strong light trying now one kind of light, now another, with a view to observing the effect of each. "I have had many opportunities," he wrote, "of testing the action of light of different sources and colours, such as sunlight, diffused daylight, moonlight, gas, lamp, and candle light, electric light from a vacuum tube, homogeneous yellow light, &c. The interfering rays appear to be those at the extreme end of the spectrum."

In the narrative just quoted, Mr. Crookes speaks of a luminous appearance that was seen by all present to hover over the vase of flowers, and of a hand that subsequently became visible to Mrs. Crookes and another of the sitters. In various portions of this work I have quoted testimony showing that these apparitions were seldom visible to all the persons present at a séance. Lord Dunraven repeatedly records this fact, so does Mr. Crookes. "The hands and fingers," he wrote, "do not always appear to me to be solid and lifelike. Sometimes, indeed, they present more the appearance of a nebulous cloud partly condensed into the form of a hand. This is not equally visible to all present. For instance, a flower or other small object is seen to move; one person present will see a luminous cloud hovering over it, another will detect a nebulous looking hand, whilst others will see nothing but the moving flower. I have more than once seen, first an object move, then a luminous cloud appear to form about it, and lastly, the cloud condense into shape and become a perfectly formed hand."

In view of these facts, attested by Mr. Crookes, Lord Dunraven, and many other observers, what becomes of the silly fable of mechanical contrivances? Will any reasoning being maintain that this theory is tenable in face of such evidence; and that, when Mr. Crookes and his friends were observing the phenomena in full light, it would have been possible for one to mistake a wax cast, glove at the end of a wire, or other contrivance for a hand; for another to fail to see anything, and for a third to behold the contrivance as a luminous cloud condensing gradually into a perfectly formed hand?

Only when fully formed, says Mr. Crookes, did the spirit-hand become visible to all present. "It is not always a mere form," he writes, "but sometimes appears perfectly life like and graceful, the fingers moving and the flesh apparently as human as that of any in the room. At the wrist, or arm, it becomes hazy, and fades off into a luminous cloud."

Here is his further testimony to these appearances:

"In the light I have seen a luminous cloud hover over a heliotrope on a side table, break a sprig off, and carry the sprig to a lady; and on some occasions I have seen a similar luminous cloud visibly condense to the form of a hand and carry small objects about.

"A beautifully formed small hand rose up from an opening in a dining-table and gave me a flower; it appeared and then disappeared three times at intervals, affording me ample opportunity of satisfying myself that it was as real in appearance as my own. This occurred in the light in my own room, whilst I was holding the medium's hands and feet.

"At another time a finger and thumb were seen to pick the petals from a flower in Mr. Home's button-hole, and lay them in front of several persons who were sitting near him.

"A hand has repeatedly been seen by myself and others playing the keys of an accordion, both of the medium's hands being visible at the same time, and sometimes being held by those near him.

"To the touch, the hand sometimes appears icy-cold and dead, at other times warm and lifelike, grasping my own with the firm pressure of an old friend."

Did Mr. Crookes, it will be asked, resort to no decisive means to assure himself of the unearthly nature of these apparitions? Yes.

"I have retained one of these hands in my own," he wrote, "firmly resolved not to let it escape. There was no struggle or effort made to get loose, but it gradually seemed to resolve itself into vapour, and faded in that manner from my grasp."

At the Tuileries in 1857 a spirit-hand, as I have already related, lifted a pencil that was lying on the table, and, in presence of the Emperor and Empress, wrote on a sheet of paper the single word "Napoleon." Mr. Crookes, during a séance in 1871, expressed the desire to witness a similar phenomenon. The result was the manifestation thus described by him:

"A good failure," he writes, "often teaches more than the most successful experiment." It took place in the light, in my own room, with only a few private friends and Mr. Home present. Several circumstances, to which I need not further allude, had shown that the power that evening was strong. I therefore expressed a wish to witness the actual production of a written message such as I had heard described a short time before by a friend. Immediately an alphabetic communication was made as follows: 'We will try.' A pencil and some sheets of paper had been lying on the centre of the table; presently the pencil rose up on its point, and, after advancing by hesitating jerks to the paper, fell down. It then rose, and again fell. A third time it tried, but with no better result. After three unsuccessful attempts, a small wooden lath which was lying near upon the table slid towards the pencil, and rose a few inches from the table; the pencil rose again, and propping itself against the lath, the two together made an effort to mark the paper. It fell, and then a joint effort was again made. After a third trial the lath gave it up and moved back to its place, the pencil lay as it fell across the paper, and an alphabetic message told us 'We have tried to do as you asked, but our power is exhausted."

The appearance of the full human figure was as rare as apparitions of hands were frequent. The why is easy to indicate. By whatever means spirits produced these impressions on the senses of sight and touch, it is obvious that to make a hand visible would be a work of less difficulty to the intelligences operating than to render manifest the full form. When the latter did appear, it was under conditions that rendered the thought of trickery impossible. There was no darkened recess with a "medium" shut inside to operate the production of a "materialized spirit" at his leisure. There among the observers sat Home; and there, distinct and separate from him, stood the phantom. Mr. Crookes' testimony concerning the phantom forms beheld by him is as follows:

"These are the rarest of the phenomena I have witnessed. The conditions requisite for their appearance appear to be so delicate, and such trifles interfere with their production, that only on very few occasions have I witnessed them under satisfactory test conditions. I will mention two of these cases.

"In the dusk of the evening, during a séance with Mr. Home at my house, the curtains of a window about eight feet from Mr. Home were seen to move. A dark, shadowy, semi-transparent form, like that of a man, was then seen by all present standing near the window, waving the curtain with his hand. As we looked, the form faded away and the curtains ceased to move.

"The following is a still more striking instance. A phantom form came from the corner of the room, took an accordion in its hand, and then glided about the room playing the instrument. The form was visible to all present for many minutes, Mr. Home also being seen at the same time. Coming rather close to a lady who was sitting apart from the rest of the company, she gave a slight cry, upon which it vanished."

I have now summarized a few and only a few of the experiences of Mr. Crookes, as related by himself. In view of them, it was not surprising that he should write to Mr. Home on April 12th 1871: "What a wonderful séance it was last night! The more I think of it, the more impressed I am with its extraordinary character. Pray do not hesitate to mention me as one of the firmest believers in you. Half a dozen such séances as that, with a few picked scientific men (I have the list of eligibles already drawn out), and the scientific recognition of these truths would be as undoubted as are the facts of electricity."

The "eligibles," with hardly an exception, declined the invitation of Mr. Crookes to co-operate in his researches.

"I confess," he told the readers of the *Quarterly Journal of Science*, in July, 1871, "I am surprised and pained at the timidity or apathy shown by scientific men in reference to this subject. Some little time ago, when an opportunity for examination was first presented to me, I invited the cooperation of some scientific friends in a systematic investigation; but I soon found that to obtain a scientific committee for the investigation of this class of facts was out of the question, and that I must be content to rely on my own endeavours, aided by the cooperation from time to time of a few scientific and learned friends who were willing to join in the inquiry. I still feel that it would be better were such a committee of known men to be formed, who would meet Mr. Home in a fair and unbiased manner, and I would gladly assist in its formation; but the difficulties in the way are great."

They proved insuperable, but they were raised by Science, not by Mr. Home. In default of a regular committee, Mr. Crookes called to his aid the scientific and learned friends to whom he refers. Only the names of Dr. Huggins and Mr. Serjeant Cox came before the public, and these in connection with only a single séance of several at which these two well-known men had been present. That séance was, as I have said, selected for publication because of the searching tests that had been applied to the phenomena observed.

"In the afternoon," wrote Mr. Crookes, "I called for Mr. Home at his apartments, and when there he suggested that, as he had to change his dress, perhaps I should not object to continue our conversation in his bedroom. I am therefore enabled to state positively that no machinery, apparatus, or contrivance of any sort was secreted about his person."

The two then proceeded to the house of Mr. Crookes. The investigators who were present that evening consisted of Dr. Huggins, F.R.S Mr. Serjeant Cox, Mr. William Crookes, F.R.S his brother Mr. Walter Crookes, and his chemical assistant.

To test the playing of the accordion, should that phenomenon occur, Mr. Crookes had prepared a cage consisting of a drum-shaped wooden frame, with insulated copper wire wound round it. The strands of wire were then firmly netted together with string, "so as to form," says Mr. Crookes, "meshes rather less than two inches long by one inch high. The height of this cage was such that it would just slip under my dining table, but be too close to the top to allow of the hand being introduced into the interior, or to admit of a foot being pushed underneath it. In another room were two Grove's cells, wires being led from them into the dining-room for connection, if desirable, with the wire surrounding the cage."

The accordion had been provided by Mr. Crookes. "It was a new one," he writes, "having been purchased by myself for the purpose of these experiments. Mr. Home had neither handled nor seen the instrument before the commencement of the test-experiments."

To test another frequent phenomenon, the alteration of the weight of bodies, Mr. Crookes had fitted up an apparatus the salient feature of which was a mahogany board three feet long.

"At each end a strip of mahogany 1&1/2 inches wide was screwed on, forming feet. One end of the board rested on a firm table, whilst the other end was supported by a spring balance hanging from a substantial tripod stand. The balance was fitted with a self-registering index, in such a manner that it would record the maximum weight indicated by the pointer. The apparatus was adjusted so that the mahogany board was horizontal, its foot resting flat on the support. In this position its weight was 3lbs., as marked by the pointer of the balance." (*Quarterly Journal of Science*, July, 1871.) It was designed by the constructor of this apparatus that Mr. Home should place his finger tips on that end of the mahogany board which rested on the table. If the index of the balance then descended, it would be conclusively demonstrated that muscular force was not the agent at work, since no pressure applied by Mr. Home's fingers to the end of the board farthest from the balance could cause the index to descend.

Both the cage and the other apparatus had been constructed without any intimation of their nature being communicated to Mr. Home "Before Mr. Home entered the room," says Mr. Crookes, "the apparatus had been arranged in position, and he had not even the object of some parts of it explained before sitting down."

The experiment with the accordion was first tried. The room was fully lighted with gas. Mr. Home sat in a low easy chair at the side of the table.

"In front of him under the table," says Mr. Crookes, "was the aforesaid cage, one of his legs being on each side of it. I sat close to him on his left, and another observer sat close to him on his right. When anything of importance was occurring, the observers on each side of Mr. Home kept their feet respectively on his feet, so as to be able to detect the slightest movement.

"Mr. Home took the accordion between the thumb and middle finger of one hand at the opposite end to the keys. Having previously opened the bass key myself, and the cage being drawn from under the table so as just to allow the accordion to be passed in with its keys downwards, it was pushed back as close as Mr. Home's arm would permit, but without hiding his hand from those next to him."

Presently the accordion played.

"Dr. Huggins now looked under the table, and said that Mr. Home's hand appeared quite still, whilst the accordion was moving about emitting distinct sounds.

"Mr. Home still holding the accordion in the usual manner in the cage, his feet being held by those next him, and his other hand resting on the table, we heard distinct and separate notes sounded in succession, and then a simple air was played. As such a result could only have been produced by the various keys of the instrument being acted upon in harmonious succession, this was considered by those present to be a crucial experiment. But the sequel was still more striking.

"Mr. Home removed his hand altogether from the accordion, and taking his hand quite out of the cage, placed it in the hand of the person next to him." His other hand remained on the table. "The instrument," writes Mr. Crookes, "then continued to play, no person touching it and no hand being near it."

The current from the battery was now passed round the insulated wire of the cage. The accordion again played. Mr. Home a second time removed his hand from it, and laid that hand upon the table, where it was taken by the observer next to him.

"Both his hands," says Mr. Crookes, "were now seen by all present. I and two of the others present saw the accordion distinctly floating about inside the cage with no visible support."

Mr. Home presently re-inserted his hand in the cage and again took hold of the accordion. It then commenced to play, at first chords and runs, and afterwards a well-known sweet and plaintive melody, which it executed perfectly in a very beautiful manner. Whilst this tune was being played, I grasped Mr. Home's arm, below the elbow, and gently slid my hand down it until I touched the top of the accordion. He was not moving a muscle. His other hand was on the table, visible to all, and his feet were under the feet of those next to him.

"Having met with such striking results in the experiments with the accordion in the cage, we turned to the balance apparatus."

I have already quoted Mr. Crookes' description of that apparatus. It is figured by woodcuts in his pages, as also are the experiments with the accordion.

"Mr. Home," writes Mr. Crookes, "placed the tips of his fingers lightly on the extreme end of the mahogany board which was resting on the support, whilst Dr. Huggins and myself sat, one on each side of it, watching for any effect which might be produced. Almost immediately the pointer of the balance was seen to descend. After a few seconds it rose again. This movement was repeated several times, as if by successive waves of the Psychic Force."

Only the scientific reader can fully appreciate the impression made by this phenomenon on the little party of scientific men observing it. Here was a downward pull applied to the balance before their eyes, when the conditions rendered it impossible for Mr. Home to make the index of that balance descend.

The board was arranged perfectly horizontally. The wooden foot screwed beneath it and resting on the table was one 1&1/2 wide. Across the upper surface of the board, at the same distance of 1&1/2 inches from the end, Mr. Crookes, with the acquiescence of Dr. Huggins, drew a line in pencil. Beyond this line Mr. Home's fingers were not at any time advanced.

"Now, the wooden foot," writes Mr. Crookes, "being also

1&1/2 inches wide, and resting flat on the table, it is evident that no amount of pressure exerted within this space of inches could produce any action on the balance.

"Again, it is also evident that when the end furthest from Mr. Home sank, the board would turn on the further edge of this foot as on a fulcrum. The arrangement was consequently that of a see-saw, 36 inches in length, the fulcrum being 1&1/2 inches from one end; were he, therefore, to have exerted a downward pressure, it would have been in opposition to the force which was causing the other end of the board to move down."

In other words, it would have been as easy for Mr. Home to have caused his chair to rise into the air by sitting on it, as to have caused the index of the balance to descend by pressing on that end of the board where his fingers rested.

When the descent of the balance was noted,

"Mr. Home of his own accord took," writes Mr. Crookes, "a small hand-bell and a little card match-box, which happened to be near, and placed one under each hand, to satisfy us, as he said, that he was not producing the downward pressure. The very slow oscillation of the spring balance became more marked, and Dr. Huggins, watching the index, said that he saw it descend to 65lbs. The normal weight of the board as so suspended being 3lbs the additional downward pull was therefore 3&1/2 lbs. On looking immediately afterwards at the automatic register, we saw that the index had at one time descended as low as 9lbs showing a maximum pull of 6lbs upon a board whose normal weight was 3lbs."

Wishing to try whether it were possible to produce much effect on the spring balance by pressure on that end of the board where Mr. Home's fingers had rested, Mr. Crookes stood on one foot at the end of the board. Dr. Huggins watched the index of the balance, and recorded that the whole weight of Mr. Crookes' body (140 lb.) when thus applied only sank the index 1lb., and when he jerked up and down 2lb. And this result was only obtained because the foot of Mr. Crookes extended beyond the fulcrum, which the fingers of Mr. Home had never passed.

"Mr. Home had been sitting in a low easy chair," adds Mr. Crookes, "and could not, had he tried his utmost, have exerted any material influence on the results. I need scarcely add that his feet as well as his hands were closely guarded by all in the room. This experiment appears to me more striking, if possible, than the one with the accordion."

On putting into the form of an article the notes of these facts made at the time, Mr. Crookes sent proofs of his paper to Dr. Huggins and Mr. Serjeant Cox. The former attested as follows the correctness of the statements it contained:

"June 9, 1871.

"Dear Mr. Crookes, Your proof appears to me to contain a correct statement of what took place in my presence at your house. My position at the table did not permit me to be a witness to the withdrawal of Mr. Home's hand from the accordion, but such was stated to be the case at the time by yourself and by the person sitting on the other side of Mr. Home.

"The experiments appear to me to show the importance of further investigation, but I wish it to be understood that I express no opinion as to the cause of the phenomena which took place. Yours very truly,

"William Huggins."

Being intended for publication, the expressions of Dr. Huggins were naturally weighed by him with the utmost caution. He wished, if possible, to give his testimony to facts without offending the ingrained prejudices of the scientific world. But "no man can serve two masters"; and Dr. Carpenter, in the name of the world of science, attacked his brother F.R.S. as venomously as if Dr. Huggins had stated a belief that the phenomena were the work of disembodied spirits.

In private, Dr. Huggins was more outspoken. "I saw Huggins yesterday," writes Mr. Crookes to Mr. Home on July 18th, 1871. "He has been doing good work with his tongue. Although a coward with his pen, he is as bold as a lion in talking."

In a lengthy letter to Mr. Crookes, Mr. Serjeant Cox not only attested in his turn the exactitude of the account of the experiments furnished by the principal investigator, but proceeded to theorize as to the origin of the phenomena which neither of the two scientific observers had done. I extract a portion of the learned Serjeant's testimony:

"June 8, 1871.

"My dear Sir, Having been present, for the purpose of scrutiny, at the trial of the experiments reported in this paper, I readily bear my testimony to the perfect accuracy of your description of them, and to the care and caution with which the various crucial tests were applied.

"The results appear to me conclusively to establish the important fact that there is a force proceeding from the nerve-system capable of imparting motion and weight to solid bodies within the sphere of its influence.

"I venture to suggest that the force be termed the Psychic Force; and the persons in whom it is manifested in extraordinary power Psychics.

"Permit me, also, to propose the early formation of a Psychological Society, purposely for the promotion of the study of that hitherto neglected Science. I am, &c., "Edward William Cox."

I believe the Society now flourishing under the name suggested by Serjeant Cox owes its origin to his efforts. He devoted much time to the investigation of the phenomena, and Mr. Home, at his entreaty, held several séances at the learned Serjeant's residence.

At one of these a person of the name of Spiller was present, who, on the publication of Mr. Crookes' papers, darkly intimated in the columns of the *Echo* that "an' he would" etc. Pressed by Mr. Crookes to explain, Mr. Spiller made several assertions concerning the séance at the house of Mr. Serjeant Cox. Not only did they furnish no explanation of the phenomena, but one and all were easily proved by Mr. Crookes to be direct misstatements of fact, conflicting with Mr. Spiller's own declaration at the time of the séance. The most important was that a light, assumed to be a spirit-light, had been seen playing about Mr. Home's hands. It was a reflection, said the veracious Mr. Spiller, "from the shining surface of Mr. H.'s monster locket." In reply, Mr. Crookes showed that no one but Mr. Spiller himself had spoken of having seen this light. It would have been strange indeed if more candid inquirers had seen it for the locket (which still exists) is not only small, but is of dull platinum. It is so covered on both sides with ornamental engraving, "that," writes Mr. Crookes, in discussing

Mr. Spiller's statements, "there is not a particle of polished platinum about it. I have," he adds, "carefully examined the optical properties of this locket. Tested in an accurate photometer, the reflecting power of each side is found to be equal to that of a silvered glass speculum less than one-tenth of an inch square."

Such were the weapons with which an attack on the testimony of Mr. Crookes was conducted by a person professing to be a scientific controversialist!

Were it worth while, I might here show, from the letters of Serjeant Cox to Mr. Home, that the former had many experiences at séances with Home which he found his theory of "psychic force" quite insufficient to explain. Always, when this was the case, the learned Serjeant proceeded to supplement his pet hypothesis by other theories, some sober, a few wild. He was a typical representative of a class of persons not uncommon, who are better fitted to observe facts than to deduce inferences from them. Mr. Serjeant Cox, untruly styled by Dr. Carpenter in the *Quarterly Review* an infatuated Spiritualist, conducted his researches with Mr. Home in a spirit of keen and sceptical inquiry. He was slow in arriving at conviction nay, even when convinced, the antagonism between reason and the evidence of his senses that Mr. Crookes found in his own mind was equally present in the mind of Serjeant Cox. Under its influence, he submitted for Home's consideration one conjecture after another respecting the origin of the phenomena, constructing them with rashness in inverse proportion to the wary scepticism with which he had investigated the phenomena themselves.

I may here mention that Serjeant Cox was present at some of the manifestations recorded by Lords Dunraven and Adare. "I remember once with you at Sydenham," he writes to Mr. Home in 1878, "seeing a hand in the daylight come over the table and hand a flower to Lord Dunraven. ... I have never seen any phenomena to compare with yours." Under the date of 1876, I shall quote an interesting letter written in that year by Serjeant Cox to Mr. Home, in which the Serjeant avows how entirely opposed to his prejudices and preconceptions were the convictions impressed on him by his séances with Home.

Desiring to experiment still further with the phenomenon of

alterations in the weight of bodies, Mr. Crookes planned an addition to his apparatus. "On trying these experiments for the first time," he explains, "I thought that actual contact between Mr. Home's hands and the suspended body whose weight was to be altered was essential to the exhibition of the force; but I found afterwards that this was not a necessary condition."

Mr. Crookes had already sent to the Royal Society a paper containing an account of his experiments made in the presence of Dr. Huggins and Serjeant Cox, at the same time inviting the two secretaries, Professors Sharpey and Stokes, to meet Mr. Home at his house. Both declined the invitation. Professor Stokes also formulated objections to the experiment made with the mahogany board and the balance, based on the assumption that Mr. Home might have exercised a pressure on the board beyond the fulcrum. In reply Mr. Crookes showed that, granting all the hypotheses of Professor Stokes, a simple mathematical formula gave the amount of force necessary to have been exerted by Mr. Home as 74lbs. "Considering that he was sitting in a low easy chair," continued Mr. Crookes, "and that four pair of sharp, suspicious eyes were watching to see that he exerted no force at all, but kept the tips of his fingers lightly on the instrument, it is sufficiently evident that an exertion of this pressure was impossible."

In another letter to Professor Stokes, Mr. Crookes wrote: "I am now fitting up apparatus in which contact is made through water only, in such a way that transmission of mechanical movement to the board is impossible; and I am also arranging an experiment in which Mr. Home will not touch the apparatus at all. This will only work when the power is very strong; but last night I tried an experiment of this kind, and obtained a considerable increase of tension on the spring balance when Mr. Home's hands were three inches off."

The apparatus in which the intervention of water was employed by Mr. Crookes consisted of the same mahogany board and spring balance, a large glass vessel filled with water being placed on the board, exactly over the fulcrum. A massive iron stand, separated by a distance of two inches from the mahogany board, was furnished with an arm and a ring. In the latter rested a wide, shallow copper vessel, perforated beneath with several holes. This vessel was so adjusted as to dip 1&1/2 inches into the water of the larger glass vessel.

"Shaking or striking the arm or the copper vessel," wrote Mr. Crookes, "produces no appreciable mechanical effect on the board, capable of affecting the balance. Dipping the hand to the fullest extent into the water in the copper vessel does not produce the least appreciable action on the balance.

"As the mechanical transmission of power is by this means entirely cut off between the copper vessel and the board, the power of muscular control is thereby completely eliminated."

To the index of the balance Mr. Crookes had soldered a fine steel point. In front of this a sheet of plate-glass smoked over a flame was made to travel by clockwork. The mark impressed on this smoked surface by the steel point registered the results of the experiment. The balance being at rest, the result was a perfectly straight horizontal line. The tension on the balance varying, the result was a curved tracing.

"The apparatus having been properly adjusted before Mr. Home entered the room," wrote Mr. Crookes, "he was brought in, and asked to place his fingers in the water in the copper vessel. He stood up and dipped the tips of the fingers of his right hand in the water, his other hand and his feet being held. When he said he felt a power, force, or influence proceeding from his hand, I set the clock going, and almost immediately the end of the board attached to the balance was seen to descend slowly and remain down for about ten seconds; it then descended a little further, and afterwards rose to its normal height. The lowest point marked on the glass was equivalent to a direct pull of about 5,000 grains."

In a subsequent experiment, Mr. Crookes removed the glass vessel, iron stand, and copper vessel, and placed Mr. Home at a distance of one foot from the remaining apparatus, his hands and feet being held. The force proceeding from him still acted on the apparatus, and the index registered an increase of weight. On another occasion, when the power appeared to be very strong, Mr. Home was placed at a distance of no less than three feet from the apparatus, his hands and feet being again held. Even at this distance the power showed itself capable of causing a marked increase of weight. "The clock," writes Mr. Crookes, "was set going when he gave the word, and the end of the board attached to the balance soon descended and again rose in an irregular manner." Calculating by the diagram that Mr. Crookes appends of the line traced on the smoked glass, the maximum increase of weight recorded during this remarkable experiment was, as nearly as possible, 1lb. 8oz. Troy. This when Mr. Home was three feet away from the portion of the mahogany board nearest to him. Could experiment be more conclusive!

Papers detailing these and other experiments were sent in by Mr. Crookes to the Royal Society. They were declined without any reason being assigned for the course taken.

Early in 1872 Dr. Carpenter exhibited to a public audience in London an experiment which he pretended to be a reproduction of that conducted by Mr. Crookes with the glass vessel of water and the copper vessel suspended above. Dr. Carpenter's design was to show that, in the words of Mr. Crookes himself, the latter "was ignorant of the merest rudiments of mechanics, and was deluded by an experiment the fallacy of which any intelligent schoolboy could have pointed out." A published protest followed from Mr. Crookes, who conclusively established the correctness of his statement: "Dr. Carpenter's experiment was not my experiment, but an unjustifiable misrepresentation of it."

"Called upon to apologize for the wrong he had thus publicly done to me," wrote Mr. Crookes, "Dr. Carpenter threw the responsibility from himself upon others whom he stated to have been his informants. I print the correspondence, and leave it to the judgment of the scientific world."

That judgment must be taken to have been unfavourable to Dr. Carpenter, whom even so friendly a critic as Professor Stokes admitted to have wholly misrepresented the experiment conducted by Mr. Crookes with the vessel of water.

The crowning and most convincing experiments of the series those in which an increase of weight was recorded by the apparatus when Mr. Home stood at a distance from it, Dr. Carpenter and other Royal Society critics passed over in silence. It surpassed even their facility of invention to suggest how Mr.

Home could possibly have influenced an apparatus that he had not touched.

In the *Quarterly Review* for October 1871, appeared the article entitled "Spiritualism and its Recent Converts" to which I have already referred. An edifying illustration of the candour and fair-mindedness of its author, Dr. Carpenter, was furnished by the fact that, for simply writing the letter quoted a few pages back, his scientific superior, Dr. Huggins, was designated by him "a convert to Spiritualism."

One would almost suspect, in reading this *Quarterly Review* article, that Dr. Carpenter's anger arose from his looking on Mr. Crookes in the light of an interloper who had usurped an inquiry that ought to have been conducted by himself. What is certain is that his criticisms took the form of a gross personal attack on Mr. Crookes, Dr. Huggins, and Mr. Serjeant Cox, to which the former felt himself constrained to reply publicly.

To the facts recorded by Mr. Crookes, and attested by Dr. Huggins and Serjeant Cox, the *Quarterly* reviewer had no reply to make, and attempted none. His plan of warfare was to attack the experimenters, and not the experiments. "No case: abuse the plaintiff's witnesses," is, I believe, a time-honoured maxim at the bar; but whether Dr. Carpenter advanced his reputation by importing such tactics into scientific controversy, I leave it to impartial judges to decide.

CHAPTER 12

Russia, Geneva, Florence, Nice

Last Journey to Russia. Second Marriage. Testimony of Professor Boutlerow. Failure of Power. Second Series of Incidents. Death of Daughter. Failing Health. The Artist Waiter. "Most Marvellous of Missionaries." Séance at Nice.

EARLY IN 1871, Mr. Home visited Russia. During his stay at St. Petersburg he enjoyed the friendly hospitality of Baron Meyendorff, the father of his old friend, and one of the principal officers of the Court. He was summoned by the Emperor as soon as his arrival became known. His Majesty welcomed him with his accustomed kindness, the remembrance of which was so prized by Home. Several séances were held at the Winter Palace; but Home followed his invariable custom on such occasions, and preserved strict silence as to the manifestations. A personage of the Court who took part in the séances was subsequently more communicative, and related two incidents that had reference to the Emperor Alexander II, and to her Majesty, the present Empress. During a séance and in full light, a spirit-hand opened a locket contrived in one of the buttons of the uniform that the Emperor wore, and containing the portrait of the defunct heir to the throne. This manifestation was followed by tiny raps struck on the button itself, that spelt out a communication confirming his Majesty's belief as to their author.

In another séance the present Empress received a token of identity not less striking, by means of a message in Danish from her grandfather, who addressed her Majesty by a pet name that he had given her in her childhood, and no one had ever employed but himself.

The Emperor Alexander II more than once signalized the favour with which he regarded Home by authorizing him to request some mark of the Imperial good-will. The only supplication that he ever addressed to his Majesty and that was granted on the spot was for the pardon of a culprit, one of whose relatives, knowing Home's interest with the Emperor, had entreated him to exert it on behalf of the condemned.

On the eve of this journey to Russia, a forecast of the future had been made to Home by the spirits. Our marriage realized it; and the object of his journey was attained by his gaining the lawsuit in which he had been involved concerning the little fortune of his first wife, unjustly disputed with him by the Countess Pouchkine, the rich heiress of his late brother-in-law, Count Koucheleff-Besborodka.

I first saw Mr. Home in February 1871. Expecting to find a personage occupied with his own celebrity, I was agreeably surprised to meet, on the contrary, a man in whom there was no trace of pretension. A smile of seductive good humour reflected a winning nature, and gave a marked charm to his expressive features. His form and bearing both denoted race. His affable disposition indicated that Scottish nationality of which he was justly proud. Such was the impression I retained of him after our conversation; but at the moment of his being presented to me, I had no power to analyze my sentiments: I heard only a voice saying to me, "Here is your husband." Home at the same instant received the same impression. It was so real, so instantaneous, that it did not even come on me with a feeling of surprise; and a mutual accord was established at once between us. The evening closed with, a very interesting séance; and all that passed at it seemed as familiar and sympathetic to me as if I had been habituated to these manifestations of the invisible watchers over us.

It was nearly six years since Mr. Home had been in Russia, and the society of St. Petersburg besieged him for séances. He held many too many, for his nervous system had recently suffered terribly from the scenes through which he had passed as a spectator of the Franco-German war.

I might fill pages with extracts from letters written to Home by his friends in Russia; but a series of proofs of the friendship and gratitude he inspired would probably have little interest for the reader. I will give, as a single example of this correspondence, a portion of one of the numerous letters of a valued friend, the Baroness de Lieven:

"St. Petersburg, March 17th, '75.

"My dearest friend, The blossoms you sent me were yet in full scent, and I kept them for many days in my room, enjoying their delightful perfume, that spoke of a better and happier land, where flowers and young lives do not shiver and fade, deprived of the blessed influence of the sunshine. ... I was deeply touched by your sending me these flowers for his birthday, my very dear Daniel; and I repeat I cannot thank you enough for them. Your letters are full of such words as nobody but yourself can find for a soul full of anguish and sorrow. You feel so keenly all that the spirit goes through in its most cruel sufferings, that your words go to the heart's deepest feelings. God bless you for it, and make your own sufferings lighter for the sympathy that you bear to others. How very much struck I was with the vision you had so many months before the unhappy day that bereaved us of our own beloved angel! How miraculous that you should have so well understood the meaning of all you saw and heard one more proof that it was so ordained long before the doom was fulfilled. Believe me, ever most affectionately, your true friend, "M. Lieven."

The Baroness de Lieven's touching letter may acquire some additional interest to English readers when they learn that it is not a translation but a transcript of the original, and a proof of the intelligence with which its amiable and gifted writer had studied the English tongue.

On the 24th of February, 1871, Mr. Home gave a lecture on Spiritualism. The hall could scarcely contain the audience. At the close of his address, he related some particulars of a séance that he had recently held in presence of a distinguished savant of the University of St. Petersburg, whose investigations of the phenomena had resulted in a recognition of their genuineness. Home, with his habitual delicacy, refrained frame naming the inquirer; and only added that, if it should prove agreeable to other scientific men to investigate the phenomena, he would place himself at their disposition; it being of course understood that he was unable to promise that manifestations should occur. On this Professor von Boutlerow (of the Academy of Science in St. Petersburg) rose from his place among the audience, and announced himself as the investigator to whom the lecturer had just referred, adding that he wished to attest the exactitude of the account of the séance given by Mr. Home, whose discretion concerning himself he fully appreciated. This action on the part of a well-known scientific man, with regard to a subject so little understood in Russia, was an honourable proof that Boutlerow possessed the courage of his opinions, and the more deserving of appreciation from the fact that such courage is very rare in Russia, as in other countries.

A committee of five scientific men of the University, including Boutlerow, was forthwith constituted, and a séance appointed for March 10th. The committee stipulated that it should take place in one of the rooms of the University, and that a table with a glass top should be provided by the investigators. This was a novel experiment, but Home raised no objection. Unfortunately, in the interval occupied by the formation of the committee and its preparations for the séance, he fell ill, and his power diminished. Frequent séances had exhausted him, and the severity of a Russian winter always tried him terribly. Unwilling to expose himself to the remarks that an abandonment of the séance would have called forth, he kept his appointment with the committee, who were enabled to verify the fact of his illness. Slight oscillations of the table were the only manifestations observed, and the investigators, overjoyed at the failure of the séance, proclaimed the fact to the world. These grave and learned men were confounded when a colleague in science gave them the following lesson:

"The explanation of this failure," wrote Mr. Crookes in the July following, "which is all that they have accused him of, appears to me quite simple. Whatever the nature of Mr. Home's power, it is very variable, and at times entirely absent. It is obvious that the Russian experiment was tried when the force was at a minimum. The same thing has frequently happened within my own experience. A party of scientific men met Mr. Home at my house, and the results were as negative as those at St. Petersburg. Instead, however, of throwing up the inquiry, we patiently repeated the trial a second and third time, when we met with results which were positive."

A second séance was appointed with the St. Petersburg

committee which the continued illness of Mr. Home prevented from taking place. The date of his departure from Russia had been fixed some weeks before; and he was unable to delay it. It was his intention to have placed himself again at the disposal of the Russian committee in the following winter; but before then our marriage had taken place; and as I did not care at all whether the scientific world was converted or not, and felt very anxious about Home's health, which over frequent séances fatigued, I entreated him not to carry out his intention.

When Mr. Home saw the Emperor Alexander II for the last time in March 1871, his Majesty congratulated him on his approaching marriage, and sent to him a ring consisting of a magnificent sapphire surrounded with diamonds. We had agreed that the wedding should take place quietly in Paris; and in October 1871, we were married there at the Russian Church and afterwards at the English Embassy. We visited England; and in December returned to St. Petersburg, where the number of fetes that were given to us on our arrival completely exhausted Mr. Home.

Professor von Boutlerow sought and obtained numerous opportunities of resuming his experiments with Home during the visit that, after our marriage, we paid to Russia, and on the occasions of subsequent visits. "I am informed by my friend Professor von Boutlerow," wrote Mr. Crookes in his papers on the phenomenon of increase of weight, "that he tried almost the same experiments as those here detailed, and with still more striking results. The normal tension on the dynamo-meter being 100lbs it was increased to about 150lbs Mr. Home's hands being placed in contact with the apparatus in such a manner that any exertion of power on his part would diminish, instead of increase, the tension."

The result of a long and scientifically conducted series of experiments was that Boutlerow in Russia fully endorsed the conclusions at which another distinguished chemist, Crookes, had arrived in England.

Because the single séance that the St. Petersburg University committee held was without result, the majority of that committee assumed that thousands of previous inquirers many of them far above their own intellectual standard had been the victims of a delusion. When men of science venture to set up such a colossus of a presumption, the sight of it may well astonish the world.

But the curious thing with certain of this class of inquirers was, that when their senses testified to facts that their prejudices denied, they meekly proceeded to class themselves with those very victims of hallucination at whom they had lately sneered. Rather than being themselves convinced, they accused their senses of being liars. The only credit they took to themselves was that they had not believed their own eyes, and were, therefore, still philosophically superior to the foolish people who had taken a fact for a fact. "In ordinary investigations," ran the creed of these invulnerable sceptics, "a fact is a fact; but the facts of Spiritualism are hallucinations. I did not accept them on your testimony shall I now believe them because my own senses have turned traitors? No! I am hallucinated thou art hallucinated he is hallucinated we are hallucinated all."

On December 26th, 1872, the *Times* published a four-column article headed "Spiritualism and Science." Its author (unnamed) had been present at two séances with Mr. Home in London.1 The first was the counterpart of that at St. Petersburg; "nothing whatever occurred" is the concise summary of the writer in the *Times*. On the second occasion he was more fortunate a sufficient reply to the hypothesis of those who would attribute the former negative result to the presence of such a sceptical and shrewd investigator. It is to be presumed that he had not parted with his shrewdness in the interval between the two séances and he furnishes emphatic evidence that he had not lost any of his scepticism. I extract a portion of his narrative:

"The room was at first well-lighted from a gas-burner overhead. To give a detailed account of everything which occurred would need more space than we can now spare. Suffice it to say, that the table was made light and heavy at our wish, that it moved in every direction, that there were vibrations of the floor and of our chairs, that on Mr. Home holding the accordion (which we took to pieces and tried, and found to be in every respect an ordinary instrument) under the table in his right hand and by the end farthest from the keys, it played a distinct tune, Mr. Home's left hand being on the table and his feet so raised as to be visible. All other hands were on the table. At the same time, and under the same conditions, a small hand-bell was rung in different parts of the space beneath the table. The gas was now turned out and the two spirit lamps lit; these gave a fair light. The raps became louder, and in the usual method directed us to take a leaf out of the table. This was done, when the table appeared to float up about eight inches off the floor, settling down again in a gentle swaying manner. The thin wooden lath lying on the cloth was seen by the whole party to be in motion. It tilted up sideways and endways, and then seemed to float backwards and forwards. Holding our hand three inches, as near as we could guess, above the cloth, the lath rose three times; the last time it touched our hand, and directly afterwards the table jumped and shook violently, and loud raps seemed to come from all parts of it and of the floor."

The *Times* writer describes other phenomena; the most notable of which was the fact that the accordion played when he held it himself. "We held it with the keys downward," he relates; "it seemed to be pushed up towards our hand, and played a few bars.

"We tried," continues the *Times* narrative, "every test we could think of. A subdued light, darkened as the evening went on, was one of the conditions we were obliged to comply with."

Hardly so, I may point out, for, on the evidence of the writer himself, the room was "at first well-lighted from a gas-burner overhead," and the movements of the table, vibrations of the floor and chairs, increase and lessening of the weight of the table, playing of a tune on the accordion, &c., took place while the room was thus lighted.

It would seem that in his secret heart the *Times* investigator felt that his determination not to accept the evidence of his own senses had much more to do with his incredulity than the fact of the light having been subdued as the evening went on, for he had the fairness to add: "Mr. Home seemed to wish to conceal nothing, and gave us every opportunity, consistent with the above conditions to satisfy our scepticism.

"By his request, we got under the table with a lamp a great many times, and insisted always on seeing his hands and feet, or on having them held firmly. As to the hand with which Mr. Home held the accordion under the table, all we know is that on one of our sub-mahogany expeditions with the spirit lamp, we saw that hand quite still, and saw the accordion moving up and down and playing music. There was nothing during the whole evening except the phenomena themselves to suggest imposture. We tried our best to detect it, but could find no trace of it. We searched Mr. Home, and found nothing whatever upon him but his clothes.

"Yet even with all this," concludes the sceptic of the *Times* triumphantly, "we are not a Spiritualist, and do not even believe in a 'Psychic Force.' 'Of course not.' The writer gives a fair and candid account of what he saw, with the exception of the somewhat misleading reference to the light; but he had evidently made his mind up, once and forever, that facts can be disputed, when they relate to the phenomena of Spiritualism. The warfare between his senses and his prepossessions is amusingly illustrated in two passages of his article. In the first he writes, "The table appeared to float up off the floor." When he penned the words, prejudice had evidently got the upper hand; the writer distrusted the testimony of his eyesight. Towards the close of his narrative he reverts to this same occurrence, and says: "We are certain that the table rose from the ground." For the moment, reason had resumed her sway; and while writing this second passage the investigator believed, if but for an instant, that what his eyes had seen they had seen.

Early in 1872, Mr. Home published that second volume of *Incidents in My Life* to which I have made occasional reference. He included in it the principal affidavits sworn on both sides during the progress of the Lyon lawsuit; and would have published the remainder in a third volume, had his health allowed him to carry out his intention of continuing his autobiography; but during the years 1872 and 1873 he passed few days that were free from, suffering.

In April 1872, we installed ourselves at Paris, hoping to enjoy there a calmer life than we had led in Russia; but our hope was shattered by a bitter trial. In the autumn we lost our child. Home, who adored our little daughter, was heart-broken by the blow; and his health failed more and more. At the moment of her parting from this world, we, and all the others who were present, heard as it were a hail of tiny sounds on the pillow where the beautiful little head rested, and in every part of the room: we heard also the sounds of music and of voices. The little coffin was laid in a vault at St. Germain, and Home expressed the desire that he might be buried there himself.

Following the counsels given to us, we passed the winter at Nice. From this moment, the health of Home became my sole care. A complete repose was necessary to him, and I entreated that he would hold séances very seldom. Change of air and scene were always of benefit to him; and in June 1873, he went to visit his friends in England; on his return we took refuge from the summer heats in Switzerland.

In November 1873, Home received news of a young friend whose acquaintance he had made two years earlier under interesting circumstances.

Shortly after the fall of the Commune, Home was in Paris; and while one day dining alone at a restaurant, he was waited on by a young man who seemed very little accustomed to the calling he was exercising. One of the impressions that Home so often received came to him at this moment, and he said suddenly to the young Frenchman, "You are not a waiter what are you doing here?"

Seeing the embarrassment that the question caused him, Home hastened to set him at his ease. His evident interest soon gained him the confidence of the other, who ended by relating his history. He was a young painter whom the siege and the Commune between them had ruined. Reduced at last to the greatest distress, he had preferred becoming a garçon de cafe to dying of hunger; and had only been exercising his new calling for three or four days when Home's notice was attracted to him.

Such a story awoke all the generous sympathies of the listener. He exerted himself so effectually to be of benefit to his new acquaintance, that he ended by finding him artistic employment in England. I have in my possession several letters to Home from his protégé, all of them written in a strain of enthusiastic affection and gratitude. "I ask myself every day," he writes in his first letter after crossing the Channel, "if I shall ever have talent enough to prove myself worthy of all the good you have done me morally even more than materially when my heart was full of bitterness and discouragement. I thank God every day for the friend He has given me, and pray Him to bless you "Alexis."

In November 1873, the writer of these words returned to Paris. Home had just before written to him, and received in reply the letter of which I translate a portion.

"Paris, 18th November, 1873.

"My dear Daniel, The years change you in nothing you are always the same generous heart, on which it is so good to lean. I cannot tell you how sad it has made me to learn the state of your health, and now I hope for better news. Send me a word from the heart that has known so often how to cheer a friend, who always blesses God for having known you.

"Alexis."

The untiring kindness of Home did not always select its objects so happily. He could not resist a tale of distress; his only impulse was to relieve. Ingratitude that would have hardened any ordinary heart had no effect on him.

We left Switzerland late in December 1873, and went to Nice. The following summer found us in Florence, where Home found, as everywhere, old friends who welcomed his coming, and added new ones to their number. He could not refuse the requests for séances pressed on him; and several took place while we were at Florence.

Mrs. Webster (an English lady residing at Florence) was one of the sitters. I extract a few lines from a letter written by Mrs. Webster to me after these séances:

"I cannot tell how to express to you how much the two séances at which I have had the happiness to be present have interested me, how deeply I am moved by what I have seen and experienced, and how grateful I am to Mr. Home, as well as to yourself, for having had the kindness to accord us these séances in spite of the critical state of his health.

"He is the most marvellous missionary of modern times in the greatest of all causes, and the good that he has done cannot be reckoned. Believe me, I am not seeking to say flattering things to him, but I speak from the depths of my soul and express my profound convictions. Where Mr. Home passes, he bestows around him the greatest of all blessings, the certainty of a future life."

We spent the winter of 1874 at Nice, and most of the ten winters following. The blue sky and brilliant sunshine of the Riviera did something to lighten for Home the burden of almost ceaseless physical suffering; and it was pleasant to him to meet many of the friends of former years. Among those whom we found at Nice in the winter of '74–5, was his old and prized friend Count Alexander de Komar. Count de Komar welcomed his arrival with joy, sought every opportunity of being in his society, and took the greatest pleasure in recalling the memories of long-past days in Paris. There was also in Nice at the time another of Home's friends of 1857, the Countess Potocka, who often joined in these conversations, and added her own memories of remarkable manifestations that she had witnessed. One evening, when the talk thus ran on the séances of 1857, Countess Potocka earnestly entreated Mr. Home to hold at least one séance that winter at Nice. A few days later, on December 23rd, we met to the number of seven at her residence. The circle was composed of the Countess Potocka, Count de Komar, the Countess de M., Mdlle. de Komar, Mons. d'Attainville, Mr. Home and myself. The salon was brilliantly lit; and on the chimney piece there were placed, in addition, two large candelabra. We had no sooner taken our places round a large table than we all felt a distinct vibration, which was communicated to our chairs and the floor of the apartment. Five raps were struck on the table a call for the alphabet; and communications to several of the sitters were spelt out. A small hand caressed Count de Komar, and rested a little while in his.

I will not describe in detail the manifestations we witnessed, but will pass at once to the startling phenomenon with the interruption of which the séance closed.

Mr. Home had passed into a trance; he walked about the room with closed eyes, then approached the fireplace an open fireplace. A large fire was burning brightly on the hearth; and kneeling down. Home bathed his face and hands in the flames, as if in water. We saw his head encircled by the flame in which it was plunged; and at the sight Count de Komar started from his chair, crying "Daniel Daniel!" At the cry, Home recoiled brusquely from his position; and after some instants, during which none of us ventured to address him, he said, in the low, clear voice with which he always spoke when in a trance: "You might have caused great harm to Daniel by your want of faith; and now we can do nothing more." We were not told what other manifestations the spirits had intended to produce. This remarkable phenomenon of bathing his face without injury in flames had been witnessed more than once previously in England.

During this stay at Nice in 1874, Home one morning, received a letter written in a hand evidently disguised. "I am here in passing," it ran; "and if you have not forgotten me, your heart will tell you what friend has the same affection for you always." There was neither address nor signature. Home puzzled over the enigma; and at last: "It is he it is he!" he exclaimed, delighted; and on my asking who: "Alexis Tolstoy, and if it is really Alexis, we shall find him at the Hotel." We went there at once; and there we found the Count, imprisoned to his room by illness and suffering severely; but always the same noble, frank, loyal, affectionate nature that Home had now known for so many years. I shall never forget Tolstoy's delight at seeing his friend, and at Home's having divined from whom the mysterious note proceeded. He was passing through Nice to Mentone, and insisted on our visiting him there. We did not fail to pay this visit; and on our departure, it was agreed that we should pass the following winter together at Florence. The project was never realized; for when the time came that should have brought Tolstoy to us, the Count had passed from this world. There remained of him here the memory of a noble nature, and the fame of a true poet.

In the spring of 1875, Home's spirit-guides prescribed to him a course to be followed for the improvement of his health; and in pursuance of these counsels we passed some months in Italy, where he experienced much relief from the remedies he had been directed to employ. We wintered again at Nice; and there met the Countess Sant' Amaro, whom Mr. Home had known twenty years before, as well as her husband. Time had not weakened or changed her friendly sentiments; and we passed some agreeable evenings at her house, where in February a séance was held. The circle consisted of the Countess Sant' Amaro, three of her friends, Mr. Home and myself. The Countess, who had long been widowed, was deeply touched by the manifestations of the evening, which were principally addressed to her. Her husband communicated several proofs of his identity; and among them there were rappings that spelt out in Portuguese a word none of the other sitters comprehended, but that the Countess at once and joyfully recognized; for it was the name by which he had been accustomed familiarly to call her. We all heard a noise as of something being torn; and at the same instant five raps demanded the alphabet. "There is no death," was spelt out; "therefore, no mourning." The Countess had never laid black aside since her husband's death. Before she could well grasp the meaning of the message, she felt some object placed in her lap; and on lifting this, it proved, to her great astonishment, to be her handkerchief, from which the black border had been torn. After that evening, the Countess laid aside her mourning.

This winter of 1875, Mr. Home saw pass from earth his friend Count Alexander de Komar, who came to him three days afterwards, and gave him the simple and touching message, "Console my children."

Numerous as are the witnesses whose testimony I have gathered together in these pages, they do not attest the twentieth part of the facts, as true as strange, that were the means of convincing thousands that,

There is not death – what seems so is transition;This
life of mortal breathIs but the suburb of the
life Elysian,Whose portal we call death

CHAPTER 13

1876–1886

During the whole of 1876, Mr. Home was occupied with the work that he published the following year under the title of *Lights and Shadows of Spiritualism.* He passed in review in those pages the phenomena both of ancient and of modern times. A large portion of the volume was devoted to an exposure of the noxious abuses that every day were making Spiritualism more and more of a byword and reproach. Home had long watched with pain and indignation the growth of those abuses; and the conviction was forced upon him that it was his duty to speak out in earnest protest. The task was neither a light nor a pleasant one. He well knew what would be the fury of the impostors who traded in sham spiritual phenomena; and that even a louder outcry would come from the enthusiasts whose self-love he wounded.

With his accustomed frankness, he made publicly known his intention of exposing the impostures that usurped the name of Spiritualism the impostures, not the impostors, be it noted; for it was not his intention to sully his pages by compiling a list of detected cheats, but simply to put too credulous persons on their guard. The manner in which his advertisement was received by some persons professing to be Spiritualists, he described in the chapter introductory to that portion of his work which dealt with the shadows the very dark shadows of Spiritualism:

"I was assailed, both openly and anonymously, with slander, lying charges, foul personalities, venomous abuse, in short, with every weapon which the most unscrupulous partisan hatred can direct against the object of its hostility. It was what I expected, and what I had been forewarned of. If the attacks made on me have moved me at moments, the support I have received from within and without, and the consciousness of the rectitude of my intentions, have made the effect but that of a moment."

The book appeared. It made no attacks on individual impostors; and the persons who had feared to find their names in its pages breathed again. Each could proclaim with reference to the facts compiled from a hundred different sources, that they concerned his neighbours not himself.

While the book was in progress, and after its publication, Home received numerous letters from friends in England concerning the very dark shadows that rested upon Spiritualism there. Among these correspondents, Serjeant Cox was one of the most frequent. The burden of the learned Serjeant's complaint was always the same that he could find nowhere else the opportunities for thorough and systematic investigation of the phenomena that he had enjoyed a few years earlier with Mr. Home.

"In the investigations in which you so kindly assisted me," wrote Serjeant Cox on March 8th, 1876, "there was nothing of this precaution and mystery. You sat with me anywhere, at any time; in my garden, and in my house; by day and by night; but always, with one memorable exception, in full light. You objected to no tests; on the contrary, you invited them. I was permitted the full use of all my senses. The experiments were made in every form that ingenuity could devise; and you were as desirous to learn the truth and the meaning of it as I was. You sat alone with me, and things were done which, if four confederates had been present, their united efforts could not have accomplished. Sometimes there were phenomena, sometimes there were none. When they occurred they were often such as no human hand could have produced without the machinery of the Egyptian Hall. But these were in my own drawing room, and library, and garden, where no mechanism was possible. In this manner it was that I arrived at the conviction opposed to all my prejudices and preconceptions that there are forces about us of some kind, having both power and intelligence, but imperceptible to our senses, except under some imperfectly-known conditions. I did not, and with subsequent extended inquiry I cannot now, arrive at the conclusion you have come to that these invisible agents are spirits of the dead."

As a pendant to the epistle of Serjeant Cox, the following letter may find a place here. It was written by a gentleman who is a relative of Lord Dunraven, and who had shared in a portion of his investigations of the phenomena:

"Atheneum Club, 11th Oct., 1875.

"My dear Home, ... I feel more than half inclined to run over to Paris, merely to have a talk with you.

"The phenomena I have witnessed through your kindness are the only things left to which I attach any hope. All the other phenomena of so-called Spiritualism of which I have been a witness except those accruing through you have been in the last degree unsatisfactory; and although I could offer no explanation of them, they seemed to me more likely to be the result of trick than of the action of disembodied spirits. Are you yourself absolutely and fully certain that the phenomena which undoubtedly occur thro' your mediumship are the acts of the spirits of those who have already lived, and that there is no other explanation possible of these phenomena? Very truly yours,

"B. Nixon."

In January, 1877, Mr. Nixon writes: "While what I have seen when you were present, and what I have heard of as vouched for by men like Crookes, Serjeant Cox and others, thoroughly accustomed to the investigation of physical phenomena and the value of evidence, seem to me to place the reality of the phenomena beyond all doubt or question whenever I have tried lately to acquire personally any fresh light or evidence, I have always been placed under circumstances and conditions of the most unsatisfactory and suspicious character."

"If anything can kill Spiritualism, it will be the follies and contemptible meanness of the Spiritualists themselves. As to the fact of Spiritualism, and the grand importance of the establishment of the reality of spirit-life, there can be no question about them, and they must be the solid comfort of every thinking man; but what ridiculous and mischievous stuff we see imported into the movement every day!"

These words were written from Italy to Home, in the spring of 1876, by a very old friend whom he had not seen for years, the well-known author, William Howitt. Mr. Howitt's convictions impressed on him by his séances with Mr. Home some fifteen years earlier were unchanged; but he had long watched with despair the condition into which English Spiritualism was sinking, and had withdrawn from all connection with the movement.

Another of Home's correspondents of 1876 was a still older friend, an Englishman by birth, an Italian by long residence the celebrated artist, Seymour Kirkup, of Florence, on whom the title of Baron had been conferred; a recognition by Italy, I believe, of his labours in connection with the poems of Dante.

"Dearest old friend," writes Baron Kirkup in April 1876: "You were very young when you knew me in Florence; and it is impossible for me ever to forget you. How I long for your new book! I never trusted these dark séances: I could have done by trick all I saw accomplished. But to deny the true because of the false is like saying there is no good coin because one has met with a bad shilling. I have seen much, and so have thousands of competent witnesses. Yours forever, "Seymour Kirkup."

"In a letter from Wilkinson lately," writes Mr. William Howitt to Mr. Home in February, 1876, "he said he had seen Crookes, who said he could not get on with his experiments on Spiritualism because the mediums in London are such cheats." Mr. Howitt's testimony to the more than unfavourable opinion of Mr. Crookes concerning the materials with which he had endeavoured to carry on his experiments after the departure of Mr. Home from England is given at third-hand, it will be noticed. None the less, it was absolutely correct. "I am so disgusted with the whole thing," wrote Mr. Crookes to Mr. Home on November 24th, 1875, "that, were it not for the regard we bear to you, I would cut the whole Spiritual connection, and never read, speak, or think of the subject again." And writing to Mr. Home nine years later, in 1884, Mr. Crookes says: "My belief is the same as ever, but opportunities are wanting."

I might multiply such plaints by the dozen from letters written about this time to Mr. Home. It never seemed to occur to the writers that their misfortunes were very much their fault. The phenomena they had witnessed and tested at séances with Home were "light-loving phenomena," as one scientific investigator, Mr. Simpson, justly styled them. The light might be daylight or artificial light, but there was always light. Home imposed no conditions on the investigator. So far from avoiding tests, he welcomed them; and the more stringent they were, the better they pleased him. Let the sceptic be never so sceptical (and I have surely accumulated in these pages sufficient testimony to the original incredulity of Robert Chambers, Dr. Elliottson, Mr. Serjeant Cox, Mr. Crookes, and a hundred other inquirers named by me), a candid, careful investigation of the phenomena always resulted in his acceptance of them as facts. He might, with Mr. Serjeant Cox, attribute the marvels he had seen and tested to "psychic force;" or, with Lord Lytton, conjecture the existence of a race of beings alien to mankind; or, with Robert Chambers, Robert Bell, and many others, feel it impossible to doubt longer of the continued existence of our lost friends and their nearness to us; but if he were honest, and honestly spoke out his mind, he invariably admitted that it was impossible to conceive of the manifestations as otherwise than genuine.

I have shown by the evidence of hundreds of witnesses that Mr. Home had no concealments, but always urged the observers present to scrutinize in the most rigid manner every phenomenon that occurred. Thousands in every country did so; and the accumulation of proof upon proof forced them to recognize, that the phenomena were neither delusions nor deceptions, but facts. Like Serjeant Cox, the inquirer might find this conviction "opposed to all his prejudices and preconceptions;" but he could only add, with Mr. Crookes, "I am conscious that my senses, both of touch and sight and these corroborated, as they were, by the senses of all who were present are not lying witnesses when they testify against my preconceptions."

Once convinced of the existence of the phenomena, investigators commonly began to ask themselves: "If they occur in Home's presence, why not in the presence of others? It is improbable that he is the sole person in the world who possesses this marvellous gift." It was natural that they should so reason, and that they should seek to test their conjectures by experiment. What was their plain duty in conducting these researches for new marvels? Surely to experiment as they had experimented with Mr. Home; to investigate only in the light, and if phenomena occurred, to subject them to a rigid scrutiny. "Where the conditions imposed are just such as are calculated to prevent detection if trickery is designed," says Serjeant Cox in one of his letters to Home, "we are bound to look with the utmost suspicion upon all that is done; and, indeed, we should refuse to take part in any such unsatisfactory experiment."

An excellent precept but did the learned Serjeant and others act upon it? On the contrary, their eagerness to experiment further was such, that when they were unable to do so under conditions favourable to the interests of truth, they resigned themselves to conditions that bore a suspicious air of having been imposed to prevent the detection of trickery. With Mr. Home they had investigated in full light; but the persons with whom they afterwards sat insisted on a darkness that would have discouraged owls. With Mr. Home they had subjected the phenomena to the strictest scrutiny and the most searching tests; but these new phenomena were too coy for either scrutiny or tests. What could result from "investigations" so conducted but loss of time and temper? Either the inquiry was abandoned in disgust when it was found that the "manifestations" obstinately persisted in refusing to occur in the light or the inquirer persisted in his discouraging task till, emboldened by previous impunity, the exhibitor of the spurious phenomena ventured on more open trickery and was convicted of imposture.

"Light," wrote Mr. Home in *The Lights and Shadows of Spiritualism*, "is the single test necessary, and it is a test which can and must be given. By no other means are scientific inquirers to be convinced. Where there is darkness, there is the possibility of imposture, and the certainty of suspicion."

It was retorted on Mr. Home by certain Spiritualists that occasionally his own séances had been held in a very feeble light. "Every form of phenomena," he replied (*Lights and Shadows*), "ever occurring through me at the few dark séances has been repeated over and over again in the light, and I now deeply regret ever having had other than light séances. What we used to term darkness consisted in extinguishing the lights in the room, and then we used to open the curtains, or, in very many instances, have the fire lit (which, if burning, was never extinguished), when we could with perfect ease distinguish the outline form of everyone in the room.

"Of another class," he justly added, "are the dark séances at present held."

Home might have also replied that the séances he held in a feeble light had been with friends who had previously tested the phenomena in a strong light and satisfied themselves of their genuineness. Those who are already convinced do not need to be a second time converted. Nor, I repeat, were his séances ever dark séances. The light might be dim but still it was light, not darkness.

The disappointing results of subsequent investigations undertaken by Mr. Crookes, Serjeant Cox, & c., so far from detracting from the value of those made with Home, added one more proof of the convincing nature of the phenomena witnessed in his presence. That they did so may easily be made clear to the candid reader, whether Spiritualist or sceptic.

A hundred English inquirers whom I might name began their investigations with Mr. Home as sceptics. They confidently expected to be able to attribute the phenomena to deception or delusion. They were compelled by overwhelming proof to recognize them as facts.

No longer sceptics but believers, they sought elsewhere for new marvels with what result? That they met with imposture, and discovered it to be imposture. Yet they were now convinced of the existence of the phenomena, whereas when, according to their shallow critics, they had been deceived by Mr. Home, they were as sceptical concerning the phenomena as any of those critics. Imposture failed to dupe them when they became believers; yet the assertion is loudly advanced that these very same observers were duped while they were still sceptics. A candid thinker will scarcely find the theory plausible.

Lights and Shadows had many readers in England and very many in America. The book was abused by the foolish and welcomed by the sensible. "I cannot understand," wrote to Mr. Home an esteemed American Spiritualist, Mr. Hudson Turtle, "why Spiritualists so oppose your book. It only tells the truth. I said in my review of your *Lights and Shadows* that it was the beginning of a new era Spiritualism here is now slowly approaching the scientific plane that I have laboured for twenty years to have it reach. I regard your *Lights and Shadows* as the opening cannonade of the battle."

"The book made you sad!" wrote Home to Mrs. S. C. Hall. "So it did me, and doubly so does the so-called Spiritualism of the day. Right-minded people have left and are every day leaving the movement. I see just such rays of 'Light' as are granted to you, but I also see 'Shadows,' which when they began to form were no bigger than a man's hand, but they have increased with a most alarming rapidity, and at last are to be found intercepting the very light we are praying and hoping for. My work is not written to obtain the praise of men; it is written to expose the falsehoods which are fast obscuring a truth which is all-important to mankind. If I had a thousand years to live on earth, I would rather speak out, and bear the heavy burden of blame which I know will be cast upon me, than remain silent, and feel the certitude that I, too, was playing a dishonest part in keeping silence."

The years with which I am dealing were years of much suffering to Mr. Home; but from time to time it was relieved in a way that surprised his medical advisers, who did not know to what to attribute these unexpected improvements in his health. They were still more astonished by the manner in which our spirit guardians sustained his physical forces beneath the burden laid on them. Again and again celebrated physicians declared his case to be hopeless; and in 1877 one of the most eminent of French medical authorities predicted that he had not three months to live. Yet he lived on, and was supported through all. I have often seen during the night a light shine round him, while a hand issuing from a luminous cloud made passes over his face, as if blessing him, and ended by making on his forehead the sign of the cross. Often the spirits dictated long communications to him; cheering him with words of encouragement and love that, above all, were needed while he was busy with his task of exposing the abuses of Spiritualism; for no effort was spared by those hostile to that task to make him renounce it. Take, for example, a sentence in a letter written from St. Petersburg in March 1876, which went so far as to say that it was improper for him to write this book "even if he had at his disposal the most convincing evidence." Nothing could be more dishonourable than the duplicity of such principles to the truth that it was Home's mission to proclaim. "No man can serve two masters;" and Home was not able to range himself on the side of such a conscience. Nor could he think, with his correspondent, that it is ever unbecoming to speak the truth. It is not astonishing that Spiritualism should sink very low in Russia, when the truth has such pioneers as this Russian champion to sustain it.

In April 1876, a leading French journal published a telegram announcing Home's sudden death. The news was speedily telegraphed to the chief newspapers in Europe and America, and the whole civilized world was thus informed that "D. D. Home had been found dead in a railway carriage while travelling between Berlin and St. Petersburg." The exact origin of the first false telegram was never traced; but it is significant that in certain quarters dark hints had been thrown out that Home would not live to complete his work. If some of the silliest of the Theosophists spoke the truth, he had been solemnly cursed by the high priestess of their superstition; and her curses, it was added, always slew. Others of his ill wishers were ether ignorant of these baleful curses, or doubted their efficacy, for Home received more than one anonymous letter threatening his life, if he persisted in his task. As he paid no attention to the threats, his enemies took his life by means of the newspapers.

Day after day during the month of April, 1876, he continued to receive from all quarters obituary notices of himself, in a dozen different languages a class of reading that it has fallen to the lot of few men, besides Home to enjoy. Some of these biographers related the facts of his life with no more distortion than was inevitable to a hasty and badly informed writer; others, French journalists especially, indulged in an unblushing license of romance that outdid anything ever published in England. It is not every day that this peculiar kind of genius obtains such scope for its exercise as the author of the false report of Home's death had afforded to it.

In May we left Nice for the baths of La Malou. "Alexander Dumas is here," wrote Home to a friend in England; "and I went to call on him yesterday. You would have laughed to see the way he stared at me, and said: 'In the first place, you died a month or two ago; and in the next place you look positively younger than when I last saw you seventeen years ago.' These baths are doing wonders for me, and I walk now without a stick."

Among the American readers of the report of Home's death was the aunt who had adopted him in his infancy and whose old age he had provided for. The following extract from a newspaper of May 1876, tells the effect on her of the cruel falsehood:

"At Elwood, on the 6th of May, passed from earth Mrs. Mary McNeil Cook, aged 70, the aunt, and mother by adoption, of D. D. Home, Esq. Our readers will be pained to hear that her departure was caused by the shock of hearing the false intelligence of Mr. Home's sudden death. A paralytic seizure was the result, and the poor lady never rallied."

Probably this announcement never reached the eyes of the inventor of the story of Home's death, and the worthy being in question may thus have been deprived of the gratification of learning what bitter pain his lie had given.

I may relate here an incident in Home's life of a date six years later. One of his friends in France was the author and journalist Henri Delaage, whose acquaintance with Home dated back to 1857. Delaage died at Paris on the 15th of July 1882. We were then travelling in Switzerland; and on July 17th arrived at Mornex, a little village near Annecy, in Savoy. Fatigued with the journey, Home had sat down to rest himself; but on entering the room a few minutes afterwards, I was surprised to see him standing at the open window looking fixedly into a large garden outside. "Look," he said, "there is Delaage;" and then added, "No, I see nothing now; and yet a moment ago he was there."

It was some months since we had received any news of Delaage, but the last had left him in his usual health. Home felt sure, however, that his friend had quitted earth; he had seen the form too distinctly to doubt of its identity; and to make certainty more certain, a few hours later we heard rappings, and the following message was spelt out: "I keep my word. H. D."

"If it was an illusion," wrote Home, the next day to Paris, in describing his vision, "I shall be much astonished; for we had made each other a promise on this subject, and I remember very well that when the report of my death was spread some years ago, Delaage said to whoever would listen to him: 'What nonsense!

If Home were dead, he would have come to tell me so' ... I await with impatience the *Figaro*, to which I subscribe, and which will certainly speak of him if he is no more of this world. Unfortunately, the numbers addressed to me go first to Loeche, so that the date of the last received by me is the 13th. If the good fellow is as usual, say nothing to him of what I have told you."

The recipient of Home's letter carried it at once to the *Paris Figaro*; and the whole story was related in that journal on July 22nd, under the heading, "Home et Delaage."

During the years that followed the publication of *Lights and Shadows*, Home's spirit-guides enjoined on him complete repose from all occupation involving mental labour or anxiety. We travelled constantly; for change of scene and climate were among the necessary conditions of his life. The summers of 1877 and 1878 saw us in Russia; and part of each was passed in the far south east, on an estate in the Government of Samara. The scenery is among the most charming in Russia; and Home was enchanted with it. "I have just accomplished a journey of 250 miles in a posting carriage," he writes to a friend in England. "Such a lovely country, my dear John. Hill and dale, forest and field, river and rivulet and lake, and in the dim distance the Ural Mountains. I am trying the celebrated cure of 'Koumis' – mare's milk prepared in a certain way. I have a Tartar who has been on the steppes many years, and nine mares are milked twice a day for me."

At Paris in 1879, Home saw a good deal of the first of American humourists, who came to one or two of the private readings to which he from time to time invited his friends, and was charmed, like all other listeners, by the alternate humour and pathos of the narrator. Home enjoyed greatly the work that Mr. Clemens had just completed, *A Tramp Abroad*; and wishing to give an idea of it to friends at St. Petersburg, had one of its most laughable episodes, the famous *Modern French Duel*, translated into Russian with the author's permission. Mark Twain's remark on receiving a copy of the translation (of which he could not read a word) was characteristic. "It seems an excellent translation," he wrote to Home, "at any rate it looks funnier than it does in English. If it has a defect, it has escaped me."

Year after year Mr. Home continued to be oppressed by the

burden of an enormous correspondence. To whatever corner of Europe we fled, hundreds of letters pursued; and it was often physically impossible for him, a constant invalid, to reply to one half of his correspondents. Spiritualists in Spain, Holland, Italy, and other countries wrote entreating him to visit them and found societies, or stimulate with his presence the vitality of a languishing cause. Inquirers sent requests for séances or for information; and correspondents by the score inflicted on him at merciless length their particular opinions concerning Spiritualism. It was happy for him that his indifference to the small troubles of life was so great and his temper so sweet, or he would have lost the latter almost every time a fresh batch of letters reached us.

His patience, and that generous belief in others which no disappointments could kill in him, were destined to be severely tried. A blind and absolute confidence had led him to deposit on a simple acknowledgment (and even for that Home did not ask) a large sum of money in the hands of one whom he believed to be a friend; and this person now refused to render up the charge confided to him. Home would not take legal proceedings to punish this breach of trust, more painful morally than materially; although his Russian advocate wrote to him: "You have a full right to reclaim this deposit, and there is no doubt that the tribunal would decide in your favour." In the end restitution of the money was made without a lawsuit; but this cruel affair gave a shock to Home's nervous system from which he never recovered. His sufferings became still more acute, his strength diminished more and more; and in the end this event cost him his life.

In September 1881, we received at Geneva a letter from my uncle, His Excellency N. Aksakoff, who was neither a Spiritualist nor a believer in the life after this. Its writer spoke of the interest with which he had read reviews of *Lights and Shadows of Spiritualism*, and of his great desire to read the book itself. He urged Home to have so interesting and valuable a work translated into French without further delay. "I wish to read your book as soon as possible," he wrote. "Have it translated and printed, and send me a copy of so honourable and interesting a work. Your affectionate friend. N. Aksakoff."

My uncle quitted this life before the translation of *Lights and*

Shadows was ready; and Mr. Home dedicated the book to his beloved memory. "As a feeble tribute," ran the inscription, "in return for the proofs of esteem and affection that he constantly gave me. I was the prouder of his friendship in that he united to the nobleness of his name that other nobleness which comes of greatness of soul and goodness of heart."

In April 1882, some weeks after his departure from this world, we received at St. Petersburg the following communication:

"He begins to believe that he lives, but he often fears that it is a dream."

Hardly had these words been spelt out when we heard sounds resembling footsteps the very step of my uncle in the apartment adjoining that in which we were; and the portiere between the two was drawn back. We saw a hand separate the curtains and then let them fall into their place. I distinctly saw the full form of the spirit as he approached us. The rappings, which had been silent for a moment, recommenced. "It is true it is true," was spelt out; "and there is my shadow" (at that instant I felt something placed in my hand), "the shadow of him who loved you dearly. The shadow of the past in no way resembles the being of the present; but affection has not changed rather, it has augmented. Take it; it is I who give it to you. You have touched my hand I have, then, a hand. I live: God is." These last words were spelt out by louder sounds, more slowly struck; as if wishing to make us feel all the reverence they expressed. Then the message recommenced: "My beloved Daniel, I love you more than ever. We must go;" and the rappings ceased. We heard again the sound of the well-known step growing gradually more distant. I lit a candle, to see what object had been placed in my hand; and found it to be a framed photograph of my uncle, that had been taken from the adjoining drawing room. It was indeed his shadow; and the phrase was characteristic, for in this world, when jesting at the notion of a future life, his habitual sarcasm had been: "You will see my shade appear to you by and by."

From that night he was often with us, and gave us the most convincing proofs, of his identity, and of his continued affection.

To relate in detail Home's life during these last years on earth would be simply to tell a story of great suffering patiently and cheerfully borne. In place of this, let me, now that I approach the close of my work, state briefly the substance of many communications made concerning the life beyond this.

The greater part of such communications were given through Home while he was in a state of trance. When he passed into this condition, the expression of his countenance became singularly sweet; "angelic," writes one who had seen him many times in the trance, Mr. S. C. Hall. There was nothing resembling excitement in these trances; look, manner, and voice were calm. "The change which takes place in him," wrote Lord Dunraven, "is very striking; he becomes as it were a being of a higher type. There is a union of sweetness, tenderness, and earnestness in his voice and manner which is very attractive." As a rule, Home's eyes were fast closed in the trance; but he moved about the room as readily and naturally as if they had been open, appearing to follow some unseen guide.

The communications already detailed as having been made in 1876 by Home's old American friend, Ward Cheney, and in 1882 concerning my uncle, show that the spirit, on passing from earth, had often the greatest difficulty in realizing the new conditions of his being; that the change seemed to him a dream. The world in which he found himself was so like this spiritually like this, not materially; himself was so thoroughly himself, that he refused to believe he had quitted earth; and the greater his attachment to earth had been, the more obstinate was his incredulity. Hundreds of communications given through Home refer to this gradual wakening of the spirit to the consciousness that the second birth called death was an accomplished fact. To some that awakening comes swiftly, to others slowly; but it does not seem that it is ever instantaneous.

One very noticeable fact with regard to these messages is that in the spirit-world the idea of good is so intimately associated with light, that of evil with darkness, that the spirits employ "light" and "good" as synonymous terms, "darkness" and "evil" as also synonymous. "We can see all light," was said in the course of one of the trance-communications, "the most beautiful combinations of light. We see the progress either of growth or decay, that is taking place in everything." "To us," another message ran, "the spirit-land of higher spheres is like a beautiful planet, luminous, shining forth as our goal and spheres higher and higher still brighten as we advance in the vista of everlasting progress."

This last word progress is the keynote of the messages, one and all. I would have written "of the teachings," but the expression would be misunderstood. Home's mission was to teach by facts, not by words. He was passive with regard to the words spoken through him in the trance, as passive as the wire that conveys the electric current. When he woke, he had no more consciousness of that which he had uttered than has the wire of the message that has just passed over it. To those who questioned him whether these supra mundane declarations were to be regarded as worthy of credence or not, he responded invariably: "Do as I do; try all communications by the help of your conscience and your reason."

Mrs. Hennings, some of whose experiences have been narrated in a former chapter, relates that she had often begun to speak to Mr. Home concerning messages given through him in the trance, and that he had always stopped her. At last, she asked him why he did so. Home thereupon explained that, as he had not the faintest recollection of anything which occurred in the trance, he preferred not to receive particulars, for they mixed themselves up in his memory with the facts of his waking life, until he became unable to separate one from the other.

It has been often objected that the widespread acceptance by humanity of the noble conception of a life of infinite progress, in place of the fancies of heaven and hell, would encourage the sinful to put off, with Felix, their reformation to "a more convenient season" that, in fact, men would abandon themselves to a life of vice here on earth, with the convenient resolution of leading a life of virtue in the world to come. One might ask in reply what the accepted teachings of heaven and hell have done for the world at large? Is its condition of today an outcome of those teachings? And, if so, is that outcome one to be regarded with satisfaction? But the true answer to such an objection is that the same revelations which speak of progress as an eternal condition of our being, speak of punishment as an eternal condition of our sins. There is no escape, say the spirit-messages. Evil and misery are one; and they who miss the knowledge of that truth on earth are preparing for themselves a terrible awakening to it hereafter. In all these communications it is earnestly inculcated that "Now is the appointed time." "If you strive earnestly and prayerfully here, you enter your true life in a state fitted for it." "Only a perfect submission to the crosses of earth can work out for you a higher and purer life." "Follow Christ's teaching, and carry out His mission." "We know all your sufferings and shortcomings, and what you have to contend with; for have not we, too, been mortals, have we not wearied on the roadside, and had our times of agony and doubt." I might go on to make scores of such extracts from even the few fragments that have been preserved of the trance-communications spoken through Home. The vast majority of those communications were never written down, and live only in the minds of the listeners.

"I shall never forget," writes one of those listeners, "the awfully thrilling way in which M. spoke through Home, the desolation of the picture she drew of her feelings. The words I do not recollect the effect of them I shall always remember."

Why, it was asked at one séance, do not spirits manifest their presence frequently to us, and aid us to shun the wrong and seek the right? As if we can judge how far spirits do actually influence us, or can form any conception of the difficulties under which they labour in seeking to make their presence known. The answer given through Home in a trance is well worthy of attention.

"You should take a higher view of it than that. You wonder why spirits do not help you. Are you not a spirit? You only have the earthly envelope about you. Rouse yourself, and help yourself; do not expect others to help you if you do not act yourself. Yet do spirits interfere in a thousand ways that you little dream of, and never notice. It is a common thing for people to say, 'If spirits are about us, why don't they manifest themselves?' Is not God everywhere? Is He not about you? Why, then, does He not manifest Himself? God has so ordained that, though many of you spend your lives looking for evidence of His existence, yet every day you pass by unnoticed the most wonderful and beautiful evidences."

A circumstance of these communications not always

sufficiently borne in mind by the recipients was that their makers experienced great difficulty in endeavouring to convey to men still in the material body an idea of the life of man in the spiritual body. They could say, for instance, that such a spiritual body clothed them that it was "exactly like the material body, only slightly smaller"; but the impression the words left was frequently either vague or erroneous. It was hard for people hearing these words to conceive of a spiritual body that took form from the spirit itself, and was beautiful or hideous as the spirit was good or evil. Our beauty or deformity in the world beyond this is of our own making; and it is here on earth that we mould our souls into one or the other form. At the touch of Death the veil of clay drops from us, and shows us as we are.

"How do you make us see you?" a sitter asked of the spirits while Home was in the trance. "Sometimes," was the answer, "we make the actual resemblance of what we were, so that we appear exactly as we were known to you on earth; sometimes we project an image that you see, sometimes we cause it to be produced upon your brain; sometimes you see us as we are, with a cloud-like aura of light around us."

In the spirit-world, as in this, likeness attracts, unlikeness repels; but far more strongly than on earth. This declaration was repeated and emphatic in the trance-messages given through Home. It is the key to some of the most difficult problems of Spiritualism. The popular conception of the happiness of hereafter is a state in which spirits can commune at will with each other. The spirits say that no such illimitable communion exists; that in the next world, as in this, there are difficulties of intercourse. Here the great obstacle is distance from those we love. We seek at will the society of a friend in the next street; we communicate less freely with one a hundred miles off; we may hear nothing for years of a third in the interior of Africa. These earthly obstacles to interchange of thought and sympathy have their spiritual counterparts. Distance in the next world is the distance of soul from soul; and it is sometimes so great as to render communion impossible. "Between us there is a great gulf fixed," are words that take a very solemn meaning in view of those declarations from the spirit-world. Consciously or unconsciously, we are working to widen that gulf every day that we live on earth; and according to our works we shall find it set hereafter between us and the evil, or between us and the good. In the latter event, declares Spiritualism, it may be bridged: but how slowly and how painfully!

Spirits tell us that the peace of the life to come is peace from the doubts, sorrows, and struggles of earth; that the adoration they offer to the Creator is obedience to His will; that their joys, the joys we cannot conceive or measure are found in forgetfulness of self and love of others. They tell us that to live for others is to draw nearer to God. "From the Eternal Source," says a trance-message spoken through Home, "goes forth the Eternal Light to which we aspire." Light Love Good; in the comprehension of the spirits of the blest, these three are one.

When the human mind tries to conceive of Eternity, it commonly falls into the error of figuring it as endless Time. In these trance communications, the spirits invariably declare that the word time had lost it's meaning for them. "We know not of time," says a message now before me; "to us yesterday, today, tomorrow are all one. Had we hours, days, years, even ages, like you, we should say time passes slowly or time passes fast. We never tire; we are eternity." That is to say, eternity does not present itself to us after death as endless Time, the passage of which we mark, but as an infinite State, wherein we progress.

A question was once asked at a séance concerning the comparative truth of different religions. The answer given through Home in the trance was: "Even the poor Pagan who bows down before his idol possesses the germ of truth, inasmuch as he worships something outside and beyond himself." It seems to me that there is a whole sermon in these words.

In March 1883, Mr. Home passed at Nice his fiftieth birthday. His health had been too feeble all winter for him to go much into society; but he received his friends as often as possible friends whose number was constantly being added to. On his birthday, the 20th of March, a crowd of the foreign colony of Nice assembled to fete the invalid, whom they surrounded with a prodigious heap of baskets and bouquets of flowers. Home, although a prisoner to his armchair and suffering severely, preserved all his accustomed exquisite affability in welcoming and thanking his friendly visitors; and complied with the general desire by reciting to them several pieces in French and English, among them a poem that I have already referred to as being one of his favourites, the "Grandmother" of Tennyson. He never rendered it with more effect; and the same was the case with the little piece that followed "Carcassonne," the masterpiece of Nadaud.

We passed the following winter in Russia, part of it at Moscow. While we were there, the Countess Tolstoy arranged an amateur performance in aid of the poor, and Mr. Home took part in it; so did my cousin John Aksakoff, the well-known Slavophil leader, not less celebrated as a poet. He had not heard Home recite before; and, the reading over, ran up to him in a transport of enthusiasm. "It was perfect it was perfect!" he exclaimed; "I never before heard anything so perfect."

Towards the close of 1884, Home predicted to me that his malady was approaching a crisis, and that it would be long and painful. He described minutely all that would happen; and, in speaking of the increased sufferings through which he foresaw that he was about to pass, said, "God, who sends the trial, knows better than we why He sends it: I trust myself wholly in His hands. I shall recover if no complication supervenes: if it does, His will be done. I am not anxious for you God will support you. I shall not suffer at the last."

All that he had predicted was realized even to the superhuman force God sent me. He suffered cruelly long and cruelly. There were intervals of repose from pain, then increased suffering. These few words tell all that need be told of the story of eighteen months.

In June 1886, the complication of which he had foretold the danger supervened, and attacking the lungs, proved quickly fatal. The last three days we both knew that all was ended for us on earth. He retained full consciousness to the last; and resignation an ineffable resignation illumined his features, as the thin thread that held the spirit to the body slowly parted. His one thought was to inspire me with strength to survive him, and to make me feel that he was but gone a little way before me; and he spoke to me much of God's great goodness to us, and of friends in heaven.

They were around him; he saw them, named them, and stretched forth his hands to them with joy. He had ceased to suffer; death came to him, as he had predicted it would come, without a pang. During these last hours, he seemed no more of this world; the soul, disengaged from all that was material, already anticipated its union with the Supreme Being and the life eternal. It was no dream, no hope to him, that life; he had prepared himself for it by his life on earth; and now, in this moment of a sublime and tranquil death, he saw it open bright before him, while slowly, painlessly, the last ties of spirit and body were gently loosed.

It was his desire, as I have elsewhere said, to be buried in the same vault with our little daughter. As she was laid in the Russian cemetery near Paris, it was necessary, I learned, for the interment to be conducted according to the ritual of the Greek Church. Our Lord pays no heed to forms, but judges each according to his works; and I had no hesitation in complying. Home had received the sacrament some days before with a devotion that deeply touched the priest, who said, in leaving him that we should rejoice and not mourn when God finds a soul so ready to be called to Him.

In quitting its earthly envelope, the spirit had left imprinted on the face an expression of celestial happiness; a peace neither of sleep nor of death, but of immortality, that seemed to say, with the Apostle, "O death, where is thy sting! O grave, where is thy victory!" That tranquil happiness did not pass from his features; and I had a photograph taken of them, in which the shadow of its beauty is preserved.

Home wished, and had always wished, that his interment should be simply conducted, and should be without show of mourning. "I desire my funeral to be as simple as possible," he wrote in his will, "and that all tokens and signs known as mourning may be entirely discarded." In accordance with his injunctions, the vanities of funereal pomp were absent from the internment; and when the service in the Russian church was performed, the priests, instead of being robed in black, wore their festival attire of white and gold. No shadow darkened that mystic and imposing service, the noble chants of which were admirably rendered. The coffin, buried in flowers and raised on a brilliantly lit dais, had nothing dismal in its aspect; it became a simple token of our loving farewell to the mortal garment of him whom God had called from earth before us.

The sentiment of all who were present at the church found expression in the words of a friend: "The whole effect was grand, solemn, and suggestive, as the full voices of the choir rose and fell in solemn cadence, and the rich soft strains of swelling harmony filled the building, dying away in distant echoes repeated from dome to dome."

Home's grave is at St. Germain. A plain cross of white marble rises from a Calvary, on which is engraved: "Daniel Dunglas Home. Born to earth-life near Edinburgh (Scotland), March 20th, 1833. Born to spirit-life: 'To another discerning of spirits' (1st Corinthians, 12th chapter, 10th verse): June 21st, 1886."

Also available from White Crow Books

Marcus Aurelius—*The Meditations*
ISBN 978-1-907355-20-2

Elsa Barker—*Letters from a Living Dead Man*
ISBN 978-1-907355-83-7

Elsa Barker—*War Letters from the Living Dead Man*
ISBN 978-1-907355-85-1

Elsa Barker—*Last Letters from the Living Dead Man*
ISBN 978-1-907355-87-5

Richard Maurice Bucke—*Cosmic Consciousness*
ISBN 978-1-907355-10-3

G. K. Chesterton—*The Everlasting Man*
ISBN 978-1-907355-03-5

G. K. Chesterton—*Heretics*
ISBN 978-1-907355-02-8

G. K. Chesterton—*Orthodoxy*
ISBN 978-1-907355-01-1

Arthur Conan Doyle—*The Edge of the Unknown*
ISBN 978-1-907355-14-1

Arthur Conan Doyle—*The New Revelation*
ISBN 978-1-907355-12-7

Arthur Conan Doyle—*The Vital Message*
ISBN 978-1-907355-13-4

Arthur Conan Doyle with Simon Parke—*Conversations with Arthur Conan Doyle*
ISBN 978-1-907355-80-6

Leon Denis with Arthur Conan Doyle—*The Mystery of Joan of Arc*
ISBN 978-1-907355-17-2

The Earl of Dunraven—*Experiences in Spiritualism with D. D. Home*
ISBN 978-1-907355-93-6

Meister Eckhart with Simon Parke—*Conversations with Meister Eckhart*
ISBN 978-1-907355-18-9

Kahlil Gibran—*The Forerunner*
ISBN 978-1-907355-06-6

Kahlil Gibran—*The Madman*
ISBN 978-1-907355-05-9

Kahlil Gibran—*The Prophet*
ISBN 978-1-907355-04-2

Kahlil Gibran—*Sand and Foam*
ISBN 978-1-907355-07-3

Kahlil Gibran—*Jesus the Son of Man*
ISBN 978-1-907355-08-0

Kahlil Gibran—*Spiritual World*
ISBN 978-1-907355-09-7

Hermann Hesse—*Siddhartha*
ISBN 978-1-907355-31-8

D. D. Home—*Incidents in my Life Part 1*
ISBN 978-1-907355-15-8

Mme. Dunglas Home; edited, with an Introduction, by Sir Arthur Conan Doyle—*D. D. Home: His Life and Mission*
ISBN 978-1-907355-16-5

Andrew Lang—*The Book of Dreams and Ghosts*
ISBN 978-1-907355-97-4

Edward C. Randall—*Frontiers of the Afterlife*
ISBN 978-1-907355-30-1

Lucius Annaeus Seneca—*On Benefits*
ISBN 978-1-907355-19-6

Rebecca Ruter Springer—*Intra Muros—My Dream of Heaven*
ISBN 978-1-907355-11-0

W. T. Stead—*After Death* or *Letters from Julia: A Personal Narrative*
ISBN 978-1-907355-89-9

Leo Tolstoy, edited by Simon Parke—*Tolstoy's Forbidden Words*
ISBN 978-1-907355-00-4

Leo Tolstoy—*A Confession*
ISBN 978-1-907355-24-0

Leo Tolstoy—*The Gospel in Brief*
ISBN 978-1-907355-22-6

Leo Tolstoy—*The Kingdom of God is Within You*
ISBN 978-1-907355-27-1

Leo Tolstoy—*My Religion—What I Believe*
ISBN 978-1-907355-23-3

Leo Tolstoy—*On Life*
ISBN 978-1-907355-91-2

Leo Tolstoy—*Twenty-three Tales*
ISBN 978-1-907355-29-5

Leo Tolstoy—*What is Religion and other writings*
ISBN 978-1-907355-28-8

Leo Tolstoy—*Work While Ye Have the Light*
ISBN 978-1-907355-26-4

Leo Tolstoy with Simon Parke—*Conversations with Tolstoy*
ISBN 978-1-907355-25-7

Howard Williams with an Introduction by Leo Tolstoy—*The Ethics of Diet: An Anthology of Vegetarian Thought*
ISBN 978-1-907355-21-9

www.ingramcontent.com/pod-product-compliance
Lightning Source LLC
Chambersburg PA
CBHW022114080426
42734CB00006B/120

* 9 7 8 1 9 0 7 3 5 5 1 6 5 *